Death or Liberty

Also by Douglas R. Egerton

Rebels, Reformers, and Revolutionaries: Collected Essays and Second Thoughts
He Shall Go Out Free: The Lives of Denmark Vesey
Gabriel's Rebellion: The Virginia Slave Conspiracies of 1800 and 1802
Charles Fenton Mercer and the Trial of National Conservatism
The Atlantic World: A History, 1400–1888
    (With Alison Games, Kris Lane, and Donald R. Wright)

DOUGLAS R.
EGERTON

Death or Liberty

*African Americans
and Revolutionary America*

OXFORD
UNIVERSITY PRESS

2009

OXFORD

UNIVERSITY PRESS

Oxford University Press, Inc., publishes works that further
Oxford University's objective of excellence
in research, scholarship, and education.

Oxford   New York
Auckland   Cape Town   Dar es Salaam   Hong Kong   Karachi
Kuala Lumpur   Madrid   Melbourne   Mexico City   Nairobi
New Delhi   Shanghai   Taipei   Toronto

With offices in
Argentina   Austria   Brazil   Chile   Czech Republic   France   Greece
Guatemala   Hungary   Italy   Japan   Poland   Portugal   Singapore
South Korea   Switzerland   Thailand   Turkey   Ukraine   Vietnam

Published by Oxford University Press, Inc.
198 Madison Avenue, New York, NY 10016

www.oup.com

Oxford is a registered trademark of Oxford University Press

Library of Congress Cataloging-in-Publication Data
Egerton, Douglas R.
Death or liberty : African Americans and revolutionary America /
Douglas R. Egerton.
p. cm.
Includes bibliographical references and index.
ISBN 978-0-19-530669-9
 1. United States—History—Revolution, 1775–1783—African Americans.
 2. African Americans—History—18th century.
 3. Slavery—United States—History—18th century.   I. Title.
E269.N3E35 2009
973.30896—dc22   2008027862

9 8 7 6 5 4 3 2 1

Printed in the United States of America
on acid-free paper

For the women in my life,
Alison
Hannah
Kearney

CONTENTS

ACKNOWLEDGMENTS

O NE OF THE FEW virtues of getting older is the large number of good friends and wise colleagues that one acquires along the way. Young scholars instinctively wish to chart their own intellectual path, and perhaps in some fashion I did. But having passed the half-century mark, I am increasingly aware of how much books are collaborative efforts. The present volume, designed as it is to pull together a series of interrelated strands of previous scholarship, never could have been written were it not for the large number of articles, monographs, anthologies, and published documents that have preceded it into print. It has been my good fortune over the years to become acquainted with most of the writers who have crafted these studies, and it is my better fortune that so many of them agreed to read sections of this book.

Richard S. Newman and Carol Berkin read the early chapters, as did Peter P. Hinks and John Ferling. All provided me with detailed and shrewd suggestions for revision, and I should probably here say that if I did not always follow their recommendations, it is only due to my stubborn determination to see matters my way. All of my previous writings have focused on Virginia or South Carolina, so I am particularly lucky to know the two leading specialists regarding slavery and freedom in New York and New Jersey, Graham Hodges and Shane White. Both provided detailed comments on sections pertaining to the northern states and caught more than a few errors. The company and good humor of Graham, a fellow resident of the Burned-Over District, help to make the cold winters of central New York more fun. Gary Nash also read portions that pertain to the North, and his encyclopedic knowledge regarding black life and white law in Pennsylvania and Massachusetts improved those chapters immeasurably.

Robert McColley has been a kind supporter for nearly two decades, but he is never shy in pointing out when we disagree on matters, which is the sign of a true friend. Eric Burin, Ronald L. Hatzenbuehler, and Stanley Harrold were also kind enough to read some of the portions on the Chesapeake, and their influence should be noticeable to anybody who writes about antislavery activism in the southern states.

As he has since our years together in graduate school, Alan Gallay cheerfully and swiftly reads any chapters that I send his way. Although his historical advice is always sound, he has clearly missed his calling as an editor, as his skill in controlling my tendencies toward wordiness is as remarkable as it is necessary. Other old friends, Clarence Taylor and Donald R. Wright, graciously put aside their own work to read my chapters, but I am as grateful for their fellowship as I am for their comments and, in Don's case, for the humorous asides and drawings he doodles along the margins.

A special debt is owed to Carol Berkin and Dan Green. The staunchest of friends, Carol provided me with invaluable professional advice during a difficult time and introduced me to Dan, agent extraordinaire. Dan continued to have faith in my vision of what this book should be about, even after it became clear that toning down the bleak conclusion made good business sense. At Oxford University Press, Susan Ferber guided the manuscript to publication with enormous care and skill, and I am deeply appreciative of her hard labors. My thanks also to copy editor Sue Warga, who helped to transform a manuscript into a book. I am grateful to Le Moyne College's Committee on Research and Development for their generous support for the maps and images.

My daughters, Kearney and Hannah, neglected to read a single page of the manuscript, and they fail to hide their boredom when I launch into yet another long story about somebody long deceased. But they are perfect in every other way. Alison Games read the entire manuscript, filling the pages with perceptive comments, penetrating questions, and indecipherable scribbles. That is not, of course, why I am so grateful to her, but she would wish me not to embarrass her by stating my reasons here. In any case, she knows why.

Death or Liberty

The Trials of William Lee

A Life in the Age of Revolution

T HANKS TO PORTRAITISTS JOHN TRUMBULL and Edward Savage, he became one of the two most recognizable slaves of the late-eighteenth-century Atlantic world. But if, unlike most enslaved Americans in the age of revolution, William Lee was captured on canvas, he was typical of bond-men in other ways. Lee lacks both a precise birth date and birth year. He first appeared in the public record in 1768, when his new master, George Washington, recorded the purchase of a teenage boy, "Mulatto Will," from Mary Lee, for the sum of £61. In recent years, a memorial erected at Mount Vernon that marks Lee's burial plot announces that he was born "circa 1750," which means that he was about eighteen when he first walked through the gates of Washington's plantation. Lee himself may not have known the date, just as he may not have known the name of his (obviously white) father. Mary was the widow of Colonel John Lee of Westmoreland County, and if she sold Will to erase a living, breathing reminder of her husband's nocturnal visits to the slave quarters, she would not have been the first Virginia widow to do so. But certainly nothing speaks more eloquently about the dehumanizing nature of slavery than the fact that the single most recognized slave in Revolutionary America lacks an identifiable birth date and recognized parentage.[1]

The young officer who purchased William, fresh from his successes during the Seven Years' War (known in the colonies as the French and Indian War), was riding through his home county of Westmoreland. Washington either heard of the estate sale at a roadside tavern or read a handbill. The ambitious planter, busily acquiring laborers for his estates, noted four slaves for sale. Two of the young men, Will and Frank, were mixed-race brothers, but the

Although William Lee can be found behind Washington in a number of paintings, he is most visible in John Trumbull's *George Washington*, completed in London in 1780. *Metropolitan Museum of Art.*

other two, Adam and Jack, were "Negro boy[s]." Like many slaveholders, Washington believed that white blood not only lightened the skin but enlightened the mind, and he preferred to employ "yellow-skinned" servants within his home. Although habitually short of cash, Washington agreed to pay three times as much for Will and Frank as for Adam or Jack. While

Adam and Jack were banished to the fields, Frank Lee was dressed in the garb of butler and installed in the living quarters in or near the big house. Older bondmen taught Will to care for his master's clothes and hair—and, rather more important, to quietly anticipate his every whim.[2]

Washington's early attitudes toward slavery were typical of a man of property bred in the colonial Chesapeake. With the death of his half brother Lawrence in 1752, Washington had inherited the estate of Mount Vernon, and with it, eighteen slaves to add to the eleven he had received upon the death of his father ten years before. His marriage to Martha Dandridge Custis, a wealthy widow, further augmented his holdings in human property, whom he managed as his own. Over the years, the enslaved population at Mount Vernon continued to grow, through both natural increase and purchase. By 1774 Washington had invested the princely sum of £2,000 in captive labor, and paid taxes on 135 slaves. Twelve years later, despite losses during the war, the number had risen to 213. The purchase of Will and the three other young men was typical of Washington's buying habits during this period, as he preferred those bondpeople "not exceeding" twenty years of age. "Let there be two thirds of them Males, the other third Females," he instructed Daniel Adams, who conducted his purchases. "All of them to be straight Limb'ed & in every respect strong and likely, with good Teeth & good Countenances."[3]

Each morning, Washington rose early to survey his lands, but William rose earlier yet to lay out his clothing for the ride. On one occasion, Lee accompanied his master, and Washington, whom Thomas Jefferson later praised as the "finest horseman of his age," was pleased to discover that Lee exhibited a natural affinity for the saddle. Like all Virginia gentlemen, Washington enjoyed the hunt, and in addition to his duties as valet, William was placed in charge of the hounds. George Washington Parke Custis, Martha's grandson, later described Lee as a "fearless horseman" who galloped "at full speed, through brake or tangled wood." Lee was "sturdy, and of great bone and muscle," and when mounted upon Chinkling, his favorite jumper, with a French hunting horn slung across his back, Lee raced after the foxes "in a style at which [other] huntsmen would stand aghast." The two men often hunted together three times a week. But traditional conventions of race and servitude, together with Washington's studiously mannered behavior, kept them from ever forming—or at least acknowledging—the sort of friendship that might have arisen had Lee been born free and white.[4]

The growing crisis with Britain brought new responsibilities for Washington. For Lee, as was the case with most African Americans, the rift brought new opportunities. The blending of egalitarian ideals with the disruption of war emboldened slaves throughout the colonies to claim the same liberties as white Americans. In the fall of 1774, as Washington put his affairs in order before leaving for the spring meeting of the Second Continental Congress, he invested fifteen shillings "for shoes, etc.," for Lee, as it would hardly do for his valet to arrive in Philadelphia wearing the scuffed boots of a huntsman. Prior to 1775, few Virginia-born slaves saw much of the world beyond their master's gatepost, but the chaos of war altered the lives of thousands of bond-people. As Lee and Washington galloped north, William's strange life grew stranger still in that he was flying *with* his master, rather than from one.[5]

On the long road to Philadelphia, William had time to think. Lord Dunmore, the last royal governor in Williamsburg, was about to offer free-dom to any slave or indentured servant who would carry a musket in the service of King George. Washington's estate would make an attractive prize for the redcoats. The general's nervous overseer admitted that the slaves at Mount Vernon regarded liberty as "sweet." There "is not a man [among] them," he admitted, "but wou'd leave us, if they believ'd they could make their escape." For white Americans, Britain was the very symbol of politi-cal oppression, but for those in servitude, English pickets meant libera-tion—if also the expectation of military service. Before the war's end, nearly fifteen thousand Africans and African Americans accepted Dunmore's offer; five thousand more, the majority of them from the nearly all-white New England states, fought on the Patriot side. Still others simply took advantage of the confusion of war to slip away from their masters' service. In a city such as Philadelphia, Lee might vanish into a back alley while on an errand for Washington and then either ride north to join the British or try to pass as a free man. But for the past seven years he had labored as a house valet, a com-paratively easy post for a slave. If he failed in his escape, Lee would almost certainly be sold into the fields, and so he had to weigh his options—and his loyalties—with enormous care.[6]

Any thoughts William had about making a run for his freedom may have been stayed by disquieting rumors within the black community that most of the bondmen who reached British lines were employed as military labor-ers. For every slave like New Jersey's Titus, who rose through the ranks and achieved the honorary title of Colonel Tye, dozens more dug trenches, cooked meals, and polished boots. Whether they found themselves in Loyalist or Patriot ranks, the casualty rates were ghastly, as white officers on both sides regarded them as little more than cannon fodder. This William discovered in June 1778 at the Battle of Monmouth Court House. Lee had "assumed unofficial command" of the slaves and valets of all the general officers, and as the day was hot, Lee and several other slaves rode to the top of a nearby hill to enjoy the cool breeze and watch the British maneuvers. Just as Lee extended his telescope to survey the field, a British artilleryman, mistaking the bondmen for Washington and his senior staff, opened fire. A six-pound ball crashed into the sycamore tree they stood beneath, "scattering but not injuring Billy Lee and his fellow servants." Washington smiled thinly as the slaves fled down the hill, but Will perhaps thought the incident somewhat less humorous.[7]

One subtle sign that his travels about the north had an impact on "Mulatto Will" was his quiet determination to be treated as an adult, which meant the adoption of a surname. Although North American slaves occasionally adopted family or occupational names for use among themselves, few masters wished to bestow upon their human property the sense of dignity a surname implied. In Washington's kinship-conscious Virginia, family connections conferred respect and rank, so slaves were denied both. Like many of the fortunate sons who peopled Mount Vernon, young George Washington Parke Custis customarily referred to the far older valet by the name of "Billy." Before the Revolution, Washington often listed his manservant in account books as "my boy Billy," but after the war, the general noted his valet had taken to "calling himself William Lee." Interestingly, while the vast majority of freedpeople in the north selected the family surname of their former master, William evidently embraced the name of Lee, as a symbolic tie either to the plantation of his birth or to the man he suspected of being his biological father.[8]

Lee's newfound sense of self-assurance appears also to have manifested itself in his choice of a spouse, as well as in his determination to have her by his side. Under Virginia law, slave families enjoyed no legal standing, but black Americans forged lasting relationships nonetheless, and wise masters recognized the calming influence of stable families in the quarters. During the summer of 1784, Lee approached Washington about Margaret Thomas, whom he regarded as his wife. While in Philadelphia, Lee had fallen in love with Margaret, who had been a slave at the time and evidently was hired out to Washington's household (what the general dubbed his "family"). Margaret was now free, and she and William begged Washington to finance her journey south. The general thought little of Margaret's character—or perhaps he did not wish to share his valet's time—but admitted that they were "attached (married he says)." Given the fact that Lee had "lived with [Washington] so long & followed [his] fortunes through the War with fidelity," the general could not "refuse his request."[9]

One would like to know the end of that story, but no evidence indicates that a Margaret Thomas or Margaret Lee ever resided at Mount Vernon. But then, as she was free, there would be no reason to expect to find her in Washington's account book. History is the past, but the past recovered imperfectly, restored to life inadequately. Like the vast majority of slaves in early America, neither Margaret nor William ever learned to read or write, and so their story comes to us secondhand, filtered through the quill pens of an elite white man who little cared to understand slave culture but had no wish to pry into the private lives of the people he owned. One assumes that Margaret came to Virginia, but given the pressures of a marriage in which the husband served at the beck and call of his busy master, the marriage may not have lasted. Or perhaps Margaret, like many black women in the early Republic, died young, for no visitor to Mount Vernon in later years mentions Lee having a spouse.[10]

Shortly before Lee took Margaret as his wife, the war had ended at York-town. With his usual sense of historical flair, Washington took leave of his senior staff by saying, "The work is done, and well done," before calling out, "Billy, hand me my horse." Having laid down his sword for the last time, the former general, like men of power and influence up and down the Atlantic coast, turned his energies to rebuilding his long-neglected businesses. Thanks to his brother's shares in the Ohio Company, together with the bounties he accrued during his years of military service, Washington owned more than 63,000 acres of trans-Appalachian land. Over the next few years, he spent springs and summers surveying his western holdings, and as always, Lee rode at his side. On April 22, 1785, while dragging heavy measuring chains, Lee tumbled over a rock and "broke the pan of his knee." He could "neither Walk, stand, or ride," so Washington was forced to construct "a sled to carry him on." Washington had hoped to spend several more weeks in the west, but Lee's mishap, he recorded in his diary, "put a stop to my Surveying."[11]

Lee continued his duties by hobbling about the mansion with a crutch or a cane. Despite the constant pain in his knee, William proved as proud as Washington proved needy. Many of the first president's biographers have been dismissive of William Lee's contribution to Washington's household. One scholar has insisted that as valet, "Will was a privileged servant with duties hardly extending beyond serving a master who needed little personal service." Without a hint of irony, however, the same writer conceded that after he laid out Washington's clothing for the day, Lee then "brushed his master's long hair." Washington himself groused that the early-rising Lee was "ruined by idleness." Echoing that sentiment, another scholar has applauded Washington for being "willing to put up with Billy Lee's afflictions," as well as for paying the unwaged, enslaved surveyor's "medical bills without an audible murmur."[12]

The complaint that men and women who drew no wages were habitually "idle" and unmotivated was heard in parlors all across the new nation. Nor are there records of anyone at Mount Vernon who sympathized with how Lee dealt with his constant pain. In an era without modern painkillers or wheelchairs, William medicated himself with ample doses of rum, earning the censure of his austere master as well as modern scholars. Without admitting that Will functioned admirably upon a shattered leg, one biographer observed only that Lee had "a gift for procuring" enough liquor to "get him drunk by evening." In this, the crippled William was unusual, since rural slaves drank far less than other laborers in early America, but also because attentive masters such as Washington demanded a sober labor force.[13]

Despite his master's admonitions, Lee continued to drink. The rum, his bad leg, or both severely limited Will's mobility, yet Washington, perhaps hoping to force his valet into sobriety, continued to send him on errands. In March 1788, he dispatched Will to Alexandria to collect the mail. A late snow had fallen, covering the town's brick walks. Unstable under the best of conditions, Lee fell again and "broke the Pan of his other Knee." No longer able to perform even the simplest task that required movement, William was now trained at "making Shoes." At about the age of thirty-eight, Lee was broken, "slow, and [in] sickness."[14]

Lee was still able to travel by carriage, and his master, despite his determination to maintain psychological distance from others, nevertheless found William's company comforting at difficult moments. In early 1789, as he prepared to leave for his inaugural in New York City, Washington paid a farewell visit to his mother. The relationship between the general and Mary Washington had ever been strained, and with Mary Washington suffering from breast cancer, her son understood that this was to be his final goodbye. Since Mary's home in Fredericksburg was but a short day trip, Washington required no valet for the visit. There was no plausible reason for Lee to accompany his master other than that Washington desired an old and familiar face. Slavery produced a host of complicated relationships, and perhaps none is harder for the modern mind to fathom than the strong, if decidedly unequal, partnership of these two men.[15]

Two days later, on the morning of April 16, the president-elect, William Lee, and aides David Humphreys and Tobias Lear boarded the coach for New York. Lee's responsibilities included procuring lodging for the group on the way north and preparing for the crowds who gathered at every stop to cheer Washington's passage. The labors proved too much for Lee, and by the third day Washington decided to leave him in Philadelphia for medical treatment. "Will appears to be in too bad a state to travel at present," Lear observed. Although Lee was in the habit of "dress[ing] his knee himself" and so was "in no need of a Doctor," Lear doubted that he could "possibly be of any service" in New York and recommended his return to Mount Vernon. But Lee insisted on joining the new president. Following consultations with Dr. William Smith and Dr. James Hutchinson, Lee's legs were fitted with steel braces that not only allowed him to travel but also enabled "him in some measure to walk" again. On June 22, much to the astonishment of Lear, Lee arrived in New York City "safe & well." He "seems not to have lost much flesh by his misfortunes," Lear added.[16]

Like many slaves who appeared briefly in the public record only to vanish again, Lee disappeared from Washington's correspondence thereafter. Circumstantial evidence, however, indicates that William remained at the president's side during his first term, which meant that "as a Butler as well as a Valette" he witnessed the parade of politicians and diplomats through his master's parlor. Did Lee have occasion to meet the squabbling secretaries of state and treasury, Thomas Jefferson and Alexander Hamilton, or perhaps their enslaved domestics, including Jefferson's quadroon brother-in-law James Hemings? We know only that early in his second term, Washington instructed Lear to obtain "a substitute for William." Nothing short of Lee's "excellent qualities" and "good appearance" would do, Washington added. The famously reserved president briefly hinted that he would miss the companionship of his longtime retainer before retreating behind a curtain of complaints about how black domestics were more a burden than a blessing. Lear chose a young slave named Christopher as Lee's replacement, and by the spring of 1794, William was again cobbling shoes in Virginia.[17]

As he approached the end of his life, Washington resolved to at last cease his ownership of other humans. In his final will, drawn up in July 1799, he proposed to free all of the slaves held under his name. Washington stipulated that aged slaves and those without parents were to be "comfortably cloathed and fed" by his heirs, and young slaves were to be educated and "brought up to some useful occupation," so that they could survive in a free society. The final clause pertained to William Lee. As "a testimony to my sense of his attachment to me, and for his faithful services during the Revolutionary War," Lee was freed immediately, paid an annuity of $30 each year for the remainder of his life, and allowed to remain in his cabin at Mount Vernon.[18]

Even by the prescribed regulations of early American legal documents, the phrasing is curious—and says much about Washington's legendary sense of reserve. Despite thirty-one years together in the saddle, in the war, and in the presidency, Washington mentioned only Will's "sense of attachment" to *him*, rather than his own affection for Lee. The Virginian, living in a society that prized composed, rational behavior, refused to reveal his true sentiments, even in his dying document. Could the man who wished not Martha but only William Lee to accompany him as he paid a final visit to his estranged, dying mother regard him as just another slave, or was Washington's "sense of attachment" for William a sentiment he dared not express? One need not suggest that Lee, if given a choice, would have remained enslaved, or that Washington's generally humane treatment of his human chattel at Mount Vernon justified his ownership of black Americans, to recognize that the shared intimacy of lives lived together in the big house sometimes allowed for tangled relationships that transcended race and class.[19]

Following his master's death and his own liberation, Lee remained at Mount Vernon. As a free man, Lee was able to come and go as he pleased, but like many of those emancipated by the Revolution, he was too impoverished and too aged and too ill to journey far. Although still a working plantation, Mount Vernon (and the president's tomb) became a common stop for sightseers. Travelers who wished to see the last of the Revolutionary generation or hear tales of the war often stopped by Lee's cabin. Artist Charles Willson Peale found William cobbling shoes in one of the plantation's outbuildings, and the two "sat alone together and talked of past days." Lee continued to drink to ease the pain in his legs, and when suffering delirium tremens was bled by a former slave, an aged mulatto named West Ford. Ironically, as was the case with the similar agonies performed on Washington by Dr. James Craik, West Ford often took too much blood and weakened his already sick patient. On one occasion in 1828, when "Westford [*sic*] was sent for to bring Billy out of a fit," Custis remembered, the "blood would not flow. Billy was dead!"[20]

William Lee's long life, although privileged and unique in so many ways, mirrored the fate of tens of thousands of Africans and African Americans during the turbulent thirty-seven years that spanned the Revolutionary era. From the end of the Seven Years' War in 1763 to the election of slaveholder Thomas Jefferson as president in 1800—the period of time covered by this volume—blacks waged their own struggle for independence. As America's white citizenry demanded liberty on the basis of natural rights and then took to the field of battle to uphold that demand, slaves such as Lee began to assert their own rights to freedom. William Lee rode beside Washington throughout the war and witnessed every campaign, from Boston to Yorktown, and like many a military servant, he was an attentive observer at each night's fireside talk of individual rights and equality. Before the century was over, the Revolution, together with the changing economy of the northern states, served to eradicate slave labor in half of the new Republic, just as it weakened it in Lee's area on the border of the South, where practical men like Washington began to diversify and plant wheat beside the more labor-intensive tobacco. William exemplified that remarkable transformation as well, for he died a free man, the beneficiary of his master's will. But no state moved to enfranchise freedmen or recompense them for decades of hard labor. William reflected that unhappy saga too. In his old age he lived an impoverished existence as a crippled alcoholic, and as he sat on the steps of his small cabin, amusing visitors with old stories of past glories and promises unkept, Lee personified a Revolution that spoke in bold terms but at best limped slowly down the path of human rights.

Not all historians, of course, would agree that the founding generation ultimately failed to practice what they preached, or that the two decades after the 1783 Peace of Paris amounted to a counterrevolution regarding black Americans. Indeed, the belief that the war with Britain marked a progressive social upheaval in black life was first advanced not by a modern apologist for the founding fathers but by Benjamin Quarles in his pioneering *The Negro in the American Revolution* (1961). Writing at a time when many white Americans were determined to deny black Americans their basic legal rights, Quarles was understandably anxious to demonstrate the black contribution to America's victory in 1781. African American involvement, his book implicitly suggested, established their right to American citizenship, both in 1776 *and* in 1961. Far from being absent during the struggle with Britain, black Americans "welcomed the resort to arms," Quarles argued, and "quickly caught the spirit of '76." Since then, a good number of formidable scholars have agreed. For all of their failings, they insist, white revolutionaries consciously abandoned a hierarchical world that reserved political power for men of gentle birth. As Gordon Wood argued in *The Radicalism of the American Revolution* (1991), the founding fathers consciously forged a philosophy that rendered inevitable the abolitionist crusade "of the nineteenth century and in fact all our current egalitarian thinking."[21]

But would William Lee agree? Would untold thousands of men and women like Lee have found anything radical about the decades in which they lived? Or would they have found the American Revolution sadly wanting and white Patriots deeply hypocritical? It may not be enough, perhaps, to judge the Revolution by what it meant to antebellum reformers, to the Civil War generation, or even to us; rather, we may need to judge it by what it meant to people such as William Lee, or Colonel Tye, or Elizabeth Freeman, or Richard Allen, or Gabriel. Their voices need to be heard, and their lives are the subject of this book.

The present volume re-creates the last four decades of the eighteenth century, as white and black Americans first struggled to assert their rights against a distant empire and then struggled yet again to define what it meant to be an American and a citizen, as well as whether a republic based upon the consent of the governed was a fraud so long as one-fifth of the population remained enslaved. Early on, as Americans articulated a sense of their natural rights, there was reason to hope that the growing crisis with Britain might result in the death of unfree labor. Virtually overnight, an institution that existed throughout the British Empire came under assault from activists of both races who grasped the ideological problem with calling themselves the "slaves of King George" yet literally holding other men and women as chattel (or being themselves enslaved). As the nation took up arms, black Americans in both camps—and a majority of African Americans ultimately cast their lot with the British—expected the conflict to result in national manumission. Should Britain prove successful in putting down the revolt, Parliament would owe a debt to thousands of black Loyalists. But if the united colonies won their independence, a new government founded upon natural rights could not easily deny liberty to formerly enslaved Patriots.

Yet deny it they did. The first part of this book explores the ways in which republican ideology and the chaos of war so weakened slavery that every northern state moved against the system by 1804, while the final six chapters chronicle the dashed hopes of black Americans. With the return of peace, white Patriots did not merely fail to enact national reforms consistent with the lofty rhetoric of the late 1760s and early 1780s. Having achieved *their* independence, most whites quickly retreated from the principles announced in the Declaration as they sought to rebuild their war-ravaged economy through the exploitation of unwaged black men and women. Although slavery gradually disappeared in the northern states, few sections of the Republic recognized African Americans as citizens or allowed them to vote during the years covered by this volume. Instead, former revolutionaries tabled practical schemes for gradual emancipation in Virginia, embedded slavery within the nation's Constitution, crafted legislation allowing southern masters to recapture fugitives in search of liberty in the North, and defined racial categories in the country's first immigration statute. America's Patriot elite knew exactly what they were doing. As Patrick Henry conceded, there was little doubt that slavery was "repugnant to humanity." But like his enemy Thomas Jefferson, he declared it impossible to free his bondpeople due to "the general inconveniency of living without them."[22]

Black Americans, however, were hardly passive victims of white authority, and although it would be false to ignore the dynamics of power and policy, it would be equally artificial to ignore what African Americans did for themselves during these decades. As it became clear that most politicians and masters had little intention of following through on their egalitarian statements, black activists pushed back hard against the rising tide of racism. Although no black American in these years was ever able to cast a ballot, former bondpeople and even those still enslaved helped to shape the politics of the early Republic through their demands and actions. As Virginia bondman Jack Ditcher insisted in 1800, "We have as much right to fight for our liberty as any men." When they could, enslaved Americans were dramatic actors in their own saga, and this book attempts to tell that part of the story too.[23]

William Lee was unusual for the connections he formed and for being among the minority of black Americans to benefit from the Revolution. Yet in so many other ways, his existence was typical of most slaves in North America during the age of revolution. The course of his long life epitomized the hopes and expectations of black Americans as well as the final, crushing disappointments of the era. As he rode west from Yorktown, Lee, like most slaves, had prayed that the independent Republic would fulfill its promise of freedom and liberty to all Americans. Lee's proud adoption of a surname, his demand that he be allowed to marry a free woman of Philadelphia, and even his elegant clothing reflected the optimism and self-sufficiency typical of his generation. So too was his manner of liberation characteristic of Chesapeake bondpeople, since Washington was just one of many planters who found it problematic to free his slaves during his lifetime. Long before Lee's death in 1828, it was all too clear that the Revolutionary generation had failed to embrace the opportunities offered by independence—and perhaps had doomed the Union to civil war. The number of enslaved Americans rose steadily over the years, from roughly 351,000 in 1760 to 893,041 by 1800, 35,946 of whom resided in the North. Even Gordon Wood has conceded that by the end of the Revolutionary era, despite manumission in the northern states, there were "more slaves in the nation than in 1760." Lee died a tragic symbol of the Republic, crippled by its inability to live up to its own Revolutionary ideals, and half free at best.[24]

ONE

Equiano's World

The British Atlantic Empire in 1763

ALMOST FROM THE TIME they learned how to walk, enslaved children learned how to lie. Wise parents taught their children how to behave when confronted by their owner, or indeed by any white person. Children had to understand the hard rules of life if they hoped to avoid ill-treatment. As they grew older, black adolescents faced far worse than a backhanded slap if they failed to master the art of obsequience. When spoken to, clever youths smiled, gazed quietly at their feet, and most of all dissembled.[1]

As both boy and man, Olaudah Equiano told more than his share of lies. He told so many contradictory stories that even today it remains unclear which were true and which were fictions crafted for self-protection or for propaganda. According to his 1789 autobiography, *The Interesting Narrative*, Equiano was born around 1745 in what is today southeastern Nigeria. At the age of eleven, he and his sister were kidnapped by three African slave catchers. After being sold and resold, Equiano was at length bought by European traders, who shipped him to Barbados. Sale into the English sugar islands usually meant a short life of backbreaking labor, but after only two weeks, Equiano was sold again, this time to Virginia, where he spent less than a month performing a child's task of "weeding grass, and fathering stones." Then once more his luck changed. Michael Pascal, a lieutenant in the Royal Navy, bought some naval stores from Equiano's master and while there took a liking to the boy. Pascal purchased Equiano, rechristened him Gustavus Vassa (after the former king of Sweden), and set him to work as a cabin boy aboard the *Industrious Bee*.[2]

While in Pascal's service, Equiano visited much of the British maritime world. During the Seven Years' War, the boy met General James Wolfe, who intervened to spare him "a flogging for fighting with a young gentleman." Equiano was in Quebec in 1759 when the British won on the Plains of Abraham, only to lose "the good and gallant" Wolfe to French shells. With the battle won, he sailed for England along with most of the fleet. Curiously, Equiano wrote nothing about the sprawling splendors of London, but ironically, having perhaps been the victim of African kidnappers, he joined Pascal in putting together a press-gang to refresh their depleted complement.[3]

At this point Equiano's tale took another curious turn. While in London he met "the Miss Guerins," two young evangelicals who fretted over the boy's soul. Informed that he faced eternal damnation, Equiano too grew "uneasy" and asked to be baptized. Pascal at first demurred, since many masters—and perhaps more than a few naval officers—regarded Anglican notions of Christian brotherhood as dangerous for impressionable cabin boys. But at last he gave way, and on February 9, 1759, Equiano was baptized at St. Margaret's Church, Westminster. Picking up his pen, the clergyman dutifully recorded these words: "Gustavus Vassa a Black born in Carolina 12 years old." If true, Equiano was no African but an American-born creole—a person born in the Americas but not of American ancestry—and he was even younger than Pascal presumably realized, since his birth year would have been 1747. Further complicating matters, fourteen years later, in 1773, when he joined the crew of the *Racehorse* during its search for the Northwest Passage, "Gustavus" told the captain that "So. Carolina" was his "Place and Country where born."[4]

So Equiano was lying to somebody; the only question is to whom. Perhaps he lied to Pascal about his age to escape the Virginia fields. Perhaps he lied to the minister at St. Margaret's due to long years of habit, although doing so just prior to baptism should have struck him as a peculiar way to achieve salvation. But by the time he boarded the *Racehorse*, he had been free for seven years, having purchased his liberty in July 1766. Perhaps he was so conditioned to creating fictions in hopes of keeping body and soul together that he saw no reason to speak the truth even when free. After all, he remained a man of color in an Atlantic world dominated by slavery. But either his early life was a tissue of lies or the stories of an idyllic childhood in Essaka that he later described in *The Interesting Narrative* were complete fabrications. In the end, Equiano's mysterious story serves as a reminder of the unreliability of the words of Africans and African Americans filtered through the pens of whites. Symbolic of this complexity is the fact that the only known painting of Equiano—as opposed to the engraved frontispiece that appeared in the first edition of the *Narrative*—may not be him at all. Although the portrait was previously attributed to Joshua Reynolds, art scholars now note that the clothing worn in it suggests the painting was done before 1765. Perhaps

Portrait of a Negro Man (left), attributed to both Allan Ramsay and Joshua Reynolds, is widely used in biographies of Equiano, but specialists date the painting to 1757–60, at which time Equiano was a boy. *Bridgeman Art Library*. The frontispiece (right) from Equiano's 1789 autobiography, *The Interesting Narrative*, is the only definitive portrait of the author. *Library of Congress*.

the well-dressed African who has proudly gazed at a generation of modern readers is yet another black man whose identity is lost to history.[5]

With his multiple and changing identities, Equiano came into contact, as he sailed from port to port, with other men and women who would choose their own identities—African and creole, black and white. They would spend the next four decades waging a war for American independence, or fighting for their freedom by picking up a musket in the name of King George, or trying to decide what liberty meant to them and to their country. Indeed, Equiano's personal saga provides ideal bookends for this larger saga. As a boy, he served in the Seven Years' War, a conflict that reshaped the map of the Americas and rendered the Revolution inevitable. By the time he died in London on March 31, 1797, while still in his early fifties, Equiano was active in the transatlantic antislavery movement. In between he had known General Wolfe, young Horatio Nelson, and abolitionists Thomas Clarkson and Granville Sharp. His fabrications notwithstanding, Equiano's astonishing life illuminates a most astonishing time.[6]

———

Normally the most astute of observers, Equiano said little about his brief journey to Canada. He described the "magnificent spectacle" of the English ships "dressed with colours of all kinds" and marveled as the marquis de

Vaudreuil, the defeated "French governor and his lady, and other persons of note, came on board our ship to dine." His autobiography contains not a single word about meeting another black person, enslaved or free, during the short period he spent in Canada in 1759. Perhaps that is not surprising. Of all the corners of the British Empire that the young mariner ever visited, what had been New France prior to the 1763 Peace of Paris had the lowest percentage of enslaved people. Yet if what the English renamed the Province of Quebec was, to borrow the words of historian Ira Berlin, a society with slaves rather than a slave society, there were still roughly 3,600 unfree workers residing in the colony. Most were aboriginal people, but at least one-third were Africans and their offspring. According to the 47th Article of Capitulation of Montreal, which protected slavery in the now-British colony, the war changed nothing in regard to unfree labor.[7]

Although primarily designed for France's Caribbean sugar islands, the elaborate 1685 royal decree known as the *Code Noir*, or Black Code, established the policies that regulated the relationship between masters and slaves in *all* French colonies. Drafted by Jean-Baptiste Colbert, the code was ostensibly designed to convert African souls and protect unfree labor from the excessive demands of cruel masters. In reality, the Black Code made but a few cursory references to instruction "in the Roman faith" before transferring control of Africans to French colonists and overseers. The code forbade priests from "conducting weddings" if the slaves lacked their masters' permission, yet ruled that all black children born of relations between slaves were to be slaves as well. Africans could not carry weapons or even "large sticks," and the list of punishments was both lengthy and gruesome. Runaways would have their ears sliced off and their shoulders branded with the fleur-de-lys; recidivists were to have their hamstrings severed. The code frowned on masters "torturing or mutilating" their human property but allowed whites to "chain [blacks] and have them beaten with rods or straps" if necessary. Since the severity of slave laws in different areas correlated to the percentage of blacks in those places, it is logical to assume that the brutality allowed by the code was more common to the slave societies of the Caribbean than in New France, yet the *Nova Scotia Advertiser* carried runaway slave notices similar to those found in every English newspaper to the south. Just to clarify that it indeed applied in New France, in 1701 Louis gave his formal consent to slavery in Canada, authorizing "its colonists to own slaves [in] full proprietorship."[8]

Accustomed to the endless varieties of slavery that existed around the Atlantic world, Equiano was silent on the multiplicity of jobs performed by slaves in Canada. Unfree labor itself was simple enough to characterize— French philosophe Charles de Secondat, the baron of Montesquieu, famously defined it as "the establishment of a right which gives to one man such power over another as renders him absolute master of his life and fortune"—but the enormous range of tasks carried out by enslaved workers would stagger modern readers, who frequently assume that slaves only picked cotton. As was typical in Britain's northernmost colonies, most blacks lived in or near towns; just over three-quarters resided in urban areas, with more than half of all slaves in Canada crowded into Montreal. Some African Americans labored along the docks, while others worked in the fisheries, but most were *domestiques* (many of them the light-skinned children of French fathers and African women). Given the region's short growing season, less than one-quarter of all slaves in Canada plowed the fields.[9]

As the relatively small number of blacks in Canada indicates, there was no serious trade of Africans up the St. Lawrence. Although the French had shipped a good many *panis*, or aboriginal slaves, to their Caribbean holdings as punishment, no reciprocal traffic in Africans developed over the course of the century. Many *domestiques* arrived with their masters from the sugar islands; typical were Toussaint, who accompanied his mistress, Milly Daccarette, from Martinique, and François, who shipped in from Saint-Domingue in 1752 with his widowed owner, Marie Cheron. The spoils of war provided a second source of slaves. In July 1745, toward the start of what Anglo-Americans dubbed King George's War, King Louis XV decreed that English-owned runaways were to be sold to French masters, with proceeds accruing to the monarchy. Although the war did not end until 1748, New England smugglers took advantage of the edict to sell enslaved crewmen to their enemy. Captain Nathan Whiting disposed of three men, including Zabud June and Jacob Toto, on Cape Breton Island, and William Pepperrell of Maine, commander of the expedition against Fort Louisbourg, either lost as a runaway or sold his slave Catto shortly after the Anglo-American expedition captured the garrison on June 17.[10]

Below the St. Lawrence lay New England. As was true further north, Britain's New England colonies were home to very few Africans. Slaves were never more than 4 percent of the region's population, and only Rhode Island, with roughly three thousand slaves in 1763, boasted a black population that was more than 6 percent. The harsh climate proved especially inhospitable to Africans, who suffered from pulmonary infections during the long winters, and it was not conducive to growing large-scale staple crops. As the mortality rate of captive Africans was twice that of white immigrants, prospective masters preferred to buy the labor of English indentured servants. Should white servants die, the capital invested in their labor was less than that required to purchase African bodies. Some New Englanders also regarded reliance upon

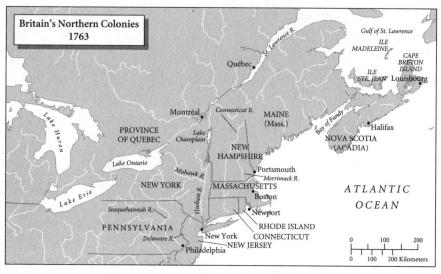

Britain's northern American colonies, 1763.

unfree labor as ungodly, since what remained of their former Puritan ethos demanded steady toil on their own part. Idle hands of an indolent master class were the devil's workshop.[11]

Not that Calvinist sensibilities, which by the mid-eighteenth century were in any case quite faded, completely prohibited slavery. African slavery was legal throughout New England, just as it was in every other colony in British America in 1763. James Otis Sr., a sixty-one-year-old justice of common pleas in Boston, owned several slaves, as did wealthy shipper John Hancock. So too did Parson William Smith, whose daughter Abigail planned to marry young attorney John Adams the following fall. Exactly how many blacks resided in New England at the end of the Seven Years' War remains a mystery, and what data do exist may have been deliberately falsified. In Massachusetts, Governor Francis Bernard reported that in 1763 the colony was home to 200,000 people—not counting Native Americans—of whom 2,221 were "negroes and mulattoes." But since slaves were counted solely for purposes of taxation, Bernard suspected that canny masters underreported their holdings. Even assuming some fraud, this means that Massachusetts was less than 2 percent black, a figure that remained constant throughout the Revolutionary era.[12]

Befitting the patchwork quality of the British Empire, pieced together through consistent conquest but sporadic settlement, the laws governing unfree labor in the New England colonies varied considerably from the *Code Noir* of the newly obtained Province of Quebec. At first glance,

Massachusetts's 1641 Body of Liberties even appeared to ban slavery. "There shall never be any bond slaverie, villinage or captivitie amongst us," admonished Article 91. But then followed the exceptions, which included "lawfull captives taken in just warres," as well as "such strangers as willingly selle themselves or are sold to us." Since the reference to "strangers" derived from Leviticus, which permitted Hebrews to purchase slaves "from among the strangers who sojourn with you," this clause bore a biblical stamp of approval. The allusion to "just warres" was also weighted with tradition, as English hostilities with the Algonquians dating back to the Pequot War of 1637 had provided settlers with a steady supply of slaves. Long before the end of the Seven Years' War, New England settlers had defined "strangers" as the ultimate outsiders: Indians and Africans. The Body of Liberties, however, never denied New England slaves the rights to marry, read, or assemble, as did the laws in Britain's southernmost colonies.[13]

As in Canada, slaves in New England tended to live in or near urban areas and were disproportionately owned by the wealthiest families. In Connecticut, home to approximately five thousand bondpeople in 1763, half of all lawyers and public officials owned slaves. So too did roughly two-thirds of those who held estates valued at more than £2,000. Most white New England slaveholders were farmers, and contemporary newspapers suggest that the minority of blacks who lived in the countryside performed a wide variety of tasks. Sale advertisements described blacks as "brought up in husbandry" or "understanding the farming business exceedingly well." Yet the majority of New England slaves worked within the household. Antoine Court, a French visitor, noted that "there is not a house in Boston, however small may be its means, that has not one or two" slaves.[14]

Slaves were particularly numerous in Rhode Island, a colony with excellent harbors but little arable land. As a result, Rhode Island ports quickly took the lead in building and fitting out the vessels that carried captive Africans to Britain's southern and Caribbean colonies. By the end of the Seven Years' War, ships owned by merchants in Bristol, Providence, and Newport accounted for 60 percent of all black cargoes to English America. Newport alone housed a population that was 18 percent enslaved, making it one of the most demographically black cities in North America. Newport contained several exceptional rum distilleries, and its merchants became celebrated on the west coast of Africa for the quality of their liquor. As Captain George Scott lamented to his Newport investors from Africa, his error was to fill his hold with anything but liquor. "Had we laid out two thousand pounds in rum, bread, and flour, it would have purchased more [humans] in value than all our dry goods." Merchants poured the profits into elegant mansions and, ironically, benevolent ventures. When the College of Rhode Island was founded in 1764, two of the signatories on the charter were John and Nicholas Brown, whose family-based company in Providence had been deeply involved in the Atlantic slave trade since 1736; at length, the university would be renamed after Nicholas Brown Jr.[15]

Since most New England slaves were not agricultural workers, historians of the region's economy continue to debate their purpose. Some argue that Africans and their offspring were critical to the economic development of northern seaports, a difficult proposition to sustain given the small number of blacks found in these colonies. Others insist that enslaved domestics fulfilled no useful economic purpose apart from serving as visible emblems of authority for urban elites. Most slaveholding New England households were not merely wealthy, however. What set them apart from other prosperous families in the region was the fact that the men who headed them conducted much of their work away from their homes. Merchants, public officials, and attorneys required either highly trained domestics to run their residences in their absence or menservants to accompany them while about on business. Such was the lot of Adam, the slave of Joshua Hempstead of New London, Connecticut. As a businessman and attorney who served also as a justice of the peace and probate judge, Hempstead used Adam to conduct a wide variety of household chores in his absence, including fulfilling Hempstead's yearly obligation to work on the public highways in town. Enslaved domestics such as Adam indicate that New England's economy was hardly dependent upon unfree labor, yet by allowing their masters to pursue new opportunities and careers, they were playing a vital role in the region's transformation from a barter economy to a capitalist market economy.[16]

What remains beyond debate is the impact these sparse numbers had on the retention of African traditions in New England. Surrounded by an overwhelming white, Protestant majority, and even living within their masters' households, blacks in Britain's northernmost colonies had little opportunity to practice African traditions or forge a culture of resistance. The hope of fashioning a viable African society became marginally more possible by midcentury, as slavers sold small numbers of Africans—rather than creoles from the Caribbean—into New England. But even then, black customs were inevitably influenced by British cultural practices. Starting around 1740, slaves in Boston and Newport began to celebrate Negro Election Day, or "Nigger 'Lection." Possibly a rite of spring in its inception, the festival came to include a parade, dances, games, and in some towns a banquet, during which slaves elected one of their own as king or governor. Slaves enjoyed the "unmolested use of the Boston Common, with an equality of rights and privileges with white people." The dances approximated a West African ring dance, but the election of a black administrator, who then appointed a lieutenant governor, justices of the peace, and sheriffs, clearly owed a debt to English political culture. Although the elected slave exerted no actual power over white authorities—or perhaps because of that fact—most masters tolerated the "Negro's hallowday" and granted their slaves a few days off. One Salem master recorded that he gave "Scip[io] 5s. and W[illia]m 2s 6d," while the Warwick owner of the E. & C. Greene Company scribbled into his account book that he had "8 days lost [due to] Negro Election."[17]

To the west of Rhode Island's profitable ports lay New York, where visitors rarely failed to comment on its large contingent of Africans. Although precise data for colonial New York are even harder to obtain than for New England, by the mid-1760s the five southern counties around the bustling port had a black population of approximately fifteen thousand. In later decades, nearly 40 percent of the white families in the city owned at least a single slave. As that percentage was even higher than in South Carolina, some have argued that portions of the city, such as the Dock Ward, constituted a true slave society—with its concomitant mentality of people as things, as belongings—rather than merely a society that owned slaves. As one visitor observed, "[I]n the vicinity of New York, every respectable family had slaves, negroes and negresses who did all the drudgery." With an enslaved population of more than 20 percent, New York was second only to Charles Town as the blackest city on the English-governed mainland. Together with western Long Island, New York City and its environs was more reliant upon unfree labor than any other colony north of Maryland.[18]

By the war's end in 1763, Africans and their descendants had lived in Manhattan for exactly 150 years, since the Dutch captain of the *Jonge Tobias* abandoned Jan Rodrigues, a "black rascal," on the island. As a result, the enslaved population was a blend of African captives, Caribbean-born laborers, and New York creoles. Prior to the start of King George's War in 1745, 70 percent of the slaves brought into New York came from the Caribbean, which meant that most blacks arrived on the docks with some knowledge of English language and culture. But in the two decades prior to the Peace of Paris, white New Yorkers reversed this pattern by importing 70 percent of their slaves directly from the African coast. Four or five vessels made the voyage each year, typically in search of young Africans who could be trained for household labor. "For this market they must be young, the younger the better if not quite Children," insisted one New York merchant. "Males are best." Even during the brief intervals of peace in the Atlantic basin, the traffic was a dangerous one. The captain of the *Sarah and Elizabeth* was chased away from the African coast by a larger French slaver as he was loading his cargo and was forced to return to New York with but nine slaves. Several years later, when the Seven Years' War formally ensued, high insurance rates dampened the trade. One of the few who tried, John Lewis of the *Catherine*, lost his cargo in 1761 when the captives below decks rose in revolt.[19]

The legal code that bound enslaved New Yorkers to their masters was derived in part from the Massachusetts Body of Liberties, yet it was also an amalgamation of ancient and modern codes that typified slave law across the Americas. When the English seized New Netherlands from the Dutch in 1664, the victorious authorities devised a set of laws named (like the renamed colony) after their patron, James Stuart, the Duke of York. The Duke's Law parroted the Massachusetts statute by promising that "no Christian shall be kept in bond slavery." In that decade, of course, most unwaged laborers in the colony were white indentured servants, and much of the code was devoted to keeping apprentices bound to their masters. Only in 1702, as the number of Africans in New York began to rise, did the colonial assembly pass an amending Act for the Regulating of Slaves, beginning with a preamble designed to clarify the proper relationship between master and slave: "Whereas many mischiefs have been occasioned by the too great liberty allowed to Negro and other slaves, it shall be lawful for any master to punish their slave for their crimes and offenses at discretion not extending to life or limb."[20]

Despite such statutes, white masters feared young bondmen, and by the eve of the Revolution, black women were the majority of the city's enslaved population. But as in other northern seaports, the demographic implications of this urban labor were not readily visible, for slave culture tended to be hidden within waterfront taverns or down twisting city alleys. In colonies such as Virginia, slaves resided in rural quarters, which meant that after the day's labor was performed, bondpeople congregated to eat, talk, sing or pray, and slumber with their spouses and children. In New York City more than half of all urban masters owned but a single slave, and even the wealthiest merchant typically owned just two or three bondpeople, so black New Yorkers tended to live in separate households from their spouses. Masters flattered themselves that because their slaves lived in close proximity to one another, it mattered little that a male butler resided in one merchant's attic, while that slave's wife lived four blocks away in another merchant's basement. As one seller put it, he preferred to auction his enslaved couple as a family, but "a few miles separation will not prevent the sale." Historians continue to insist that northern slavery was of a milder variety than that found in South Carolina or Jamaica, and in many ways it was, yet a young bondman who could visit his family only on Sundays might not have agreed.[21]

As in New England, enslaved New Yorkers fused European holidays with West African traditions. This became easier following the importation of large numbers of Africans after midcentury. Originally the religious holiday of Whitsunday or Pentecost—Pfingsten in German—New York's Pinkster was practiced anywhere there was a healthy Dutch cultural presence. "All the various languages of Africa, mixed with broken and ludicrous English, fill the air, accompanied with the music of the fiddle, tambourine, the banjo, [and] drum," noted one observer. Another described the election of "Old King Charley," a "Guinea man" from Africa, who rode at the head of a parade astride his master's horse before dismounting to lead a "Congo dance as danced in their native Africa." Charley then demanded tribute from each tent placed along the parade. In another example of the racial world turned upside down, Charley charged each black man's tent one shilling, but each white man's two.[22]

Festivals that permitted slaves even a small amount of liberty were rare moments and much to be prized. Most slaveholders frowned on any celebration that weakened the supremacy of the master class, and they understood that holidays like Pinkster—in which domestics might be absent for several days—gave blacks an opportunity to make a run for their freedom. This even Equiano discovered in 1765, when his ship first touched Philadelphia's docks. His owner, Robert King, allowed him to market a few goods of his own, and Equiano promptly "sold [his] goods there, chiefly to the Quakers." As Philadelphia was the most populous city in British America, with an enslaved labor force of nearly 10 percent, King feared that Equiano might simply vanish into the city's numerous back alleys. Equiano responded indignantly that had he chosen to flee, he could have escaped in any number of ports. "I thought that if it were God's will I ever should be freed," he insisted, "whilst I was used well, it should be by honest means."[23]

Perhaps because of this, Equiano said little about meeting other slaves while in Pennsylvania. Had he done so, he might have noted that in Philadelphia as in New York City, the vast majority of masters owned just one or two slaves. But there the similarities ended. The entire colony of Pennsylvania was then home to roughly 4,500 enslaved men and women; by comparison, New York colony had four times that population of Africans and creoles. In Pennsylvania, blacks constituted only 2.3 percent of the overall population, whereas New York was 13.9 percent black. In New York, however, slavery had spread far into Long Island and up the Hudson River Valley, which accounted for the larger number of blacks. In Pennsylvania, as in New England, slaveholding was predominantly an urban affair. Philadelphia merchants and shopkeepers owned one-third of the city's slaves. Philadelphia's mayor, William Masters, owned thirty-one slaves; other masters included Benjamin Franklin and assemblyman John Dickinson.[24]

Unlike the legal codes in New York and New England, which appeared to frown on unfree labor while leaving exceptions enough for a master class to emerge, the first ordinances of Pennsylvania, the Laws Agreed upon in England, said nothing about slavery. But as merchants and shippers began to settle in Philadelphia with their black domestics, the Quakers who dominated the colonial assembly fashioned a body of laws designed to allow one person to own another. The 1726 Act for the Better Regulating of Negroes in This Province not only devised a caste system on the basis of race but also placed a number of restrictions on free blacks. Since the colony included a large number of white indentured servants, the assembly drew a sharp line between those who served for a set number of years and those who served for life. Magistrates tried whites and blacks in separate courts, and penalties for the latter were far harsher. Slaves could leave their masters' homes only with written passes, and "drinking in or near any house or shop where strong liquors [were] sold" was outlawed. As in other colonies, whites generally assumed that free blacks posed a dangerous model of upward mobility to their enslaved brethren; consequently, the 1726 code inflicted harsher regulations on freedmen. Any master who wished to free his servant was required to post a prohibitive £30 bond against the possibility that the former slave might prove a financial drain on the city. Blacks were always in danger of being reenslaved. "[A]ny free negro fit and able to work" who was judged to be idle could be bound "out to service" from year to year as any two magistrates saw fit. Freedmen risked enslavement "during life" for marrying a white woman, and the colony could take children away from freed couples, even if the family in question was neither poor nor negligent.[25]

Within just a few years, the harshness of the code was softened by the changing attitude of the Society of Friends toward human bondage. In the 1730s, Benjamin Lay, a former Caribbean planter who had relocated to Philadelphia, began to preach that his fellow Quakers should divest themselves of the sin of slavery. By the following decade, John Woolman, a Quaker from New Jersey, joined Philadelphia schoolmaster Anthony Benezet in urging that the Friends' leadership become "conscience reformers." With stunning swiftness, antislavery brotherhood swept through Quaker meetinghouses, and in 1758 the Philadelphia Meeting formally voted to act against slavery. Having perhaps heard of their denunciation of slavery, Equiano gave in to his "curiosity" and attended a Quaker service. Much to his surprise—for West African spirituality was every bit as patriarchal as European religions—he saw only "a very tall woman standing" in front of the hall, "speaking in an audible voice something which [he] could not understand."[26]

The black mariner did not know that the Friends, despite their pretensions of claims to Christian charity, merely encouraged their membership to cease the buying and selling of black bodies. It would be nearly two decades before the Yearly Meeting threatened "disownment" as the penalty for noncompliance. Some Quakers obeyed the spirit of the law, rather than the intent, by promising to free their bondpeople only after they reached the age of thirty or thirty-five. Even those who did liberate their slaves believed that the demands of brotherhood extended only to actual freedom. Quakers expressed little desire to bring African Americans into their meetinghouses, and most failed to educate their former servants, despite the leadership's recommendation and the absence of a law prohibiting teaching slaves to read or write. If Philadelphia boasted a slightly higher percentage of free blacks than other cities in English America, slavery nonetheless remained firmly entrenched in the City of Brotherly Love. Had Equiano glanced at the city's gazettes, he would have noticed the usual smattering of runaway slave notices. One fugitive "named Pen," who preferred to call himself James Pemberton, absconded while being returned from jail, fleeing with Cuff, who had already "run away several times" and tried to "board vessels in Philadelphia harbour." The two slaves, their master churlishly noted, evidently practiced what others only preached, since Pemberton "pretends to be very religious."[27]

Not for nothing did Pemberton and Cuff head for the waterfront. One curiosity that Equiano never noted specifically, because it was far from curious in his experience, was the large number of black and African mariners in the late-eighteenth-century maritime world. Not only did slaves swarm the docks in every port city, but a good number of those who sailed Atlantic waters were slaves and free blacks. In the ships that sailed from Philadelphia, at least one-quarter of the crewmen were Africans or African Americans; the number of black mariners on vessels from Providence hovered around 30 percent. On one ship sailing out of Pennsylvania, only five of fifty crewmen were native-born white Philadelphians. Even more than English America itself, the English maritime industry—as well as the Royal Navy—was a virtual Babel of languages and nationalities. If clever, able-bodied men such as Pemberton and Cuff could make it to the docks, a good many captains would sign them on with no questions asked. Indeed, even captains had a difficult time holding on to their enslaved mariners, who often jumped ship in search of liberty and better conditions. The aptly named Captain John Waterman advertised for his slave Joe, who fled from the brig *Catherine* the moment it reached Philadelphia. Joe was "Virginia born" and had twice been branded, including once with a large *F* (for "fugitive") on the left breast. He "speaks good English," Waterman admitted, "and will attempt to pass for a free Man."[28]

As they sailed south from the city, down the Delaware River into the bay, mariners could espy the Delaware coast to their west. Although agricultural slavery existed to one extent or another in all of Britain's American empire, Delaware was the beginning of the great plantation districts. Because the small colony kept no statistics prior to the first federal census of 1790, the exact number of Africans and black Americans in the region is hard to determine, though it clearly had a declining number of African-born slaves by 1763. While New York began to import greater numbers of Africans after midcentury, Delaware mirrored its southern neighbors by increasingly relying on a domestic slave population that reproduced itself naturally. Although the percentage of Africans in the colony's enslaved populace had dropped from 50 percent to 33 percent in just over a decade, an Anglican minister described the labor force as speaking "a language peculiar to themselves, a wild confused medley of Negro and corrupt English." For every two acculturated black Delawareans whose language and religion reflected numerous generations of native-born slaves, visitors such as Equiano might encounter one man like Congamochu, who bore "many large [ceremonial] scars on his belly and arms in his country fashion" and spoke of little besides the village and the wives he had left behind in Africa.[29]

What set Delaware apart from England's colonies to its south—and a factor that explains the state's later willingness to embrace voluntary emancipation—is that by the end of the Seven Years' War, very few men like Congamochu labored in tobacco fields there. Its inferior lands had been eclipsed by soils better for tobacco production in Maryland and Virginia, and as early as the 1740s, even large planters instructed their slaves to plant wheat and corn beside tobacco. Because corn required less attention from field workers, prudent masters hired out their surplus labor for short periods of time to nearby farmers who owned no slaves. Even as the colony's economy shifted toward corn and cereal crops, slaves lived in larger units than in the urban North, allowing for black families to live and work together. The declining number of Africans in the rural colony—together with the fact that whites in Delaware outnumbered blacks by four to one—meant that African cultural traditions survived only with difficulty. Visitors to the region failed to remark on any celebration or festival that rivaled New York's Pinkster holiday.[30]

No obvious geographical landmark indicated precisely where the coast of colonial Delaware gave way first to Maryland and then to Virginia's Eastern

Shore, but all mariners knew that roughly 150 miles below the entrance to the Delaware Bay lay the opening to the far larger Chesapeake Bay. Near the top of the bay sat the port of Baltimore. Despite its advantageous location, adjacent to the wheat-producing lands of western Maryland, together with the rich tobacco plantations in the eastern portion of the colony, the town was small by northern standards. Legislation that authorized the construction of "Baltemore Town" was signed in 1729, making the town roughly a century younger than Boston. Three decades later, Baltimore had grown little and was home to but three hundred residents. Apart from sleepy ports such as Baltimore, however, the Chesapeake was very black. Demographically as well as geographically, it rested between the extremes of the northern colonies, with their white majorities, and the English colonies of the lower South and Caribbean, with their steadily increasingly black majorities. In 1763, the Chesapeake was home to roughly 170,000 slaves, and Virginia was the most populous British colony. By comparison, bondpeople in the northern colonies totaled 35,000, while the enslaved populations of the Carolinas and Georgia amounted to 70,000, with another 183,000 slaves residing in the English sugar islands of Jamaica and Barbados. Where Africans and black Americans rarely constituted more than 4 percent of any New England colony's population, slaves numbered above 40 percent in Maryland and Virginia, a proportion great enough to worry the master class, but not high enough to produce the sort of terror and paranoia common to whites in the plantation districts of the Caribbean and lower South.[31]

By the time Equiano sailed into Chesapeake Bay in 1757, the Virginia countryside was dominated by enslaved creoles. As in Delaware, the natural increase of the black population allowed planters to reduce the number of Africans imported by midcentury. In the year that Captain Pascal purchased young Equiano, only 15 percent of the adult slaves in the colony were recent captives from Africa, and most of these were sold into the newly cleared lands of the western piedmont. One could still find a few men like Jack, whose "Cuts down each Cheek" betrayed "his Country Marks," or Neptune, whose teeth were "fil'd sharp" and whose back displayed "many small Marks or Dots running from both Shoulders down to his Waistband," but they were the exception. Despite the fact that he "landed up a river a good way from the sea," Equiano "saw few or none of our native Africans." Far more common was the girl called Ann Dandridge, who arrived at Mount Vernon, Virginia, in 1759. Although a slave like her mother, Ann's father was the recently deceased planter John Dandridge, whose white daughter, Martha Dandridge Custis, was the wife of Colonel George Washington. Ann had been a childhood playmate for Martha's children Jacky and Patsy, although they did not

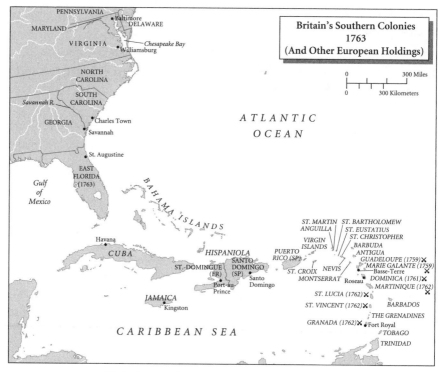

Britain's southern American colonies, 1763.

then know that she was their aunt. Ann would become free only in 1802, liberated by her half sister Martha.[32]

Large landholders like Washington represented but 10 percent of Virginia's white population, yet they controlled at least half of the colony's productive assets. Middling yeomen—men who owned small farms and worked the land with one or two white indentured servants or slaves—made up another 30 percent of the population, while a significant percentage of Virginia males owned no property at all and eked out a marginal living as tenants, servants, or unskilled day laborers. Virginia landowners well understood the economic and social power they derived from their enslaved labor force. As one white minister conceded during the same year that Equiano arrived in the colony, "to live in Virginia without slaves is morally impossible."[33]

If the minister in question never bothered to explain the connection between morality and chattel slavery, Virginia legislators understood the need to codify their rapidly growing slave population. As early as 1705, the House of Burgesses replaced earlier, piecemeal legislation with a comprehensive slave code. Borrowed in part from the Barbados statute of 1661 and the

Carolina code of 1696—as well as from ancient German and Spanish feudal law books—the lengthy statute remained in place with minor alterations until the early years of the Revolution. Although seventeenth-century legislation and court decisions revealed considerable ambiguity when it came to holding mixed-race children or Christianized Africans as slaves, the 1705 statute removed any lingering uncertainty on matters of race and bondage. "All servants imported and brought into the Country [who] were not Christians in their native Country," the burgesses declared, "shall be accounted and be slaves. All Negro, mulatto and Indian slaves within this dominion shall be held to be real estate."[34]

Real estate, of course, rarely resisted its condition at the point of a sword, and on this matter Virginia slave law utterly defied the rules of logic. As one judge observed in later years, a "slave is not in the condition of a horse," for he has "mental capacities" and an innate moral sense of right and wrong. Yet should any troublesome bondman, not unlike an unbroken horse, "happen to be killed [during physical] correction, the master shall be free of all punishment as if such accident never happened." The code even allowed habitual runaways to suffer dismemberment and the loss of a foot. But most of the brutality happened away from the courts, on isolated farms and plantations. As one overseer bragged to visitor Philip Vickers Fithian on the eve of the American Revolution, he had invented a method to deal with "Obstinacy, or Idleness" among field hands. He stripped slaves and tied them to a post, after which he took "a sharp Curry-Comb" and brushed the slave "severely til he is well scrap'd." The overseer then forced another slave to scour the wounds for several minutes "with some dry Hay" and "then salt him, & unlose him." Even the most recalcitrant African, he laughed, "will [then] attend to his Business."[35]

As this story indicates, the vast majority of slaves in Virginia spent their days surrounded by wheat and tobacco. By the time Equiano arrived in the colony, large-scale Virginia planters divided their estates—which often contained vast but noncontiguous acreage—into smaller units, or quarters. The number of slaves assigned to each quarter varied, but on most plantations, each contained about twelve "hands." On some units, the sex ratio was balanced, which meant that many families lived in nuclear units. But in other units, such as those owned by John Parke Custis, there were twice as many men as women, which suggests that many Virginia bondmen, like enslaved fathers in New York City, saw their families only on Sunday. Near the big house of the master, slaves resided in small villages of cabins. At Monticello, Thomas Jefferson directed his slaves to "build the Negro houses near together [so] that the fewer [black] nurses may serve" the enslaved children. But in the distant quarters, blacks often slept in barn attics or lofts in outbuildings. Planter Joseph Ball admitted that his slaves "must ly in the Tobacco house," and traveler J. F. D. Smyth described spending the night in a crude hovel with six slaves and their overseer. "[H]ogs lay under the floor, which made it a swarm with flies."[36]

Although masters such as Jefferson preferred to house their slaves in close proximity to one another, there is no little reason to suspect that blacks objected, and even English visitors to the colony correctly guessed that black Virginians were replicating West African village organizations. Whether Equiano was a Nigerian or a creole, he was familiar with communal family compounds that "present the appearance of a village." In the evening, bondpeople gathered in the quarters to eat and whisper news from within and without the plantation. Visitors to the big house, even as they were entertained with violin and harpsichord, frequently reported hearing the distant music of "banjar" and "quaqua" (drum) wafting up from the quarters. On occasion, whites such as Randolph Jefferson, Thomas's younger brother, would "come out among black people, play the fiddle and dance half the night." But in 1763, a time when the harsh patriarchalism of the colonial South had yet to soften into the cloying paternalism of the post-Revolutionary era, few whites flattered themselves welcome guests at night in the quarters.[37]

Equally unwelcome were the Anglican clerics, who came to minister to "the unimproved Capacities of these poor Creatures" (as one Methodist preacher bluntly put it). Encouraged by reformers in Britain, a number of Virginia Anglicans began as early as 1738 to instruct black creoles in their brand of Christianity. Masters like Equiano's Michael Pascal worried that the Christianization of their labor force might prove disruptive to proper control, although the colony's 1705 slave code had put an end to the practice of bondpeople applying for freedom on the grounds of conversion. But the "inoffensive and pious behavior" of Anglican clergymen, who well understood whence their salaries derived, won over all but the most suspicious planters. The Church's determination to maintain a clergy educated in Britain, however, destroyed any appeal Anglicanism might have held for the enslaved. Those who embraced Christianity—and few Africans expressed much interest in abandoning their early spiritual customs—turned to the Baptists and Methodists, whose lay clergy fanned west across Virginia just after 1760. Black converts found within these revivals the flexibility to practice their traditional religions even while adopting aspects of their new country's dominant faith.[38]

As a growing number of black Virginians embraced dissenting brands of Christianity, their masters fretted about a potential connection between those who rebelled against the established order of the Anglican hierarchy and those who rebelled against the social order of the southern colonies. Planters rightly feared that enslaved congregants would use the idea of God's love as a foundation from which to argue for basic human rights. Others worried that some bondmen would go further still. Decades before, in 1730, "black Christians [from] the Congo" had organized a large conspiracy in which freedom was clearly defended in Catholic religious terms. Two hundred rebels assembled in Norfolk and Princess Anne counties, where they followed Congolese traditions of electing officers and dividing into military units. The insurgents planned to rise on a Sunday when whites would be unarmed and at church. Although they succeeded in "commit[ting] many outrages against the [white] *Christians*," the militia, together with some obliging Pasquotanks, chased the Congolese into the Great Dismal Swamp. At least twenty-four Africans were summarily executed, and five more black Christians, recognized as leaders of the plot, were tried and hanged. In the aftermath, Governor William Gooch instructed all able-bodied men "to carry with them their Arms" as they attend "their respective Churches or Chappels on Sundays."[39]

The real danger to white authority, of course, was not a growing number of evangelized bondmen but simple demography. As Equiano sailed south, he noticed that the ratio of Africans and black creoles to whites grew larger with each passing colony. The Charles Town he visited in 1766 was the blackest city on the English mainland. South Carolina was 60 percent black, and the great plantation districts that lined the Cooper and Ashley rivers were even more so. In the Carolinas, as in the British Caribbean, only the daily imports of Africans kept the black population growing, since as many as one-third of all Africans imported into the lowcountry died within the year from malaria or yellow fever. By the end of the Seven Years' War, importers such as Henry Laurens negotiated the sale of more than seven hundred Africans during a single year. By feeding the market for labor—for a 10 percent commission— merchants like Laurens and Gabriel Manigault became two of the wealthiest men in the English colonies. Each boasted a yearly income that exceeded £2,500, exactly ten times what Charles Town's most highly trained physicians and attorneys received for their services.[40]

If merchants in Newport supplied the capital for the trade with Africa in these years, South Carolina supplied the buyers. By the early 1760s, the traffic in Africans had begun to dwindle in the Chesapeake, but the voracious economy of the lowcountry demanded ever more black bodies. For approximately 150,000 blacks—roughly one-quarter of all Africans imported into the English mainland—Sullivan's Island, just off the coast of Charles Town, served as the leading entrepôt. "Never was there such a pulling and hawling for negroes before," Laurens crowed in 1755. "Had there been a thousand, they would not have supplied the demand." Carolinians preferred slaves from the Gold Coast or Senegambia; white Protestants regarded enslaved Catholic Kongo-Angolans as troublesome, and "Callabars" (Ibos) as melancholy and suicidal. "Callabar slaves won't go down when others can be had," Laurens warned Richard Oswald, his Scottish supplier of Africans. Yet as historian Donald R. Wright has cautioned, it was European traders and buyers, rather than the Africans, who spoke in ethnic terms. A "person was a 'Bambara' or an 'Ibo' in the eyes of the enslaver rather than the enslaved," he notes.[41]

Since the colony continued to import nearly two thousand slaves each year, it followed that there were far fewer black converts to Christianity in the lowcountry than in the Chesapeake. Carolina whites did not begin in earnest to convert their bondpeople until long after the Revolution, and even then, planters along the Cooper continued to fret—more so than their Virginia counterparts—that any preacher who wished to acquaint enslaved Africans with the *entire* Bible was fit for "a room in the Lunatic Asylum." For the few masters who did wish to Christianize their labor force, African religiosity proved stubbornly resistant to conversion. African minds were hardly the uncommitted "heathen" slates whites believed them to be, and as one bold Carolina bondman explained it to a meddling white minister, they believed "the preachers and the slaveholders to be in a conspiracy against them."[42]

When Equiano visited the Carolinas, the vast majority of Africans cultivated indigo and waded fields of rice rather than harvesting cotton. Planters relied on the technical expertise of Africans purchased directly from the Windward Coast, a region long accustomed to producing rice. In the earliest days of the colony, Carolina masters, many of whom began as young planters in the Caribbean, attempted to force their laborers to adopt the West Indian "gang system," in which they supervised groups closely and kept them in the fields all day. Black workers fought back in a guerrilla war against tools and animals, until planters grudgingly accepted the compromise of the "task system." Under this system, planters subdivided their rice fields into parcels of roughly a hundred square feet. Individual slaves worked each plot, but once that task was complete, the bondperson's time became his own. The task system quickly spread beyond the rice fields. Masters assigned black women a precise number of bushels of corn to pound into meal; children weeded an exact number of feet; sawyers produced 600 feet of pine or 780 feet of cypress. Using their own time, slaves grew garden crops beside their cabins or kept fowl, which they bartered in Charles Town on Sundays in exchange for clothing and other goods.[43]

The patchwork quilt nature of the empire's slave laws was nowhere more evident than in South Carolina. The original 1669 Fundamental Constitutions of Carolina, drafted in part by Royal Africa Company investor John Locke, expressly granted masters authority "over Negro Slaves, of what opinion or Religion soever." Conventional wisdom holds that it was modeled on the earlier Barbadian Code for a model, but evidence also suggests Barbados sugar planters, finding no clear framework in English Common Law, borrowed many of *their* provisions from feudal statutes. In the wake of the 1739 slave rebellion near Stono River, South Carolina, the assemblymen revised their body of laws. The comprehensive twenty-four-page code of 1740, commonly known as the "Negro Act," covered every possible aspect of slave life. As the title indicates, the legislation drew few distinctions between bond-people and free blacks, as it empowered rural patrollers and city watchmen to stop and interrogate any black on sight. So sure were colonial legislators that Africans and their descendants were meant to be slaves that the lengthy bill mentioned free blacks only four times, twice to mandate that freedmen be treated as human property in the courts.[44]

As both the harshness and Caribbean origins of the Negro Act indicate, the farther south one traveled, and the higher the proportion of slaves one encountered, the more draconian were the laws designed to uphold unfree labor. Masters enjoyed the right to discipline their slaves to death, and the Carolinas witnessed cruelties surpassing those in Virginia. Courts meted out brandings, whippings, ear croppings, gibbeting, hangings, and burnings; in one peculiar case, a runaway was sentenced to be "severely whipped and pickled, on three several days around the square of Charles Town." What transpired on isolated plantations far upriver was more gruesome yet. Around 1760, Michel-Guillaume-Saint-Jean de Crèvecoeur, a young adventurer traveling about the colonies, came across a large "cage, suspended to the limbs of a tree, all the branches of which appeared covered with large birds of prey." As he got closer, he could see that the bars held a live slave, although "the birds had already picked out his eyes." Hearing somebody nearby, the slave cried out first for water, and after Crèvecoeur put water to his lips, the African begged him to "puta some poison and give me." The Frenchman's host calmly explained that the slave had murdered his overseer; he had been suspended for two days.[45]

Equiano put Charles Town behind him as soon as he "disposed of some goods on [his] own account." But when his master's ship landed in Savannah, Georgia, a "worse fate than ever" befell the black mariner. Although slavery had become legal in Georgia in 1751, over the next decade most Africans and African Americans arrived in the colony with their masters, or were purchased from South Carolina or the Caribbean. By the end of the Seven Years' War, the enslaved population of the colony amounted to 36,000, or 40 percent of the total populace, high enough to threaten white control and excite white paranoia. This Equiano discovered one Sunday night as he sat with other slaves behind the house of a Dr. Perkins. The doctor and a white employee arrived home drunk and were displeased at finding some "strange negroes in his yard." The two men beat Equiano badly, but despite his severe wounds, the city watch carried him off to jail the next morning. Only when his captain began to fear that Equiano had run off did he begin a search. The beating left Equiano in bed for the next sixteen days, and he was not able to resume his duties for another two weeks. His captain, Thomas Farmer, consulted several attorneys, "but they told him they could do nothing" for Equiano, as he "was a negro."[46]

By the end of 1766 Equiano's wounds had healed and he was once more in the Caribbean. According to his later *Narrative*, the vessels he sailed never touched the docks of Florida, and little wonder. British diplomats had traded the Cuban port of Havana (which they had captured in 1762 but were unable to maintain due to malaria) for Spanish Florida. Few shippers carried anything but African bodies into the new colony. Richard Oswald, a British investor (and future diplomat) who did considerable business with Henry Laurens, sent 106 captured Africans directly from his slaving factory on the Sierra Leone River. During 1771, the peak year of importation during the period of British control, English investors shipped one thousand Africans into Florida, mostly from the Gold Coast and Guinea Coast of West Africa, from Gambia, and from Angola.[47]

For all of his travels throughout Britain's northern empire, Equiano spent most of his time as a mariner in the Caribbean, the wealthiest part of the British Empire and also its most disproportionately African in population. The English part of the North American mainland was where Britain dumped its dispossessed poor, its surplus population, whereas the sugar islands of the Caribbean were where European investors amassed enormous fortunes. By Equiano's time, the English West Indies produced 100,000 tons of sugar each year. English and American consumers heaped sugar into their tea, basted their meats with it, and transformed it into rum, the staple of life for the Royal Navy, and, ironically, when mixed with cool water into grog, the opiate of slaves.[48]

Jamaica was far and away Britain's most valuable possession in the Americas. Equiano described it as "a very fine, large island, well peopled, and the most considerable of the West-India islands." If the English mainland— apart from South Carolina—was predominantly white, with an African

American minority population, the reverse was true in the Caribbean. At the end of the Seven Years' War, the population of Jamaica was just over 200,000 (larger than both New York and South Carolina), yet fewer than 21,000 whites resided in the colony. Due to the wretched diet afforded slaves, together with brutal labor regimes and cruel treatment in an already unhealthy disease environment, at least one-third of all Africans imported died within three years. Their numbers were replenished by daily importation of fresh captives, most of whom arrived from the Gold Coast and the Bight of Biafra. "There were a vast number of negroes" there, Equiano reported, and "as usual, exceedingly imposed upon by the white people."[49]

If anything, life in Jamaica proved even deadlier for white immigrants than for Africans. During Equiano's time on the island, fully one-third of all white children born in Kingston died before their first birthday. Few immigrants lived to celebrate their fortieth birthday, and white indentured servants, on average, perished by age thirty-three. Although these grim conditions were well known in Britain, whites continued to arrive on Jamaica's shores. For the lucky few who survived this "seasoning" process, the chance to grow rich beyond the imagination was a real possibility. By 1763, Jamaica's planter class boasted some of the wealthiest men in the empire. Per capita white wealth in mid-eighteenth-century Jamaica was an astonishing £2,201, by comparison to £42 sterling in England and £60 in the mainland colonies. Put another way, the average white person in Jamaica was 57.6 times as rich as the average white person in the New England colonies. British aristocrats might have enjoyed the social status that accompanied ancient lineages, but Jamaican planters accrued far greater riches by working Africans to death than any English noble could extract from his tenants.[50]

If slave codes and discipline grew harsher in proportion to the percentage of blacks to whites, it is hardly surprising that visitors to the islands, including those hardened by contact with other slave societies in the West, recorded countless horror stories of beatings, tortures, rapes, and murders. On some occasions, particularly brutal masters recorded their own violations of African bodies, a testimony to the barbarous sensibilities common in the colony. Diarist Thomas Thistlewood, who served as an overseer before acquiring a small estate, relished the very act of listing the punishments meted out. During the course of a single year, he beat thirty-five of the forty-two slaves under his control—some of them two or three times—and prescribed fifty lashes for the smallest infraction. In one instance, he flogged a woman "for wishing [aloud] she was dead already." Another, who "threaten'd to Cutt his own throat," was "Whipp'd, gagg'd, & his hands tied behind him so that the Mosskitoes and Sand flies might torment him." In 1758 alone Thistlewood raped twenty-three women a total of 179 times. Although a harsh and cruel master, he was probably unusual only in keeping a precise accounting of his acts; Equiano's *Narrative* indicates that his behavior was the norm among whites on Jamaica.[51]

Conventional wisdom holds that absentee landlords were crueler masters than landlords who lived on their estates, and with notable exceptions, that may well be true. For London capitalists who invested in the Caribbean sugar fields, Africans were merely figures scrawled in a ledger book. Across English America, slaves experienced varied treatment based upon crops, climate, and the percentage of Africans in the population, but also due to rates of absentee ownership. For most of the eighteenth century, Virginia planters lived on their estates, while masters in coastal South Carolina, in imitation of their grandfathers' Caribbean experience, spent much of their year enjoying society in Charles Town. Absentee ownership was most troublesome in the islands, since a good percentage of plantation owners resided in Britain and ran their estates through men such as Thistlewood. In St. Kitts, absentee masters owned half of the estates, and out of seventy-seven proprietors in tiny Tobago, only twenty lived on the island.[52]

Conditions in the islands favored the survival of women over men. It was not that the labor black women performed was easier, for they toiled long hours planting and harvesting cane and dragging bundles to the mill. But the tasks reserved exclusively for men, from operating the boiling houses to running the distilleries to hauling freight along the docks, proved particularly murderous. Typical was the brief life of a slave described in plantation records only as Deborah or Debby. Born on the island to an enslaved woman named Katey and to a black father her white owner little cared to name in his account book, Debby was sent into the fields at the age of eight as a "gleaner," cleaning up the remains of a crop after the main crew. From age nine to fourteen, she cut grass, then was assigned still harder work. Finally, at the age of twenty-one, her master placed her in the main "gang," which cut the cane. Despite producing three daughters, she rarely left the fields until reaching the advanced age of twenty-nine, when her abilities were downgraded from "able" to "weak." Given the less demanding task of shepherd, Debby died at the age of thirty-seven. Taking up his account book, her master recorded a typically grotesque epitaph: "lost her arm, subject to fits, and ill disposed."[53]

Cruelty was so common in the British Caribbean that Equiano's autobiography often reads like a ghastly list of "chains, and other instruments of torture," including the "iron muzzle, thumb-screws, &c." Along the quays at St. Kitts, he watched as newly arrived Africans were "branded with the initial letters of their master's name," while in Montserrat he saw one slave "staked to the ground, and cut most shockingly" with a whip before his ears were shaved "off bit by bit" for the crime of consorting with a white prostitute. To best illustrate their power—and the deadly risk one assumed in challenging it—most slaveholders required that blacks witness the execution of their fellows. Hangings were at once a potent symbol of the power of the state over individual black bodies and a gruesome lesson of the futility of resistance to white domination. Nothing was more successful in inducing passive behavior than to be forced to watch as loved ones kicked helplessly at the end of a noose.[54]

Far to the south and east of St. Croix lay the considerably larger island of Barbados, frequently the first port of call for vessels sailing from Britain or the African coast and Equiano's original destination (provided that he was telling the truth about his African origins). Despite the fact that Equiano's vessel arrived in Bridgetown, the colony's busiest port, in the evening, "merchants and planters" poured up the gangplank to inspect the cargo. One local merchant bragged that Barbados was "worth all the rest" of the colonies "which are made by the English," and while Jamaican shippers might disagree, Barbados sent more than six thousand casks of sugar to Britain each year. Producing such quantities of sugar involved more than merely harvesting cane. For each gang that was set to work cutting, several other groups of ten to twenty slaves performed a myriad of other labors. According to one observer, landlords ordered some bondpeople "to weed, some to plant, some to fall wood, some to cleave it, some to saw it into boards, some to fetch home," while male gangs attended the "Boyling-house, Still-house, and Cureing-house; [and] some for Harvest." As in other British islands, "the life of a negro," as Equiano put it, was held in "small account."[55]

The hub of this vast Atlantic empire was London, a sprawling metropolis where Equiano would settle upon obtaining his freedom. At the time, the city was home to between five thousand and seven thousand blacks, a small fraction of London's one million people. As was the case in New York and Philadelphia, blacks performed a variety of tasks. A few lived in elegant townhouses and wore the embroidered coats and powdered wigs typical of upper-class domestics; one servant, Francis Barber, often appeared in portraits behind his famous employer, Dr. Samuel Johnson, and was nearly as recognizable as William Lee would come to be. Far more earned poor livings as waiters in taverns, but the majority were mariners who rented squalid rooms in the dockside parish of St. George. London masters rarely had to resort to harsh punishments to keep their servants in order, since flight meant escape into an urban world of poverty and want. As one bondman later admitted,

"I did not know how to get my living; and therefore I did not like to leave the house."[56]

As Equiano's travels reveal, by the eve of the American Revolution the African and African American populations and societies of the British Empire were of different historical eras and ethnic origins. Though the majority of blacks enslaved in the colonies in 1763 had been shipped out of West and Central Africa, they embodied a diverse range of cultural backgrounds. Africans had lived in New York City since the day that Dutch mariners abandoned Jan Rodrigues in 1613, and in Jamestown since 1619. By the time Equiano was sold into Virginia, he encountered creoles who were seventh-generation slaves, and captives from Angola and the Guinea coast newly arrived in Georgia, South Carolina, and the Caribbean. These newcomers spoke different languages and practiced different religions. Some held to the spiritual traditions of their homeland, while many black Americans fused those beliefs with the Christian creeds of their masters. Their labor enriched white men and women on both sides of the ocean and helped to make the British Empire the formidable military machine it had become by 1763. Both Africans and black creoles were prepared, however, to take advantage of the coming dislocation and chaos of the Revolutionary era, and a good many black men and women were to play a leading role in sparking the fires of liberty that soon blazed across the North Atlantic world.[57]

TWO

Richard's Cup

Slavery and the Coming of the Revolution

I F EQUIANO SERVES AS a reminder of how little we know about the existences of most slaves, the bondman now known only as Richard presents an even greater puzzle. Although hired out to arguably the most celebrated American of the late eighteenth century, a man whose pen and prose helped to "invent America," Richard makes but sporadic appearances in the documentary record. It is not even known from whom Thomas Jefferson hired Richard's time. Yet Richard's brief service in Philadelphia reveals the cruel irony of the decades that followed 1763. While Equiano's career charted a map of the British maritime Atlantic world, Richard personified the hopes and dreams of black Americans during the early years of the Revolution. Although we can never know for sure, as Richard listened to men of influence dub themselves "the slaves of King George," and as he watched his temporary master craft the Declaration of Independence, he must have believed that a new day of liberty was about to dawn in Britain's American colonies.[1]

In the early spring of 1775, a small group of Virginians began to prepare for their journey north to Philadelphia for the Second Continental Congress. Among them was Thomas Jefferson, chosen to stand in for his distant kinsman, the ailing Peyton Randolph. The tall, reedy, red-haired planter desperately wished to make an impression on the Congress, but unlike the voluble Patrick Henry, Jefferson lacked a voice that could shake the rafters. A grand entrance would have to do. To pull his phaeton, he purchased a fourth horse, an animal named General, a postillion whip, and green decorations for the harnesses. To complete this impressive picture, he hired two slaves: Jesse, to ride postillion, and Richard, as his manservant.[2]

Over the next few weeks, as Jefferson's entourage bumped across the roads toward Philadelphia, the young politician splurged a bit to spruce up his new servants. On June 14 he tossed Richard three English shillings "to pay for washing," and three days later he bought him a comb. On several occasions, Jefferson simply handed Richard a few coins. To the extent that Richard was a slave, and so probably unaccustomed to being paid anything, Jefferson possibly flattered himself a benevolent master. Perhaps also his determination to arrive in style on the national stage led him to open his purse in a previously unaccustomed fashion. In early July, Richard was given cash enough to purchase a linen shirt; one week later Richard again received funds for "washing," and when his clothes required "mend[in]g," Jefferson paid for that too.[3]

Just prior to his departure, Jefferson had recorded a precise list of the "Number of souls in my family," by which he meant the people who resided under his patriarchal control. His Monticello "family" numbered 117. Just below himself on the social pyramid sat his wife, Martha, and his daughter, Patsy. Then came sixteen free white overseers and craftsmen, their wives and children, and eighty-three slaves. Since many of his slaves had been trained as house servants, one wonders why Jefferson felt the need to hire a valet for Philadelphia. Quite possibly, he wished to leave his domestic slaves with Martha, who was rarely well. More likely, he realized that time spent in a northern city with a large number of slaves might ruin a bondman by exposing him to dangerous dreams of autonomy, and so renting a servant would corrupt only the property of another man.[4]

Jefferson had resumed his seat in Congress in May 1776 when word arrived of the resolutions passed by the Virginia convention, which instructed its delegates in Philadelphia to propose independence. To nobody's surprise, Jefferson, the celebrated author of *A Summary View of the Rights of British America*, was appointed to the committee charged with drafting a manifesto justifying revolution. Charged with handing Jefferson cups of tea while his master scribbled was Richard. Few slaves knew how to read, but those who did tended to be domestic servants, and perhaps Richard peered over Jefferson's shoulder as he picked up his quill pen to write the words that shook an empire. "We hold these truths to be self-evident, that all men are created equal," Jefferson wrote in his slow, deliberate fashion, "that they are endowed by their Creator with certain inalienable rights; that among these are life, liberty, and the pursuit of happiness."[5]

Whether Richard could read those words or heard them read aloud in the streets of the city, the fact remains that he was one of roughly 600,000 Africans and black Americans living in those colonies that would ultimately endorse the Declaration of Independence and thus ratify the notion that Jefferson's country was to be a new kind of society, a world based upon liberty and natural rights rather than monarchical power. As the historian Herbert Aptheker once observed, it "is indeed one of the most painful and yet most revealing facts in American history that the author" of this founding document "was himself a slave-owner." That Jefferson savored the rich irony that the man handing him cups of tea while he wrote these glorious sentiments was held "to labor under the lash" is far less certain.[6]

William Lee survived long enough to benefit from the promise of the Revolution, even if he also lived to see that most black Americans did not. Richard, by comparison, vanishes from public view after 1776, making him the perfect symbol of the hopes and aspirations of Africans and their children as the growing rift between Britain and its American colonies fostered a new spirit of liberty and equality. The emergent articulation of natural rights— nowhere more eloquently stated than in Jefferson's Declaration—not only led many masters to question their ownership of slaves but also strengthened the hand of the enslaved themselves by creating an ideological context in which they could advance their demands for freedom. As elite critics of imperial policies began to disparage their lack of political rights and advance the principles of universal liberty, their involvement in unfree labor increasingly presented an obvious dilemma. How could Americans "complain so loudly of attempts to enslave them," one Patriot wondered, "while they hold so many hundreds of thousands in slavery?"[7]

————

For the British government, victory over France in 1763 was a mixed blessing. The triumph was decisive, but in the process Prime Minister William Pitt amassed a staggering debt of £122,603,336. The annual interest alone amounted to more than half of Britain's typical peacetime budget. To put this in perspective, three years later, in 1766, a slave as valuable as Equiano purchased his freedom for £70. Moreover, Britain had conquered a vast territory inhabited by French Catholics and native people hostile to London's control, and so the new young king, George III, was determined to maintain the size of his army. Parliament expressed no desire to force its colonists to finance the debt, but most members thought it simple justice that residents of North America pay a portion of the cost of its defense. Slaves, of course, were not directly affected by the litany of taxes and acts that Britain imposed on the settlers, but they could not help being politicized by the language of protest. Laboring in craft shops, taverns, or elegant parlors, slaves overheard their masters' increasingly heated discussions of American rights, and they would not be slow in applying those rights to themselves.[8]

Over the course of the 1760s, white colonists frequently claimed that the British government consciously plotted to reduce them to the condition of "slaves." Colonial pamphleteers may have been employing a recognizable rhetorical device or may have been advocating the rights of black slaves. Either way, the development of this American self-awareness during the thirteen years before 1776 was of critical importance, since claims of "enslavement" by King George forced white elites to examine their long-held preconceptions, and in some cases to act upon them. At the same time, Africans and black Americans used this growing consciousness to assert their own privileges as Americans.[9]

Curiously, this connection between the alleged "enslavement" of white colonists and the black men and women those colonists actually owned was initially advanced by James Otis Jr., a wealthy Boston attorney. Although one historian has suggested that it was the harsh reality of southern plantation life that slowly fashioned an "identification between the cause of the colonies and the cause of the Negroes bound in chattel slavery," Otis was not a resident of a colony heavily populated by African Americans. (His father, however, owned several domestic slaves, and one wonders if a particular household cruelty witnessed by the young James transformed him into an early abolitionist.) Otis's conflation of white and black rights, moreover, first appeared just *before* the end of the Seven Years' War. Speaking in 1761 before the Superior Court of Massachusetts against the Writs of Assistance—general search warrants that empowered customs officials to enter warehouses without probable cause—Otis insisted that British policies violated the rights of Massachusetts residents. Before concluding his remarks, however, he advanced the startling claim that *all* colonists, "black and white, born here, are free born British subjects, and entitled to all the essential civil rights of such." Otis lost the case, but not before an original point had been made.[10]

Three years later, in a series of essays entitled *The Rights of the British Colonies Asserted and Proved*, Otis went farther still. Again observing that all "colonists are by the laws of nature free born," he denounced "slavery [as] so vile and miserable an estate of man, and so directly opposite to the generous temper and courage of our nation," that he could not conceive of any *"englishman"* who might try to defend it. In language reminiscent of a later era, Otis slashed away at the racist logic that allowed one man to own another. "Does it follow that tis right to enslave a man because he is black?" Otis reasoned. "Will short curl'd hair like wool, instead of christian hair, as tis called by those, whose hearts are as hard as the nether millstone, help the argument? Can any logical inference in favour of slavery, be drawn from a flat nose, or long or short face?" What began as a rhetorical comparison between colonists and slaves turned into a defense of the natural rights of "all men, white or black."[11]

Otis's support for racial egalitarianism was unusual in that it was advanced by an American who was speaking about political theory rather than Christian brotherhood. Religious voices, such as Woolman and Benezet, had long been raised in opposition to unwaged labor. And at almost the same moment, European Enlightenment thinkers began to condemn the practice on the basis of economic practicality. In 1748, French philosopher Charles-Louis de Secondat, baron de Montesquieu, published a detailed attack on slavery in *The Spirit of the Laws*. "The state of slavery is in its own nature bad," he wrote. "It is neither useful to the master nor to the slave." His reasonable tenor, together with his rank among the French nobility, gave his work precisely the sort of gravitas that appealed to affluent readers in the British and French colonies. In the same fashion, Adam Smith's *Theory of Moral Sentiments*, published four years before Otis's pamphlet, castigated slavery on pragmatic grounds. It was as unwise as it was cruel, Smith argued, "to reduce [blacks] into the vilest of all states, that of domestic slavery, and to sell them, man, woman, and child, like so many herds of cattle, to the highest bidder in the market."[12]

Despite these seemingly progressive statements regarding racial justice, the few blacks who managed to read or overhear such words objected to more than just the moderate prose. Otis did not merely assail the presence of racial slavery in New England but came perilously close to attacking the very presence of slaves *themselves*. Unlike Britain's Caribbean sugar colonies, Otis insisted, the northern colonies were no debased "compound mongrel mixture of *English*, *Indian*, and *Negro*." Rather, they were home to "freeborn *British white* subjects, whose loyalty has never yet been suspected." Otis's central point was that white Bostonians, being racially similar to Londoners, were better able to appreciate English traditions of liberty than men "of the stamp of a creolean planter." His words made it abundantly clear that while he believed slavery to be wrong, he also suspected that people of a darker hue were not yet prepared for the political responsibilities of freedom. Indeed, the entire context of Otis's tirade was the ideological slavery that Britain was imposing on its colonies, not the social slavery that colonists imposed on Africans.[13]

None of this is to imply that Otis's public rhetoric was inconsequential. Woolman and Benezet had denounced slavery on the grounds of Christian charity, whereas Montesquieu and Smith criticized unwaged labor as legally imprudent and economically unwise. Otis was the first influential voice to bring up the notion of natural rights. Still, apart from raising a few eyebrows among his more staid colleagues, Otis risked little by publishing his views.

In far greater peril were the enslaved New Englanders who took his words as solemn promises to be acted upon. Not coincidentally, blacks in and around Boston promptly began to sue for their freedom, which required both courage and financial resources. In late 1766, Jenny Slew dragged her master into a Salem court, arguing that her enslavement was illegal on the grounds that her mother was white. The Essex County court ruled in her favor and awarded her damages and court costs "of four pounds lawful money." John Adams witnessed the proceedings and noted that "there have been many" such cases. Three years later, Quaker merchant William Rotch encouraged a black whaler named Boston to sue for his freedom. When a Nantucket jury granted Boston his freedom, the owner threatened to appeal, and Rotch hired Adams, who won the case. "I never knew a jury by a verdict to determine a negro to be a slave," Adams observed. "They always found him free."[14]

That a man as legally cautious as young John Adams took this case indicates just how quickly ideological freedom for white men became associated with literal freedom for black men. With good reason, blacks in northern seaport towns came to believe that a new day was dawning. Prior to the end of the Seven Years' War, upper-class colonists, like wealthy Englishmen in the home island, hailed Britain as the land of freedom. But in the wake of the 1765 Stamp Act debates, during which one officer bragged that he "would cram the stamps down American throats at the point of his sword," the image of Britain was transformed, and not for the better. Critics of the crown loudly denounced Britain as a "kingdom of slaves" and toasted the colonies as the "country of free men." Although northern whites defined political slavery as the denial of the right of self-government rather than the actual enslavement of their bodies, this rhetoric of bondage became a constant and standard part of the dialect of resistance. Enslaved and free African Americans even joined white colonists in the streets as the demands for freedom became ever more violent. In New York, Joseph Allicocke, a mixed-race office clerk, was honored for his role in the Stamp Act riots by being dubbed "general of the Sons of Liberty." Allicocke and his white allies routinely met to plot at the Queen's Head Tavern, a center of resistance owned by "Black Sam" Fraunces, a Jamaican freeman of mixed ancestry.[15]

Given the necessity for the members of the emerging Patriot faction to remain in contact with one another through Committees of Correspondence, it was no coincidence that elite voices in Philadelphia soon joined this discussion. Among those to pick up his pen in support of Otis was Dr. Benjamin Rush, an Edinburgh-trained physician who had only recently returned to his native Pennsylvania. In his 1773 "An Address to the Inhabitants of the British Settlements in America, upon Slave-Keeping," Rush became one of the first scientists to suggest that Africans in their native lands were "equal to the Europeans." Although it had been commonplace among educated whites to regard blacks as inherently "inferior to the inhabitants of Europe," Rush argued that all "the vices which are charged upon the Negroes" were the "genuine offspring of slavery." Montesquieu and Smith had condemned slavery as an unsound public policy only; to insist that black skin no more "qualifies [Africans] for slavery" than white skin justified Euro-American liberty was a truly radical proposition that had previously been heard only at night in the slave quarters.[16]

Although Rush was in no position to know whether a general loathing for slavery pervaded "all ranks in every province," he was far more correct than those modern historians who argue that the rise in antislavery opinion was "slow and sporadic." Pamphlets such as those penned by Otis and Rush, with their inescapable rhetoric of liberty and equality, were read and reread across the North, often by ministers who transformed them into blistering sermons. "For shame," thundered Connecticut's Nathaniel Niles, "let us either cease to enslave our fellow-men, or else let us cease to complain of those that would enslave us." Connecticut theologian (and former slaveholder) Samuel Hopkins even structured his *Dialogue Concerning the Slavery of the African* as a Puritan homily. To hold another as property, he promised, was a "sin of a crimson dye" and explained "the calamities [God] has brought upon us" in the form of British policies. Within an astonishingly brief period, slavery had been denigrated from a common practice to "a very great and public sin" in much of New England and Pennsylvania.[17]

A similar hypocritical sense of sin, or at least unease, over enslaving black Americans permeated the mainland colonies south of Pennsylvania as well. Late-eighteenth-century newspapers' practice of reprinting entire stories and essays allowed for the northern conflation of political and literal bondage to seep into southern publications. The Williamsburg *Virginia Gazette* routinely reprinted lengthy essays from the *Boston Gazette*, and so the Massachusetts refrain that Britain sought to "enslave her own children" was soon heard in Virginia's capital as well. (One indication of the complexity of this discourse in the Chesapeake, however, was that publisher William Rind printed an advertisement for Jupiter, a runaway slave, on the same page as the *Boston Gazette* essay.) Virginia whites were particularly sensitive on this issue, since enslaved labor was the cornerstone of their economy. Yet as masters who resided in a slave society, they knew far better than any Boston clergymen what it meant to be a slave, and they based their haughty sense of independence on the fact that they were neither black nor dependent upon others. So when Boston pamphleteers warned them that ideological dependency was precisely what Parliament had in mind, they regarded the threat as literal, not rhetorical.[18]

Perhaps no man better articulated this curious analogy than George Washington, whose long familiarity with the exercise of capricious authority over slaves such as William Lee led him to grasp London's capacity for abusing paternal controls. In letter after letter, Washington fretted that Britain intended to "make us as tame, & abject Slaves, as the Blacks we rule over with such arbitrary Sway." Although regarded today as a far less abstract thinker than Jefferson or Adams, Washington instinctively employed the rhetoric of resistance to slavery precisely because he had witnessed white masters misbehave with impunity. When he insisted that Parliament hoped to "fix the Shackles of Slavery upon us," he selected that metaphor because he had seen shackles fastened upon black men too often. William Lee conceivably thought his owner a hypocrite for fearing the same "abject state of slavery" in which he held others, yet Washington described the cruelties of bondage so eloquently because he knew them so well.[19]

Other Virginians, like many northern pamphleteers, quickly grasped the insincerity of their behavior. Among them were Richard Henry Lee and Arthur Lee, brothers and heirs to one of the greatest fortunes in the colony. As was the case with many who came to question "the nature & Consequences of Slavery" in North America, Arthur Lee had studied abroad, in his case in Britain, where he was influenced by Adam Smith. Building on a short pamphlet he had published in London three years before—as well as upon opinions his brother Richard expressed in private correspondence—Arthur Lee penned a lengthy "Address on Slavery" for the *Virginia Gazette* in early 1767. He declared freedom "the birth-right of all mankind, of Africans as well as Europeans." Because no person ever "consent[ed] to be our Slaves," the practice was "a Violation both of Justice and Religion." Although the essay contained the obligatory references to slavery as "dangerous to the safety" of white society and "destructive" to Virginia's economic health—as well as customary attempts to blame slavery on "British merchants"—Lee concluded with an audacious demand for the "abolition of Slavery."[20]

Nor was Lee's an isolated voice. No better reminder exists of the close ties that emerged between the small number of powerful men who organized to resist British authority than the exchange of letters between Robert Pleasants and Patrick Henry. Pleasants, a Quaker planter who had emancipated his slaves before hiring them back as paid laborers, sent his Virginia acquaintances a series of articles by Anthony Benezet. Among the recipients was Henry, an attorney of the middle ranks who had risen into the upper class through his purchase of slaves. Henry conceded that he had been "drawn along by the general inconvenience of living without" slaves, yet he could not "justify it." While he had once thought little of the practice, in a day "when the Rights of Humanity are defined & understood with precision," slavery was clearly "inconsistent with the Bible and destructive to Liberty."[21]

As encouraging as these declarations sounded, the proposition that slavery was wrong primarily because it was harmful to *white* society was a prominent feature of these essays and letters. Had slavery never been introduced into Virginia, grumbled George Mason, "we shou'd not at this Day see one Half of our best Lands in most Parts of the Country remained unsetled." Worse than the deleterious impact unwaged labor had on the economy was its ethical impact, "the ill Effect such a Practice has upon the Morals & Manners of our People." Even Arthur Lee speculated that the slaves' debased condition "proceeds from a native baseness that fits their minds for all villainy." Yet if verbal expressions of planter guilt typically failed to translate into even private manumissions, in some cases they had an impact on black lives. In the wake of the Townshend Revenue Act of 1767, which levied import duties on paint, glass, paper, and tea, Virginians—again protesting that Parliament intended to reduce them into "a Wretched & miserable State of Slavery"—formed the Nonimportation Association to boycott British goods. Prodded by Richard Henry Lee, adherents promised "not to import any Slaves, or purchase any" Africans "until the said Acts of parliament are repeale'd." Admittedly, an agreement that equated humans with other imported goods, such as "chairs, tables, [and] looking glasses," was hardly an eloquent manifesto for human rights. But Virginians never again imported many Africans into their colony.[22]

Even in slave-heavy South Carolina, the mainland colony destined to be the most resistant to any public discourse on the evils of bondage, the comparison between political and chattel slavery appeared early. "Whatever we may think of ourselves," the editor of the *South Carolina Gazette* charged in June 1769, "we are as real SLAVES as those we are permitted to command." Before the end of the Seven Years' War, such talk, one visitor observed, had largely been limited to "the negroes," but as in the Chesapeake, white Carolinians were all too conversant with phrases such as "with a Rod of Iron." On some occasions, critics of the crown went beyond language and employed physical symbols of enslavement. When news arrived in Charles Town that the Stamp Act had been repealed, Equiano reported that "the guns were fired, and bonfires and other demonstrations of joy shewn." Yet he also witnessed many of the white sailors in the crowd wearing blackface to indicate that the crisis was not over yet, and that they remained the slaves of King George.[23]

For all the speed with which the language of political enslavement became the common currency of the emerging Patriot elite, Jefferson's

Richard—like tens of thousands of Africans and African Americans in the British colonies—instinctively made the connection far faster, typically at the first moment a white colonial shouted for his freedom. Just prior to Equiano's visit, white artisans had taken to the streets of Charles Town in protest of the Stamp Act, chanting "Liberty, liberty," and carrying a large flag with the word emblazoned across it. Several weeks later, according to Henry Laurens, black Carolinians began "crying out 'Liberty'" themselves, until daily patrols put a temporary halt to black gatherings. Three decades before, the uprising at Stono River had shown whites that slaves knew how to exploit political divisions among the master class, and so it comes as no surprise that Laurens regarded the growing crisis with Britain as "more awful & distressing than Fire, Pestilence, or Foreign Wars." Other residents of the city worried "that slaves in Charles-Town are not under a good regulation."[24]

That proved to be an understatement. It took no more than two weeks before black Americans ceased "crying out" for liberty and began to organize for their freedom. In mid-January 1766, South Carolina's lieutenant governor, William Bull Jr., informed a nervous assembly that "One Hundred and Seven Negroes had left their plantations" in an "Intended Insurrection" in Colleton County. The *Virginia Gazette* reported that many firearms were "found concealed," while masters at several plantations discovered that the touchholes in their own guns had been plugged up. At precisely the same moment, the unwaged servants of George Mason acted upon his public criticism of their enslavement by planning a revolt. Two more conspiracies surfaced the following year in Loudoun and Fairfax counties, and in Hanover, forty slaves belonging to Bowler Cocke rose, seized the overseer, and whipped him "from neck to waistband." When the county militia attempted to restore order, the rebels took refuge in a barn. In the battle that followed, whites killed three slaves and wounded five more; blacks dubbed the mêlée "bloody Christmas." Elsewhere in the colony, in a vain attempt to reestablish white control, authorities hanged seven bondmen. To serve as a lesson to the living, the magistrates ordered the heads of four to be "cut off and fixed on the chimnies of the courthouse."[25]

The extent to which enslaved people, routinely denied access to information and even a rudimentary education, understood the contemporary political debates remains unknowable. But white contemporaries were almost certainly correct in suspecting that they knew far more than they let on. In some cases, of course, imperial regulations infringed upon black bodies in very unambiguous ways. As Britain struggled to maintain the size of its navy in the decade after 1763, press-gangs swept through waterfront taverns with little regard for color and forced more than a few slaves into service on King

George's "floating hells." Mobs resisting royal forces cut across racial lines. In 1765, roughly five hundred "Sailors, boys, and Negroes" rioted against the king's men in Newport, Rhode Island, and two years later, "Whites & Blacks all arm'd" assaulted a press-gang in Norfolk, Virginia. In 1768, a crowd of black and white sailors rioted in Boston. As one white Bostonian put it, he "preferred death to such as a life as [he] deemed slavery" aboard a British man-of-war.[26]

Much to the embarrassment of elite Americans, shrewd British observers could not resist commenting on the fact that scores of those calling themselves the slaves of King George actually owned black men and women as human chattel. As the English Tory Samuel Johnson famously phrased it, "How is it that we hear the loudest *yelps* for liberty among the drivers of negroes?" Even some English writers who believed that American colonists had a legitimate point about their lack of representation in Parliament mocked the comparison. "With what consistency or decency," wondered one, could American Patriots "complain so loudly of attempts to enslave them, while they hold so many hundred thousands in slavery?" In at least one celebrated case, a visiting merchant was able to query Americans in person. While conducting business in Philadelphia, Richard Wells grew weary of hearing white Americans complain while watching black Americans unload cargo along the docks. "Were the colonists as earnest for the preservation of liberty" as they claimed, he huffed, "they would enter into a virtuous and *perpetual* resolve, neither to import, nor to purchase any slaves introduced amongst them."[27]

Conveniently for Johnson and Wells, a British judge, in perhaps the most celebrated English court case of the eighteenth century, complicated American cries of enslavement at precisely that moment. The trial dealt with the fate of one young African, known to history only as James Somerset. Born and enslaved in West Africa, the eight-year-old boy had been resold into Virginia in the spring of 1749, where he was purchased by Charles Steuart and rechristened Somerset. Two decades later, Steuart and his manservant left Boston (where they had resided for the previous four years) for Britain on business. But when it came time to return to Virginia, Somerset fled his master and "absolutely refused" to go. Running out of both tide and patience, Steuart had Somerset arrested and clapped aboard the *Ann and Mary*, a ship then lying in the Thames. Having concluded that Somerset—who had adopted the forename of James upon being baptized at St. Andrew's Church in London—was no longer docile enough to be his slave, Steuart hired Captain John Knowles to transport him to Jamaica, "to be there sold."[28]

At this juncture, philanthropist and well-known British abolitionist Granville Sharp entered the fray. A correspondent of Philadelphia's Anthony

Benezet and friend and counselor to Olaudah Equiano, Sharp heard of the case from members of London's black community and approached William Murray, earl of Mansfield and lord chief justice of the King's Bench (the highest common-law court in Britain), in hopes of obtaining a writ of habeas corpus against Captain Knowles. No attorney himself, Sharp also contacted Francis Hargrave, an inexperienced but eager young barrister, and convinced him to volunteer his services to Somerset. The case lumbered through eight lugubrious hearings from February into the early summer of 1772, during which time Lord Mansfield hinted darkly of the dire consequences the case might have for Britain's Caribbean interests and quietly urged both sides to settle. Neither did. Steuart wanted his investment back, while Sharp hoped to establish a larger precedent.[29]

By June 22, the lord justice could delay no longer, and before a crowded court he read out a prepared statement, lasting less than a minute, according to one witness. "The state of slavery is of such a nature," he began, "that it is incapable of being introduced on any reasons, moral or political; but only by positive law." Parliament, over the centuries, had codified various forms of unfree labor, from indentured servitude to apprenticeship, but never anything "so odious" as permanent, hereditary slavery. As a result, nothing in common law existed to hold James Somerset in bondage so long as he remained in Britain, and no statute compelled him to return to the Americas. "Whatever inconveniences, therefore, may follow from the decision, I cannot say this case is allowed or approved by the law of England," Mansfield concluded, "and therefore the black must be discharged." As he finished, the black men and women present slowly rose and bowed toward the bench.[30]

Slaves around the empire immediately grasped the implications of the case. As word of the Somerset decision spread from ships to back alleys to farms to plantations, slaves along the Atlantic seaboard openly discussed the prospect of freedom. In September 1772, the *Boston Gazette* explained the situation to anybody who could read—or be read to. "[A]s Blacks are free now in [Britain], Gentlemen will not be so fond of bringing them here as they used to be." In the fall of 1773, the Williamsburg *Virginia Gazette* reported the attempted escape of an enslaved couple who hoped to reach Britain, "a notion now too prevalent among the Negroes, greatly to the vexation and prejudice of their masters." South Carolina journals carried runaway slave advertisements that did more than hint of slaves inspired by Lord Mansfield. Among those who took flight was Bacchus, who relieved his master of "a Purse of Dollars" for back pay, changed his name to John Christian, and was expected to "attempt to get on Board some Vessel bound for Great Britain, from the Knowledge he has of the late Determination of Somerset's Case."[31]

Mansfield tried to craft his decision narrowly so that he might find for Somerset without freeing other slaves in England. As petty slaveholder Benjamin Franklin chortled, for all of its reputed "love of liberty," the British legal system only succeeded "in setting free a single negro." But as John Christian's flight demonstrated, what mattered most was how black and white Americans *perceived* the case's outcome. Caribbean landlords besieged allies in Parliament to clarify the law by "securing property in negroes and other Slaves [throughout] this kingdom." Edward Long, a Jamaican planter and former vice-admiralty court judge, mailed a lengthy rebuttal to Hargrave in which he argued that the ramifications of the Somerset decision would be immeasurable. Not only might the Caribbean economy collapse as thousands of black laborers swarmed toward Britain, but the ethnic nature of England itself should suffer. The "lower classes of women," Long reasoned, being "remarkably fond of blacks, for reasons too brutal to mention," might so contaminate English blood through intermarriage that the island's population might resemble Portugal's "in complexion of skin and baseness of mind."[32]

As Long's bizarre missive indicates, Lord Mansfield's ruling forced those with investments in Britain's Caribbean islands to ponder their place within the empire. While friction increased between Britain and its mainland colonies, the severe reality of sugar slavery meant a speedy parting of the ways between North America and the Caribbean. The powerful West Indian lobby had long seen to it that its interests were maintained, and legislation such as the Sugar Act of 1764 was designed to tax the importation (rather than the exportation) of Caribbean molasses. In the immediate aftermath of the Seven Years' War, a few white radicals on islands such as St. Kitts had raised their glasses to "the Independency of America," but even before the Somerset case such toasts had become increasingly rare. The high proportion of Africans on the sugar plantations led to feelings of insecurity among the white minority population and therefore a paranoia whose intensity reflected the Caribbean's racial demographics. If white masters in Massachusetts quickly recognized the hypocrisy in complaining of their political enslavement by Britain, wealthy landlords in Barbados instinctively saw the madness in such rhetoric.[33]

Due in large part to the withdrawal of British forces northward into French Canada toward the end of the Seven Years' War, slave revolts shook the Caribbean islands. In Jamaica, slaves plotted for their freedom in 1760 in what came to be known as Tacky's Revolt. Among the leaders were Tacky, whose name translated into Akan as "chief," and Aponga, who had probably witnessed a riot between press-gangs and sailors in Boston. Tacky was captured and beheaded, but his followers fought on for nearly a year, until sixty whites and nearly four hundred slaves lay dead. Conspiracies or revolts erupted nearly every year thereafter: in Bermuda and Nevis in 1761, in Jamaica in 1765 and 1766, and in British Honduras, where officials banished nearly five hundred of Tacky's captured soldiers. Despite Dr. Samuel Johnson's public toast "to the next insurrection of the Negroes in the West Indies" and Lord Mansfield's ruling, Caribbean planters gambled that their lives were safer within the potent shelter of Great Britain rather than in a feeble alliance with mainland patriots. By 1770, the year of the Boston Massacre, when "lobsterbacks" became the visible symbol of royal tyranny in Massachusetts, the colonial assemblies of Nevis, Montserrat, St. Kitts, and Tobago petitioned King George to station additional redcoats in the islands.[34]

The Caribbean colonies grew increasingly estranged from their mainland brethren as the crisis with Britain grew warmer. A good number of Caribbean landlords spent much of their lives in London, a reminder that the web of empire tied each colony to Britain. As one visitor to St. Kitts marveled, the colony was "almost abandoned to overseers and managers, owing to the amazing fortunes that belong to Individuals, who almost all reside in England." So while legislation such as the Stamp Act gave rise to mainland rebels like Patrick Henry and James Otis, the sugar islands produced only Samuel Martin of Antigua, who opposed the tax but resisted any movement for independence. If any one moment defined the growing estrangement of Britain's mainland colonies from its Caribbean holdings, it came in 1772. The Somerset decision forced slaveholders such as Washington to calculate the dangers *within* the empire, but sugar planters like Martin, surrounded by black majorities on each island, fretted about the dangers of life *without* British military might.[35]

As mainland merchants fought back against parliamentary controls with economic boycotts, the gulf between the continent and the islands grew. Caribbean residents required New England fish and Pennsylvania corn to feed their slaves, and any shortage of essential foodstuffs could lead to further rebelliousness. Since Boston Patriots boycotted any British island that submitted to the Stamp Act, there could be no neutrals in the emerging contest. Stamped documents were tossed onto bonfires in the mainland colonies, and some colonists advocated starving the "Creole Slaves," that is, the Caribbean master class, through a complete embargo of provisions. "Can no Punishment be devised for Barbados and Port Royal in Jamaica," John Adams fumed, "for their base Desertion of the Cause of Liberty? Their tame Surrender of the rights of Britons? Their mean, timid resignation to slavery?" A few colonists observed that the presence of large numbers of redcoats in the Caribbean prevented the handful of dissenters from burning the stamps, but the truth was that nervous sugar planters welcomed the royal presence. Fearing further servile unrest in the wake of Somerset, the Jamaican Assembly even urged the governor to appoint regular army officers to supervise the colony's ill-trained local militia.[36]

Given the determination of the Caribbean islands and the lower colonies to maintain controls over their labor force, it comes as no surprise that the movement for independence on the part of black Americans began in those northern seaports where white authority was always the most lax. In Boston on the afternoon of March 5, 1770, forty-seven-year-old Christopher (or Crispus) Attucks was drinking in a pub with other mariners when he glanced up as a British soldier entered the tavern to enquire about part-time employment. Since Britain paid its soldiers so poorly, redcoats found it necessary to take odd jobs along the docks, which served to depress the wages of American workers. Hearty mariners such as Attucks—the *Boston Gazette* described him as a "well-set" man, six feet two inches tall—also faced the dangers of press-gangs. As a runaway slave of African and Nantucket Indian ancestry, Attucks was unprotected by colonial law, and might have remained silent. Instead he rose and joined the other patrons in cursing the soldier and hounding him from the pub.[37]

As evening descended, the sailors, whose number had grown to nearly thirty men, left the tavern. With Attucks in the lead, the mob, derided by John Adams as a mixture of "saucy boys, negroes and mulattoes, Irish teagues and outlandish jack-tarrs," headed for the Customs House on King Street. Attucks poked one sentry with a large stick and denounced the redcoat as a "lobster," while others rained rocks and chunks of ice down on the terrified soldiers. Above the catcalls, somebody shouted, "Fire." One shot rang out. After a pause, the eight British soldiers unloosed a volley, wounding eleven men and killing five. Among the dead lay Attucks, the first "martyr," as Adams later conceded, of the American Revolution.[38]

Attucks had risked life and limb not for an ideology but in the cause of sailors' and workingmen's rights. However, that mattered little to most Bostonians. Samuel Adams organized a procession to carry his coffin—and those of three others—to Faneuil Hall, where he lay in state for three days. Samuel's cousin John defended the accused soldiers with an overtly racist appeal, suggesting that Attucks's visage "would be enough to terrify any person," but within three years he adopted Attucks's moniker as a pseudonym in a public letter on liberty. Abigail Adams agreed that it "always appeared a most iniquitous scheme" to "fight ourselves for what we are daily robbing and plundering from those who have as good a right to freedom as we have."[39]

Admittedly, the whites who revered Attucks the most included those who had long despised slavery. Five years before the massacre, Samuel Adams's wife, Elizabeth, had received a female slave named Surry as a gift. The family accepted the present on the condition that she cross their threshold as a free woman. (Surry resided with the Adams family for decades as a paid servant.) When Adams took up his pen to denounce the monarchy as "bigoted to the greatest degree to the doctrines of slavery," it was no idle metaphor. A few days after the shootings, Adams was among the ten thousand mourners who marched behind the four hearses as they bore Attucks and the other "martyrs" to Boston's Middle Burying Ground, where the city erected the first funeral monument to a black American.[40]

Other slaves and freemen from Massachusetts colony soon donned uniforms in an overt demand for political inclusion. When British troops under the command of Major John Pitcairn marched out of Boston for Lexington, blacks numbered among the roughly seventy minutemen who took their stand on the village green. Prince Estabrook, a "Negro man," was wounded but lived to fight another day, as were Pompey of Braintree and Cato Wood of Arlington. Peter Salem, a slave of the Belknap family, had been freed just before the skirmish so that he might enlist in the Massachusetts militia. Salem survived the encounter and lived, in a curious turn of events, to shoot and kill Pitcairn two months later at the Battle of Bunker Hill. Twenty-two-year-old freeman Lemuel Haynes not only penned one of the first patriotic ballads of the fight, "The Battle of Lexington," but proudly insisted that he be identified as "Lemuel a young Mollato" on the manuscript's title page.[41]

With free and enslaved black Bostonians almost daily adding their names to the casualty rosters, a good many whites hoped to repay them for their sacrifice, all while ending their colony's participation in the Atlantic slave trade. Even before the fighting erupted at Lexington and Concord, Samuel Adams had introduced into the Assembly a bill designed to limit the "unnatural and unwarrantable custom of inslaving Mankind in this province" by banning "the importation of slaves into the same." The measure failed that year, but in 1771, in the wake of the Boston Massacre, Adams tried again, only to have his successful legislation vetoed by Governor Thomas Hutchinson. Finally, in June 1774, the General Court once more passed the bill, just as tensions between Hutchinson and the colonists collapsed into armed hostilities. Connecticut and Rhode Island banished the traffic from their borders the same year, and Pennsylvania doubled its tariff on imported Africans in a move designed to tax the trade out of existence. Although Adams's efforts were completely altruistic, his crusade was aided by the soft market for new Africans in the northern colonies. In the wake of Parliament's Coercive (or Intolerable) Acts, moreover, colonists moved to ban all trade with Britain, including trade in slaves.[42]

Primarily because the importations of the previous decade had produced a glut of Africans in the Chesapeake, Maryland joined the campaign against the traffic in humans in 1771. Like Pennsylvania, colonial legislators did not ban the trade outright but, perhaps in an effort to avoid a veto by the royal governor, instead sought to kill it by imposing a duty of £8 for each slave brought into Maryland. New Jersey legislators followed suit with an even higher tax of £20 per head, although the council rejected the plan. But North Carolina banned the importation of Africans in August 1774, and even frontier Georgia, typically an eager importer of fresh bodies, did so as well less than a year later. Already flush with Africans, the Virginia Assembly had been taxing African imports since the late 1760s with the quiet permission of the royal governor. But in 1772, the House of Burgesses ostentatiously announced its intentions of increasing the tariff on "a Trade of great Inhumanity." An offended Parliament promptly disallowed the higher tax, which permitted white Virginians to renew the tired complaint that they had never desired enslaved workers, who had been forced upon them by the crown. Still, no king had compelled ambitious whites to purchase Africans. By the end of the Seven Years' War, planters hoped to curtail imports primarily because they feared the growing body of slaves among them. As George Mason worried, "the primary Cause of the Destruction" of Rome had been "the Introduction of great Numbers of Slaves." Attacking Parliament with progressive legislation and model constitutions nobody expected to pass was in part a way for guilty slaveholders to absolve themselves from any complicity in creating an unwaged population whose very existence was clearly at odds with American rhetoric of the early 1770s.[43]

Even American defenders of slavery as a benevolent institution found it difficult to defend the horrors of the Middle Passage. Tory voices, otherwise willing to endorse the actions of the crown, and well aware that Britain dominated the Atlantic slave trade, fell silent when it came to the commerce in human bodies. Prodded by the New Englanders, the Continental Congress, as part of its larger nonimportation program, passed a resolution on April 6, 1776, that "no slaves be imported into any of the thirteen United Colonies." Faced with a national boycott on Africans, the House of Burgesses finally banned any further imports two years later. Although the congressional prohibition, as much a slap at Parliament as an egalitarian statement on human rights, did nothing to impede the intercolonial traffic in slaves, the 1776 resolution nonetheless stood as the first *national* step in what would become a very long crusade against human bondage. Activists like Samuel Adams hoped that it would be but the first step toward American liberty, not the last.[44]

Black Americans, particularly those in New England, had no intention of either letting the drumbeat of liberty cease or turning control of the movement over to white activists. Their first peaceful, collective response to their condition took the ancient English form of petition, the way Englishmen and colonists had long voiced their grievances to crown and Parliament. By early January 1773, with increasing numbers of Americans confronting the chasm between liberty and enslavement from the pulpit to the battlefield, black Bostonians believed the time had arrived to force those in power to translate their disquiet into legislative action.[45]

The first petition bore only the signature of freeman Felix Holbrook, but it spoke on behalf of "many Slaves, living in the Town of Boston." Delivered to Governor Hutchinson, the colony's council, and the legislative General Court, the brief petition adopted the language of Christian obsequiousness. "We desire to bless God, who loves Mankind, who sent his Son to die for their Salvation," Holbrook insisted, shrewdly emphasizing his Christian faith. He even promised to "be obedient to our Masters, so long as God" desired them to remain in bondage. No discussion of political or natural rights appeared in the document, although Holbrook did stress the practical benefits of having more free taxpayers "to bear a part of the Public Charges." Neither did Holbrook presume to suggest any particular "Laws proper to be made, in relation to our unhappy State." Instead, he concluded with a humble prayer "for such Relief only," which might not injure the rights of "our Masters; but to us will be as Life from the dead," perhaps a hint toward gradual, compensated emancipation.[46]

Several days after, the assembly appointed a committee to address Holbrook's petition. But with Massachusetts finally achieving some unity on political issues, wealthy Americans feared creating new divisions over black freedom. "[W]hile we are attempting to preserve ourselves from slavery," fretted merchant and slaveholder John Hancock, "we also take into consideration the state and circumstances of negro slaves in this province." While sympathetic to the petitioner, John Adams stressed the importance of forging a truly continental movement for independence, and any alliance with New York or Virginia required silence on the issue of slavery. After three days of deliberation, the committee voted to table the petition until the next session. Holbrook promptly led a delegation to the home of Governor Hutchinson, where he was informed that instructions from London rendered any assistance impossible.[47]

Holbrook was back within three months. His second petition, dated April 20, 1773, carried three additional signatures—those of Peter Bestes, Sambo Freeman, and Chester Joie—but a hardened tone as well. Apart from a passing reference to "civil and religious liberty," the document eschewed spiritual pieties in favor of a bold statement on the "spirit of *freedom*, [which] seems to fire every humane breast on this continent." Gone were the vague hints of reform. Instead, in an indication that the black community in Boston was aware of antislavery news around the larger Atlantic basin, the petitioners recommended the Spanish system of *coartación*, which allowed slaves to purchase their freedom or extra time with the money they earned during the "one day in a week [when they] work for themselves." In a blunt assault on the consciences of Boston's merchant elites, Holbrook observed that "[e]ven the *Spaniards*, who have not the sublime ideas of freedom that English men have," accorded their laborers a modicum of human rights. As free blacks, the four suggested that at some future date they might abandon Massachusetts for "the Coast of *Africa*," but in the meantime they demanded "that ample relief which, *as men*, [they] have a natural right to."[48]

As men! With each passing month, the black petitioners grew bolder in their language, and their rhetoric increasingly mirrored the emergent discourse on the inalienable rights of men. In May 1774, just after the Boston Tea Party and the resulting Coercive Acts, "a Grate Number of Blackes" submitted a third petition. This time, the petitioners included slaves as well as freemen, and the recipients were not only members of the colonial assembly but also General Thomas Gage, British commander in chief in America, recently arrived to replace the ineffective Hutchinson as governor of the Massachusetts Bay Colony. Although the document is unsigned, its phrasing indicated the petitioners were less educated than Holbrook. But the brief statement demanded the same "naturel rights" to freedom "in common with all other men" and reflected Lockean ideology in its insistence that "we are a freeborn Pepel and have never forfeited this Blessing by aney compact or agreement." The petitioners also betrayed an awareness of the Somerset decision in their reminder that English common law "doth not justifi but condemns Slavery." This time, the authors went so far as to request that the assembly pass an act for gradual emancipation that would restore their "Natural rights" and liberate their children at the age of twenty-one. This petition, like the previous two, elicited no official response.[49]

That was hardly an end to it. While the spread of information throughout the black community is hard to trace, word of the Massachusetts activities evidently sailed down the shoreline with black mariners, or traveled with the menservants of wealthy merchants and planters, or perhaps even was spread through the letters of the small number of literate freemen. Black activists across New England picked up their pens in hopes that at least one legislature would extend liberty to those who literally bore the shackles of slavery. Eight bondmen from Salem, Connecticut, called upon the assembly to recognize black Americans as fellow "friends of freedom," and a number of "Negroes in the Towns of Stratford and Fairfield" also observed "the flagrant Injustice" in advocating "the Cause of Liberty" while holding others "to perpetual Slavery." Nineteen slaves from New Hampshire reminded the legislature "that the God of nature made us free," while Lemuel Haynes, the mixed-race veteran of Lexington, was blunter yet. "Liberty is Equally as pre[c]ious to a Black Man, as it is to a white one," he asserted in a widely reprinted essay, "and Bondage Equally as intolarable to the one as it is to the other." Caesar Sarter, an African sold into Massachusetts, went farther still in his 1774 "Essay on Slavery," published in the *Essex Journal*. "[L]et that excellent rule given by our Saviour, *to do to others, as you would, that they should do to you*, have its due weight with you."[50]

The Stratford petitioners promised not to adopt "violent measures" to cast off their "grievous Yoke," but other bondmen were not so timid. The fact that enslaved Americans had adopted the language of natural rights clearly unnerved conservative dissidents. Limus, after knocking on his master's door to say farewell, audaciously informed his stunned owner that he "will be free, that he will serve no Man, and that he will be conquered or governed by no Man." Near Boston, Abigail Adams informed her husband of "a conspiracy of the negroes." The matter was "kept pretty private" and was allegedly revealed by a slave "who endeavored to dissuade" his fellows from their actions. If a plot did exist, it confirmed the worst fears of white Patriots, as the slaves, weary of appealing to the colonial assembly, approached General Gage, "telling him they would fight for him provided he would arm them" and support their liberation.[51]

Rumors of the petitions reached the southern colonies in a matter of months. In November 1774, a band of Virginia slaves met to elect a leader "who was to conduct them when the English troops should arrive." Young James Madison, a member of the Committee on Public Safety in Orange County, could not decide whether he was more surprised that African Americans might elect a leader or that they "foolishly thought" the British might repay their rebellion "with their freedom." He did, however, beg his Philadelphia correspondent not to spread the story for fear of inciting similar conspiracies in Pennsylvania. Yet Madison's pleas did nothing to quell black rebelliousness in the Chesapeake. Shortly thereafter, a Prince William County court charged a slave named Toney with insurrection, and three days later, planters in nearby Chesterfield County were "alarm'd for an Insurrection of the Slaves." In Norfolk, magistrates passed a "Sentence of death" upon two slaves; one of them, Emanuel, was the bondman of militia lieutenant

Matthew Phripp. Clearly, the language of liberty, once unchained by white orators, was difficult to contain or qualify.[52]

Similar incidents of black resolve emerged even in the lower colonies. In Beaufort, North Carolina, planters jailed, whipped, and cropped forty black men and women for complicity in "a deep laid Horrid Tragick Plan" for freedom. Just to the south, in Pitt County, the local Committee of Public Safety granted a patroller's request to summarily "shoot any Number of Negroes above four" found off their master's estates, especially if "armed." In South Carolina, rumors spread along the docks that British governor William Campbell sailed into Charles Town's harbor with muskets for "an insurrection amongst the Slaves." No guns were found, but local authorities hanged and burned Thomas Jeremiah, a free black pilot, for allegedly colluding with the British. In that same year of 1775, white South Carolinians also executed a slave named George for preaching that "the Young King," George III, had "set the Negroes Free," but that local dissidents refused to honor his decree. The ghastly deaths of Jeremiah and George indicated the determination of South Carolina to quarantine any discussion of black freedom. Yet in a curious way, the indictment of "sedition"—rather than the traditional charge of "insurrection"—implied that both men were political actors capable of making informed decisions, an indispensable requirement of all citizens in a free society.[53]

If the petitions in New England and the intrigues farther south served to alter the tone of the debates on black liberty, white reformers of humble origins helped to keep the antislavery movement alive. Thomas Paine, the son of a Quaker staymaker, wrote his first essay on slavery soon after his arrival in Philadelphia in late 1774. The essay, published in the *Pennsylvania Journal* on March 8, 1775, denounced unfree labor in daring, muscular language rarely found in pamphlets drafted by gentlemen revolutionaries. Using the pen name "Humanus," Paine romantically portrayed Africans as having "lived quietly" as "industrious farmers" before European traders had "debauched them with liquors." He struck a political nerve by observing that "the wicked and inhuman" English might choose to enslave any prisoner they captured in their "unnatural wars." With what "consistency, or decency" could white Patriots "complain so loudly of attempts to enslave them," so long as they themselves "enslave many thousands more, without any pretence of authority?" Unique among white reformers was Paine's stubborn refusal to even acknowledge the existence of race; he wrote as if the unwaged workers he defended were of European ancestry. As a radical evangelical, Paine excoriated the "pretended Christians" who defended the system by "alledging the Sacred Scriptures to favour this wicked practice." Since no human would ever willingly sell his body, Paine insisted, a black Pennsylvanian "who is proper owner of his freedom, has a right to reclaim it, however often sold."[54]

Goaded into action by the increasingly undeferential demands of black essayists and petitioners and inspired by such righteous fervor, a significant number of white Patriots began to move decisively against slavery. In 1774, an assemblage of New York City rum distillers unanimously voted not to refine syrup or molasses designated for the Atlantic slave trade. Nor were these sentiments limited to northern seaport towns. The same year, Virginia planter George Mason mourned his colony's participation in slavery, as it obliterated "the Dictates of Humanity, & all other finer feelings of the Soul." In early 1775, several dozen parishioners in St. Andrew's Parish, Georgia, adopted a resolution denouncing slavery as an "unnatural practice" forged in "injustice and cruelty, and highly dangerous to our liberties." At a time when discussions of liberty and natural rights rang from every pulpit, filled every tavern, and packed every courtroom, growing numbers of white and black activists had good reason to hope that if independence came, Americans would not merely be exchanging kings, but that the "very wrong foundation" the colonies were based upon might be swept away.[55]

The defining moment in laying the proper foundations for an independent republic arrived on June 7, 1776, when Richard Henry Lee introduced into the Continental Congress a resolution demanding the dissolution of "all political connection" between the colonies and "the State of Great Britain." Four days later, a committee was appointed to draft a statement justifying and announcing American independence. Composed of John Adams, Roger Sherman, and slaveholders Benjamin Franklin, Robert R. Livingston of New York, and Thomas Jefferson, the committee delegated the task of crafting the first draft to Jefferson. Returning to his rented lodgings on Market Street, Jefferson began to write.[56]

Over the course of the next seventeen days, Jefferson labored over his draft, while Richard hastened to brew the tea. The document opened with a bold avowal of American ideals before moving to a lengthy list of grievances against King George. In an often-told story, Jefferson squirmed silently as Congress edited and amended his work. One of the passages dropped completely blamed both domestic slavery and the Atlantic trade on the monarchy in general and George III in particular. Why Jefferson thought this charge justified, since white settlers in Virginia had been willingly purchasing Africans since 1619, remains unclear. Quite possibly he hoped that by attacking slavery in the Declaration, America might silence British critics such as Samuel Johnson. More likely, Jefferson wished to relieve his new country—and, more profoundly, himself—of the guilt of importing hundreds of thousands of Africans before taking up arms in the cause of liberty. If Jefferson could prove that his innocent countrymen had been forced to involve themselves in a detestable institution by a distant tyrant, they might yet flatter themselves the champions of liberty, rather than the hypocrites Johnson insisted them to be.[57]

John Adams, who fought to retain the eliminated charge as a "vehement philippic against negro slavery," was equally distressed by the omission. But even in its expurgated form, the Declaration remained a powerful indictment of social inequality. What remained was the promise of "inalienable rights" in the new nation, most particularly "liberty." When planter Landon Carter, friend and mentor to George Washington, first perused the document he stood dumbstruck. Assuming that the Declaration was meant to be taken literally, he feared he would have to free his slaves. Evidently many of his bondmen had the same thought. Having heard the news from domestic slaves returning from Williamsburg, eight of Carter's slaves stole a gun, a "bag of bullets and all the Powder," and "ran away" in pursuit of happiness.[58]

As the stunned Carter's response indicates, Jefferson's proclamation was far more than a declaration of independence from the British Empire. So long as the mainland colonies remained within the English fold, their political system was hierarchical and class-based. Power flowed downward, from king to Parliament to royal governor to colonial assembly, and from those institutions to what Patrick Henry once dubbed the "well-born," who lorded above "the lower orders" and dependent populations of servants and slaves. But a republic implied no such thing. Under Jefferson's unforgettable formulation, governments derived "their powers from the consent of the governed," and so authority emanated from "the people." In a monarchical world, one man, much like one monarch, enjoyed command over another, but in a republic—no matter how restricted the franchise might be—"governments [were] instituted among men" based on a mutual contract of all sovereign individuals within that society. Ancient statutes might exist within each new state to protect slavery, but African Americans and nervous masters like Carter understood that such laws no longer had any rational basis. Enslaved Americans had never accepted their condition, but now, with the stroke of Jefferson's pen, slavery had become a national ideological problem.[59]

History has a curious way of not turning out as expected. But gazing backward only from an unhappy later date—say, the firing on Sumter—conceals the hopes and dreams of those present at the nation's founding. For black Americans, the Declaration was no hollow pretense but rather a solemn pledge. "[We] have in Common with all other men a Natural and Unalienable Right to that freedom which the Grat Parent of the Unaverse hath

Bestowed equally on all menkind," one northern freedman insisted in a clear appropriation of revolutionary rhetoric. As Americans faced the grim prospect of war with Britain, slaves and freemen stood ready to use the conflict to advance freedom's cause. As Lemuel Haynes wrote in an appeal to white Patriots, "If you have any Love to yourselves, or any Love to this Land, if you have any Love to your fellow-men, Break these intollerable yoaks." By then, Congress had adopted the Declaration on the Necessity of Taking Up Arms. But whether Haynes's plea would be taken to heart would be up to the five thousand blacks who would serve in the Continental Army, the nearly fifteen thousand blacks who would opt for the Loyalist ranks, and the small number of white politicians who would spend the next quarter century retreating from the promise of 1776.[60]

THREE

The Transformation of Colonel Tye

Black Combatants and the War

B ORN IN 1754, the same year the Seven Years' War began in western Pennsylvania, Titus grew to maturity during the two divisive, politicized decades preceding the fighting at Lexington and Concord. Together with five other slaves, Titus lived on his master's farm near the village of Colts Neck, in Monmouth County, New Jersey. On the eve of the Revolution he was one of roughly 8,200 slaves in the colony, which stood second only to New York among northern colonies in both the number and percentage of African Americans. Titus's owner, John Corlies, was a Quaker, but not a very godly one, and he stubbornly resisted manumitting his bondmen despite numerous visits from church elders who prodded him to do so. Some Friends sought to balance their economic needs with the demands of their faith by manumitting their slaves when they reached the age of twenty-one. But as 1775 dawned, Corlies made no move to follow that practice and liberate Titus. Unhappily for Corlies, however, he was as good a pacifist as he was an abolitionist, which is to say that he was not one at all, and so Titus had been raised in a household that hardly cherished the ideal of peaceful resolution.[1]

As a young man, Titus was "not very black [and] near 6 foot high." Like many farm slaves of the period, he wore "a gray homespun coat, brown breeches, [and] blue and white stockings." Although Corlies had afforded his slaves "no learning [and was] not inclined to give them any," on such a small farm, Titus was surely aware of the Quakers' unsuccessful attempts to persuade his irascible master to adhere to the Friends' directives regarding manumission. The town was about forty miles by road from New York, so reports of the larger Atlantic world were never long in reaching rural

Colts Neck. By 1774, Lord Mansfield's decision was common knowledge among the county's black population, and worried masters in Shrewsbury and Middletown peppered Governor William Franklin with remonstrances, complaining of their bondmen's growing "Impudence." Slaves and free blacks, they insisted, were "running about in all times of the Night Stealing and Taking and Riding Peoples Horses," and they heaped blame upon the "deluded King," who encouraged their "Domestics to cut the throats of their Masters."[2]

Although rumors of British judicial support, together with Titus's suspicions that his master was holding him in bondage that violated God's will, played a role in his decision to flee the Corlies farm, it was the dramatic news that reached Monmouth County in early November 1775 that served as the final inspiration. Virginia governor John Murray, fourth earl of Dunmore, declared martial law, and Chesapeake bondmen were flocking to his standard. On the same day that Dunmore finally offered freedom to any "indent[ur]ed servants, negroes [who were] willing to serve His Majesty's forces to end the present rebellion," Titus threw down his hoe and began walking toward Williamsburg. He tarried only long enough to gather "a quantity of clothes," which he tied up into a bundle "drawn up at one end with string." Corlies promptly advertised for his capture, promising a reward of "three pounds proclamation money."[3]

THREE POUNDS Reward.

RUN away from the subscriber, living in Shrewsbury, in the county of Monmouth, New-Jersey, a NEGROE man, named TITUS, but may probably change his name; he is about 21 years of age, not very black, near 6 feet high; had on a grey homespun coat, brown breeches, blue and white stockings, and took with him a wallet, drawn up at one end with a string, in which was a quantity of clothes. Whoever takes up said Negroe, and secures him in any goal, or brings him to me, shall be entitled to the above reward of *Three Pounds* proc. and all reasonable charges, paid by

Nov. 8, 1775. § JOHN CORLIS.

The day after Lord Dunmore announced his proclamation, the future Colonel Tye fled his master's New Jersey farm. John Corlies placed a number of advertisements in Pennsylvania newspapers. This November 22, 1775, announcement appeared in the *Pennsylvania Gazette. American Antiquarian Society.*

For more than two years, Titus vanished from the sight of history. But in the summer of 1778, around the time that the Society of Friends "disown[ed]" John Corlies for the sins of drinking, cursing, and slaveholding, he resurfaced. Fighting alongside white Tories at the June 28 Battle of Monmouth was Colonel Tye, the African American whom historian Graham Russell Hodges described as "one of the war's most feared Loyalists, white or black." Titus's new name and title were revealing. Although the British military rarely granted formal commissions to black officers in the Americas, they often bestowed such titles out of respect, particularly in the Caribbean. During the battle, Tye captured Captain Elisha Shepard of the Monmouth militia and, in a reversal of the authoritarian controls whites typically exerted over blacks, dragged him back to imprisonment in British-occupied New York City.[4]

Throughout 1778 and 1779, Tye launched a series of surprise raids across northern New Jersey, foraging for food and supplies. Operating out of a forested base called Refugeetown on Sandy Hook, Tye and his guerrilla followers targeted wealthy, slaveholding Patriots during their night assaults. Since white farmers typically owned but a few slaves, unlike the case farther south, whites and blacks in New Jersey knew one another intimately, and so many of Tye's raids took on the quality of angry reprisals for past mistreatment. On July 15, 1779, Tye led "about fifty negroes and [white] refugees" in a foray into Shrewsbury, during which they made off with eighty cattle, twenty horses, and two well-known white inhabitants. British soldiers in New York badly needed the meat, and Tye and his men were paid in gold guineas; the seizure and imprisonment of slaveholding Patriots earned Tye no cash but provided him with enormous satisfaction.[5]

As Tye's forays continued, terrified white Patriots begged Governor William Livingston for assistance. The fighting in the area grew particularly malicious. Tye murdered militiaman Joseph Murray in his home in retaliation for Murray's past summary executions of local Loyalists. On September 1, 1780, Tye led a small band of African Americans and Queen's Rangers to Toms River in hopes of capturing Captain Josiah Huddy, a man infamous among Tories for his swift execution of captured Loyalists. Huddy was briefly taken prisoner but managed to escape when a party of Patriots surprised Tye's small army. Tye took a bullet in the wrist during the mêlée. Gangrene set in, and Tye died several days later. In a curious coda to the affair, Loyalists later recaptured Huddy and clapped him aboard a British prison ship. Angry Tories dragged him ashore and hanged him on the coast of his native Monmouth County. His executioner was a black soldier.[6]

As Tye's stunning transformation from rustic farmhand to guerrilla officer indicates, the six years of combat that began with Lexington and ended at

vn created new opportunities—as well as new dangers—for African
ans. Like all wars, the American Revolution disrupted established
elations. If the egalitarian rhetoric of the early 1770s challenged the
;ical framework of human bondage, military service allowed thousands
oι ᴗᴗᵣdmen to liberate themselves. For black Americans who resided in the
New England colonies, service with the American Continental Army (or with
the newly created state militias) became the path to freedom. A far larger
number of blacks in the middle and southern colonies found that casting
their lot with His Majesty's forces proved the wisest gamble. As the historian
Benjamin Quarles put it, the role of the black soldier in the Revolution "can
best be understood by realizing that his major loyalty was not to place nor to
a people but to a principle."[7]

———

Although young James Madison had once sneered at the thought that Virginia
slaves were capable of electing a black officer "who was to conduct them when
the English troops should arrive," he also had no doubts that should "america
& Britain come to an hostile rupture," an "Insurrection among the slaves may
& will be promoted." Nor was that a unique fear among southern Patriots, all of
whom, however, cast black Americans in the passive role of people whose lives
would be acted upon by distant white authorities. John Houston and Archibald
Bulloch, two delegates to the Continental Congress from Georgia, also worried
that the British might stir up slaves against their American masters.[8]

Such concerns were hardly the irrational apprehensions of whites. Should
the dissent of the late 1760s erupt into open warfare, Britain would be foolish
not to employ every means possible to subdue the rebellion. In fact, had Madison been privy to the private correspondence of King George's administrators, he might have been more anxious. Due to the precarious nature of peace
after 1763, Britain had long weighed the impact of large numbers of slaves
in its southern colonies. In "case of a war," Governor Dunmore informed his
superiors in 1772, "the people [of Virginia], with great reason, tremble at the
facility that an enemy would find in procuring Such a body of men, attached
by no tye to their Masters or to the Country." In North Carolina, Governor
Josiah Martin complained to London of rumors that he "had formed a design
of Arming the Negroes, and proclaiming freedom to all such as should resort
to the King's Standard." Martin was no conspirator, but slaves in the eastern
counties of Pitt and Beaufort nonetheless began to discuss a "Tragick Plan"
to burn their masters' plantations before turning themselves over to the royal
"Government for their Protection."[9]

White southerners preferred to believe that the king's men lurked behind
servile unrest, but the truth was that politicized black Americans aggressively

advanced their own cause. In April 1775, Lord Dunmore, hoping to squash any movement toward armed independence, ordered the seizure of gunpowder in Williamsburg. When members of the House of Burgesses publicly condemned the act, an "exceedingly exasperated" Dunmore exploded. He "swore by the living God" that if white Virginians did not alter their behavior, "he would declare freedom to the slaves & reduce the City of Williamsburg to ashes." If war came, Dunmore lectured a group of startled slaveholders, "all the Slaves" would fight "on the side of the [royal] Government." The governor hoped only to scare the burgesses, but several days later he awoke to find a delegation of blacks requesting an audience. Having heard of Dunmore's tirade from "one of his [own] servants," the slaves boldly "offered to join him and take up arms." The stunned governor ordered them "to go about their business" and "threatened them with his severest punishment, should they presume to renew their application."[10]

Perhaps Dunmore's reaction was designed to placate nervous slaveholders, but most likely it was the honest response of an affronted aristocrat with considerable slaveholding investments in Virginia and the Caribbean. Nevertheless, the bondmen's offer of service set Dunmore to thinking. As his administration grew increasingly alienated from white Virginians, it was logical to search elsewhere for support. On May 1, Dunmore wrote to the earl of Dartmouth, suggesting that if given arms enough, he could "collect from among the *Indians*, negroes and other persons" an army sufficient to maintain control of the colony. Word of Dunmore's ruminations spread quickly if not accurately. Only two weeks later, General Thomas Gage wrote to Dartmouth from Boston: "We hear that a Declaration his Lordship has made, of proclaiming all the Negroes free, who should join him, has Startled the Insurgents."[11]

Gage thought the policy a sound one. By mid-June, he warned Secretary of War William Barrington that if tensions in Massachusetts grew much worse, "we must avail ourselves of every resource, even to raise the Negros, in our cause." For their part, African Americans around the Chesapeake had no intention of waiting for British policy to solidify. When British troops from St. Augustine arrived in Norfolk, that July, lowcountry slaves began to flock toward English lines. The presence of foreign soldiers, one Virginian fretted, created "exceeding bad effects" upon slaves in the nearby counties. Heightened patrols were no match for black resolve, as "Slaves eloped from their Masters." Norfolk residents appointed a deputation to call upon Captains John McCartney and Matthew Squire, the respective commanders of the *Mercury* and the *Otter*, who assured the group that they would never encourage runaways. Despite these promises, not only did both men welcome slaves aboard their vessels, but Squire also found employment for fugitives who paddled out to the *Otter* while it lay in the York River.[12]

Not surprisingly, white Loyalists along the southern tidewater found themselves suspect in the eyes of their planter neighbors. Samuel Kemp went so far as to place a letter in the Williamsburg *Virginia Gazette* denying reports that he "had endeavoured to exasperate the Negroes to rise." But even as Kemp was drafting his denial, far across the Atlantic the king's government was discussing an "expedition against the Southern Provinces in North America." On October 15, 1775, Lord Frederick North, the prime minister, advised King George on "the perilous situation" of Virginia and the Carolinas due to "the great number of their negro slaves, and the small proportion of white inhabitants." Eleven days later, William Henry Lyttelton, the former royal governor of both South Carolina and Jamaica, rose in the House of Commons with "a proposal for encouraging the negroes in that part of America to rise against their masters." Angry members—particularly those with financial interests in the Caribbean—shouted down Lyttelton's idea as "horrid and wicked," and Parliament voted against his motion. Even so, a policy of black freedom in the name of military exigency was coalescing at the highest levels of the British government.[13]

Only one month later, Dunmore finally acted. During the previous June, Dunmore had quit Williamsburg and taken refuge aboard the sloop-of-war *Fowey*. Realizing that the majority of the gentry stood against him, the governor at last decided to make good on his threat. "Lord Dunmore sails up and down the river," wrote a horrified Norfolk resident, "and where he finds a defenseless place, he lands, plunders the plantation and carries off the negroes." On November 7, 1775, Dunmore's roving flotilla became larger still when he declared martial law and announced that he would free "all indent[ur]ed servants, Negroes, or others, (appertaining to Rebels), that are able and willing to bear Arms" with "His Majesty's Troops." As the caveat of service implied, his proclamation was inspired by the expediency of war rather than by humanitarian concern, but that meant nothing to enslaved Virginians, their frantic masters, or bondmen such as Titus.[14]

As slaves sought to turn the political chaos in the colony to their advantage, white Patriots assured one another that their unwaged servants remained faithful. Writing from Williamsburg, Robert Carter Nicholas reported that white "Tories of Norfolk are said to be the Ringleaders" of any movement to arm Virginia slaves. Although rumors held that "great Numbers of Slaves from different Quarters have graced their Corps," Nicholas insisted that Dunmore was "using every Art to seduce the Negroes." Collective self-deception, however, could not disguise the fact that any bondman within safe distance of

British lines "flocked to [their] Standards." In early December, Virginia militiamen captured "Negro George," who had fled his master's plantation near Suffolk. Under questioning, George confessed that "there are 400 Blacks" in Norfolk, "besides Soldiers and Tories." The runaways had been far from idle, as "the intrenchment at Norfolk was nearly compleated," and they had begun to "mount their Cannon yesterday on the works, twelve peices."[15]

By that date, "the king of the blacks," as the *Virginia Gazette* branded Dunmore, marched south toward Great Bridge, a shipping point between Norfolk and the Carolinas. Before Dunmore's six hundred men—about half of them blacks—could fortify the narrow causeway, militiamen from Virginia and North Carolina attacked. According to some reports, the former bondmen wore sashes emblazoned with the words "Liberty to Slaves," but the raw recruits were no match for local whites long accustomed to armed patrols. Under withering fire, Dunmore's men fell back toward the *Otter*. In the fighting on December 9, Patriots killed more than one hundred Loyalists and captured eighteen wounded prisoners, two of them former slaves. Dunmore's "Ethiopian Regiment" was decimated, and the bloodied survivors limped back to their camp in Norfolk.[16]

If the debacle at Great Bridge kept Dunmore from enlarging on what as yet remained a very local proclamation, it did nothing to stem the tide of black refugees flooding out of the counties near Norfolk. Creative slaveholders tried a variety of measures, including propaganda, to curtail the nightly disappearances. Robert Carter, one of the largest slaveholders in the colony, assembled the bondpeople at his Coles Point quarters and warned them of Dunmore's perfidy. The governor promised freedom for those who fought, Carter cautioned, but actually schemed to sell them to "white people living in the West [Indian] Islands." The black men sadly shook their heads at such treachery and vowed to "take [their] wives, Children, [and] male and female acquaintances" and flee into the woods at the first sight of a British vessel. Pleased by this response, Carter was stunned to learn that the moment a privateer landed near Coles Point, thirty-two blacks placed "themselves under the care and direction" of British forces.[17]

Try as they might, slaveholders were unable to prevent news of the larger world from reaching their slaves, in part because enslaved workers craved information, but also because their plantations were not as isolated as they appeared. Because of the need to roll the enormous hogsheads of tobacco onto waiting vessels, most large estates were situated along Virginia's inland waterways, where slaves heard stories of foreign affairs. In light of the Somerset ruling, it was not hard for bondmen to believe that Dunmore's offer of freedom was sincere. Although unable to travel much beyond Norfolk, the governor harbored any runaway who could reach his lines. Nine slaves from southern Maryland set sail for Norfolk "in an open boat," and three more boarded what they erroneously took for a British vessel, swearing to shed "the last drop of their blood in Dunmore's service." In early January 1776, Virginia militiamen captured "[u]pwards of thirty of Jack Dunmore's hopeful gang" and placed them "under a strong guard." When returned to their masters, many runaways simply tried again. The fact that British soldiers were increasingly willing to encourage slaves "to leave their masters [and] to take up arms against them" only convinced irresolute masters to endorse calls for independence. By late March, one white Patriot argued the necessity of taking up arms in this "most just and holy war, and in which Heaven has peculiarly favoured us." Another Virginian, even more irony-challenged, also denounced Dunmore's "many attempts" to "enslave us."[18]

That Virginia's planter class and not the royal governor had literally enslaved others was something that many Patriots had been trying very hard *not* to come to grips with for thirteen years. But with British boats raiding tidewater estates, the planters could no longer avoid this reality. On July 19, a British patrol foraging for water put ashore at Mount Vernon. The captain demanded supplies and, aware of whose land he stood upon, offered protection for any slaves who desired freedom. Seventeen "of General Washington's servants," men and women alike, accepted the offer and boarded the small craft. Among those who sought liberty was thirty-six-year-old Harry Washington. Later that month, young Ralph Henry, who like his celebrated master cherished liberty over death, stumbled safely through British lines.[19]

By the time that Henry found freedom with the redcoats, however, Dunmore's camp suffered the problems of too many refugees and too little food. Wealthy Loyalists in the tidewater either had been alienated by Dunmore's promises of black liberty or simply found it too dangerous to ferry fresh food to the beleaguered British garrison. In desperation, the governor had to send black refugees who knew the Chesapeake well on nightly excursions to plunder nearby plantations. Militiamen captured one foraging party of "one white and sixteen blacks" herding livestock toward Norfolk. Then smallpox hit the camp. Within weeks, gravediggers were so overwhelmed by their nightly tasks that they resorted to mass burials. Finally, on August 6, 1776, Dunmore's fleet abandoned the Chesapeake. Those African Americans healthy enough to travel—roughly three hundred men, women, and children—sailed with him. When the Virginia militia overran the camp, they discovered a number of "miserable wretches left behind," most of them dying of fever. Terrified of disease, the soldiers set fire to the hastily built shanties, burning alive some of the remaining inhabitants.[20]

As Dunmore's flotilla sailed north toward New York City, word of his brief experiment in black freedom spread. In the City of Brotherly Love, urban masters found their domestics every bit as unruly and recalcitrant as had Virginia landlords. According to the Philadelphia *Evening Post*, one white "gentlewoman" was "insulted" when a black man refused to step off the sidewalk into the street as she passed. When she chided him for not knowing his place, he spat: "Stay you d[amne]d white bitch 'till Lord Dunmore and his black regiment come, and then we will see who is to take the wall." Six hundred miles to the south in Charles Town, magistrates charged a bondman with "inticing other slaves to desert on board [a British] man of war," while nightly patrols arrested slaves who sought to paddle canoes out to the royal sloop *Cherokee*. Hoping to minimize the damage, desperate editors changed the word *Negroes* to N*****s in newspaper accounts of Dunmore's proclamation, but nothing could dissuade South Carolina slaves such as Thomas Jeremiah from believing that "the War was come to help the poor Negroes."[21]

As was the case with Lord Mansfield's ruling, the widespread perception in the black community that Dunmore—and the British government—was an enthusiastic liberator was more perception than reality. Even while issuing his November 1775 proclamation, Dunmore declined, as the *Virginia Gazette* noted, to apply it "to his own bondsmen." Despite debate in Parliament and discussions between Lord North and King George, Britain had devised no clear policy nor issued any universal decree. London's initial policy was to maintain the status quo; Parliament was trying to defuse a rebellion, not incite a social revolution. Any blanket policy, moreover, would liberate the human property of slaveholding Loyalists as well, and as London was painfully aware, Dunmore's failed experiment with black troops had "united every Man" in Virginia against him. Indeed, as one Patriot crowed, white "Men of all ranks resent the pointing [of] a dagger to their Throats, thru the hands of their Slaves." Blacks in the southern colonies might believe otherwise, but throughout 1775 and 1776, British policy toward African Americans was, in the words of one historian, both "hesitant and disjointed." And it was that vacillation that provided the new American government with a unique opportunity.[22]

When it came to American policy, any unified response was hampered by the decentralized nature of the government and the military. The Continental Congress was created to forge a united response to British policies, not to govern the united colonies. Worse yet, there was not a single military command but rather fourteen separate armies. Each colony (or state, after 1776) maintained its own militia comprised of citizen-soldiers who enlisted for a short term, usually three to six months. Farmers, mostly, rather than trained soldiers, militiamen had become infamous during the Seven Years' War for their tendency to run during combat. Then there was the Continental Army, raised and financed by the national Congress. Beginning in 1777, Continental troops signed on for lengthier terms of service, usually three years or the duration of the conflict, and as the war dragged on, their superior training showed. But as the military wing of what passed for a national government, George Washington's Continental force reflected the nation's unease when it came to employing black soldiers.[23]

Although white Patriots were not anxious to enlist African Americans into the military—even if free—potential black Patriots proved surprisingly willing to enroll. As Quarles observed, enslaved Americans fulfilled the basic requirements of a revolutionary combatant. They "had little to lose in goods or lands" and "lacked a sentimental or blood tie with England." Whereas white Patriots loudly demanded liberty while refusing it to others, black Americans who were denied ownership of their bodies and labor deeply valued the principles white Americans professed to hold dear. Particularly in urban areas, where the discourse of natural rights was incessant, blacks well understood that a new political order was being forged, and if they were allowed to fight for their country, their demands for freedom and inclusion could not easily be ignored.[24]

Within just a few months of declaring independence, the American government faced a severe crisis in military manpower. During the late summer of 1776, Congress passed legislation creating an eighty-eight-battalion Continental Army. Each state was urged to contribute an assigned number of soldiers, based upon estimates of that colony's prewar white male population. But recruiters reported that white farmers preferred a shorter enlistment in their state's militia, who fought on familiar terrain close to home. Many white enlistees soon thought better of their decision and promptly deserted. Even in the northern states, however, free blacks had little to desert to. Many masters also sought to fulfill their duty to the new country by sending a bondman in their place. "There are in the Massachusetts Regiments some Negroes," reported one surprised officer. Another conceded that "the Negro can take the field instead of his masters; and, therefore, no regiment is seen in which there are not negroes in abundance, and among them there are able-bodied, strong and brave fellows."[25]

When George Washington arrived in Cambridge to take command of Continental forces, he was stunned by the sight of black men bearing muskets and the easy familiarity that existed between white and black New England soldiers. At a council of war in October 1775, he urged an end to the recruitment of blacks, and either because they wished to please their commander, or because many of the northern commanders were themselves slaveholders, the officers unanimously agreed "to reject all Slaves, & by a great Majority to reject Negroes altogether." The sluggish pace of recruitment, however, compelled the general not to purge those "free Negroes who [already] have Served in this Army," and he informed Congress that unless instructed otherwise he would continue to reenlist black soldiers. Upon receiving Washington's letter, Congress referred the question to committee, which in February 1776 concurred that black men already under arms might remain, but recruiters should admit no new black soldiers.[26]

As the committee's vote in Congress indicated, Washington was hardly alone in his dismay over black troops. Despite his abhorrence of slavery, John Adams endorsed the ban on African American soldiers. "We have Causes enough of Jealous Discord and Division," he fretted, and white southerners would "run out of their Wits at the least Hint of such a measure." Nor was Washington's prohibition a new one. State militias traditionally barred blacks from service, although these bans were frequently ignored during times of war, and African Americans had fought in every colonial conflict, including the Seven Years' War. But pragmatists such as Adams recognized that crippling divisions over race hardly assisted the Patriot cause.[27]

There was a logic to Adams's concerns, but ultimately the national prohibition on black troops proved untenable. Even in the Continental Army, troop turnover was a consistent problem. Over the course of the war, approximately 400,000 men enlisted in the national military, but it was rare for more than 14,000 Continentals to be on active duty at any given moment. By 1776, the British had about 35,000 seasoned troops under arms in America, and Washington's decision nearly resulted in the demise of the American cause. The mainland colonies in rebellion were home to roughly 500,000 slaves and free blacks, and every day that the American government tarried in recruiting black soldiers provided Britain with the opportunity to opt for a firm course of freedom. Although Congress never formally repealed the ban, Washington's lieutenants quietly began to allow state recruiters to enlist freemen to complete their troop quotas. Since these troops were incorporated into the national army, Congress even reluctantly agreed to compensate masters up to $400 for each slave they volunteered. By war's end, roughly 5,000 African Americans served in the Continental Army. If General Washington ceased to grouse about black soldiers, it was in part due to the fact that he learned to be content with the recruits sent him, but also because the sight of large numbers of black men in his service grew increasingly commonplace.[28]

Far fewer African Americans served in the state militias. One of the reasons that militiamen enjoyed briefer periods of service than Continental soldiers was that they had families, farms, and businesses to return to. Former slaves such as Devonshire Freeman, who claimed nothing more than an "old violin or fiddle" as his sole piece of property, were more inclined to sign up with Washington's army. For men whose labor had never earned a penny, even meager pay appeared attractive. Moreover, whites who frowned on armed blacks were less inclined to worry if local African Americans volunteered for lengthier tenures in national forces that served far away; militia service, by comparison, often kept armed freedmen near the place of their previous enslavement.[29]

The New England states, despite—or because of—their small black populations, enlisted more black militiamen than any other region of the new nation. As early as April 1775, when riders Paul Revere and William Dawes alerted Massachusetts to the British march on Lexington and Concord, African Americans like Job Potomea and Isaiah Barjonah of Stoneham and Cuff Whitemore of Cambridge turned out to fight. Twenty-two-year-old Lemuel Haynes joined Captain Lebbeus Ball's militia company that month, and shortly thereafter he took part in the siege of Boston and the firefight at Bunker Hill. No sooner was independence declared, one visitor reported, than every Massachusetts regiment included "a lot of Negroes." The seeming contradiction between Massachusetts's small African American community and their willingness to fight for the United States was easily explained. Home to a white majority that comprised 96 percent of the state's population, Massachusetts Patriots felt little paranoia over the prospect of armed blacks and so welcomed their participation. In exchange, black soldiers such as Haynes hoped that their service could force white masters to recognize their "undeniable right to Liberty."[30]

The desperate need for healthy young men also trumped race in neighboring Connecticut. On the eve of Congress's vote of independence, the new state revised its militia act to require all males between the ages of sixteen and sixty to serve, with the exception of members of Congress or the state assembly, Yale tutors and students (an indication that class privilege was not erased by revolutionary fervor), and "Negroes, Indians, and mulattoes." Within a year, the legislature agreed to allow masters to liberate healthy slaves, a move that slaveholders interpreted as permitting them to enlist their bondmen as substitutes. So many did that the assembly again revised its militia act so as to encourage substitutes, and in 1781 the state even raised a segregated unit of African American soldiers. The black privates served under white officers.[31]

Rhode Island's motivation arrived with British troops. In 1778, British forces captured Newport and occupied much of the state. In response, the assembly approved legislation that freed black men provided they agreed to serve for the duration of the conflict; their owners were compensated up to £120 for each freedman. As in Connecticut, black recruits served under white officers. Cuff Greene, Dick Champlin, and Jack Champlin became the initial recruits for the First Rhode Island Battalion, led by Colonel Christopher Greene, a former Quaker. The fact that Cuff and Christopher shared a sur-name perhaps suggests that the former bondman adopted his officer's name for his own, or even that the two men were once master and slave; quite possibly Colonel Greene finally embraced his faith's belief in liberty even as he abandoned its principle of pacifism. Like Private Greene, most recruits came from the black communities around the North and South Kingstown town-ships. Hoping to prevent their bondmen from joining without their consent, some masters indentured their slaves to white relatives who lived far from the front, while others tried to scare slaves into believing they "would be sent to the West Indies and sold as slaves" if captured by the British.[32]

Despite such arguments and obstacles, approximately one in four able-bodied male slaves in Rhode Island eventually served in the First Battalion (later called the Black Regiment). During those years when many white mili-tiamen turned defeatist and straggled home, black soldiers served in twice the proportion of their numbers in the overall Rhode Island population. Unlike in Connecticut, where black soldiers were doomed to remain lowly privates, courageous African Americans (and Indians) such as Bristol Prime, Narragansett Perry, George Sambo, and Peter Mohawk eventually became noncommissioned officers, and although the regiment largely fought in New England, it also saw combat in New York and even Virginia.[33]

As for New York, the state's confused policy suited its geographic posi-tion as a northern state with a large black population. On the eve of conflict in 1775, the assembly updated its Militia Act so as to allow freemen to fight, but not enslaved "bought servants." But within the year, as Patriot forces battled unsuccessfully to keep the British from taking New York City, the legislature grew so desperate that it welcomed all comers. Particularly as the militia required manual laborers to construct fortifications, the state needed black muscle every bit as much as military prowess. Slaves who could provide their own "shovels, spades, pick-axes and hoes" were enlisted without ques-tion, and the state openly encouraged aged masters to provide young bond-men in their stead. More aristocratic New Yorkers grumbled, and General Philip Schuyler protested that African American soldiers "disgrace our arms," but pragmatists, including the general's son-in-law, Alexander Hamilton, understood that continuing manpower shortages meant the military had to learn to ignore race.[34]

Pennsylvania proved to be a unique case, not merely because of the state's smaller black population, but also because of the former colony's long tradition of merchant conservatism and Quaker pacifism. In and around Philadelphia, most blacks found freedom by running for British lines, but a small number of African Americans found refuge in the maritime service. Slaves and freemen, of course, had sailed aboard Pennsylvania's ships for decades, and local privateers recruited heavily along Philadelphia's docks. Among them was young James Forten, the great-grandson of an African captive and son of a free black sailmaker. Educated at Anthony Benezet's school, Forten hoped that black participation might help transform the War for Independence into a true American Revolution. Although only fourteen, Forten was tall and athletic, and his ability to repair a sail whitened his skin in the eyes of Captain Stephen Decatur. Young men such as Forten were also aided by the Continental Congress. Fearful that the more lucrative privateers would drain the national navy of experienced sailors, Congress required one-third of a privateer's crew to be "landsmen." Decatur had previously lost one ship by skimping on prize crews, and so Forten was far from the only black man to sign aboard the twenty-two-gun *Royal Louis*.[35]

As always, the policies pursued south of Pennsylvania were more complicated. The colony of Virginia had long banned slaves from serving in its militia on the grounds that arming Virginia's sizeable black minority would enable bondmen to turn their muskets against their masters. As one general admitted, the "dominion over the black is based upon opinion," that is, the ability to convince the enslaved population of their powerlessness. "[L]ose that and authority will fall." Among those who expressed no desire to revise colonial statutes in this regard was Thomas Jefferson, the state's governor from 1779 to 1781. Not only did he support the legislature's refusal to allow slaves to enlist in the Continental Army, navy, or state militia, but in October 1780 he signed into law a bill that promised white recruits a signing bonus of "300 acres of land plus a healthy sound Negro between 20 and 30 years of age or 60 pounds in gold or silver." So aware was the governor that his constituents were white men resentful of any assaults upon their property rights that he denied Baron Friedrich Wilhelm von Steuben's request to employ black laborers to construct military works. "The executives have not by the laws of this state any power to call a freeman to labor even for the public without his consent," he lectured the apoplectic general, "nor a slave without that of his master."[36]

The demands of military necessity quickly eroded early-eighteenth-century racial barriers in the Virginia militia. Virginia recruiters, like their Continental counterparts, began their own propaganda campaign to counteract the widespread perception in the slave community that a British victory would mean that "all Negro slaves will gain their freedom." Although neither Jefferson nor the legislature formally amended the colonial prohibition on black service, militia officers spread the word that masters could send able-bodied slaves as substitutes. Some whites promised willing bondmen their freedom at war's end. Others hinted that if America won its independence, the state assembly could hardly deny them their freedom. Shortly after the siege at Yorktown, a few masters attempted to renege on such assurances. The legislature finally acted. Confessing it "contrary to principles of justice" to reenslave men who had stepped forward to serve after their timid masters had not, the assembly declared black militiamen "fully and completely emancipated, and shall be held and deemed free in as full measure."[37]

Even so, state militias took every opportunity to make it abundantly clear, as one historian has aptly put it, that black soldiers were to be "utilized rather than welcomed." Even in the North, white officers used black recruits primarily as manual laborers. Whites instinctively thought of former bondmen, who had performed hard labor before the war, when it came time to assign the jobs of cooks, personal valets, wagon drivers, and drummers. If black recruits outside of Connecticut served in integrated units, they performed segregated jobs *within* their units. As Private Obed Coffin groused, many of these assignments reflected a conscious attempt on the part of the state officer corps to remind blacks that military service would not elevate them to the level of citizen. Yet in the midst of battle white officers never hesitated to place a musket in every available hand, even if black. James Cooper spent most of his days as a cook with the Virginia militia, but when his unit was attacked by British forces at West Point, he fought as did any white combatant.[38]

If southern states armed even freed slaves only reluctantly, Britain's Caribbean possessions were positively terrified by the thought of black men with muskets. As early as 1776, the effects of war-induced food shortages began to be realized. According to the Jamaican slave Pontack, bondmen were talking rebellion as "they were angry too much with the white people, because they had taken from them their bread." English journalists sought to keep Caribbean masters among the Loyalist ranks by printing stories that American Patriots planned to smuggle guns and ammunition to the islands' slaves. Although this step was never taken, the English press—and absentee planters residing in London—would have been more horrified had they read the letters diplomat Silas Deane submitted to John Jay, the antislavery (if slaveholding) chairman of the congressional committee on foreign affairs. "*Omnia tentanda* [all things must be tried] is my motto," Deane insisted. Since Lord

Dunmore offered liberty to slaves in Virginia, Deane proposed "the playing of their own game on them, by spiriting up the Caribs in St. Vincent's, and the Negroes in Jamaica to revolt." Bondmen such as Pontack, of course, hardly needed Deane or other elite rebels to explain the virtues of liberty, but they did need the tools, and the Connecticut-born Deane, whose state actively armed blacks, was happy to oblige.[39]

Trying all things was evidently Lord North's motto as well. In the wake of General John Burgoyne's invasion of New York, which culminated in a stunning American victory at Saratoga in October 1777, London opted for a new "southern strategy." By shifting the theater of war to the states below Pennsylvania, Parliament hoped to enlist the aid of what it prayed was a vast number of potential Loyalists, as well as to shut off the export of commercial crops that provided necessary collateral for foreign assistance. Even at this stage of the conflict, Britain had not formally resolved on a course of black liberation, but combatants on both sides understood that British hopes in the South were predicated on disrupting its plantation economy and utilizing large numbers of black troops and laborers. The bloodless seizure of Savannah in late December 1778 marked the commencement of North's new strategy. With the young frontier state of Georgia quickly subdued, residents of South Carolina braced for the expected invasion.[40]

By late spring British forces led by General Augustine Prevost had reached the outskirts of Charles Town. Governor John Rutledge ordered the state militia to defend the besieged city, but fewer than three hundred soldiers turned out to oppose the several thousand troops under Prevost's command. Patriots did, however, volunteer nearly three hundred bondmen as gang laborers to dig a series of trenches along the Neck, the narrow spit of land that connected the city peninsula to the mainland. Rutledge and his council briefly debated the emergency use of enslaved troops but agreed that it would be both impractical and "inexpedient" to do so. Prevost withdrew only when word arrived that General Benjamin Lincoln's forces were approaching, but not before tarrying long enough to liberate nineteen slaves from the estate of Major Thomas Pinckney.[41]

At least one son of South Carolina privilege thought Rutledge wrong. Even before the British retreat, twenty-three-year-old John Laurens, the eldest son of planter-politician (and slave importer) Henry Laurens and Eliza Ball of Charles Town, had come to believe that only the wholesale employment of black troops could salvage the American cause. Educated in Geneva and London, where he met abolitionist Granville Sharp, Laurens returned to the colonies with enlightened views regarding slavery, so much so that he (unsuccessfully) urged his father to free their "able bodied Slaves, instead of leaving me a fortune." An enthusiastic supporter of independence, Laurens's connections won him a post as aide-de-camp to George Washington, but being in the inner circle did nothing to alter his view that he was also responsible for alleviating "the groans of despairing multitudes, toiling for the luxuries of merciless tyrants."[42]

As he brooded over the situation from the bleak, frozen landscape of Valley Forge, Pennsylvania, Laurens conceived of a plan to liberate and arm thousands of black Carolinians. Perhaps influenced by the anonymous Philadelphia pamphleteer "Antibiastes," who in his 1777 *Observations on the Slaves and Indented Servants* advocated a "general emancipation of [any] Slaves" who enlisted in the American army and navy, Laurens hoped to "reinforce the [white] defenders of liberty with a number of gallant soldiers." Writing to his father, then president of the Continental Congress, on January 23 and again on February 2, 1778, Laurens described the "two-fold" benefits of arming former bondmen. Echoing the hopes of the black militiamen who fought in New England, Laurens assumed that military service "would advance" the political claims of "those who are unjustly deprived of the rights of mankind." Expecting his father to respond that Africans and their descendants preferred "their ignominious bonds" to risking their lives for "the untasted sweets of liberty," Laurens insisted that only years of "servitude," rather than any natural incapability, had rendered enslaved Carolinians "debased." Laurens implored his father not to dismiss his proposal as "the chimera of a young mind," but to instead applaud it as "a laudable sacrifice of private interest, to justice and the public good." And with British forces marching south, an army "of 5,000 black men, properly officer'd" by experienced whites, "might give us decisive success in the next campaign."[43]

Laurens found time enough to post further thoughts about his "black project" to his reluctant father that interminable winter. Despite his insistence that this was no mere fantasy of a youthful radical, Laurens advanced arguments that would carry little weight with Congress and were sure to backfire in the Carolina lowcountry. Should the elder Laurens succeed in obtaining "the sanction of a Recommendation from Congress," he could "have the glory of triumphing over deep rooted national prejudices" and the country "may perhaps have reason to call you her deliverer." For his part, John insisted, he would be content "to transform the timid Slave into a firm defender of Liberty and render him worthy to enjoy it himself," a dream not shared by white men and women along the South Carolina coast, who wished to obtain their independence while holding on to their enslaved labor force and class prerogatives.[44]

Either because he preferred to work through the proper political channels or perhaps due to Washington's notorious disinclination to discuss slavery even with his senior officers, Laurens evidently had not raised the proposal with his commander. Instead, it fell to Henry Laurens, writing from Philadelphia, to bring the plan to Washington's attention. Writing in mid-March, the elder Laurens unexpectedly embraced the idea. "[H]ad we Arms for 3000 such black Men, as I could select in Carolina," he maintained, "I should have no doubt of success in driving the British out of Georgia & subduing East Florida before the end of July." But while Laurens alluded to letters he had received from Charles Town and the "greatly distressed" situation of South Carolina, he declined to mention that the proposal to arm slaves originated with one of Washington's own junior officers, an omission that revealed just how provocative the congressman understood the scheme to be—as well as just how detrimental it could prove to John Laurens's future military and political career.[45]

Washington wrote back immediately. The general maintained he had never "employed much of [his] thoughts" on the idea "of our arming Slaves," and so his response constituted "no more than the first crude Ideas" on the proposal, though his cautious, consciously vague answer suggested otherwise. It was "a moot point" at present, Washington observed, since the British had yet to formulate a coherent policy on black troops. Should South Carolina do so, the British would promptly follow, and the question "then must be, who can arm fastest, & where are our Arms?" Falling back on an excuse that white Virginians often employed in later years in response to plans for gradual emancipation, Washington also fretted that freeing some young men while holding others in bondage could "render Slavery more irksome to those who remain in it."[46]

Although Washington's refusal to endorse the proposal weakened it considerably, Henry Laurens pressed ahead. Among those in Philadelphia who favored the proposal were South Carolina's William Henry Drayton and Daniel Huger, the governor's envoy. While neither man was enthusiastic, Huger informed Laurens that South Carolina simply could not raise any more militia regiments since, ironically, most whites preferred to remain "at home to prevent Insurrections among the Negroes." Laurens successfully referred the entire matter to his five-member congressional committee, which opted to turn Washington's pessimistic arguments—and white South Carolinians' fears—into strengths. If the state recruited slaves as soldiers, there would be fewer "Enterprising and vigorous" bondmen to plot rebellions, or for Britain to incite into "revolts, and [plantation] desertions." Consequently, on March 29, 1779, the Continental Congress formally recommended that "the states of South Carolina and Georgia, if they shall think the same expedient, to take measures immediately for raising three thousand able bodied negroes." Black recruits could not exceed thirty-five years of age, and they received "no pay or [land] bounty" and had to return their arms after the conflict. But if they served "well and faithfully," they were to "be emancipated" at war's end and "receive the sum of fifty dollars." Each master would be compensated up to $1,000 for his or her lost property.[47]

The resolution was heartily endorsed by those congressmen who grasped the implications of arming three thousand aggressive young bondmen in the state with the highest percentage of slaves. If the South Carolina assembly put the plan "into effect," observed William Whipple of New Hampshire, it would "lay a foundation for the Abolition of Slavery in America." John Jay of New York was pleased to hear that "an essential part of the plan [was] to give them their freedom with their muskets." In hopes of pressuring South Carolina to act, Congress even commissioned John Laurens as a lieutenant colonel, provided that he lead the proposed regiment. In April, the young officer galloped south to prod his state into action. "I am pleased with your success, so far," wrote Colonel Alexander Hamilton, "and I hope the favourable omens, that precede your application to the Assembly, may have as favourable an issue."[48]

Only too well did South Carolina legislators understand the not-so-secret abolitionist agenda lurking within Laurens's plan. Three years before, Henry Laurens had warned his son that "the Laws and Customs of my Country," not to mention "the avarice of my Country Men," opposed the "dangerous doctrines" of liberty. Now the rancorous debate within the assembly proved the elder Laurens prescient. "We are much disgusted here at the Congress recommending to us to arm our Slaves," thundered Christopher Gadsden. Both Edward and Governor John Rutledge angrily denounced the proposal, which was "received with horror by the planters." In the end, the vote was approximately 100 to 12 or 13, with Henry Laurens among the minority. Instead, the assembly agreed to award confiscated slaves to white volunteers as signing bonuses, hoping that human rewards might eliminate any need to arm black men. A more vigorous endorsement on Washington's part might have convinced South Carolina's planters to accept the plan. Yet Gadsden's characterization of Congress's resolution as "a very dangerous and impolitic step," as well as his description of the "great resentment" it caused, suggests that most wealthy white South Carolinians would have preferred to lose the war rather than win it as middle-class farmers. "White Pride & Avarice are great obstacles in the way of Black Liberty," sighed David Ramsay, another of the lonely voices in the debate. John Laurens promised to "continue [his] utmost efforts for carrying the plan of black levies into execution," but his pragmatic friend Hamilton advised him that any hopes of passage were "very feeble." Henry Laurens abandoned the fight and prepared to sail for Europe on a diplomatic mission, where he would be captured by the Royal Navy and imprisoned in the Tower of London.[49]

No evidence exists to prove that British generals were aware of the assembly's vote, but with redcoats stationed in nearby Savannah, the furious denunciations of Laurens's proposal was surely known from New York City to St. Augustine. With the conflict continuing to be a stalemate in the north, Sir Henry Clinton, the British commander in chief in North America, decided to follow up the successful Georgia campaign with yet another invasion of South Carolina. Since large numbers of New York and New Jersey runaways had sought refuge within British pickets, Clinton's staff thought it necessary to clarify the status of African Americans residing in Manhattan. On June 7, 1779, David Jones, the commandant of New York, publicly announced that "All Negroes that fly from the Enemy's Country are Free," and he warned his soldiers, "No person whatever can claim a Right to them—Whoever sells them shall be prosecuted with utmost severity." Because Jones drew no distinction between refugee women and black men who might serve, his order of protection went far beyond Dunmore's more limited and pragmatic offer four years before. Since 1775, most black Americans had regarded His Majesty's forces as potential liberators, but Jones's pronouncement evidently convinced the wavering; within a short period one British officer complained that so many black women and children fled toward the city that they allegedly became "a burden to the town."[50]

Later that month, as General Clinton prepared to abandon his headquarters in Phillipsburg, New York, for the southern states, he issued his own proclamation. Dated June 30, his announcement, unlike Jones's statement, revealed its military motivation. He admitted that his intentions were to neutralize the Continental Army's growing "practice of enrolling Negroes Among their Troops." But like his junior officer, Clinton promised "to every Negro who shall desert the Rebel Standard," regardless of gender, "full security within these Lines [and] any Occupation which [they] shall think proper." Although Clinton's statement applied only to bondpeople who belonged to "Rebel[s]," while leaving intact the property rights of white Loyalists, in practical terms the British policy, as historian Thelma Foote suggests, "destabilized the long-standing colonial relations of domination that had confined slave revolts to untenable, sometimes suicidal acts of defiance." In effect, a bondman who exchanged his work clothes for a red jacket was engaging in a state-sponsored slave rebellion.[51]

Unwilling to allow his Carolina prize to escape a second time, in February 1780 Clinton and eleven thousand men landed on the coast roughly thirty miles below Charles Town. In desperation, General Benjamin Lincoln begged the state assembly to comply with Congress and raise a regiment of freed slaves. Just before his departure, Henry Laurens again endorsed the proposal in committee on the grounds of "publick utility." The committee's report promised to pay a fair market value for any young bondmen who served, and it pledged "ample reparations" to owners for any slave killed or wounded. But even as siege guns hurled cannonballs into the city, the assembly voted only to raise a unit of "1,000 Negroes" to act as oarsmen and sailors aboard Carolina naval vessels. With the Royal Navy already blockading Charles Town's harbor, the legislature's position was both insufficient and absurd. On April 13, Governor Rutledge and leading members of his council escaped the city, but by nightfall of the following day, Clinton's land siege was airtight. Lincoln offered to surrender the city if he and his men were allowed to retreat safely. Clinton refused, and so the question was not if Charles Town would fall, but when.[52]

On May 12, Lincoln accepted the inevitable and surrendered his entire army of fifty-five hundred men. Clinton once more announced that he intended to "use slaves against their masters" as he prepared to invade west into the vast Carolina frontier. But as Lord North hoped to discover a hidden cache of white Loyalists in the lowcountry, Clinton also let it be known that while he planned to honor his promise to liberate any slave who belonged to a rebel master, he would also be scrupulous in returning the runaways of Tory owners. His chief lieutenant, Lord Charles Cornwallis, even issued a proclamation warning residents of the state not to attempt to liquidate any debts they might owe to "the merchants in Great Britain" by selling off "any lands, houses, or negroes, without having first obtained a license to do so from the commandant." Thousands of Carolina bondpeople, knowing what life they faced on coastal plantations, immediately risked the dash. As Boston King later wrote, he "determined to go to Charles-Town, and throw myself into the hands of the English." So many did so that British forces in the city found themselves awash in a tidal wave of black refugees. "[A]ltho' I was much grieved at first, to be obliged to leave my friends, and reside among strangers," King added, "the happiness of liberty, of which [he] knew nothing before," was a moment he never forgot.[53]

It was one thing for Henry Clinton to offer liberation to New York or Carolina bondpeople; what to do with the thousands who paddled across the Ashley and Cooper rivers was quite another matter. The general intended that healthy young men be sent into combat, but quickly training raw recruits to shoot, to function as a unit, and to stand in the face of withering fire was no effortless task. At the very least, every slave who crossed into British-held territory was one more bondperson that Clinton could put to good use and whom the Patriots could not employ. Because the initial refugees escaped from the plantations immediately around Charles Town, they knew the terrain and could serve as guides into the backcountry. Thomas Johnson, for one, volunteered to show some British scouts the safest route to the strategic crossroads of Monck's Corner. A Patriot patrol surprised the small band, and while Johnson and the redcoats escaped, the Americans beheaded another black guide and left his head on a post as a warning to other runaways. Undaunted, Johnson, his spouse, and their two young children remained steadfast in their support of the British cause, and Johnson continued to serve with Clinton.[54]

For siding with the British, former slaves such as Boston King and Thomas Johnson won their liberty, but little else. Upon arriving in occupied cities, black refugees typically had to build their own shelter and scavenge for food. The supply of food from the countryside dried up, and British encampments frequently faced starvation. Freedpeople huddled together in tent cities along side streets and back alleys, and even by eighteenth-century standards, hygienic conditions proved primitive. The limited quantities of medicines were reserved for active troops, and so black women and children, inadequately protected by foreign soldiers, perished by the thousands. Some young, single women acquired food and housing by forming sexual relationships with British soldiers. South Carolina Loyalist Samuel Mathis confided to his journal that "it was not uncommon for persons to let out the Negro girls to British Officers." Since so many aristocratic English and Hessian officers regarded Americans of any race as their social inferiors, the disdain they expressed for impoverished refugees was hardly surprising. Captain Johann Ewald, who served with Clinton and Cornwallis in South Carolina, sneered at the "comical [and] motley clothing of the black" refugees who "had plundered the wardrobes of their masters and mistresses, divided the loot, and clothed themselves piecemeal with it." The "strange baggage train" of refugees "looked rather like monkeys," the German liberator added.[55]

Black soldiers earned a modicum of respect from their royal commanders, although British and German behavior toward black troops ranged from honest admiration to open hostility. But by the time British forces captured Charles Town, some former slaves had worn red jackets for five years. One unit, the Black Pioneers, included a few of the soldiers who had fought beside Dunmore at Great Bridge. Over the next few years, the regiment grew as young runaways signed on after General Clinton swore that at war's end, they "shall be entitled (as far as depends on me) to their freedom." In 1777, as the Pioneers marched toward Philadelphia, muster rolls recorded the presence of 172 men; three months later, after occupying the city, the regiment had increased to 200. Others hailed from Georgia and South Carolina. Thomas Peters, who rose to the rank of sergeant, recorded that the unit was "regularly supplied with provisions and decently clothed." The black soldiers received the same rations and pay as white soldiers, although white officers led the unit. One member of the Pioneers, John Provey, who had been a gentleman's manservant, was put to work as Clinton's second secretary.[56]

Far more numerous were the black Loyalists who served as guerrilla raiders and foragers. Although Clinton's advancing army badly required foodstuffs, a key reason to employ black partisans to swoop down onto farms and plantations was to terrify southern whites. Jean Blair, a Patriot who resided near Windsor, North Carolina, was alarmed by reports of "two thousand of them out in different Partys." What "they find in the houses they plunder." One of the British officers who led these raiding parties was Colonel Banastre Tarleton. Although the young baronet came from a family who had made their fortune in slave trading and sugar plantations, he quickly grew to respect the fearless runaways who followed him into the Carolina interior. "Bloody Banny" Tarleton understood that part of his job was to demoralize civilians, and on one occasion, Tarleton and his "armed Negroes" broke into a plantation mansion and so terrified the mistress that she "could not support [her]self, and later gave way to a violent burst of grief." Tarleton may even have been with the foraging unit that briefly seized the Silk Hope plantation, "bound the overseer" to a tree, "& whipped him most unmercifully." Tarleton and "the enemy's Negroes" so terrorized the countryside that South Carolinians like Eliza Wilkinson never walked roads but "with heavy hearts."[57]

For the most part, however, British forces utilized runaways in support capacities. As the war shifted to the southern states in 1778, African Americans who lived near the vast inland river systems assisted the Royal Navy as pilots and guides. Romantic tales of freedmen serving with the Connecticut militia or racing down Carolina pathways beside Tarleton ultimately serve to conceal the sad truth that both armies primarily wanted black men for their muscles. When Captain Ewald discovered the British redoubts across the Stono River to be little more than "heaps of sand," he ordered "thirty Negroes" to find "axes and shovels [and] repair the works." During Clinton's brief siege of Charles Town, when it came time to transport "heavy pieces, munitions [and] provisions" across the Ashley River, British officers were dismayed by the "lack of horses" until one redcoat suggested that "Negroes [be] used to drag these things to their places." Colonel Tarleton was clearly among the minority of officers, as he took some pleasure in the liberation of recruits. On one occasion, after Patriot forces hid all available boats to hinder the progress of the British army, several bondmen approached his patrol to tell him "where some were secreted." The clever colonel even paid rural slaves to pretend to be British "deserters" and "communicate false intelligence."[58]

Unhappily, Tarleton's acceptance of his black comrades placed him in a minority. The attitude of most officers resembled the attitude of king and prime minister: black liberation was a means to an end, not an end in itself. By 1778, some members of Parliament had concluded that the New England colonies were lost to British control, but the invasion of the South gave them hope that Britain might resurrect a new, plantation-based American empire out of colonies stretching from the Chesapeake through the Carolinas and across the Caribbean. To that extent, British policy was fundamentally conservative, in that it aimed to restore the colonial status quo, and that meant plantation agriculture. When John Cruden proposed raising an army of ten thousand African Americans to occupy the southern mainland, he wanted it "clearly understood" that freed soldiers were "to serve the King for ever, and that those slaves who are not taken for his Majesty's service are to remain on the plantation, and perform, as usual, the labor of the field." When black refugees demanded too many rights in occupied Charles Town, British officials simply imprisoned those men regarded as "dangerous to the community" in the same "large Sugar House" along Broad Street where slave trader William Savage had previously stored captive Africans. As historian Sylvia Frey has observed, "[T]he British army acted as both a sword and a shield, challenging and conserving the system at the same time."[59]

For the most part, the majority of Africans and black Americans regarded themselves as neither Patriot nor Loyalist, but as independent actors in a drama that was largely written by white men of power on either side of the Atlantic. Because nearly twenty thousand blacks fought for one side or the other, it is easy (if erroneous) to see the war as a two-sided struggle. But the fighting assumed a triangular nature, since several hundred thousand slaves tried to use the chaos of war to their own advantage. Although the attempts by bondpeople to take advantage of the disorder were most pronounced in southern colonies, where the conflict between white Loyalists and Patriots frequently resembled a civil war, blacks endeavored to capitalize on the Anglo-American struggle anywhere the skirmishing turned fierce. In the frontier county of Ulster, New York, slaveholder Johannes Schoonmaker overheard two of his bondmen plotting to burn nearby homes and slaughter the masters within. When taken into custody, the two slaves and their confederates were discovered to have considerable shot and powder in their possession. Much to the surprise of Patriot authorities, the rebels had no intention of fleeing east toward British lines. Instead, they planned to escape west into Iroquois territory.[60]

Perhaps because they could not admit that their black servants just wished to be free, white southerners consoled themselves that British officers had seduced their slaves into running off. In reality, most slaves simply slipped away when the opportunity presented itself. In southeastern Virginia, the number of runaways hiding in the Great Dismal Swamp mushroomed, as white Patriots, preoccupied with Clinton's invasion, lacked the time to pursue their errant property. Some young bondmen, having heard of the "ill treatment" accorded black soldiers by the British, opted instead to roam the countryside in small bands, living off the land and "procuring [other] slaves" as they hid from both armies. Before the outbreak of hostilities, runaways were scarce in number, since bondmen had few places to run to, few permanent refuges to hide in. But by 1781, one Virginia planter complained, "a great number of slaves which were taken by the British Army are now passing in this Country as freemen."[61]

The story was much the same in the northern states. During the six years of fighting, the black fugitive population in Philadelphia doubled in size, even as the number of African Americans held there in bondage shrank. In New York City, which remained under British control from 1776 through the fall of 1783, blacks freed themselves by the hundreds, while hundreds more bondpeople from neighboring counties sought liberty by relocating into Manhattan. So many "female Negroes with their children" arrived in the city that the British general James Patterson thought them "a burden to the town" and instructed one Loyalist ferryman to "prevent" any more runaways from crossing "the North [Hudson] River." But black Loyalists turned a blind eye to incoming refugees when it was their turn to guard ferry landings at Fort Lee and Fort Delancey. By 1779, census takers counted more than twelve hundred blacks who had recently arrived in Manhattan. One band of enterprising Jersey runaways rolled logs down the gorge near Weehawken, lashed their makeshift raft together, and paddled across the Hudson to freedom.[62]

While uncounted numbers of slaves liberated themselves along the eastern seaboard, British fortunes in the South shifted. Believing the rebellion in South Carolina on the verge of collapse, Clinton returned north, giving General Charles Cornwallis responsibility for the pacification of the backcountry. Harassed by General Nathanael Greene, Cornwallis steadily lost terrain into the summer of 1781, until British troops in the lower south held only Savannah and Charles Town. Seeking to cut the flow of supplies from the upper South into South Carolina, Cornwallis marched his army north into Virginia, hoping to achieve decisive results. His soldiers—white and black alike—continued to raid across the "undefended part of Virginia," making off with "Negroes plate &c," and one patrol even returned to "gen Washington's plantation," but ultimately failed to crush Patriot morale. While Cornwallis retained between four thousand and five thousand black recruits around Yorktown and Portsmouth, smallpox and typhus hit his swampy camps, killing perhaps 60 percent of his troops. The black Loyalists among his ranks chose to remain with the British, but many runaways, realizing that defeat was imminent, offered their services to nearby French officers, praying that they would find a new home in Paris, rather than be sold into the French Caribbean. "We gained a veritable harvest of domestics," chuckled one French officer.[63]

Even as British raiders under Tarleton reached as far west as Charlottesville—where they liberated a number of Governor Thomas Jefferson's slaves—Washington and his French ally spied an opportunity to land a devastating blow in Virginia when he learned that a large French fleet under the comte de Grasse had set sail from Saint-Domingue for the Chesapeake. After feigning an attack on Clinton in New York, the Franco-American allies raced toward the tidewater. With de Grasse's fleet bottling up any retreat into the Atlantic, Cornwallis was forced into a siege at Yorktown. Among those marching south with Washington was Rhode Island's First Battalion. As one French officer noted, "[T]hree-quarters of the Rhode Island regiment consists of negroes, and that regiment is the most neatly dressed, the best under arms, and the most precise in its maneuvers." And, the officer might have added, they had besieged British lines that protected several thousand southern blacks.[64]

British protection, however, was often worth very little. As Cornwallis's beleaguered forces ran short of food and water, he ordered the smallpox-ridden runaways huddled within his lines driven out of camp. One Patriot soldier described "herds of Negroes" turned adrift "with pieces of ears of burnt Indian corn in the hands and mouths." Johann Ewald, the Hessian officer who had served beside black troops, judged Cornwallis's order as shameful. "We had used them to good advantage," he wrote, "and set them free, and now, with fear and trembling, they had to face the reward of their cruel masters." Several hundred former slaves, sick and dying, tried to flee into the nearby woods, but Washington had them seized and held until advertisements could be placed to locate their rightful owners. Several of those rounded up, evidently, had escaped from Mount Vernon. On Friday, October 19, Cornwallis struck his regimental colors in surrender. For the African Americans who sought freedom under Britain's flag, it was a tragic end to a war they hoped would liberate a nation. Glancing about him as the British stacked their arms, young St. George Tucker noted the black bodies strewn about the field. "An immense number of Negroes have died in the most miserable manner in York."[65]

Although the surrender of Cornwallis's forces severely damaged Britain's capacity to wage the war in the southern states, there was little reason to believe that the conflict was at long last concluded. Washington shouted, "Billy, hand me my horse," and he and William Lee galloped for Mount Vernon for what both assumed would be a brief respite. Among those who planned to fight on was the Earl of Dunmore, who landed in British-occupied Charles Town in December 1781 and was increasingly enthusiastic about the use of black troops. Roughly seven hundred black Loyalists still guarded the access routes to Charles Town, and Dunmore now hoped to raise as many as ten thousand blacks to hold the lowcountry for his king. Together with commissioner John Cruden, Dunmore spent the month of January devising his elaborate plan, which he forwarded to General Clinton on February 2, 1782. Building on earlier proposals floated by both Patriots and Loyalists, Dunmore recommended freeing South Carolina slaves in exchange for military service; both freedman and former master were to receive compensation. As in John Laurens's plan, African American troops would serve under white officers—Dunmore immodestly advanced his own name here—but as blacks gained experience and as vacancies appeared, blacks might be promoted into noncommissioned ranks.[66]

When the news of the Yorktown debacle reached London, however, a disgraced Lord North fell from power in March 1782, and neither General Clinton nor the new administration pursued Dunmore's idea. Yet as peace negotiations in Paris slowly lurched forward, sporadic skirmishes continued along the Carolina seaboard. In February, Loyalist Benjamin Thompson pieced together a mounted unit of whites and runaway slaves, who raided south toward Savannah, liberating slaves as they rode. To put a stop to the forays, Washington dispatched the gravely ill John Laurens to the coast. Near the Combahee River, his group encountered a larger unit of Loyalists dug in along the banks of the river. Without waiting for "the main body of the detachment" to arrive, Laurens attacked and was mortally wounded. Ironically, the young patrician who had yearned to lead black Patriots into battle in the name of antislavery reform was most likely shot by a Carolina freedman. More tragic yet, his death on August 27 came exactly six months to the day after Parliament voted not to continue the war in North America.[67]

Modern readers tend to think of wars as a series of battles, and of peace as the cessation of armed hostilities. But for black Americans, whether Patriot or Loyalist, whether soldier or noncombatant, the events at Yorktown were as much a beginning as an end. The African Americans who remained in the new republic struggled to rebuild shattered families, fashion churches and schools and communities, adopt new names and personal identities, and, most of all, launch crusades to end human bondage across a nation that professed to be forged in liberty. As the historian Willie Lee Rose insisted, "the real meaning of the Revolution for America's black people" had little enough to do with battles or treaties. Its importance "was more subtle" and rested upon the continuing national debate as to the meaning of freedom, the "new opportunities the general disruption of society afforded," and most especially the critical social and demographic changes that emerged out of the struggle between Parliament and colonial elites.[68]

FOUR | # Quok Walker's Suit
Emancipation in the North

A LTHOUGH SETTLED BY WHITES as early as 1673 and just forty-six miles west of Boston, Worcester, Massachusetts, remained a rustic farm community at the start of the Seven Years' War. In that year, a farmer named James Caldwell purchased three slaves from Zedekiah Stone, "all sound & well for the Sum of One hundred & eight pounds." They were twenty-year-old Mingo, his wife, a "negro wench named Diana, about nineteen years of age, with child Quaco, about nine months old." (Kwaku, an Akan day-name, was often given to boys born on a Wednesday.) For the better part of the next decade, as was typical of so many Africans and black Americans, Mingo's family then vanished from the public record. But in 1763 James Caldwell died intestate. A court-appointed committee drew up an inventory of Caldwell's property, granted the customary one-third to the widow, Isabell Caldwell, and placed the remainder in trust with a guardian for James's adolescent children. Mingo's family was assigned to the widow's share.[1]

As Quaco (or Quok) grew older, he heard of events to his east in Boston. Emboldened by the endless talk of liberty that pervaded even rural Massachusetts, he pressed his owners to consider freeing him when he reached adulthood. According to what Quok later told one court, James Caldwell had agreed to liberate him at the age of twenty-five, a figure Isabell purportedly reduced to twenty-one. But within three years of James's death, Isabell married again. Her new husband, Nathaniel Jennison of the nearby town of Barré, already owned eight slaves, and as far as Jennison was concerned, if a revolution was to be fought, it would be waged in the name of property rights rather than human rights. As the head of his household, Jennison and not Isabell made such decisions. She was his "lawful wife," he swore, by which he "became possessed of the said Quork as his own proper negro slave."[2]

When spring arrived in 1781, the young man, now twenty-eight years old and calling himself Quok Walker, decided he had been patient long enough. In early April he simply abandoned Jennison's household for the nearby farm of John and Seth Caldwell, James's younger brothers. Furious, Jennison demanded that Walker return immediately, but the young revolutionary replied that he was "a free man, & not the proper negro slave of the said Nathaniel." At that, Jennison rounded up several of his white farmhands and marched to the Caldwell farm. They attacked Walker "and threw him down and struck him several violent blows upon his back and arm with the handle of a whip" before dragging him back to Barré and locking him in a barn. One of the Caldwell brothers "heard a screaming" and ran in from the fields. He shouted to Jennison that his "brother said always [Walker] should be free at 25," but Jennison warned Caldwell to stop "maliciously" interfering "with his said servant."[3]

How Walker escaped the barn remains a mystery, but clearly he was no longer safe in Worcester County. Yet neither could he flee for Boston. At least one of his brothers remained enslaved on the Jennison farm, and the only whites who had ever tried to help him—the Caldwell brothers—lived just down the road. Had Walker been born in a different era or in a different part of the Americas, he surely would have done what determined young bondmen had long done: fly for the nearest seaport in hopes of finding a new life on the high seas, or wade into the hinterland in search of a maroon colony of runaways. Instead, with the war nearly won and Revolutionary republicanism upheld, Walker, now styling himself a "yeoman," did what any proud American with a grievance would do. On June 12, 1781, with the assistance of the Caldwells, he hired Levi Lincoln, the most able attorney in the county, and filed suit for unspecified damages in the local Court of Common Pleas. Significantly, Walker dragged Jennison into court on charges of assault and battery only. Walker did not sue for his freedom, which he simply assumed was the natural right of all Americans living in a post-1776 world. So began the case of *Walker v. Jennison*, the first of six trials involving one or both of these antagonists that would help determine the future of slavery in Massachusetts.[4]

As Walker's inclination to adopt legal means suggests, black Americans immediately expected the Revolution to offer not merely new opportunities for freedom but also full participation in the new political order. The thirteen united colonies began to write thirteen new state constitutions, and industrious "yeomen" such as Walker anticipated that these documents would live up to the egalitarian ideals of their Revolutionary age. But for all of his strength of purpose, black activists like Walker needed the assistance of benevolent whites such as the Caldwell brothers, just as he required the legal aid of reform-minded attorneys such as Levi Lincoln. It would be this combination of African American activism and legal action on the part of white reformers that would finally force every state supreme court or legislature north of Delaware to eliminate slavery. This struggle was not to be easily won, and the gradualist laws they achieved revealed the extent to which racism remained a crippling national phenomenon. Yet even more than black participation in the military, it was these victories that gave black Americans enormous hope and allowed them to believe that they enjoyed the power to begin the world anew.

————

The reasons the northern courts and legislatures ultimately gave way when faced with the demands of black and white reformers, while the states along the southern coast did not, remain a topic of considerable debate. A number of scholars point to the egalitarian ideology of the era and insist that a nation forged in liberty could not tolerate the contradiction of chattel slavery. Others emphasize the hypocritical failings of white republicans and instead note that post-1783 immigration into northern seaports and an acceptance of free wage labor doomed the already failing system of black slavery. Still others point to the importance of black military service in eroding old colonial laws that protected slavery. In states such as Connecticut, large numbers of black soldiers returned to their communities to form the core of a visible and frequently armed free African American community. At least 20 percent of the men listed as black heads of household in Connecticut's 1790 census had served in the Patriot forces. With so many African American veterans in the state population, legislators had little recourse but to recognize that the necessary controls for those still enslaved simply could not be maintained.[5]

Evidence exists in ample measure to support each interpretation. Clearly, several decades of incessant demands for liberty and natural rights established the common belief in the sanctity of personal freedom. If the basic core of slavery was the notion that human beings could be "animalized" and debased to the level of things, the outpouring of speeches, pamphlets, sermons, editorials, petitions, and, most of all, declarations after 1763 challenged that belief. Yet if the rhetoric of inalienable rights laid the basis for black freedom, economic factors cannot be ignored. In the urban North, white workers understood that unskilled bondmen who tramped the docks on their rare moment off in search of a single day's salary depressed wages (already low due to the depression that followed the 1783 peace treaty). Although they often cared little about the plight of black Americans, white workers pressured state politicians to end slavery. Since northern employers found new sources of labor in farm boys moving to urban centers, or in the renewed flow of immigrants from Europe, employers and merchants had little reason to maintain an ideologically and morally problematic form of labor.[6]

Every reform movement, however, regardless of basic causation, requires a human factor. As historian Graham Russell Hodges suggests, slavery ultimately died in the northern states due to an uneasy alliance between elite white reformers—evangelicals, legislators, and attorneys—and African American agitators, who signed petitions, hired lawyers, crafted tracts, reminded assemblies of their service during the conflict, or simply ran away in search of a new life. As Hodges aptly notes, it was "the unceasing efforts of blacks themselves" that set unfree labor on the road to extinction in the years prior to 1804. Typical of those who appealed to the patriotism of Massachusetts slaveholders was Lemuel Haynes, a veteran of the battle at Lexington. "If you have any Love to yourselves, or any Love to this Land, if you have any Love to your fellow men," he wrote, "Break these intolerable yoaks." Others adopted a more personal approach. When Captain William Whipple of New Hampshire wondered why his slave Prince was so depressed, the bondman— who as an oarsman had helped to row Washington across the Delaware on Christmas night in 1776—shot back: "[Y]ou are going to fight for your liberty, but I have none to fight for." Stunned by this response, Whipple promptly agreed to liberate Prince.[7]

None of these factors, however, explains why black and white activists were able to pass laws for gradual emancipation across the North but failed to do so in the southern states. Virginia too boasted its share of reformers, and some of the most eloquent denunciations of unfree labor emanated from within its borders. It is, however, clear that slavery died in those states where the percentage of blacks was small, where the labor they performed was as easily undertaken by free wage laborers, and where men and women who owned slaves lacked a deep ideological or psychological commitment to the system. Perhaps the best formulation that can be achieved is that when the Revolution arrived, creating a relentless discourse on natural rights, chattel slavery expired in those sections of the country that were "societies with slaves." In the border South areas, properly characterized as "slave societies," the ideology of liberty briefly weakened but did not eradicate slavery, while in the lower South, states with the highest percentage of Africans and black Americans, the white minority hastened to rebuild their shattered plantation world.[8]

Given this, it was hardly surprising that the first state to move decisively against slavery was the newest state and the one with the smallest number of slaves (as well as the lowest percentage of blacks). Long claimed by both New Hampshire and New York, Vermont emerged as the fourteenth state in early 1777. On the next July 4, a handful of delegates, meeting in the Windsor Tavern during a raging thunderstorm, drafted an astonishingly egalitarian constitution. The document, which allowed for unrestricted male suffrage regardless of property or even taxation, denounced unfree labor as a violation of "natural, inherent, and unalienable rights." Any bondman already within the state or "brought from over sea" was to become free upon reaching "the age of twenty-one years," while black women were to be liberated "at the age of eighteen years." Masters received no compensation. Because of the frontier nature of the state, none of the men who crafted the document had any idea how many slaves resided in Vermont, but the number was clearly minuscule. So foreign was slavery to the Green Mountains that when Reverend David Avery arrived from Yale soon after to accept the pulpit of a Congregational church, his own parishioners refused to pray with him because he owned a female slave.[9]

For antislavery activists, however, one of the coveted prizes was the critical state of Pennsylvania. Although hardly home to the nation's largest black population, Pennsylvania was regarded as the cradle of the Republic due to its long association with the Continental Congress (which in 1777 evolved into the national Congress in accord with the provisional Articles of Confederation). Philadelphia was the largest and most sophisticated of American cities; should emancipation be achieved in this middle state, ripples of liberty might spread up and down the Atlantic coast. Because the state's population as a whole was just less than 3 percent black, reformers hoped the task would be simple. Ever since the colonial assembly had imposed high import duties on African bodies, unfree labor had been on the decline. Artisans preferred to hire white immigrants and servants during the decade before 1775, and the Quakers whom Equiano noticed during his stay there were increasingly active in their abolitionism. Still, four years after Jefferson drafted the Declaration in his rented home near the statehouse, roughly four hundred Philadelphians owned 539 slaves, and two hundred residents of adjacent Chester County held an additional 493 people in bondage. Moreover, as a result of their pacifist refusal to bear arms against King George, the Quakers had damaged their standing in the popular mind.[10]

As early as 1775, the city's abolitionists organized what would become the nation's first antislavery organization. On April 14, a handful of reformers—most of them Quakers—met at the Sun Tavern and formed the Society for the Relief of Free Negroes Unlawfully Held in Bondage. Large journeys often begin with tiny steps, and the group's preamble made it clear that their main goal was the liberation of already free "negroes and others" who were kidnapped and forced back into slavery, rather than the complete liberation of all of the city's bondpeople. The group met only three more times that year, and not once during the course of the fighting. It fell, therefore, to Philadelphia's "divers Negroes" to take the lead in what quickly became a more radical crusade. As they peppered the legislature with petitions, literate blacks adopted the Quakers' deferential tone, conceding that "an address from persons of our rank is wholly unprecedented." But unlike their white neighbors, the petitioners assaulted the central "question of slavery or liberty." In the midst of a bloody war for liberty, one petitioner observed, their state should take the lead in restoring "the common blessings" that all Americans, regardless of race, "were by nature entitled to." As Pennsylvania's slaves had not "by any act of ours deprived our selves of the common rights of mankind," they were fully as deserving of sovereignty as any wealthy merchant of the city.[11]

Less eloquent bondmen delivered a similar message with their feet and thereby helped to dismantle the institution of slavery. Any slave in any society who ran away, of course, was always engaged in what one scholar has called "a forceful but highly personal act of rebellion." But Philadelphia slaves could not be unaware of the debate over emancipation. By fleeing their masters, young men knew they were exacerbating the economic headaches already faced by whites living in a city under siege or under British occupation. Masters always had to weigh the costs against the benefits of holding others in slavery, and since the majority of runaways were skilled young men—the most valuable of human commodities—even a small number of successful escapes damaged an already weakened system. Moreover, runaways now found allies. When Ned absconded from nearby Lancaster County, he encountered "two [white] gentlemen" who "gave six dollars to a lawyer to help them set him free." Dan fled Lancaster "in company" with a white man and "endeavour[ed] to pass as a freeman," as did Michael Hoy, who posed as the "servant to a white man he is supposed to have gone off with." Still another runaway, Charles, having heard of the Society for the Relief of Free Negroes, assured suspicious whites that he had "been set free by the people called Quakers."[12]

Charles knew what he was about. Chief among the city's white reformers was Anthony Benezet, one of the society's founders and a longtime advocate of religious education for blacks. (Hoping to advance moral improvement beyond Pennsylvania's borders, Benezet also corresponded with Granville Sharp, James Somerset's benefactor.) Benezet went further than most Quakers with his sharply worded denunciations of slaveholding Patriots who demanded their own freedom from Britain while denying the fundamental "rights of man" to their black domestics. Benezet was in frequent contact with Dr. Benjamin Rush and pamphleteer Thomas Paine, who had criticized slavery as "contrary to the light of nature" almost from the moment of his arrival in the colonies in 1775. Perhaps in no other American locale was the alliance between black activists, rebellious bondmen, and well-connected, determined white Christians as powerful as in Philadelphia.[13]

Even so, the fact that resolute reformers such as Benezet and Rush saw little success until the last years of the war serves as a reminder of the resilient nature of American racism even in the City of Brotherly Love. Among those who refused to be swayed by the words of his friend Rush was Charles Willson Peale, the painter today most identified with the portraits of the founding generation. As an Episcopalian, Peale listened to the arguments of the Society for the Relief of Free Negroes and conceded the immorality of slavery but declined to liberate his domestic Phyllis on the grounds of property rights. Scots-Irish Presbyterian farmers residing in Chester County submitted a 1779 petition to the legislature arguing that emancipation would burden the state with a sizeable population of "lazy" freedpeople who preferred private charity over hard labor. Faced with the threat of British occupation as well as bitter domestic debates over chronic inflation, food shortages, and price fixing, the state assembly declined throughout the late 1770s to add to their legislative headaches by debating emancipation.[14]

Convinced that the moment was at hand was Irish-born evangelical George Bryan. A Presbyterian whose Scots-Irish background rendered him palatable to farmer-slaveholders, Bryan had risen through state politics by 1778 to serve as acting president of the Supreme Executive Council. Decrying slavery as "the opprobrium of America," he warned the legislature of the dangers to potential European alliances of allowing the world "to see a people eager for liberty holding Negroes in bondage." But Bryan was clever enough to disguise his egalitarian beliefs in pragmatic rhetoric. Large numbers of bondpeople had fled with "our late invaders," he hinted in a reminder that yet another British invasion might sweep away what remained of Philadelphia's black population. Bryan also published a series of essays in county newspapers designed to win over rural slaveholders. Although he again observed that "all men are born equally free," Bryan generally stayed clear of ideological critiques. Instead, he claimed to find it painful that the Quakers, "who we [Presbyterians] think have but clouded views of the gospel," were far ahead of other denominations on this question. He also cleverly turned allegations of black indolence against proslavery advocates. Far from threatening to impoverish the state through emancipation, Bryan argued, it was his conservative opponents who hindered economic growth by maintaining a potentially disloyal class of men and women who had little motivation to labor.[15]

By late February 1780, Bryan had completed a draft of his lengthy bill. As clerk of the legislature and a staunch abolitionist, Paine read the manuscript, which filled seven printed pages. Whether the uncompromising Paine agreed with the hardheaded pragmatism of the draft is a different question. Having failed for two years to bring antislavery legislation to a vote, Bryan understood that success required conceding ground to the opposition. Although, as an evangelical, he devoutly believed it his Christian duty to set "the oppressed free," he was an astute enough politician to appreciate that "loosing the bonds of wickedness" often necessitated compromise. One of Bryan's friends described the bill as a "law for freeing of Negroes hereafter born," and the depressing truth is that the statute immediately freed no slaves. Believing it was the best he could achieve, Bryan introduced his bill on March 1, 1780, fully nineteen months before the surrender at Yorktown.[16]

Following a lengthy preamble that promoted the common but useful fiction that the kings of Britain had fastened slavery upon the unwilling colonists, the statute featured thirteen legalistic sections that detailed the future "condition of those persons who have heretofore been denominated negro and mulatto slaves." The most critical of the sections was the second. Every child born after the passage of the bill who would have been a slave had "this act not been made" was to be considered a "servant" by his or her master "until such child shall attain unto the age of twenty-eight years." Like any white indentured person, such a black child was entitled to "relief in case he or she be evilly treated by his or her master or mistress, and to like freedom dues" at the date of liberation. The act freed not a single black Pennsylvanian. Bondpeople born before March 1 were not covered by the statute, and exempted also were "domestic slaves attending upon delegates in Congress from other American states" (provided that they remained in the city no more than six months at one time). Section eight empowered masters to pursue runaways into "any other state" to retrieve their errant property. Nor did the bill address the question of black citizenship. Most of all, in a time when the average life expectancy for blacks—whether slave or free, male or female—was between thirty-three and thirty-four years, serving until the age of twenty-eight was tantamount to laboring without compensation well into middle age.[17]

As a result, militant white reformers and black activists denounced the bill as too timid, and they feared (with great accuracy, it turned out) that Pennsylvania's act might become the model for other gradual emancipation laws across the nation. Opponents pointed out that not only was a black woman born on the last day of February 1780 doomed to live her life out as a slave, but if she bore a child before her fortieth year in 1820, that child would not be liberated until the far-off day of 1848. (Only in 1847 did Pennsylvania finally pass a second statute freeing those remaining aged slaves not covered by the 1780 law.) As Quaker David Cooper huffed, white Patriots were announcing to their slaves that "we will not do justice unto you, but our posterity shall do justice unto your posterity."[18]

Yet the fact that the legislation denied no current master his property rights and achieved black emancipation over a two-generation grace period without costing state taxpayers any revenue was its strongest selling point, so far as George Bryan was concerned. Even this painfully gradualist statute failed to win over delegates from the slaveholding regions in western Chester, Lancaster, and Westmoreland counties. The majority of Bryan's fellow Presbyterians abandoned him and voted against the bill. So furious were many rural Pennsylvanians that in the next election, many of those who had voted for the bill were denied reelection, and slaveholders wasted no time in submitting petitions demanding its repeal. As legal historian Leon Higginbotham observed, when measured against the standard of "total freedom or complete equality"—or against the founding generation's own egalitarian rhetoric, perhaps—the Pennsylvania act reveals "significant deficiencies." Although it was to serve as the model for other northern legislation, it was the most restrictive of the five gradual emancipation laws that would be passed before the end of 1804. But, as Higginbotham adds, when evaluated within the context of a century that regarded unwaged labor as a global norm, "Pennsylvania significantly distinguished itself from most of its northern neighbors by being the first to initiate legislation for the gradual demise of slavery," and in fact it did so while British forces remained on American soil.[19]

The realization that slaves would continue to tramp the streets of Philadelphia for decades more, however, only spurred Pennsylvania radicals into further action. For most reformers, the law of 1780 was not the culmination of a great crusade but rather the first step in what activists now understood would be a long battle for equality. In February 1784, just a few months before Benezet's death at the age of seventy-one, a group of eighteen reformers—six of them survivors of the short-lived Society for the Relief of Free Negroes of 1775—met to reconstitute their defunct organization. Despite retaining their original name, this time there was no charade about existing merely to assist freed blacks kidnapped into bondage. Living in what was again the Republic's capital (the Congress having constantly relocated during the war to avoid capture), the group's members hoped to first eradicate slavery in Pennsylvania before advancing their demands for abolition onto the national stage. This would be no easy task. Few wealthy merchants joined the society in 1784; its members, most of whom were Quakers, hailed from the middle class. Three hatters and three shoemakers were among the initial members, as were two tailors, hardly the sort of occupation guaranteed to impress affluent members of Congress. Benezet, however, lived long enough to present Congress with a petition demanding the closure of the Atlantic slave trade. Signed by more than five hundred Quakers, the petition was granted a hearing on the floor of Congress but resulted only in a vaguely worded resolution encouraging the fourteen state legislatures to "enact such laws as to their wisdom may appear best calculated" to resolve the question.[20]

Finally, in 1787 the group reorganized for a final time. In the process, they took a new name, the Pennsylvania Society for Promoting the Abolition of Slavery, a significant change in heralding the group's radical new direction. Although middle-class shopkeepers and artisans remained the backbone of the society, the new set of officers was clearly chosen to garner national attention. Hilary Baker, soon to become the city's mayor, was among them, as were Thomas Paine and physician Benjamin Rush (who promised to free his slave William Grubber the following year). But certainly the most illustrious recruit was the aged statesman Benjamin Franklin, recently returned from his diplomatic service in France. As one of the two most famous Americans—the other being George Washington—Franklin's name was sure to win over other prosperous and powerful Philadelphians. At the age of seventy-nine, and so burdened with gouty feet that he could barely walk, Franklin was expected to do nothing more than lend his considerable cachet to the organization. But at least he was no longer a slaveholder. His last remaining slave, George, whom Franklin had obtained as a debt payment, had passed away six years before, in 1781.[21]

It was this more aggressive organization that succeeded in revising the 1780 statute in an "explaining" act of 1788. Although the second bill did not achieve immediate emancipation, as the society's black allies hoped, it did put an end to many of the "ills and abuses" that arose from loopholes and "defects" in the earlier act. More than a few "ill-disposed" masters had tried to circumvent the key provision of the 1780 law by briefly carting pregnant slaves across state lines into Delaware, Maryland, or New Jersey so that their children were not technically born in Pennsylvania. The amending law put an end to that practice by extending the freedom year of twenty-eight to any child for whom Pennsylvania was the primary residence. In particular, Virginia congressmen residing in Philadelphia had learned to send their enslaved domestics home periodically so that they would not be in the city for the six consecutive months that would make them subject to the statute; the new law halted that practice as well by making the six-month period cumulative over the course of any year. The statute also prohibited the sale of young bondpeople into another state where they would "lose those benefits and privileges" of eventual freedom. But perhaps the most compassionate clause was section five, which levied a £50 fine on any master who "separated or removed a wife from her husband or child from his or her parent to a distance of greater than ten miles."[22]

If Pennsylvania's initial law became the model for other state acts of gradual emancipation, the one state where piecemeal legislation proved unnecessary was Massachusetts. As was typical in the states where slavery was abolished either during or shortly following the war, the colony had never proven particularly hospitable to African slavery. By the eve of the Revolution, Massachusetts was only 2 percent black. Notions of inalienable privileges and the duty to struggle for them were more deeply embedded in the home of Crispus Attucks than in any other corner of the Republic. Old religious sensibilities, even as they adapted to changing economic times, frowned on the sloth implicit in having another perform one's labors; the same deeply ingrained instincts that propelled John Adams out of bed each morning at five to read his Bible, memorize another legal precedent, or walk his fields led him to regard unwaged labor as a sinful "black cloud." To all of these factors working for emancipation, Adams later added the demands "of labouring white people, who would no longer suffer the rich to employ these sable rivals so much to their injury."[23]

In no state was the tradition of petition by free blacks and even enslaved African Americans stronger, and the resolve witnessed by literate black activists since the day that Felix Holbrook had submitted his petition in 1773 (see chapter 2) only increased with independence. On January 13, 1777, Prince Hall and seven other men publicly demanded that Massachusetts grant them "the Naturel Right of all men." Hall, born to a British father and a mixed-race mother in Barbados, had achieved freedom in 1770 before founding the first lodge of black Masons in the Americas. Well aware of proposals for gradual emancipation being discussed in other states, Hall pointedly called upon his white neighbors to practice "the mild Religion of Jesus" by liberating all "Slaves after they arive at the age of Twenty one years." Hall's petition led a legislative committee to draft "an Act for preventing the practice of holding persons in Slavery," although the bill never came to a vote. Undeterred, black mariner Paul Cuffee and six others "of the African extract" demanded legal satisfaction in February 1780. Twenty-one-year-old Cuffee observed that blacks had "cheerfully entered the field of battle in the defence of the common cause" and paid the same taxes as "the white people," although long years of slavery had deprived blacks from "enjoying the profit of our labour." Raised amidst the familiar cry against taxation without representation, Cuffee requested that black residents "be free from paying tax" so long as they were "not alowed in vooting in the town meating" or having their voices "ever heard in the active Court of the jeneral assembly."[24]

If such reminders of Revolutionary hypocrisy were not particularly welcome in the corridors of power, they clearly resonated with many of the state's common folk. Adams's uncharitable insistence that white workers opposed slavery because they feared their wages would be depressed by cheaper black labor was certainly correct, but that was only part of their complaint. Much of their hostility toward slavery was purely ideological. When the first draft constitution was circulated across Massachusetts in 1778, a good many whites objected on the basis that blacks were excluded from voting "even tho they are free and men of property." The entire town of Sutton united to reject the document, as it only added "to the already acumulated Load of guilt lying upon the Land [for] supporting the slave trade [against] the poor innocent Affricans who never hurt or offered any Injury or Insult to this country." Should Massachusetts neglect to liberate "every person within the State [at] 21 years of Age" and allow freedmen "all [their] earnings," white Patriots would only be "bringing or incurring more Wrath upon us." Slightly chastened, the state revised the proposed constitution so that it erased the color barrier for voting, but added nothing about gradual emancipation.[25]

In a society as culturally litigious as Massachusetts, that left it to blacks such as Quok Walker and whites like the Caldwell brothers to pursue human rights through the state's legal system. African Americans, of course, had pursued their rights through the courts almost since the end of the Seven Years' War, although these cases typically concluded on technical points— such as Jenny Slew's 1766 insistence that her mother was white—rather than on grander ideological theories of inalienable rights. But at almost the same moment that Levi Lincoln filed suit against Nathaniel Jennison on behalf of Walker, another slave filed a similar suit. Together, the two cases effectively ended slavery in Massachusetts. The bondwoman in question was Elizabeth, or Bett for short, or sometimes even Mum Bett. Born around 1742 in the town of Claverack, New York, Bett grew up in the western portion of Massachusetts. As a young woman, she was buffeted about due to the vagaries of her various masters' lives. Originally the property of Pieter Hogeboom, she became the slave of Colonel John Ashley when the latter married Hogeboom's daughter, Annetje. In 1773, Ashley and a young attorney named Theodore Sedgwick helped draft the Sheffield Declaration, which proclaimed all people to be "free and independent of each other." Then, according to one account, in early 1781 Bett found herself in the midst of an angry dispute between her sister Lizzie and Annetje, and when her mistress swung a heated fire shovel it was Bett and not Lizzie who received a burn on her arm, the scar of which "she bore until the day of her death." Furious, Bett marched out of Ashley's house and vowed never to return. Determined to remain free, Bett arrived at the Stockbridge doorstep of attorney Sedgwick, who had already served one term in the state assembly. Sedgwick agreed to take the case and obtained a writ calling for Bett's release, and also for that of Brom, another of Ashley's slaves.[26]

As the August 1781 court date approached, Sedgwick worried about what grounds he might use to secure Bett's freedom. Unlike the simultaneous case of Quok Walker, there were no veiled promises of future liberation upon which to construct a case. Sedgwick approached Tapping Reeve, one of the most respected legal minds in Connecticut, to serve as co-counsel. Together they hit upon a brilliant strategy. The final state constitution of 1780, like many documents of the period, opened with a flowery preamble: "All men are born free and equal." By ratifying that statement of rights, Sedgwick insisted, Massachusetts effectively nullified earlier (if ambiguous) legislation supporting unfree labor. When the Court of Common Pleas finally met in Great Barrington, Sedgwick argued that Bett and Brom were not "legal Negro Servants" at the time the writ was issued, since the constitution had banned the institution the previous year. Although jury foreman Jonathan Holcomb did not refer specifically to Sedgwick's argument, he agreed they could not legally be "Servants of the s[ai]d John Ashley during life" and assessed damages against the colonel of thirty shillings.[27]

Outraged by what was clearly an act of judicial activism, since the drafters of the state Bill of Rights hardly meant for their florid language to be taken literally, Ashley appealed the case to the state Supreme Court, which was set to ride circuit through the county in October. By the fall, however, the next round of trials in the ongoing *Walker v. Jennison* cases had been decided, and Ashley evidently decided that the winds of revolutionary change were against him. He dropped his appeal, "confessed Judgment for thirty shillings damage and Cost of suit," and returned home to face an aggravated Annetje. As for Mum Bett, she accepted a position as paid servant in Sedgwick's household and adopted a more appropriate name for a liberated woman of the new Republic, Elizabeth Freeman.[28]

Quok Walker's case was at once more trivial but in the end also more momentous. It was trifling in that it began in June 1781 as a "common assault & Battery" suit, yet it ended by reaffirming Sedgwick's Mum Bett argument in the state's highest court. In the first round, heard in the Worcester Court of Common Pleas, attorney Levi Lincoln merely asserted that Nathaniel Jennison's behavior violated "the peace & the laws" of the state. The jury agreed and awarded Walker the impressive sum "of Fifty Pounds in lawful gold or silver." Not asked to take a position on Walker's freedom—Walker continued to maintain that he had become free at age twenty-one thanks to promises made years before by Isabell Caldwell—the jury simply found against Jennison's brutality. The same court, therefore, saw no difficulty in finding for Jennison in a second suit, this one filed against the Caldwell brothers. In this case, also filed in June 1781, Jennison charged that his wife's brothers had deprived him of the rightful labor of "a certain negro man named Quarko." Levi Lincoln and Caleb Strong defended the Caldwells, but the jury found them guilty of meddling in Jennison's property rights and assessed damages of £25.[29]

A number of legal historians have declared the two jury decisions "clearly contradictory." Yet as the first jury was called upon to rule not on Walker's legal status but only as to whether an assault had taken place, there was no incongruity in the second jury's finding that John and Seth Caldwell had injured Jennison's income. Admittedly, few states would have heard cases regarding the physical abuse of an unruly bondman. But as Theodore Sedgwick's son later insisted, "instances of cruelty were uncommon" in Massachusetts, so it is hardly surprising that Jennison's neighbors took him to task for excessive violence against a dependent. In any case, both sides appealed to the Superior Court of Judicature, and in January 1782 Jennison filed a petition asking for a stay in Walker's judgment on the grounds that his attorney, John Sprague, had neglected to file the proper appeal papers. Lincoln and Strong were back once more, defending the Caldwells in their appeal, and in this round, the question of Walker's status was central to both sides. William Stearns, Jennison's new attorney, began with the curious assertion that Walker was "a slave by his own consent" and that, consent or not, he had become human property in 1754 when James Caldwell bought the infant from Zedekiah Stone. For the first time, Lincoln argued that Walker was free due to promises made by his second owners, but unlike Stearns, he could present no documents to prove that assertion, and Isabell Caldwell was long deceased. Judge Nathaniel Peaslee Sargent, having heard of the previous year's Mum Bett decision, ignored the question of alleged promises of manumission and instead drew the jury's attention to the state constitution's "free and equal" clause. Not only did Walker win this round as well, but the court slapped a criminal indictment against Jennison for extreme brutality.[30]

Perhaps the most stubborn man in a region renowned for stubbornness, Jennison, unlike Colonel Ashley, refused to concede defeat. On June 18, 1782, he petitioned the state assembly, pleading that they review Sargent's verdict. Jennison protested the Superior Court's literal reading of the state constitution and hinted that if Sargent's ruling went unchallenged, every master's property rights in Massachusetts stood in danger. He had been "deprived of ten Negro Servants by a judgment" of the court, he fumed, and should the assembly approve of that decision, he requested that he "be freed from his obligations to support said negroes." Since neither Walker nor any other of Jennison's slaves wanted anything more than liberty, his petition was as irrational as it was petulant. Yet it had an effect. Scared legislators agreed that Sargent had overstepped his authority, and they crafted a bill for gradual emancipation along the lines of that recently passed by Pennsylvania, which at least would guarantee slaveholders a few more decades of uncompensated labor. The bill passed the House but failed to achieve a second reading in the Senate.[31]

Finally, in April 1783 the Supreme Judicial Court arrived in Worcester. Since judges often wore several hats in the early Republic, it was not unusual that Sargent sat on the state's highest court as well, a fact that hardly pleased William Stearns, who continued as Jennison's attorney. The question mark was Chief Justice William Cushing, who had owned a slave, Peter Warden, as late as 1779. Cushing had much to consider. Even in the highest court, a jury would decide Walker's fate, but the chief justice enjoyed the right to prod the panel in one direction or another. A narrow verdict could liberate Walker on the grounds of alleged promises, while a broad ruling would uphold Sargent's decision and so endanger slavery throughout the state. There was also the precedent of the Somerset decision, which had been widely (if incorrectly) reported in the *Boston Gazette* and the *Middlesex Journal* as liberating fourteen thousand British slaves. Like Lord Mansfield before him, however, Cushing was aware that tradition rather than unambiguous statute allowed for slavery in Massachusetts. As chapter 1 notes, Section 91 of the 1641 Body of Liberties banned "any bond slaverie, villinage or Captivitie amongst us." A qualifying clause allowed for the use of "lawfull Captives taken in just warres," which often had been used against the Algonquians, but as an enlightened jurist, Cushing was hardly prepared to rule that nine-month-old Quok had been a legitimate prisoner of war.[32]

Levi Lincoln's brief to the court urged a broad ruling. He and Strong appealed for the first time to notions of Christian brotherhood, and he also endorsed Sargent's reading of the "free and equal" clause, a wise move since Sargent again sat before them. For his part, Stearns ignored the previous ruling and simply sought to prove that Walker was the legal property of Jennison. The case did not last long, and Cushing's directions to the jury were equally brief. He began by summarizing the two positions. "Fact proved," he began, "Quack is a slave," or at least was one as a child before coming of age and inheriting the promises of "his master Caldwell, and by the widow." But the central questions were two: were the laws of colonial Massachusetts clear as to slavery, and if so, had they been overturned by the constitution of 1780? Almost from Cushing's first words, it was clear that Walker had again won. It is true that "the right of Christians to hold Africans in perpetual servitude, and sell and treat them as we do our horses and cattle," was widely practiced in earlier days, Cushing conceded, "but nowhere [was] it expressly enacted or established" by Massachusetts law. Moreover, the Revolution swept away "whatever sentiments have formerly prevailed" regarding the ability of one person to own another. A new and "different idea has taken place with the people of America," he added, "more favorable to the natural rights of mankind." It was in this spirit of liberty that the authors of the Massachusetts constitution declared "that all men are born free and equal—that every subject is entitled to liberty, and to have it guarded by the laws." In short, Cushing concluded, "the idea of slavery is inconsistent with our own conduct and Constitution." Massachusetts juries rarely retired to deliberate; instead they simply huddled to the side of the courtroom. This one needed but a moment to agree with the chief justice.[33]

Contrary to popular myth, Justice Cushing's ruling did not immediately liberate every slave in Massachusetts. But like Lord Mansfield's decision eleven years before, the Quok Walker case made it clear that no law existed to protect chattel slavery, and in fact it went further than the 1772 ruling by announcing bondage to be in violation of the state's constitution. Because Cushing ruled from the judicial bench rather than legislated from the state assembly, the burden of proof remained with enslaved men and women such as Walker and Bett. But since slavery was now proclaimed to be unconstitutional in Massachusetts, if individual slaves took their masters to court, the slaveholders would clearly lose. Most bondmen, and nearly as many masters, assumed that slavery was now illegal. During the following year, Zachariah Johonnot of Boston left some money in his will to Caesar, "formerly my Negro Man Servant now a Freeman," and Joseph Gardner, a physician, directed his heirs to see that a man named Sharp, "who was formerly my servant before he was free, should not suffer or come to want." Less benevolent masters were not as charitable. William Royall, who owned a large farm in Canton, was so outraged by the decision that he hired a gang of white toughs to seize his slaves and sell them into perpetual bondage in Barbados. Two of his slaves, Hector and Pero, managed to escape and maintained their liberty through threats of violence. Had they known of Royall's intentions earlier, they swore, he "would not have lived" so long.[34]

Royall was the exception. To the extent that Cushing's ruling could have been overturned by the state assembly—the principle of judicial review not yet being clearly established—or through an amendment to the constitution, the decision stood largely because it enjoyed widespread public support. Gazing back from the vantage point of 1795, abolitionist Jeremy Belknap conceded that the Walker case was critical, yet he also believed that slavery was ultimately "abolished here by publick opinion; which began to be established about 30 years ago" in the wake of the Seven Years' War. Reverend John Eliot agreed: "The cause of abolition of slaves in the State may be traced entirely to the sentiment of the people." Such views slighted the hard work of black activists such as Walker, Bett, and Paul Cuffee, not to mention the dedication shown by white progressives like Lincoln and Cushing. Yet it is also true that their actions were allowed to succeed simply because unwaged labor was so unimportant to Massachusetts's economy. Blacks were, as John Adams admitted, "unprofitable servants." When the first federal census was conducted in 1790, the Massachusetts rolls listed not a single slave.[35]

In one novel case, a former Massachusetts slave followed up her emancipation with a petition demanding decades of back pay. After being sold away from Africa around 1725 at the age of twelve, Belinda had labored as a domestic of Isaac Royall, a Loyalist who fled his Medford mansion in 1775. Three years later, the state seized Royall's property and assets, in the process liberating the aged Belinda and her invalid daughter, Prine. Facing an impoverished dotage in Boston, Belinda presented the state assembly with a petition in February 1783, requesting an annual pension taken from the proceeds of Royall's estate. Belinda insisted that she was "denied one morsel of [Loyall's] immense wealth, a part whereof hath been accumulated by her own industry." Perhaps because Loyall was a Tory who abandoned Massachusetts for Britain, the legislature agreed to Belinda's request and awarded her an annual pension of £15 to be paid from the rent of his home. The assembly, however, was less anxious to pay reparations to the former bondpeople of Massachusetts Patriots.[36]

The remainder of New England was easier yet. In Rhode Island, skilled bondmen had long hired their time for wages during their off hours, and so they were nearly as integrated into the regional economy as were free blacks or white craftsmen. Thanks to the mixed-race First Rhode Island Regiment (which included a number of Indians as well as blacks), the state was home to a large number of recently freed veterans, all of whom could be counted on to participate in the liberation of their relations and friends. Their ally was Moses Brown, a businessman and philanthropist who had broken with his slave-trading family upon converting to the Society of Friends. Even before the Treaty of Paris was ratified in 1783, Brown penned countless pamphlets and essays for the *Providence Gazette*. During the following year, he submitted a petition calling for immediate emancipation. Now that his country was founded upon "the blessings of liberty," Brown argued, slavery represented "a national evil, with accumulated guilt." Encouraged by the number of influential signatures on the petition, a legislative committee drafted a bill that not only abolished slavery but levied heavy fines for those involved in the Atlantic slave trade. Since the Brown family was hardly the only one to acquire vast sums through the buying and selling of African bodies, it was unsurprising that the full legislature rejected the bill by two to one. Under pressure from black veterans and white Quakers, however, the legislature conceded that slavery was "incompatible with the Rights of Man" and passed a far more conservative substitute. Under this law, all children born after March 1, 1784, would become free after reaching the age of eighteen if women and twenty-one if men. Each town was expected to pay for the upbringing and education of black children. Slaveholders might also liberate any healthy bondperson between the ages of twenty-one to forty without assuming any financial responsibility. The final bill, however, said nothing about Rhode Island's participation in the traffic in humans outside of the state.[37]

The tendency of reform-minded politicians to borrow legislation from neighboring states was particularly conspicuous in Connecticut. Black petitioners and white evangelicals lobbied the assembly to emancipate the state's more than six thousand slaves as early as 1776. One minister pointedly observed that leading Patriots prayed for God's assistance through public days of fasting, yet they had not "let the oppressed go free." A 1777 statute that encouraged masters to manumit healthy young bondmen who could serve in the military led to the emancipation of several hundred slaves, and as elsewhere in New England, black veterans took the lead in protecting those kinsmen still in slavery. At war's end, Roger Sherman chaired a committee to revise the state's laws. His colleague, the aptly named Richard Law, lifted Rhode Island's act almost verbatim, including its emancipation date of March 1, 1784, with the exception of raising the number of years of uncompensated service freed bondpeople owed their masters to twenty-five for both genders.[38]

The last New England state, New Hampshire, proved a curious exception, since it neither freed slaves through the courts nor gave them freedom by legislative action. Here too black petitioners appealed early on to Revolutionary justice. In 1779 Prince Whipple, the celebrated oarsman, urged the legislature to abolish slavery on the basis of "humanity, and the rights of mankind," but the assembly failed to liberate even the tiny number of slaves (674) who then resided in the state. When the drafters of New Hampshire's constitution included a preamble similar to that of Massachusetts by proclaiming that "all men are born equal and independent," reformers took heart, only to hear Justice Simeon Olcott of the state supreme court announce that it had long been "Custom & Practice in this state" to "hold [blacks] in Servitude" and that independence had done nothing to alter that. The 1790 census revealed 158 slaves still living in the state, although that number plummeted to 8 by 1800. Still, it was not until 1857 that the assembly finally passed the unequivocal Act to Secure Freedom and the Rights of Citizenship, which made every resident of New Hampshire a citizen.[39]

Given that the relative speed with which states moved against slavery correlated to the size of their black population and the importance of unwaged labor to their economy, it came as no shock to reformers that the path to liberty was far rougher in New York. According to the state's first postwar census of 1786, New York as a whole was home to 18,889 African Americans, who constituted 8.5 percent of the population, a decline from 1771, when blacks equaled 13 percent of the population, a drop due largely to the exodus of black Loyalists out of the state. Moreover, slaveholding tended to be concentrated in New York City and on the large farms that dotted the banks of the Hudson River, making Manhattan second only to Charleston as the demographically blackest city in the United States. Holdings were generally small, however, and the majority of bondpeople worked as domestics or as assistants to craftsmen. Among Manhattan's elite—the merchants, shippers, and attorneys who dominated the city's political life—slaveholding was especially prevalent. The richest 10 percent of Manhattan's population owned more than half of the city's taxable property and roughly 40 percent of the city's enslaved men and women. In the most fashionable neighborhoods, few households eschewed the practice, which meant that while the state as a whole could hardly be described as a "slave society," many merchants demonstrated the sort of ideological commitment to, economic interest in, and even psychological dependence on the system that was typical of the Carolina lowcountry.[40]

Despite this, for one brief moment at war's end it appeared that New York might follow Pennsylvania's path to gradual freedom. At the state's 1777 constitutional convention, delegate Gouverneur Morris sought to include a statement declaring that "every being who breathes the air of this State shall enjoy the privileges of a freeman." Morris failed in his attempt, but in 1781, even as Manhattan remained a British-occupied city, the assembly manumitted those bondmen who served in either the state militia or Washington's army. Although that number was small compared to the number of black Loyalists, it meant that aggressive young men mustered out of their units expecting a better future. Even before that, county governments had often liberated bondpeople who belonged to white Loyalists, and in 1784 the legislature announced that known Tories had forfeited their property, including that in slaves (a declaration that foreshadowed the federal government's Confiscation Acts of 1861 and 1862).[41]

When the legislature next convened in the spring of 1785, antislavery men believed that sufficient votes for emancipation existed in both chambers. The question was what form that emancipation might take. Hoping to guide potential legislation, gradualists published copies of Pennsylvania's statute in New York journals. Others advocated immediate emancipation, among them twenty-nine-year-old Aaron Burr, who was himself a slaveholder. The son of a Presbyterian minister (and the grandson of Calvinist theologian Jonathan Edwards), Burr was raised in a slaveholding household, but also a somewhat benevolent one in which slaves and indentured servants were taught to read. His sister Sarah was married to Tapping Reeve, one of Mum Bett's attorneys, and as a veteran of Valley Forge, Burr had served alongside black soldiers. When Burr's proposal for the unconditional abolition of slavery came to the floor, however, it failed by an overwhelming vote of 33 to 13.[42]

The House then set to work on a far more conservative statute, one even more restrictive than Pennsylvania's. Not only did the act demand the customary two decades of uncompensated service from those set to be emancipated, but also proslavery legislators, recognizing that antislavery forces had enough votes to secure passage of this bill, introduced a series of amendments that sought to replace slavery with a very limited form of freedom. The bill finally sent to the Senate denied freedmen the right to a "legal vote," and it also stated "that no negro, mulatto or mustee whatsoever, shall hold or exercise any office or place of trust, nor shall be admitted [as] a witness or juror in any case civil or criminal," which meant that black New Yorkers could never be tried by a jury of their racial peers. The Senate demanded that the latter amendment be removed. The House agreed but by a comfortable ratio retained the language barring black voters. "It would be greatly injurious to this state if all the negroes should be allowed the same privileges as white men," one legislator reasoned. Without some level of political segregation, New York could witness the "shame" of racial egalitarianism, with a "General Quacco here [and a] Col. Mingo there" in the legislature. The assembly then passed the entire bill by a vote of 36 to 11. Although still hoping for a more radical bill, Burr grudgingly voted with the majority.[43]

The next, stunning turn of events proved to be both a victory for social justice and a failure of pragmatic policy. When the bill arrived on the desk of Governor George Clinton, his advisory board urged him to veto it on the grounds that it was "repugnant to the principle on which the United States justify their separation from Great Britain." Under the state constitution, colonial property requirements for voting were largely maintained. But as any male resident could theoretically obtain the requisite assets, Clinton's councilors regarded the vote as a potentially universal right, rather than a "Priviledge [denied to] Freemen." On March 30, Clinton agreed and vetoed the measure. Curiously, the fact that its gradualist provisions held some New Yorkers in bondage while eventually liberating those lucky enough to be born after 1785 was unobjectionable, while the fact that those who became free remained second-class citizens was denounced as an "odious Distinction." The governor also observed that the bill would create social unrest in future years. Those blacks freed but denied basic legal rights would remain a "class of disenfranchised and discontented citizens" with no attachment to the state or its laws.[44]

If Clinton and his council expected the legislature to promptly pass a more progressive act without the offending clauses, they were to be as disappointed as the black New Yorkers who awaited freedom. Instead, the assembly crafted a completely new bill that sought merely to weaken slavery by banning future importations of bondpeople into the state. The statute was designed only to mollify the anger of antislavery activists, since in practice the law was wholly ineffective. Masters still enjoyed the right to relocate into New York and bring slaves for their own "personal use," and they could later legally sell their chattel to other state residents. Some recent immigrants into the state simply evaded the law by redefining their slaves as long-term servants. Upon moving into the state, one former New Jersey resident listed his bondman as "free" but serving a ninety-nine-year period of indentured servitude. To the extent that the original 1785 statute was the best law the assembly was inclined to pass, enslaved New Yorkers might be forgiven for admiring the governor's sense of justice while regretting that his veto produced an impasse to further reform. It would be fourteen long years before the assembly again took up the question.[45]

Faced with this intransigence at the highest levels of government, reformers moved outside the system. When it became clear that the assembly might pass, at best, a highly restrictive law, a band of thirty-three abolitionists met at the home of innkeeper John Simmons on January 25, 1785, to organize the New York Society for Promoting the Manumission of Slaves. Some of its members were Quakers, although unlike Pennsylvania's Abolition Society, the majority were not. A number of prosperous attorneys and rising politicians, from John Jay (the future Supreme Court chief justice and governor) to Alexander Hamilton and Aaron Burr, lent their names to the organization, although the actual running of the society fell to its less prestigious members, mostly shopkeepers and merchants of modest means. Believing that the "benevolent Creator" had endowed all people with "an equal Right to Life, Liberty and Property," the founders drafted thirteen bylaws to govern the society. Most of the rules dealt with mundane matters, such as the election of officers, the keeping of records and dues, and even the expulsion of members "deem[ed] unworthy of continuing." None of the rules demanded that members divest themselves of their human property.[46]

When asked about this obvious inconsistency, members replied that it was "inexpedient" to exclude slaveholders, since so many men of influence in Manhattan owned domestics. If pressed to release their bond servants, masters might "gradually withdraw their services," leaving behind only those shopkeepers who enjoyed no influence in the corridors of power. Among those who confessed to being "very inconsistent as well as unjust" was society president Jay, who owned six bondpeople in 1785. Before the Revolution, Jay confided to a British abolitionist, "very few" men of standing "doubted the propriety and rectitude of" owning other humans. Although old attitudes had changed for the better, it was "not easy to persuade men in general to act on that magnanimous and disinterested principle." Nor was Jay alone. Merchant Robert Troup, who crafted the society's Lockean preamble, owned two slaves. Of the 120 men who joined the society in its first five years, at least 27 owned slaves. Another 8 who did not appear in the 1790 census or owned no slaves that year acquired bondpeople by 1800. In fact, not until 1809—twenty-four years after its founding—did the society finally adopt a resolution demanding that its members free their slaves.[47]

Another slaveholding member was attorney Alexander Hamilton, whose marriage into the influential Schuyler family brought him wealth and political connections, as well as black servants. (At the time of his marriage, Hamilton's father-in-law, Philip Schuyler, retained twenty-seven slaves at his Albany mansion and his mills near Saratoga, which made him one of the largest slaveholders in the state.) Despite his wartime friendship with John Laurens and his "support and encouragement" of the use of black troops, Hamilton appears to have owned or hired enslaved domestics until the day of his death. In 1781, shortly after his marriage, he rented a slave belonging to George Clinton for his wife, Eliza. Fourteen years later, Schuyler wrote to inform Hamilton of "the Negro boy & woman" he "engaged" for the pair. Hamilton promptly mailed Schuyler a check for $250 "for 2 Negro servants purchased by him for me."[48]

So reluctant to practice what they preached were many members of the society that when in November 1785 Hamilton produced an internal committee report regarding this awkward problem, even his painfully gradualist proposal went nowhere. Hamilton suggested that members who owned slaves younger than twenty-eight should agree to manumit those bondpeople at the age of thirty-five. Those between the ages of twenty-eight and thirty-five were to become free after seven more years of uncompensated labor, and those above the age of forty-five (which put them well beyond the period of valuable labor) should be freed immediately. Despite the fact that Hamilton's proposed timetables were conservative even when compared to gradualist plans passed in nearby states, society member Melancton Smith effectively killed the plan by deferring its consideration to a later meeting. What the society again convened, a new committee ruled instead that members were free to retain or liberate their slaves as they wished and not as the organization saw fit.[49]

With these sorts of tepid allies, black New Yorkers understood that the task of liberation fell to them. One of the leading activists was William Hamilton, the mixed-race son of Alexander Hamilton. Weary of waiting for white New Yorkers to end "slavery and oppression" in what they insisted was "a land of liberty and equality, a christian country," Hamilton called on society president Jay to ask what the society intended to do to eradicate "the scandal of this country [so] that it might be called a free nation." Another activist was Peter Williams Jr., the city's first black Episcopal priest. Born into slavery, Peter became free at the age of five when his father, who had first purchased his own liberty with money earned as a cigar maker, bought his son's freedom as well. Peter Williams later returned the favor by using his church's assets to buy bondpeople and allowing them to pay the debt back over time. By 1799, such methods of self-purchase produced 97 percent of all manumissions in New York.[50]

As elsewhere across the North, young bondmen refused to wait for wealthy white men such as Jay to act, and seized their liberty by running away. During the first years after the British evacuated New York Harbor, the number of runaways advertised in the city's newspapers plummeted; as rumors of impending legislative emancipation spread through Manhattan's back alleys, bondmen waited for the assembly to act. When it failed to do so following Clinton's veto, countless numbers of young men (who ran away twice as often as did young women) abandoned their masters' homes. Some fled for Philadelphia or New England, having heard rumors of emancipation in those locales, while most simply remained in the city. As Manhattan grew rapidly after 1783, enslaved artisans with marketable skills encountered numerous white employers who asked few questions of those eager to work. Typical was Jack, who was "African born, but speaks good English." A "good cook and a butcher," Jack gambled that his trade would secure him employment.

Successful flights in turn fueled the growth of a free (legally or otherwise) black community willing to shelter other young bondpeople fleeing into the city from the countryside. As the runaway advertisements in rural New York journals revealed, more than one-third of those gone missing were thought to be heading toward Manhattan. Notable also was how many advertisements warned against "harbouring or employing" those being sought, compelling evidence that many were sheltering or hiring them.[51]

Despite this, support for abolition actually weakened in the decade after 1785. In the counties with the largest number of bondpeople—King, Ulster, and Albany—masters continued to fear that should state manumission come, the crime rate would soar, as could their tax rates, since they would be responsible for the maintenance of impoverished freedpeople. Other slave-holders hinted they might endorse abolition, but only with new and cruel amendments to any proposed statute, such as their right to sell troublesome young bondmen into the southern states (traditionally one of their most effective punishments and forms of labor control). As the state's black population began to increase following the war's end—from 18,889 in 1786 to 25,983 in 1790, more than twice the number of slaves in Delaware—masters once more grew reliant upon unwaged labor, and entrepreneurial artisans increasingly bought enslaved assistants rather than turning to white apprentices. Most troubling of all, Manhattan's merchant elite, which controlled the assembly, began to replace shopkeepers and middling artisans as the city's typical slaveholders.[52]

No better illustration exists of this mounting proslavery sentiment than the comprehensive slave code passed by the assembly in February 1788 (the first all-inclusive black code in New York since 1730). Nominally designed to plug inadvertent loopholes in the 1785 slave importation act, the legislation outlawed the resale of bondpeople brought into the state after that year. It also banned the practice of professional slave buyers coming into the state and pretending to be permanent residents simply for the purpose of purchasing bondpeople to be resold in Georgia or South Carolina. But these modest reforms masked the legislature's determination to affirm slavery's continued legality in New York. In response to black activists who hoped that the egalitarian spirit of the Revolution might erode harsh racial walls, the bill clarified matters. All "blacks, mulattoes, or Mestees" who were enslaved as of February 22—the date the statute finally passed—remained in that condition unless "properly manumitted" by their owners, and their children "shall follow that state and condition of the mother." Baptism did not alter enslavement, and those abolitionists inclined to hire or assist runaways faced stiff fines. Americans liked to insist that black slavery was an unhappy legacy of British rule, but with the passage of this statute, white New Yorkers could no longer make that claim.[53]

Proslavery advocates hoped the 1788 bill would put an end to further agitation, but black activists continued to lobby for reform. Beginning in 1792, one or two courageous statesmen volunteered to craft a gradual emancipation act with each new legislative session. Most bills failed to emerge from committee. But in 1795, John Jay resigned as the nation's chief justice to run for governor on the Federalist ticket, and slaveholder or not, Jay continued to defend his association with the Manumission Society. One supporter feared that Jay might "not have many Votes from the *Dutch Inhabitants*" of Ulster County, since "a great majority [of them] possess *many Slaves*." Another Federalist worried that Jay's Republican opponents planned to "descend to the lowest subterfuges of craft and chicane" in spreading the rumor that he intended "to rob every Dutchman of the property he possesses most dear to his heart, his slaves." For his part, Jay adhered to his long-held position that while "every man of every color and description has a natural right to freedom," the "abolition of slavery must necessarily be gradual." Whether his supporters spread the word that Jay continued to own slaves is less clear. (As late as 1809, Jay sold his domestic Zilphah for being disobedient.)[54]

Although the election was close, Jay carried the day. Reformers and black activists also took heart in January 1798 when Aaron Burr resumed his old seat in Albany. Painfully aware that immediate emancipation was less likely to succeed than fourteen years before, Burr began to push for a gradualist statute modeled after Pennsylvania's. Although one of the nation's leading Republicans, Burr obtained only modest support from within his own party, while Governor Jay secured almost twice as many Federalist backers for emancipation. New York Republicans, as elsewhere in the new nation, were predominantly farmers, artisans, or petty shopkeepers, while the Federalist Party attracted merchants and urban attorneys, who owned domestics as symbols of wealth and social standing but understood that unwaged labor was a clumsy, ineffective relic of a precapitalist age. Hamilton and Jay might own slaves, but they recognized that bonded labor made little sense in the world of Adam Smith and could only hinder the development of the capitalist society they wished to create. Ironically, the same party that attracted so few immigrant or working-class votes, in New York at least, was also the party of abolition.[55]

In its final form, the bill that reached the assembly floor in 1799, like that of Pennsylvania nearly two decades before, freed not a single slave on the day of its passage. Instead, the law promised eventual freedom to those black children born after July 4 upon reaching the age of twenty-eight for males and twenty-one for females. Delegate Erastus Root tried to reduce the period of required servitude on a plea of "Divine Law" to twenty-one and eighteen, the ages required of impoverished white children bound out for service, but slavery was too deeply embedded in New York to be reformed by an appeal to religion. Should masters wish to divest themselves of black children, they might turn them over to the state overseers of the poor at age one. Curiously, the state agreed to pay a maintenance fee of $3.50 each month per child, even if the caretaker was the former master, making this abandonment clause a veiled form of compensated emancipation. Even these concessions failed to win over many Republicans, and the final vote of sixty-eight to twenty-three largely fell along party lines. Aaron Burr broke ranks to vote with the majority, and Governor Jay signed the bill with "unfeigned pleasure." That pleasure, however, did not stop Jay from selling his "difficult" slave Phillis to an owner who promised to manumit her within two years. The governor chose not to free her himself, as he did not want to be "chargeable with her maintenance."[56]

As activists such as William Hamilton understood too well, the 1799 law was as much a prod toward further reform as it was something to celebrate. The number of slaves in New York State declined very slowly, and not until the census of 1810 did the figure in Manhattan drop to 947. The cost of maintenance proved so burdensome to state budgets that the assembly repealed that part of the statute in 1812, after which masters resorted to selling black children to southern states, where their enslavement would become permanent. Although this practice skirted the 1788 act and defied the spirit of the 1799 law, avaricious slaveholders simply found, or paid off, justices of the peace willing to concur that the bondpeople agreed to their purchase. Only in 1817 did the assembly pass a true emancipation act, when it freed those luckless bondpeople born before July 4, 1799, reduced the age of manumission to twenty-one for both genders, and set the date of 1827 as the final moment of liberation in New York State.[57]

Of the lands north and east of the Chesapeake Bay, that left only New Jersey to reconcile the principles of the Revolution with the ownership of slaves. As was the case in neighboring New York, enslaved labor was far more important to the state's rural economy than it was in New England. Men like Titus had long plowed the farms of Monmouth County, and if Quakers in the western regions urged emancipation, white farmers in the war-ravaged eastern counties regarded unwaged labor as their surest path back to solvency. So resistant were slaveholding agrarians that when in the immediate aftermath of the war Governor William Livingston proposed statutes for the gradual abolition of slavery and a ban on the further importation of slaves into the state, the entire assembly promptly voted only to consider the latter. Livingston regarded slavery as "utterly inconsistent, both with the principles of Christianity & humanity; & in Americ[a]ns who have almost idolize[ed] liberty." Not only did the legislature disagree, but the law finally passed in February 1786 set fines for importation so low that violators regarded the penalty as a minor nuisance. Nor did the act liberate bondpeople illegally brought into the state. The law did, however, ban African Americans freed in other states from entering New Jersey.[58]

For the next eighteen years, abolitionists and proslavery advocates argued their respective cases from the pulpit, the printing press, and in the state's newspapers. Quaker David Cooper penned a vitriolic pamphlet, *A Serious Address to the Rulers of America, on the Inconsistency of Their Conduct Respecting Slavery*, which accused New Jersey slaveholders of committing "treason" against the American ideal of natural rights. When that failed to advance his cause, he led a procession of eleven other Quakers into the assembly to present a widely circulated petition signed by "the most respectable names in the State." The *New Jersey Gazette* championed reform and routinely carried letters and editorials demanding emancipation. But the conservative *New Jersey Journal* just as routinely fired back. One writer, adopting the ironic pseudonym "Impartial," insisted that the state constitution protected property rights in humans just as it upheld other forms of chattel ownership. Adopting a view commonly heard across the southern states over the next eighty years, Impartial therefore maintained that only individual masters, and not the state, could emancipate the slaves. Any gradualist attempts to end the system, he added, should await a feasible plan to resettle emancipated bondpeople "in a separate region."[59]

Masters, of course, looked even less favorably on any scheme for the colonization of freed blacks, who constituted their agricultural labor force, than they did on proposals for gradual emancipation. Finally in the spring of 1804 proslavery forces gave way. Enough Republicans joined the solid block of Federalists to adopt what had become the traditional gradualist statute. Bondmen born after July 4, 1804, were to become free upon reaching the age of twenty-five; for female African Americans the age of liberation was twenty-one. As elsewhere across the North, bondpeople born before that date were damned to remain slaves for life unless New Jersey saw fit to later pass a second law liberating them (and it never did). Since the act was copied from New York's statute as well as from the much earlier law of Pennsylvania, masters might abandon black children to the overseers of the poor. So many did so that within four years, fully $12,000 (roughly one-third of the state's budget) went to fund abandonment programs. Worse yet, the 1804 act allowed whites to sell their chattel beyond state boundaries, and most issues of the *Journal*'s pages carried advertisements for the sale of young blacks. Among those listed for sale was twenty-six-year-old Bett, listed as a "slave for life," as she was born in 1788, well before the passage of the gradual emancipation act. As late as 1861, as the young men of New Jersey marched off to fight in the Civil War, whites held eighteen African Americans as "apprentices for life." Less enamored of polite euphemisms, census takers categorized them as "slaves."[60]

As luckless bondwomen such as Bett understood all too well, the series of gradualist laws set in motion twenty-four years before in Pennsylvania was just the beginning of what would be a lengthy struggle for equality and human rights. Quok Walker and other black activists across the North might demand an immediate end to slavery, but all too often their white allies were willing to accept the sort of lingering compromises they never would have agreed to had those provisions applied to their own spouses or children. John Adams saw no contradiction in bragging that he "always employed freemen, both as domestics and laborers," while insisting that the "abolition of slavery must be gradual and accomplished with much caution and circumspection." Within the span of just over two decades, reform-minded white politicians succeeded in setting unfree labor on the road to extinction in every state north of New Jersey. But far fewer whites advocated political rights or full citizenship for former slaves. Having freed young black men and women, elite reformers typically believed their task to be done. All too often, the decline of slavery in the North was caused by an influx of cheap white labor, as was the case in New Jersey, or the sale of healthy young bondmen into Georgia or South Carolina. According to the census of 1810—put another way, thirty-five years after Lemuel Haynes risked his life at Lexington and Concord—there remained some 27,000 slaves in the North, compared to about 50,000 free blacks. As historian Alfred F. Young has aptly written: "It was a grudging emancipation."[61]

Nor did the demise of slavery mark a change in the way that white northerners viewed their black neighbors. The egalitarian spirit of the Revolution helped to eliminate unfree labor, but that hardly meant that most white Patriots embraced the dream of a more racially egalitarian society. Even many reformers who supported black demands for liberty wanted little to do with African Americans after those initial goals were achieved. When asked about the innate mental ability of freedpeople, the best that Alexander Hamilton offered was a weak endorsement: "[T]heir natural faculties are probably as good as ours." Franklin agreed in a curious double negative, saying blacks were "not deficient in natural understanding." The hope that African Americans would somehow vanish along with slavery was a constant refrain. Speaking to an English traveler, one New York merchant repeated "the general opinion which prevails here" that "when emancipated" the city's black population "will dwindle away and soon disappear," as had "the Indians" before them.[62]

Northern emancipation was as penurious as it was grudging. Apart from the carefully disguised compensation clauses in New York's and New Jersey's statutes, northern assemblies were reluctant to expend public funds in the cause of emancipation. The young black men and women who became free in their twenties were given nothing more than what their former masters might care to grant them. Legislatures were, however, anxious to pass new laws clarifying the degraded position of the freed blacks who lived among them. Even as Patriots in Massachusetts crafted the egalitarian preamble to their state constitution, they passed a 1778 law granting adult taxpayers the right to vote, "excepting Negroes, Indians, and mulattoes." Eight years later in 1786, the assembly restored the colonial prohibition against marriage between whites and blacks (or Native Americans), with a new clause announcing any such preexisting unions null even if performed by white ministers. Massachusetts, like many northern states, worried that manumissions in the border South would result in black migrations into New England, and so in 1788 yet another act forbade African Americans not born in the state from residing within its borders for more than two months. Responding to these laws in the *Independent Chronicle*, one black observer sarcastically wondered why the assembly did not also deny the franchise to men "for being long-nosed, short-faced, or higher or lower than five feet nine" inches. "A black, tawny or reddish skin," he argued, should not be "so unfavorable in hue to the genuine son of liberty, as a tory complection."[63]

If racism remained a national dilemma, New Jersey's statute nonetheless meant that after 1804, slavery was increasingly a sectional problem. While in 1763 slavery had been legal within Britain's western empire from Quebec City to Barbados, the northern areas, unlike those below the Mason-Dixon line, had never truly been slave societies. Now the efforts of black activists and their reluctant political allies had divided the newly independent nation into sections, with the North endorsing free wage labor and the South remaining proslavery. But the division of the Republic into free wage labor sections and proslavery regions, which in hindsight appeared to be inevitable, did not have to happen that way. Even as reformers continued their labors across the North, a host of activists carried their struggle into the upper South. Especially in Virginia, the state with the largest number of black Americans, white elites might have made very different choices from the ones they eventually did.[64]

FIVE

Absalom's "Meritorious Service"

Antislavery in the Upper South

AMONG THE MANY SIGNIFICANT EVENTS in his life, Absalom decided later, the most critical was the day he "bought [himself] a primer." Saving the pennies he earned from performing Sunday odd jobs near his master's thousand-acre farm in Sussex County, Delaware, the young slave "begged to be taught by any body that I found able and willing to give me the least instruction." His master, Abraham Wynkoop, a merchant as well as a farmer, evidently recognized Absalom's ambition and ability; as the boy approached the age of thirteen in 1760, Wynkoop put him to work inside the house. Absalom was delighted to be away from the fields, although this also meant he only saw his mother and six siblings long after the workday was done. His near apprenticeship to the merchant, as well as his rapidly growing literacy, increased the cultural distance between Absalom and those bondpeople who worked Delaware's farms and plantations. His solitude rendered him introspective, or "singular," as he later described it.[1]

Finding that most of his days were spent traveling north to Philadelphia, in 1762 Wynkoop decided to sell his farm and move his business to the bustling city. With no further need for farmhands, he sold Absalom's mother and siblings, taking only the literate fifteen-year-old with him as his clerk and handyman. The move severed all ties between Absalom and his family but introduced him to a rapidly growing freed urban community. During the day, Absalom had to assist his master in running the store, but in 1766, around the time of his twentieth birthday, Wynkoop permitted him to attend Anthony Benezet's school for freedmen. Either Absalom's master regarded the request as fair recompense for the day's diligent labor or he thought that further education for his clerk might advance his own interests.[2]

Like most urban slaves, Absalom lived in his master's house, probably in the attic or basement. Wynkoop's neighbors, Thomas and Sarah King, also owned a young slave, a domestic named Mary. The girl caught Absalom's eye, and she was attracted to the bright, determined young man. In 1770, when Absalom was twenty-three, the two married in St. Peter's Anglican Church, where both Wynkoop and the Kings worshiped. Perhaps it was at this point that Absalom adopted the surname of Jones. (When or why he chose that name remains a mystery, although the surname of Jones was commonly adopted in the next century by Delaware's freedpeople.) Mary was right to be impressed by her husband's ferocious work ethic. Although both wished to become free, Jones thought it wiser that Mary be liberated first, since that meant their future children would be born free. He penned an eloquent appeal for his wife's freedom, and together with her father he carried it to "some of the principal Friends" in Philadelphia. Impressed by his draft, some Quakers agreed to loan him the required £30, while others offered "donations." Even as the war threatened, Jones "made it [his] business to work until twelve or one o'clock at night" after his duties at Wynkoop's business were complete, "to pay [back] the money that was borrowed to purchase her freedom."[3]

Much to his dismay, Jones discovered that his growing reputation for industry worked against him. By 1778, he had paid off his wife's debt and wished to purchase his own liberty. Wynkoop, however, saw scant logic in manumitting such an assiduous clerk. Yet when the British captured Philadelphia and offered freedom to any bondpeople who evacuated with them, Mary and Absalom chose to bide their time. Instead, the clerk used the money he had put aside to purchase a substantial house in the southern Dock Ward in January 1779. The Jones family became neighbors to Thomas McKean, the chief justice of Pennsylvania, and also to Cyrus Griffen, a congressman from Virginia who was none too pleased to find himself residing next to a half-free, half-slave black couple.[4]

In 1784 Wynkoop finally gave in and agreed to sell Jones his freedom. Perhaps it was the fact that Jones agreed to continue to working for his former master as a paid assistant that persuaded Wynkoop to free the thirty-eight-year-old bondman. No record remains of what price Wynkoop demanded, or whether Jones bargained on the grounds of age and nearly four decades of uncompensated labor. Wynkoop did insist, however, on noting that he agreed to liberate Jones in reward for his long and "meritorious service." Jones, who

Former Delaware slave Absalom Jones was sixty-four years old when he sat for celebrated Philadelphia portraitist Raphaelle Peale in 1810. *Delaware Art Museum.*

would go on to be ordained the first black minister in the Episcopal Church, typified those men and women who became free in the border South in the years just after the Peace of Paris. Although the northern states and British Canada abolished slavery through their political systems, the border states of Delaware, Maryland, and Virginia ultimately failed to achieve black liberation. Instead, bondpeople, acting as individuals, ran away or patiently saved their meager earnings to purchase freedom. Within a changing economy and a region wracked by British invasion, some white Patriots reconciled their own demands of liberty with their private behavior by manumitting some or all of their slaves. Others, who simply could not envision a world without unfree labor or who feared the consequences of liberating the roughly 328,000 blacks who resided in the Chesapeake region, advanced increasingly racist excuses for why they could not do so. "[W]e have the wolf by the ear," Thomas Jefferson famously rationalized, "and we can neither hold him, nor safely let him go."[5]

———

Absalom Jones's boyhood state was just twenty miles downriver from Philadelphia. A southern colony but never a plantation society, Delaware was home to approximately nine thousand blacks at war's end, which meant the state was approximately 80 percent white. Yet Wynkoop's cavalier attitude toward Absalom's mother and siblings was hardly typical of Quok Walker's Massachusetts and in fact resembled views Equiano discovered in Georgia and South Carolina. When the colony debated banning private manumissions in 1767, legislators derided free blacks as "idle and slothful" and replaced its 1740 slave code with a far tougher statute. In theory, the revised statute was passed to ban the cruel practice of masters manumitting aged or crippled bondpeople so as not to have to support blacks who could no longer work for them, but Quakers suspected that the real motivation was that too many whites were liberating young and healthy bondmen, precisely the sort of model of black self-reliance the colony could not abide. Yet unlike nearby Virginia, where private emancipations required the governor's consent, Delaware masters retained that right, provided they posted a crushing £60 bond for each "Mulatto or Negro slave" they chose to set free.[6]

When it came to statewide emancipation, the usual correlation between the percentage of slaves, the economy of the region, and Revolutionary ideals held as true in Delaware as elsewhere in the young Republic. Although the assembly never came close to passing legislation for gradual emancipation, in 1787 the state reversed course by passing the first of several statutes designed to encourage private manumission. The law permitted masters to free healthy slaves without posting a bond for their maintenance and good behavior. Lawmakers also sought to reduce the number of bondpeople within the state by prohibiting the importation of slaves into Delaware and "declar[ing] free" all those imported in defiance of the ban (although it also outlawed the sale of slaves outside the state as a measure of protection for black families). Support for the measure was particularly strong in the northernmost county of New Castle, home to a sizeable Quaker population. Among them was John Flynn, who freed his bondpeople after being persuaded that chattel slavery was "incompatible with the royal Law of our Blessed Lord." Warner Mifflin agreed: "[I]t is a Sin of a deep Dye to make Slaves of fellow Creatures."[7]

The relative absence of Friends in Absalom's Sussex County helps to explain the lack of enthusiasm for the 1787 statute in the southernmost region of the state. Yet in no section of Delaware would emancipation have come easily had not agriculturalists continued the long-underway transition from export commodities to less labor-intensive cereal crops. Even so, the historian William Williams insists that "more than economic imperatives" lurked behind "the extraordinary number of manumissions" that took place in the wake of the Revolution. Petitioners to the state assembly begging for emancipation often quoted the Declaration of Independence and described slavery as "unjustifiable upon any principles of reason or justice." John Dickinson, who served as a congressman both from Delaware and from Pennsylvania, was the largest slaveholder in the state when he freed his thirty-seven slaves in 1777. Yet even as he publicly denounced slavery as antithetical to American ideals, he privately admitted that his slaves had simply become a "burden." The fact that the British burned two of his country estates during the war further complicates attempts to disentangle antislavery motives, as does the fact that Dickinson's wife was a devout Quaker.[8]

Perhaps the inability of Delaware's master class to sell their surplus bondmen down the coast into Georgia explains the slow collapse of slavery in the state. And the success with which young men ran away certainly damaged the system. As elsewhere, when states either passed laws for gradual emancipation or encouraged private manumissions, the sudden emergence of a free black community not only provided models of upward mobility but also served as a source of assistance for runaways. Nor could wary whites assume that every African American they encountered on the road was a runaway. One master worried that Stephen, his elusive bondman, could create a forged pass "so well drawn that it will deceive, if not attentively examined." Charles and Sam borrowed papers from liberated friends in Wilmington in their flight toward Philadelphia. By the 1810 census, roughly 78 percent of Delaware's blacks were free (compared to 63 and 42 percent in New York and New Jersey, respectively).[9]

Five times the size of Delaware, Maryland posed a daunting task for those who desired an end to slavery. Despite the dislocation of war, the black population actually increased through natural reproduction to 83,000 by the conflict's end. As the city of Baltimore rapidly expanded, urban whites began to purchase skilled bondmen from rural counties. So many black artisans were drawn into Baltimore that until 1810, white masters were eight times more likely to procure slaves from outside the city than they were to sell their surplus bondpeople to nearby farms and plantations. This increase in the black population, together with the city's booming economy, allowed many whites who had not previously owned slaves to do so. In the first seven years after the Peace of Paris, the proportion of property-owning whites in Charles County increased from 47 to 60 percent. The rising number of bondpeople also meant that Maryland, like Delaware, banned the further importation of Africans. The state had laborers enough.[10]

In fact, many large-scale tobacco planters had far too many field hands. Tobacco production had been in decline on Maryland's Eastern Shore since the 1740s, and the dislocation of war only accelerated that pattern. Even before the Revolution, Maryland masters attempted to remain solvent by reducing the number of manufactured items they had to purchase, and that meant training bondmen to perform skilled tasks. One reason rural masters were able to sell enslaved craftsmen into Baltimore after 1783 was because they had a surplus pool of black artisans. So many young bondmen had been trained as carpenters or blacksmiths that in St. Mary's County fully 20 percent of male slaves above the age of sixteen performed nonagricultural labor. Although a growing black population might seem like good fortune to prospective masters, it could also prove dangerous, since they quickly found themselves with more slaves than they could employ or feed. As one visitor to the state observed, everything "bears the stamp of slavery," including the "parched soil, the badly managed farming, the ramshackle houses, and the few scrawny cattle that look like walking skeletons." So many agriculturalists gave up and migrated west into the fresh lands of northwestern Virginia and Kentucky that between 1790 and 1800 the slave-heavy counties of Calvert, Charles, and St. Mary's shrank in terms of both white *and* black populations. Southern Maryland particularly looked "as if it had been deserted by one half its inhabitants," worried another visitor.[11]

Yet the Maryland assembly never seriously debated the prospect of gradual emancipation, despite the encouragement of Quakers and Methodists, inspired by the example of the Pennsylvania legislature. In September 1789, influential politicians also added their voices to the call for reform by meeting in Baltimore to organize the Maryland Society for Promoting the Abolition of Slavery. Founding member Luther Martin, the state's attorney general and the owner of domestic servants, denounced slavery as "inconsistent with the genius of republicanism." It had "a tendency to destroy those principles on which it is supported," for it "lessens the sense of the equal rights of mankind, and habituates us to tyranny and oppression." Black Marylanders rejoiced to hear one of the state's leading officers condemn chattel slavery as antithetical to the Republic's political ideals, but Martin's words echoed the common refrain that slavery was evil for what it did to elite whites, rather than how it divided enslaved families or denied them the fruits of their hard labor. The state assembly, in any case, promptly censured Luther's organization.[12]

As always, demands for social justice were most frequently heard by those whose economic stake in the system of slavery was declining. As Maryland masters diversified by planting wheat and other cereal crops beside their export product of tobacco, they discovered they needed a considerable workforce only during the fall harvests. For the remainder of the year, those slaves not trained as skilled craftsmen were underemployed, yet they required the same food and clothing. It made far more sense for wheat farmers to hire white harvest hands or free blacks for the season and then release them when the work was finished. This knowledge, admitted Assemblyman William Pinkney, permitted passage of the 1790 statute that overturned the colonial ban on manumissions by will. Never would "agriculture, commerce, or manufactures flourish," he argued, "so long as they depend on the reluctant bondsman for progress." A good number of hard-pressed masters agreed, for within twenty years the free black population of Baltimore equaled the number still enslaved there.[13]

Even then, whites tended to award freedom primarily to those slaves who enjoyed some special tie to the white household, either as long-serving, uncomplaining domestic servants or because they had biological ties to the white family. The federal census of 1790 revealed that in Charles County, nearly 90 percent of those listed as free black household heads were classified as "mulatto." The number of households run by a black female—nearly one-third—was also far higher than was the case with white households, indicating that light-skinned domestics were far more likely to be manumitted than aggressive young men. In short, those most likely to stridently demand their freedom in Maryland were also those least likely to get it.[14]

By century's end, much of Maryland resembled southern Pennsylvania. With no rich hinterland to expand into, masters had to abandon the state if they wished to move west. Having already begun to switch from tobacco to cereal crops, a good many slaveholders found it feasible to embrace the ideals of the Revolution by manumitting their surplus bondpeople. By the census of 1800, roughly twenty thousand blacks, or 16 percent of Maryland's black population, were free. Although the state had the largest free black population in the Republic, approximately eight out of ten blacks in Maryland remained enslaved twenty years after the siege at Yorktown. Still, the trend revealed a split in the Chesapeake. Delaware and Maryland stumbled toward black freedom, while Virginia proved a far more complicated tale.[15]

Boasting a total population of nearly 600,000 in 1782, some 270,000 of whom were black, Virginia was the most populous and powerful state in the Union. Not only were its population and geographical expanse impressive by late-eighteenth-century standards, but the state's population began to shift westward even before the fighting ended. In 1780, to better protect its new political order from British armies, Virginia relocated its capital up the James River to Richmond, a move that mirrored the inland migration of farmers and small planters who marched their bondpeople west to escape the wartime chaos of the tidewater counties. Although the eastern edge of the state remained heavy in slaves, there was a clear shift in Virginia's black population into the fresher lands of the Piedmont. This vast hinterland, perhaps more than any other feature, explained Virginia's faltering, befuddled course of action regarding slavery in the two decades after Yorktown. Yet as the residence of approximately 40 percent of the nation's black population, Virginia was destined to play a critical role in the Republic's future. Had Virginia followed Pennsylvania and New York into gradual emancipation, the subsequent history of the United States likely would have been far different.[16]

For a time, the migration westward that slowly spread unfree labor across much of the state revealed an institution in chaos. In truth, this migration began as flight. When Lord Dunmore offered liberty to young bondmen in 1775, he triggered a massive departure of slaves along Virginia's extensive waterways. Precisely how many Virginia slaves gained their freedom during the years of combat remains unclear. Jefferson placed the number around thirty thousand, but the correct figure is surely far smaller. Wherever redcoats marched, such as along the James River valley, they left behind a trail of burned bridges and wrecked warehouses—and disappeared slaves. By some estimates, just under five thousand black Virginians evacuated with the British, not including the freedpeople who died near Yorktown. A far larger number of slaves used the British invasion as an opportunity to escape their captivity without going over to the redcoats. Whatever the final tally, the Revolution created a severe labor shortage in the eastern section of the state, the export-based region that fueled Virginia's prewar wealth. Although the departure of black Loyalists should have come as welcome news to those politicians who regarded unwaged labor as fundamentally antirepublican, the decrease in the Tidewater's productive capacity served only to convince others that an economic recovery in the 1780s required a complete restoration of the slave system.[17]

Despite slave flight, the number of bondpeople in Virginia continued to grow at an annual rate of 2 percent, thanks to the natural increase common to an already large population. By 1782, Virginia was 37 percent black, and its African American population was 270,000. Despite the loss of young bondmen—the next generation's fathers—there were 105,000 more slaves in the state in 1782 than in 1776. For those ambitious young planters preparing to move into the Piedmont, this was all to the good. But for those agriculturalists who intended to stay put, large black families were a recipe for economic disaster. Returning to Mount Vernon after years of campaigning, George Washington discovered he had "more working Negros by a full moiety, than can be employed to any advantage in the farming system." The export market for tobacco plummeted during the war and remained low throughout the 1780s. As was the case in Maryland, Virginia planters shifted toward cereal crops. For small farmers in search of extra hands during harvest season, the former slaves who freed themselves during the war provided ready labor. If a war-torn state and an economy in transition were often the prelude in other parts of the Republic to an act mandating gradual emancipation, or at least to an easing in the legal codes that kept some Americans in chains, Virginia met that criterion.[18]

But what allowed Massachusetts masters to give up the fight in the wake of the Quok Walker decision was not merely a state increasingly tied to the demands of mercantile capitalism. Nor was it even a decade or more of liberty's rhetoric. It was the minuscule number of bondpeople within Massachusetts. In Virginia, by comparison, enslaved blacks *were* the state's working class. The Caldwell brothers befriended self-styled "yeoman" Walker because they recognized him as just that, a fellow tiller of the soil. By comparison, the great Chesapeake planters described themselves as "farmers," but these gentlemen agriculturalists never expressed the smallest desire to pick up a hoe. If an insignificant slave population was the third ingredient necessary for radical reform, that element was much missing in Virginia. "Virginia republicans had the decency to be disturbed by the apparent inconsistency of what they were doing," observes historian Edmund Morgan. "But they were far more disturbed by the prospect" of releasing more than a quarter million laborers. Perhaps the simple truth is that Massachusetts got off easy; progressive reform always came easiest when it picked nobody's pocket.[19]

Guilt enough could be found. The enlightened spirit of the age reminded Virginia Patriots that their Creator—to borrow the word commonly embraced by deists—endowed their black property with the same inalienable rights they claimed for themselves. Even as they publicly denounced Dunmore as an enemy to peace, they conceded the justice of his liberation. Since planters had spent the past two decades comparing their political enslavement at the hands of King George to the enslavement of Africans in Virginia, they could not ignore the implications of their rhetoric. One year after the ratification of the peace treaty, Richard Henry Lee admitted that "both reason & experience" indicated that slavery was "the greatest [of] human evils."[20]

If Virginia's black population hardly mirrored that of Pennsylvania, neither ideas nor pamphlets respected state boundaries. Thanks to the Quaker Robert Pleasants, Patrick Henry obtained and read a copy of Benezet's denunciation of the slave trade. In a confession as tortured as any produced by the Revolutionary gentry, Henry admitted that he could not "justify" his earlier purchase of slaves. An anonymous essayist, writing just before the Peace of Paris, was less equivocal. "Whilst we are spilling our blood and exhausting our treasure in defense of our own liberty," he wrote in the *Virginia Gazette*, "it would not perhaps be amiss to turn our eyes toward those of our fellow men who are now in bondage under us." Well aware of the recent act of emancipation in Pennsylvania but critical of gradualism, the writer feared "divine retribution" should Virginia fail to act immediately, and wondered, with the truce not yet finalized, "how can we expect [God] will decide in our favor?"[21]

Indicative of the intellectual confusion then reigning among Virginia's planters was the case of Billey, the domestic servant of James Madison. Billey resided with his master for four years in Philadelphia, and when in 1783 Madison returned south, he decided to reward his servant by selling him to a Pennsylvanian so that Billey could become free after six years. As a devout republican, Madison had come to understand that Billey too "covet[ed] that liberty for which we have paid the price of so much blood, and have proclaimed so often to be right, and worthy the pursuit, of every human being." Yet there was more to the story than merely Madison's growing awareness of his own hypocrisy. After so many years among Philadelphia's free blacks, Madison judged Billey to be "too thoroughly tainted" by freedom "to be a fit companion for fellow slaves in Virginia." In short, Madison's liberality was tempered by fears of what stories Billey might spread in the quarters. Nor did the Virginian see fit to simply free Billey by leaving him in Philadelphia; by selling him to another master, Madison was able to flatter himself a humanitarian even while turning a small profit.[22]

If there was one consistency for men such as Madison and Henry, it could be found in their steadfast refusal to openly address the issue or to examine their own motives. For an otherwise enlightened generation who questioned every topic imaginable, the disinclination of these brilliant statesmen to confront their irresolute course baffled northern reformers. Even if the antislavery moment in Virginia was of short duration, as many scholars suspect, the admissions that slavery was, to borrow Henry's term, an "Abominable Practice" were undoubtedly sincere. But acting on these confessions and liberating hundreds of bondpeople, as opposed to the occasional Billey, was quite another matter. Many masters assuaged their guilty consciences with the conviction that the very progress of the age might somehow magically eradicate the stain of slavery. "I believe a time will come when an opportunity will be offered to abolish this lamentable evil," Henry hoped, and Jefferson agreed: "[T]he hour of emancipation is advancing, in the march of time." For gentlemen who could not imagine plowing their own fields or, as in the case of George Washington, combing their hair without the assistance of a bondman, the belief that time would fix what they chose not to came as welcome delusion.[23]

To the extent that Virginia planters ever thought deeply about the matter, they unanimously concluded—as had generations before them—that if Africans and their descendants were endowed with natural rights, they were also sure to misuse them if given the chance. Long before the war's end, George Mason, that most antislavery of Virginia slaveholders, warned Jefferson that emancipation should only follow a statewide program of grammar schools for young bondmen. "If they were not educated before being freed the first use they would make of their liberty would be loafing," he concluded. Once again, Jefferson agreed. Like Mason, he never considered the possibility that freedpeople might work harder if they were working for themselves. "A black, after hard labour through the day, will be induced by the slightest amusements to sit up till midnight, or later, though knowing he must be out with the first dawn of the morning." Given their belief in black inferiority, Virginia's planter class was, as historian Robert McColley has aptly observed, "in the peculiar position of repeatedly describing an evil and then proceeding to insist that nothing could be done about it."[24]

Planters possessed a near monopoly on political clout, but activists outside the halls of power tried to make the Revolution a truly radical affair. Among those most disinclined to pass the question of unfree labor on to the next generation were Quakers Warner Mifflin and Robert Pleasants. In the years immediately preceding the war, Virginia's Quakers were much like their brethren in Pennsylvania or New Jersey: theologically opposed to the sin of slavery but often reluctant to manumit their few bondpeople. But after much prayer, during which God demanded "greater vigilance [against] sin," Mifflin not only freed his slaves but persuaded his father to do so as well. The stirring words of Jefferson's Declaration encouraged him to move beyond his immediate family, and after speaking at his local meeting he succeeded in convincing "most of our members" to liberate their slaves. Because they did so in violation of Virginia's 1723 statute that banned private manumission, Quakers began to pepper the assembly with petitions demanding the state validate these manumissions. Quakers such as Mifflin represented few Virginians, yet their stubborn determination to uphold "the great principle, that freedom is the natural rights [sic] of all mankind" gave them influence beyond their numbers; perhaps three out of four members of Virginia's Society for Promoting the Abolition of Slavery were Quakers.[25]

Larger in number if somewhat less resolute in practice was Virginia's Methodist community. Although the denomination's abolitionist phase barely outlasted the 1780s, a number of Methodist ministers responded to Revolutionary ideals by liberating their domestic slaves, witnessing deeds of manumission, and preaching antislavery sermons from the pulpit. The Reverend Edward Mitchell hailed from a prominent family and inherited fourteen slaves. Upon gaining his birthright, he liberated them at once, stating simply that "it is contrary to the Principals of Christianity to hold our Fellow Creatures in Bondage." Other ministers tried to recruit leading planters—such as George Washington—to publicly endorse their crusade, and when that failed they turned to petition. The "ever Memorable Revolution can be justified on no other principles but what do plead with greater force for the Emancipation of our slaves," read one 1785 petition to the legislature. James Madison assured Washington that the petition was promptly tabled with "much indignation."[26]

Some young bondpeople celebrated the success of the Revolution by liberating themselves. Twenty-four-year-old Peter, once a slave near the Great Bridge in Norfolk County—which meant he surely knew of the fight black Loyalists had waged there—was spotted in North Carolina, "where he passed for a freeman." The equally "brazen and impudent" Sukey, who could "wash, iron, and cook," quit her owner's home for "some town," where she would "attempt to pass for a free wench." Young Prince of Richmond, who decided that his skill at weaving rope might earn him a position in a free port, armed himself with his master's "brass barreled holster pistol," which he threatened to use when briefly captured by a suspicious white in Elizabeth City. As had been the pattern before the war, most of those who stole themselves possessed a marketable skill. Few field hands appeared in the runaway advertisements. Most were like Francis, a "tailor by trade" who hoped to "get on board some vessel" and begin life anew with a decent wage, but perhaps the most determined was General, a tailor who vanished despite "having lost both his legs, cut off near the knees, which being defended by leather, serve him instead of feet."[27]

A few young men proved even more "brazen and impudent." When faced with white intransigence, some Virginia bondmen picked up weapons, as had their masters when they heard of the battles at Lexington and Concord. One officer in Accomack County heard whispers in the spring of 1782 of "a conspiracy of tories, British and negroes," and four years later, another nervous planter informed Patrick Henry of a "dangerous insurrection" of the slaves in Cumberland County. The rumblings unnerved so many whites that one militia colonel found it impossible to stockpile muskets, since private individuals "secrete them and Say they will do it for their own Defence against insurrections of Slaves." If runaways in search of individual freedom served as a painful reminder that a truly egalitarian America had yet to be created, chattel who plotted for mass liberation forced state authorities into politically untenable positions. When John Tayloe's Billy was caught aiding the British army in 1781, he was "Indicted for Treason" and sentenced "to be hanged by the Neck untill Dead," a judgment that implied Billy was a citizen and a political being. In fact, under Virginia law the "said Slave Billy" was just a piece of moveable property officially lacking in free will.[28]

Faced with these legal contradictions, the Virginia government slowly lurched toward reform, but in a curiously contradictory fashion indicative of a region burdened by a huge number of slaves. When George Mason proposed his Declaration of Rights in 1776, delegates to the Virginia Convention objected to his statement that "all men are by nature equally free and independent" on the grounds that it might lay the basis for black citizenship. Robert Carter Nicholas wondered how a fellow slaveholder could write that blacks deserved any "inherent rights," and Edmund Randolph argued that "slaves not being constituent members of our society could never pretend to any benefit from such a maxim." At length, the Declaration was saved when Edmund Pendleton modified the offending clause by adding the words "when they enter into a state of society," since none of the delegates believed their slaves to be part of the social contract. From the moment of its inception, Virginia pursued a path of quiet progressive reform followed by a conservative counterresponse.[29]

One year later, the General Assembly banned the further introduction of African slaves into the state. In a bill drafted by Thomas Jefferson, the law "exempted from all Slavery or Bondage" any slave brought into Virginia, even those born in the colonies and imported from another state. This rather bold pronouncement, however, was balanced by the clause that clarified the status of runaways from other states, since no slave "absconding" from neighboring masters would become free upon entering Virginia. Even some white supporters of the law conceded that this ostensibly humanitarian act masked the fact that planters such as Jefferson and Mason had laborers enough. Reformers regarded the law as only the first of many progressive steps toward emancipation, but the fact that Virginians could still sell their surplus workers within the state—at artificially inflated prices—raised suspicions that the act was hardly inspired by antislavery sentiments.[30]

Even more revealing were two laws passed in 1779. As the war dragged on, the always cash-poor planter class found itself unable to pay the necessary wartime taxes, which traditionally fell on land. Particularly given the chaos that reigned across the countryside, the assembly was unable to obtain consistent assessments and instead levied a £5 poll tax "for all negro and mulatto servants and slaves." Here, at least, was a financial disincentive to own other Virginians as chattel. But within two months, the legislature raided the increased treasury to compensate state residents for any "Loss or Damage" caused by invading British forces. Drafted, ironically, by George Mason, the statute did not specifically mention property in slaves, but it did include any possessions burned, destroyed, or carried away from "helpless Individuals, contrary to the principles of Humanity." As Richard Henry Lee indicated in 1781, all "unfortunate owners" of slaves should receive £5 from "the public treasury for each" runaway. In short, the legislature imposed a poll tax on slaves, but used those funds to compensate masters who had lost "the negroes now with the enemy."[31]

Perhaps no greater indication of the assembly's haphazard course exists than its 1780 bill to enhance the size of the state's beleaguered militia. Facing the threat of a new invasion with declining recruits, the legislature voted to grant every new militiaman who promised to serve for the duration of the war a bonus of £60 in hard currency or 300 acres of western land together with "a healthy, sound Negro" between the ages of ten and thirty. These chattel bonuses were to be seized from planters who owned more than twenty slaves, and the planters, in turn, would be compensated over an eight-year period. To the extent that the bill hoped to enlist farm boys who regarded slave labor as the path to prosperity, the statute served to spread the plantation system westward and increase the percentage of whites who owned bondpeople. At about the same time, the assembly passed a second law exempting the "distressed bretheren" of South Carolina and Georgia from the law of 1777, so that white refugees from the lower states could "bring their Slaves" into Virginia. "Thus amidst many mistakes some good has been done," a pleased Richard Henry Lee reported.[32]

But other sorts of petitions arrived on the desks of assemblymen, not all of them submitted by "distressed" planter refugees from the Carolina lowcountry. One request arrived from George, the domestic slave of the deceased John Thornton. He had "received repeated assurances from his late master that he would set him free at his death," but now George discovered that the statute of 1705 banning private manumissions without the consent of the government stood in the way of his liberty. George prayed that a reform "act may pass for that purpose." The petition was properly obsequious in tone and was accompanied by testimonials from Thornton's children testifying to their father's desire to free George. The humble domestic, of course, was precisely the sort of loyal retainer freed by private manumission in other parts of the Chesapeake, and so the House of Delegates sent the matter to committee with instructions to consider George's request.[33]

The resulting law of May 1782, An Act to Authorize the Manumission of Slaves, laid the groundwork for George's manumission. Yet to an extent, the law reflected the emphasis on personal liberties so central to the age of revolution as much as it revealed any growing liberality toward black Virginians. The same generosity of spirit—as legislators saw it—that admitted white refugees and their human property into the state was inclined to allow John Thornton's children to honor their father's dying words to a faithful manservant. Unlike the manumission acts passed by Pennsylvania and New York that eventually *forced* masters to free their slaves, Virginia's reform merely *permitted* any white so inclined, "by his or her last will and testament, or by any other instrument in writing," to "emancipate or set free, his or her slaves." Had George's new owners wished to retain him as their bondman, his petition and others like it never would have gone to committee, which suggests that the 1782 statute was ultimately about the rights of white citizens to dispose of their property as they saw fit.[34]

Virginia's inability to achieve a political consensus regarding the future of slavery was revealed in three more laws, two of them passed in 1783. The first pertained to slaves who had served in the state militia. As manpower reserves declined, Virginia authorities had been willing to look the other way when masters misrepresented their bondmen as free men so that they might serve as substitutes. With the return of peace, more than a few owners planned to renege on promises of freedom in return for military service. Planter-legislators angrily denounced this as "contrary to the principles of justice," though the statute they passed liberating all bondmen who had served in the state militia affected but a small number of slaves. Nor did their desire to reward black Patriots stop the assembly from punishing the human property of white Loyalists when in 1783 it authorized their "public" sale, as well as the auction of bondpeople purchased by the state during the war as manual laborers in military support services. But then, shifting direction yet again, in 1787 the state made it a capital crime to knowingly sell a freedperson back into slavery.[35]

Having taken these steps, why did Virginia not go further at that time and consider gradual emancipation, especially since to the north, statutes facilitating individual manumissions typically preceded laws for statewide abolition? In 1776, when Jefferson served on a committee with George Wythe and Edmund Pendleton to revise the state's antiquated criminal code, he allegedly devised a plan for gradual emancipation. A decade later, Jefferson insisted that although he had never prepared an actual statute, he had crafted "an amendment" for statewide manumission "to be offered to the legislature whenever" the package of revisions "should be taken up." But did such an amendment really exist? Other revisions to the criminal code rendered slave law harsher than before, such as a new prohibition against slaves testifying in court against whites. If Jefferson prepared such a detailed plan, it was never brought before the legislature when the assembly debated the proposed revisions. In fact, several of Jefferson's proposed revisions regarding slave law were rejected by the assembly, not because they were too progressive but because they were exceptionally restrictive.[36]

What is beyond dispute, however, is that Jefferson devised a plan for gradual emancipation sometime in 1783 when, he later claimed, it appeared that Virginia was preparing to craft a new state constitution. Even then, he showed his proposal to few if any legislators. The unfinished document fleshed out what he insisted in his *Notes on the State of Virginia* was his 1776 proposal, under which young slaves "should continue with their parents" until "the females should be eighteen, and the males twenty-one years of age, when they should be colonized" outside of the United States. According to the draft constitution, only those slaves born after December 31, 1800, would be covered. This meant that Virginia's already large slave population was to increase for another seventeen years, although deferring freedom until a later date was typical of northern manumission laws as well.[37]

What set Jefferson's plan apart from northern bills for gradual emancipation was the stipulation that black Virginians, once freed, be forcibly removed and shipped back to the lands of their ancestors. Jefferson's plan to colonize freed young men and women away from their still-enslaved parents raised few eyebrows in a society that habitually separated enslaved relations through sale. But what doomed Jefferson's scheme was the problematic detail that he intended to strip the state of its principal laboring class. Jefferson reasoned that white Virginians, who could not imagine residing in a state inhabited by what in 1800 would be twenty thousand freedpeople, might never liberate their slaves if that meant "a compleat incorporation of the latter into" civil society. Left unsaid was who would till the lands once African Americans were removed, or how many planter-politicians would embrace a scheme that sought to deny them field hands. Moreover, one of the most popular features of Pennsylvania's gradual emancipation statute was that it cost the state nothing, but Jefferson's plan burdened his always tax-poor state with decades of deportation and settlement costs. As the duc de La Rochefoucauld-Liancourt astutely observed when visiting Virginia in 1796, Jefferson saw "so many difficulties in their emancipation, even postponed, [and] he adds so many conditions to render it practicable, that it is thus reduced to the impossible."[38]

According to one celebrated historian, Jefferson and Madison "ardently desired" gradual emancipation, but if so, these two supremely influential statesmen had little to show for their efforts. Instead, it fell to individual slaveholders who took advantage of the 1782 law to liberate approximately ten thousand black Virginians in the years prior to 1806. Although unfree labor was not set on the road to extinction in Virginia, the number of bondpeople voluntarily manumitted was just slightly less than the number liberated through gradual emancipation in New Jersey and greater than the number freed in Connecticut and Rhode Island combined. As the historian Eva Sheppard Wolf observes, the manumission deeds filed in Virginia in the decade after the war "were impressive for the radical sentiments they evinced" when it came to "feelings of fellowship between blacks and whites, which contrasted sharply with Virginia's codified separation of the races." James and Matilda Ashby, for example, liberated their slaves Peter, Parris, and Pleasant after acknowledging that "freedom from a state of Slavery [was] the natural & proper right of the black people as well as white." It was God's "wish that the Black People should be free as well as the White people in society," declared another manumitter. At a time when Virginia's leading intellectuals advanced racially based excuses for inaction and schemes for the wholesale removal of freedpeople, these simple testimonials to egalitarian brotherhood serve as a reminder that at least some Virginia whites "ardently desired" black freedom.[39]

Factors other than Revolutionary ideals also shaped the pattern of manumissions. During the 1780s, manumitters disproportionately tended to be Quakers, Methodists, and Baptists. Older Tidewater counties, where the soil was damaged by tobacco production, were more likely to foster manumissions than the fresh lands of the frontier. Urban masters were also more inclined to free individual slaves than were rural slaveowners, although towns and cities tended to reverse gender trends. That is, in the countryside, men were slightly more likely to be manumitted than were women. But in urban areas, just more than half of those freed were women. Urban slaves, of course, enjoyed the opportunity to hire their time away from their masters, and female domestics and laundresses earned small amounts of cash from white neighbors, which they used eventually to purchase their freedom. Perhaps also the close proximity of slave to master (and especially mistress) within urban households allowed for greater bonds of friendship and affection than typically found on large estates. Diana Hoggard of Norfolk freed her domestic Judy as recompense "for many faithful services rendered," a phrase used also by Nancy Cox to explain her manumission of Jemima. Manumitted men tended to be slightly older than women—on average 26.8 years compared to 25.1 years—but both sexes were young enough to disprove the myth that masters freed only aged bondpeople no longer capable of productive labor.[40]

None of this is to imply that black Virginians waited passively for their masters to free them. Many bondpeople, as was the case with Absalom Jones, scrounged for paid labor during their off hours in hopes of buying their own bodies, which typically took years. Francis Drake was hardly unique.

He saved for years to buy his liberty, and then he saved for another four before he had money enough to purchase his daughter Catherine and his son. Jerry, who lived in Alexandria, promised his owner "four more years" of diligent labor while he hired out portions of his day to a white neighbor in hopes of raising the agreed-upon fee. Masters, of course, were under no obligation to liberate their slaves no matter how much cash they had put aside, and so whites who did so were probably more accepting of Revolutionary ideals than their planter brethren, if every bit as penurious. In Norfolk, at least 39 percent of manumissions were the result of self-purchase, a transaction that concluded with money changing hands in exchange for a legal deed of freedom. Slave societies were filled with contradictions, but few were greater than the fact that human chattel, as legal nonpersons, became party to the sort of transaction allowed only to free citizens. This incongruity led masters like George Herdon to quit-claim his three slaves' "*persons* as well as their *Services* and estate[s]" and Enock Foley to sell Fanny to herself by releasing "his controul" over her.[41]

So too did the language of manumissions change over time. If manumission deeds witnessed just after the war spoke in the language of egalitarianism, by the 1790s private emancipations tended to be granted, or sold, as a reward for years of loyal behavior, or even in exchange for promises of a specified term of intense labor (since unwaged labor had no other positive incentives to spur hard work). By liberating only those men and women who had demonstrated unusual fealty to their masters, these manumissions actually reinforced Virginia's caste system, since it taught young slaves that the ultimate path to freedom was obedience. Some masters even went so far as to let it be known that, provided their slaves behaved, they planned to free them in their wills. By comparison to whites troubled by their Christian consciences or by the Revolutionary spirit of the age, masters who waited until they were six feet underground to free their bondpeople were hardly eloquent critics of the system.[42]

Yet in one celebrated instance, one of the wealthiest planters in the state chose to fulfill the promise of the Revolution by steadily manumitting all of his 452 bondpeople. Robert Carter, scion of one of the oldest families in the state, determined upon an "immediate but a Gradual Emancipation," in which he would free at least fifteen slaves every January 1. After carefully drawing up a list of his bondpeople, their quarters, and their ages, he decided to first liberate "the Oldest of my Slaves," while all "Male and Female Slaves" below "the Ages of 21 and 18 Years" were to be automatically freed when they reached those ages. Although many planters who liberated their entire labor force in their wills had no children to pass their estates on to, Carter had several sons and heirs. More unusual yet was the fact that Carter encouraged his former bondpeople to remain in his employ as free wage laborers. Gloucester Billy, who had sailed Carter's tobacco down the Chesapeake aboard the *Betty*, continued to do so, but now he drew wages. Carter even rebuffed complaints from his white neighbors that his lands were becoming havens for runaways. When Mary Lane wrote to ask for Carter's assistance in finding a missing slave, he bluntly refused: "I cannot consistantly furnish Means to continue a practice manifestly Oppressive to Mistresses & Slaves."[43]

Both Madison and Jefferson professed to favor emancipation, but they refused to consider the possibility that black and white Virginians could continue to live side by side as free people. "Deep rooted prejudices entertained by the whites [and] ten thousand recollections, by the blacks" prohibited peaceful coexistence, Jefferson famously insisted. Interracial harmony was "rendered impossible by the prejudices of the Whites," James Madison added, "prejudices which proceeding principally from the differences of colour must be considered as permanent." By comparison, Carter not only evicted white tenants he regarded as lazy but also rented out his lands to former bondmen. In August 1792 he instructed his overseer to "dispossess" one "Mr. Holcomb" and replace him with "Negroes Jo[seph] Reid & Anthony Harris" as the "occupiers of the aforesaid Tenement." During the following year, he rented farms to two former bondmen, Prince Johnston and Samuel Harrison, allowed their still-enslaved children to reside with them, loaned them poultry and milk cows, and offered them tasks that allowed them to pay their year's rent after several weeks of work. So pleased was Carter with his experiment in free wage labor that he began to began to liberate his remaining slaves well ahead of schedule.[44]

Few planters followed Carter's lead. Yet the number of free blacks in Virginia mushroomed in the two decades after Yorktown. The 1790 census revealed that the number of freedpeople had surged to 12,766 (or 4.2 percent of all blacks), and that figure more than doubled to 30,570 (or 7.2 percent) by 1810. As a proportion of the black population, freed Virginians were a smaller percentage than in the northern states, but in real numbers, more than half of all free black Americans lived in the upper South. The rise of this free black caste did not indicate that most planters envisioned an end to slavery, but for white reformers and freed black activists, the relative harmony found on Carter's farms proved that a republic of free citizens might yet be achieved in their lifetime.[45]

The census of 1790, it appears, inspired some would-be abolitionists to again push for a statewide plan for emancipation. As New Yorkers once again took up legislation for gradual manumission, they provided an impetus for like-minded emancipators elsewhere to press for plans in their own states. Among those inspired to pick up the pen was planter and slave-holder Fernando Fairfax, a northern Virginian familiar with Jefferson's dream of emancipation and colonization from his recently published *Notes on the State of Virginia* as well as an unpublished 1775 proposal for compensated emancipation drafted by Levi Hart of Connecticut and widely circulated within reform circles. In December 1790, Fairfax published his "Plan for Liberating the Negroes within the United States" in the *American Museum*, a leading Philadelphia journal, in hopes of reaching a national audience. Like Jefferson, Fairfax believed that gradual emancipation could only be accomplished through removal. Former "prejudices, sentiments, or whatever they may be called," Fairfax worried, "would be found to operate so powerfully as to be insurmountable." Black men had a "natural right" to be freed, but if allowed to remain in the United States, they might also wish "the privilege of intermarriage with the white inhabitants."[46]

Sometimes the chief virtue of a poor idea is that it leads to a better one. Congress took no action on Fairfax's proposal, but one of its readers was St. George Tucker. Although married into one of Virginia's prominent families, Tucker derived his principal living not from the land or politics but from teaching law at the College of William and Mary while serving as judge on the state's general court, two sinecures that allowed him to speak his mind regarding slavery more freely than men who had to run for public office. Like many upper-class Virginians, Tucker harbored suspicions as to the "marked physical and intellectual inferiority" of blacks, yet unlike many of his generation, he believed that eradicating slavery required more than eloquent denunciations buried within private correspondence. Well aware that slavery was collapsing in the North, the professor decided that research was in order. He took up his quill and wrote a long series of queries to Jeremy Belknap, one of Boston's leading Congregational ministers.[47]

Tucker's January 1795 missive contained the usual Virginia excuses for the continuing existence of slavery—that early-eighteenth-century colonists had attempted to limit the importation of Africans only to be stymied by "the influence of the [Royal] African Company in England"—yet there was no doubt where he stood on the question. "The introduction of slavery into this country is at this day considered among its greatest misfortunes by a very great majority," Tucker insisted. Understanding that "slavery has been wholly exterminated from" Massachusetts, he wondered how this had been accomplished, "whether by a general and simultaneous emancipation," or gradually "by declaring all persons born after a particular period free." Belknap circulated Tucker's eleven queries to a number of correspondents, among the most prescient of whom was James Sullivan. Hoping that Tucker might be persuaded to drop the standard condition of removal, Sullivan observed that the cost of mass colonization not only was far greater than any southern writer had estimated but exceeded even "more than the Treasury of the United States could possibly bear." Yet as Virginia was clearly not Massachusetts, gradual emancipation there "must be slow in its progress, and ages must be employed in the business."[48]

At length, Tucker agreed. Although Jefferson continued to think otherwise, Tucker conceded that "the difficulties and expence of an attempt to colonize 300,000 persons" rendered removal impractical. Armed with this data, Tucker drafted *A Dissertation on Slavery: With a Proposal for the Gradual Abolition of It, in the State of Virginia.* The pamphlet, published in Philadelphia in the summer of 1796, ran to more than one hundred pages. Although it was hardly the sort of proposal that would find much support in the free black community, it at least established a basis for discussion. Tucker suggested that every black woman born after "the adoption of the plan [should become] free" at the age of twenty-one. Any of her children, regardless of gender, born after that birthday, would be born free. All freed blacks were to "voluntarily [bind] themselves to service for a year before the first day of February annually," or it would be done for them by the overseers of the poor. No freed slaves could vote, hold office, or acquire "any estate in lands or tenements, other than a lease not exceeding twenty-one years." Neither could they bear arms, marry whites, serve as an attorney, or prepare a will.[49]

What made Tucker's plan different from previous Virginia plans for gradual emancipation was its specificity—down to what sort of blanket black women were to be granted at age twenty-one—and the fact that it did not require freedpeople to be colonized outside the nation's borders. Although Tucker hinted that some former slaves might be inclined to migrate into the Spanish colonies of Florida or Louisiana, forced emigration, Tucker insisted, was both cruel and financially impossible. His assumption was that most blacks would remain in Virginia as a landless and politically powerless agricultural working class. Financial concerns aside, this was a frank recognition that most planters would never permit an end to slavery unless they could retain their black labor force. In his proposal, Tucker emphasized, the "earth cannot want [black] cultivators." In short, his plan allowed the gentry to abolish slavery while retaining their class prerogatives.[50]

Tucker respectfully presented his plan to the General Assembly, where with little fanfare and even less discussion, *A Dissertation* was "ordered to lie on the table." A dejected Tucker forwarded copies to Jefferson and Madison, telling the former that he hoped the hostile "reception that it met with from some individuals" in the assembly was not indicative of "its merit." But the legislature's refusal to implement or even seriously consider Tucker's gradualist scheme was tantamount to a collective, if possibly unconscious, decision to retain slavery. Jefferson's noncommittal response was characteristic of both the man and his class. He hoped Tucker knew of his "subscription to [the pamphlet's] doctrines" but added that any "mode of emancipation" must be a "compromise between the passions, the prejudices, & the real difficulties which will each have their weight in that operation," as if Tucker's conservative plan was not all of those things.[51]

Although the assembly, despite occasional petitions to do so, exhibited no serious interest in repealing the 1782 statute for private manumissions, legislators increasingly found small ways to hinder the activities of antislavery activists. Some bondpeople, in imitation of Quok Walker, pursued freedom suits on various grounds, usually due to a deceased master's promise of eventual freedom not honored by the heirs. Such suits freed few slaves, but whites regarded them as a nuisance, and by the mid-1790s nearly thirty cases were pending in Virginia courts. In response, one assemblyman rose to denounce the "menacing" efforts of the Richmond and Alexandria antislavery societies. Another, worried about news from across the border, railed against the "impropriety" of Pennsylvania activists assisting Virginia bondpeople. Slaveholders lobbied the legislature to take action. "This Society," complained one, was "infusing into the slaves a spirit of insurrection and rebellion which might eventually destroy the tranquility of the state." In 1795, the General Assembly responded by banning organized antislavery societies from representing black claimants in court, and three years later they outlawed society members from sitting on juries that dealt with freedom suits. At about the same time, the Rhetorical Society of Richmond debated whether "the slaves in Virginia should [be] emancipated at present." Not much to anybody's surprise, the membership decided in the negative.[52]

Even less promising was the fact that the generation reaching adulthood in the two decades after Yorktown was more interested in rebuilding war-shattered estates than in fulfilling the Revolution's egalitarian legacy. For every Robert Carter, who was sixty-four years of age when he began to liberate his slaves, there were young men such as his own sons, who sought to overturn his deed. One even bought new slaves from Virginia traders while he freed Carter family slaves in compliance with his father's wishes. More tragic yet were the actions of self-proclaimed abolitionists. In December 1796, the same year in which he published his *Dissertation on Slavery*, St. George Tucker sold four of his slaves—a woman and her three daughters—to William Haxall, a Petersburg slave trader. Tucker had hoped to realize no less than £200 for the family, given "the high price of negroes at present." Haxall urged him to sell the four separately at public auction, but Tucker settled for less to keep the family together. Perhaps Tucker felt secure in the knowledge that the bondwoman would not have been covered by his gradualist scheme in any case.[53]

If anything, the Revolution strengthened slavery as much in western Virginia as it weakened it elsewhere in the Chesapeake. The end to British imperial restraints along the frontier allowed for the slave regime to move westward. Instead of freeing all or part of their surplus slaves, many young planters and petty slaveholders either carried their bondmen into the fresh lands due west of Virginia (which became the fifteenth state, Kentucky, in 1792) or sold them to those who planned to relocate. As elderly masters, freed from British laws of primogeniture (which bequeathed property intact to the eldest male), divided their holdings among their children, stable black communities and families were torn asunder. Jefferson sold or bestowed upon his family roughly 160 slaves between 1784 and 1794; like Tucker, he preferred to sell families as a unit but regarded the solvency of Monticello as the most important factor in any transaction. Planters always assured themselves that they sold their human chattel only out of financial necessity. Typical was David Meade, who lamented being "so unfortunate as to be under the necessity of selling Slaves," as if he were the true victim of the transaction.[54]

The expansion of slavery across the state and into eastern Kentucky helped to bring about a reformulation of the relationship between master and slave, as the harsh patriarchal ethos of the colonial era gave way to the ideal of paternalism. Planters unwilling to manumit their labor force increasingly soothed their scruples by emphasizing their responsibilities to their black retainers. "[L]et us treat the unhappy Victims with lenity," insisted Patrick Henry, as "it is the furthest advance we can make toward justice." As planters expanded their acreage or diversified into cereal crops, labor patterns, slaves' duties, and even hours spent in the fields became the subject of endless negotiations between white and black Virginians. Masters literally held the whip hand in this relationship, but bondpeople proved to be tenacious bargainers, demanding time on Sundays to work their own provision grounds or to earn a few dollars for extra labor. Wise masters learned not to drive their slaves too hard, especially the young men, since the result could be a slower pace of labor, an increase in runaways, or even open revolt. When overseer William Elson made too ready use of his whip, a handful of slaves struck back, "cut[ting] his throat from Ear to Ear with an Axe." But young rebels paid for such resistance with their lives, and most African Americans found safer ways to challenge their owners' authority.[55]

Scholars continue to debate precisely when paternalism appeared in the southern states, as well as what factors allowed for its maturation. Some point to the end of North America's involvement in the Atlantic slave trade in 1808 and the emergence of a wholly creole slave population with no memory of freedom in Africa and few hopes of liberation in the United States, a phenomenon already present in Virginia with its large native-born slave class. Others attribute the evolution of ruthless patriarchalism into paternalism to the moderating influence of evangelical Christianity, while yet other historians regard it as only a pose adopted by planters to disguise the cruelty of their regime. If Chesapeake slavery became somewhat less harsh in the decades after the war, it was because planters wished to make it more permanent and create a stable slave society. In the process, masters increasingly adopted the excuse that maintaining unfree labor was their responsibility to those who lived on their lands and under their care. As was so often the case, Jefferson put it best: "To give liberty to, or rather, to abandon persons whose habits have been formed in slavery is like abandoning children."[56]

Virginia's intellectual elite was less willing to concede that their ownership of slaves helped to produce a sense of social equality among whites. So long as black Virginians, even if freed, remained a politically degraded caste, the poorest white man could feel superior based upon his allegedly superior pigmentation. As British diplomat Augustus John Foster observed, artificial social distinctions remained far greater in the postwar North than in the southern states. Virginia slaveholders, he concluded, "can profess an unbounded love of liberty and democracy in consequence of the mass of the people, who in other countries might become mobs, being there nearly altogether composed of their own Negro slaves." To the modern eye, slavery and liberalism appear a glaring contradiction, but in the context of early national Virginia, the former helped to foster the latter. In Massachusetts, John Adams fretted about the common man, who like Daniel Shays rose in rebellion against hard times, but Virginian paternalists, as the historian Edmund Morgan wrote, could outdo New England in their republicanism "because they had solved the problem: they had achieved a society in which most of the poor were enslaved."[57]

How should posterity judge the American Revolution in the state of Virginia, home to statesmen-philosophers, the state of origin of drafters of both local and national declarations, domicile of four of the first five presidents, and, perhaps not coincidentally, home of the largest number of enslaved Americans in the postwar period? According to historian Gordon Wood, the imperial divorce may not have brought about social equality, but its principles laid the groundwork for the "anti-slavery and women's rights movements of the nineteenth century." The founding generation liberated but a few slaves, yet their ideals "set in motion ideological forces that [ultimately] doomed the institution of slavery" and "led inexorably to the Civil War." But would Absalom Jones agree? Was freedom for the few, often purchased after decades of toil, enough to characterize the American Revolution as revolutionary? As Alfred F. Young has argued, the question is not what later generations accomplished but what those who dubbed themselves Patriots achieved. "[O]ne could argue as easily that the failure of the Revolutionary generation to destroy slavery made the Civil War inevitable," Young observes.[58]

One Revolutionary figure who decided to practice what he preached was the aged George Washington, but not easily and not in a way that persuaded others to follow his lead. Despite his experiences during the war, when he both led black militiamen into battle and faced the fire of black Loyalists, the squire of Mount Vernon found it difficult to cut his ties to unfree labor. But as William Lee's saga attests, as the general reached the end of his life, he decided to act independently. In his final will, dated July 1799, Washington quietly freed all of the slaves he owned outright upon his death. (He was unable to liberate Martha's slaves, in part because they technically belonged to her first husband's estate and had to be passed down to his descendants, but also because Martha evidently did not share Washington's increasingly antislavery sentiments.) Whereas his neighbor Fairfax thought it impractical to allow freedpeople to remain in Virginia, Washington stipulated that his aged slaves be "comfortably clothed and fed" by his heirs, and he created an apprenticeship system so that his younger field hands might be "brought up to some useful occupation."[59]

Admirable though that was, did he, and did his generation, do enough? Washington was no Robert Carter, heir to a vast fortune but politically obscure. Known even then as "the sword of the Revolution," the statesman who walked away from power by declining a third presidential term was the most revered man of his generation. Yet it is hard not to conclude that when it came to potentially unpopular antislavery crusades, Washington simply lost his courage. "Some petitions were presented to the Assembly, at its last Session, for the abolition of slavery," he confided to Lafayette, "but they could scarcely obtain a reading." How might events have turned out differently had Washington publicly endorsed those petitions, or Tucker's gradualist plan? According to one biographer, "modern-day moralists" regret that he failed to do so, but so too did several hundred thousand black Virginians. The theory that nothing was done about slavery in Virginia because nothing could have been done is a circular argument that is most often advanced, as the historian Gary Nash has noted, by scholars "eager to excuse mistakes and virtually never by those writers on behalf of victims of the mistakes."[60]

Are such condemnations "thoroughly ahistorical and presentistic," as one biographer has charged? Are critics of the Founders applying "our own superior standards of political and racial justice" to an earlier time? If this debate is simply reduced to a political equation, so the desires of disenfranchised black Americans are not taken into consideration, there were still a large number of Quakers, urban artisans, and nonslaveholding small farmers who favored emancipation. Absalom Jones was typical of those blacks in the Chesapeake who became free in that his liberation resulted not from state action or white liberality but from his own hard work and determination. Perhaps the final word on this should go not to a twenty-first-century historian but rather to a contemporaneous voice. "[F]rom the mouth to the head of the Chesapeake, the bulk of the people will approve" of abolishing slavery, one wrote, "and it will find a respectable minority ready to adopt it in practice," an elite "minority which for weight and worth of character preponderates against the great number, who have not the courage to divest their families and property." Perhaps watching as these elegant words were penned was the slave Richard, a cup of hot tea in hand.[61]

SIX

Captain Vesey's Cargo
Continuity in Georgia and the Carolinas

BORN IN THE OLD PORT TOWN of Warwick in the British colony of Bermuda, Joseph Vesey was thirty-four years of age when in the fall of 1781 he first laid eyes on the boy he would later rename Telemaque. Since 1767 Vesey had sailed the Caribbean, mostly in the employ of Joseph Darrell, a wealthy South Carolina merchant, providing rice, wine, and Africans for Charles Town. Vesey first visited the city in July 1770, and in 1774 he invested his earnings in a plot of land that ran from Canal Street to Round O Road. By then he had been promoted to the post of master, and he proudly named his new property "Capt. Vesey's Avenue."[1]

By the coming of the Revolution, Vesey thought himself enough a Carolinian to side with the Patriots. The British naval blockade of the North Atlantic coast served both to shut down Joseph Darrell's trading company and to draw Captain Vesey into the conflict. In the fall of 1775, William Drayton, the chief member of the Secret Committee of Five (a group executive created to govern the colony), ordered Vesey to take a detachment of troops and cruise the coast "to the northward of Charles-Town bar, in order to speak with and warn all vessels" that British warships guarded the harbor's entrance. Because Vesey enjoyed nearly a decade's experience running rum and slaves up South Carolina rivers, the young captain was especially suited to guide Patriot shipping "to some other port or inlet in this colony."[2]

The Revolution proved to be lucrative for Captain Vesey. As a privateer and the master of the armed pilot boat *Hawke*, Vesey was entitled to the lion's share of what he could drag into southern ports. In early 1776, Vesey's crew bested a British brigantine in Mediterranean waters and hauled their captured prize all the way back to the Stono River. By the fall of 1778, Vesey received a new letter of marque in Annapolis, Maryland, authorizing the crew of his newest ship, the sloop *Adriana*, to plunder British shipping in the name of the Republic. Evidently, Vesey's earlier prizes had paid handsomely. Not merely was he listed as master of the *Adriana*, but he posted the $5,000 bond as well. Together with the Charles Town firm of North and Trescott, he claimed part ownership of the fifteen-gun sloop.[3]

As the war dragged on into the early 1780s, Vesey began to contemplate a return to his former profession. When his home port of Charles Town was occupied by the British in May 1780, Vesey decided that supplying the Caribbean with Africans would turn as handy a profit as plundering British shipping, and at far less risk to his ship and crew. The French entrance into the Revolutionary conflict meant that Continental slavers were diverted to war use and so were incapable of meeting the insatiable demand for laborers in the French sugar colony of Saint-Domingue. In the fall of 1781, the *Prospect* docked near the fort at Charlotte Amalie in the Danish colony of St. Thomas. There Vesey purchased a cargo of 390 slaves for resale at the French port of Cap François. Among the slaves was a handsome boy of Coromantee descent, whom the captain guessed to be "about 14 years old." Impressed by the youth's "beauty, alertness and intelligence," Vesey retained the slave as a cabin boy and, befitting his new status, gave him a new name as well: Telemachus, or Telemaque, the wandering son of Odysseus and Penelope.[4]

Following the signing of the preliminary peace treaty in late 1782, British forces prepared to evacuate still-occupied Charles Town. On December 14, the British flotilla sailed out of South Carolina's main harbor; shortly thereafter, Captain Vesey and the boy, now roughly sixteen years old, alighted on Charleston's docks (as it was rechristened in an attempt to disguise its kingly origins). For the next seventeen years, Telemaque labored as Vesey's manservant, helping to run his home at 281 King Street as well as his business office on East Bay. On occasion, it was Telemaque's unhappy task to appear at the docks to sign in the captain's human cargo, such as Vesey's 1786 consignment of "sundry non-Enumerated Goods" from Bermuda, which included four adult "wench[es] and Child at the Breast." Telemaque's responsibilities, together with the long days spent in a predominantly white household, forced him to speak English, and since the captain's business would suffer if left in the hands of an unlettered servant, Vesey taught the young man to read as well.[5]

If the young domestic led an unusually privileged life for a South Carolina slave, in other ways he was typical of the roughly 86,000 blacks who would be sold into Georgia and the Carolina lowcountry in the twenty-five-year period before the United States ceased its involvement in the Atlantic slave trade. If proposals for gradual emancipation were already well under way in the northern states, the impact of the American Revolution on the lower states—where the percentage of slaves was long the highest and the number of black Loyalist refugees by far the greatest—was just the reverse. In the Chesapeake, planters such as George Washington fretted about declining tobacco prices and calculated the costs of maintaining too great an unwaged labor force. But agriculturalists in the lower South planned to rebuild their shattered plantation empires by importing thousands of young men like Telemaque. As one planter put it bluntly: "South Carolina and Georgia cannot do without slaves."[6]

————

Captain Vesey's adopted home on the South Carolina coast was a forlorn city at war's end, as was most of the southern lowcountry from Norfolk to Savannah. No county that offered an easy landing for British forces escaped the fighting unscathed. But to the extent that the Revolution in Georgia and the Carolinas collapsed into a triangular conflict, in which South Carolina's black majority either openly sided with the British or used the chaos of war to escape their bonds, the warfare south of Norfolk was especially ruinous. Guerrilla raiders destroyed bridges, burned public buildings, and razed warehouses, all of which were critical for the resumption of commerce and travel. White Patriots returning to the region reacted to the devastation with stunned horror. Georgia was "almost overrin by a handfull of Men" who "ravaged the Country," reported Rawlins Lowndes, "carrying with them a great Quantity of Cattle and other Stock—and many Negroes." Another reported that Georgia was stripped of "all her Cattle, Horses and other live Stock" necessary for getting the next season's crops into the ground. John Lewis Gervais returned to his South Carolina plantation in February 1783 to discover that the "British have carried off all my Negroes and they have either destroyed or carried off all my horses." Redcoats used Gervais's home as a battlefield hospital and burned his furniture for warmth, leaving him "nothing but the land which thank God they could not carry away."[7]

Central to all of these complaints was the endlessly repeated assertion that British officers had "carried off all [the] Negroes." So common was this allegation that South Carolina politicians even alluded to black infidelity in the state's first constitution of March 1776. Britain had "excited domestic insurrections—proclaimed freedom to servants and slaves, enticed or stolen them from, and armed them against their masters." Yet perceptive observers understood that the British invasion of the southern colonies was merely an opportunity for, not the cause of, black restiveness. When British forces landed in North Carolina, patrols searched "every Negro's house" in Wilmington for arms. Janet Shaw, an Englishwoman stranded in the state, recognized that most bondpeople were not loyal to King George; they simply wished to be free. "My hypothesis is," she observed, "that the Negroes will revolt" as soon as redcoats neared the town. Long familiar with the weapons of domination, the lowcountry's white minority responded with a new level of ferocity. "We keep taking [slaves] up," admitted Colonel John Simpson, "examining and scourging more or less every day." When Georgians discovered that several hundred black refugees from the Savannah area had congregated on Tybee Island, hoping to be evacuated by the Royal Navy, Colonel Stephen Bull recommended extreme measures. "If they cannot be taken," Bull suggested, it "is far better for the public and the owners" of the runaways for them simply to "be shot." Perhaps, Bull added, they could be murdered "by the Creek Indians," as that would create a useful "hatred or aversion between the Indians and negroes."[8]

Despite, or perhaps because of, such atrocities, black refugees continued to tramp down the roads toward Savannah, which remained occupied by British forces from 1778 through 1782. The exact number of bondpeople who reached British lines and were evacuated at war's end remains unclear, with Patriot estimates running as high as six thousand and British records suggesting a lower figure of thirty-five hundred. As the British retreat began, so many slaves reached their camps that the redcoats were forced to appropriate anything that floated. When naval vessels proved inadequate, Loyalists turned to private vessels, but even those ships were insufficient to ferry the refugee population to British Florida. As the teeming flotilla began to sail away from Savannah, "many Indians, refugees, and Negroes" paddled toward St. Augustine in canoes and rafts. Still other African Americans tried to reach Florida by wading through the coastal swamps. Perhaps as many as five thousand blacks fled the state, while a similar number perished from disease or combat during the war. Georgia's prewar black population of roughly fifteen thousand dropped by two-thirds within a decade.[9]

The number of slaves who escaped from South Carolina during the British evacuation was even greater. General Nathanael Greene estimated the state lost five thousand to six thousand blacks, but the number of slaves who were carried away by white Loyalists may exceed that figure. Quite possibly as many as ten thousand Africans and African Americans quit South Carolina during 1782. Planters in St. John Berkeley Parish returned home to discover that nearly 50 percent of their prewar labor force of fourteen hundred had fled. The Reverend Archibald Simpson, a slaveholding minister at the Independent Presbyterian Church, discovered that his estate near Stoney Creek had been occupied by both armies and several hundred refugees. In the wake of the conflict, the county was abandoned. "All was desolation," Simpson scratched into his diary, "and indeed all the way [back home] there was a gloomy solitariness." Every field and plantation he passed revealed "marks of ruin and devastation. Not a person was to be met with."[10]

As in Savannah, the desperate, chaotic evacuation of black and white refugees from Charleston defied precise accounting. The mass exodus from Charleston and the islands that lined its harbor lasted for three weeks, and there were so many small transport craft that British authorities despaired of keeping track. Most sailed for St. Augustine, though a small number scattered toward New York, Jamaica, and even Britain. During the four years from the British invasion of the southern colonies through the fall of 1782, South Carolina lost roughly twenty-five thousand slaves—nearly one-third of the former colony's black population—to death, disease, internal flight, and emigration. To the extent that South Carolina's black majority had been the colony's laboring class, the loss of so many slaves meant that the region faced a critical juncture in its history. But planters along the Ashley and Cooper rivers, unlike their brethren in Virginia, had never fretted about the large number of bondpeople in their midst. White Virginians were bothered enough by the egalitarian ideals of the Revolution to respond with their habitual inconsistency, but the lowcountry's planter class never doubted that the wisest response to the devastation of war was to rebuild their plantation empires.[11]

Three hundred miles down the coast from Charleston, the old Spanish fort at St. Augustine became the convenient, if temporary, asylum for Loyalists escaping the southern states. Having demanded East Florida—the peninsula and lands east of the Perdido River—as spoils of war in 1763, Britain was now obligated to return it to Spain under the provisions then being finalized in Paris. During the brief era of British control of East Florida, the plantation system along the St. Marys and St. Johns rivers expanded rapidly, with slaves working rice and sugar fields and orange groves. During most of the British interregnum, blacks had come to outnumber whites by two to one, but with the arrival of refugees from Georgia and the Carolinas, the ratio moved closer to three to one, a proportion the Spanish quickly sought to reverse.[12]

South Carolina had far longer experience in controlling its black majority. In the spring of 1783, just after Captain Vesey settled in Charleston, the legislature agreed to Andrew Pickens's request to raise a new company of rangers in hopes of eradicating backcountry guerrillas. Anticipating a lengthy campaign, the governor recommended purchasing additional ammunition for the militia units, but a year later, residents of Orangeburg continued to pepper the assembly with petitions demanding a special company of rangers to bring "to justice" both white and black Loyalist partisans "lurking in that Neighborhood." Since militiamen regarded black guerrillas as runaways and slave rebels, rather than as legitimate enemy combatants, they often resorted to summary execution of those captured. Francis Marion regarded the white partisans he sought as "ex-Tories," but the black skirmishers he captured were not granted that status. Like Washington, who fought for liberty while being served by William Lee, the Swamp Fox rode beside his manservant Oscar Marion, one of the nine of his slaves (out of two hundred) who did not escape to British lines during the conflict.[13]

It was easy to see why white Carolinians were so terrified by black maroon settlements. Every group of successful runaways, particularly those who were armed and living within fortified communities, presented an attractive haven for those who sought to flee their masters' estates. The impulse to be free was ever present among enslaved Carolinians; the question was where to escape to. Runaway advertisements placed shortly after the British evacuation reveal that most bondpeople fled west into the woods or along the coast into deep river swamps. As was the case during the war, families continued to escape in groups. One newspaper told of Old Ross, a fifty-six-year-old Ibo woman who led two daughters, a son-in-law, a son, and a grandson away from the plantation of Mary Thomas. Slave catchers and militia units patrolled the waterways; in 1793 the state of North Carolina made it a capital crime for white watermen to help slaves escape the state. More creative masters attempted to coax their slaves back onto their lands. Joseph Turpin placed an advertisement assuring Rinah, who had fled with the British in 1781, that if she would just return, all "shall be forgiven."[14]

The vast majority of Carolina bondpeople, of course, were unable to evacuate with the British or locate a fledgling maroon colony in the swamps. But the dramatic decline in the number of slaves in the lowcountry meant that even when threatened by the whip, blacks were well aware of the need for their muscles and the importance of their labor. One lowcountry mistress reported her bondpeople to be even more "insolent" than usual "and quite their own masters." Long accustomed to working on the task system, which afforded them some small measure of autonomy, Africans and black Carolinians took advantage of the immediate postwar chaos to gain even greater self-sufficiency.[15]

Newly assertive bondpeople could not know the precise number of lowcountry slaves who had made good their escape, but the dislocation and devastation was impossible to miss. Although South Carolina boasted a prewar white population of less than one hundred thousand, the state had spent the staggering sum of $5.4 million to prosecute the war. The loss of black refugees meant more than merely a decline in the number of laborers; on the eve of the conflict, Georgia's slaves represented a capital investment of roughly $3.3 million, and now nearly two-thirds of those bondpeople had died or fled. Independence meant an end to trade with the British Caribbean, and planters who had sold their rice to Jamaica and Barbados had to locate new markets. Before the war, South Carolina exported approximately 130,000 barrels of rice, but in 1785 that figure plummeted to 50,000 barrels. Yet independence did not mean that private debts to British merchants were erased, and as planters sought to rebuild their estates, they simply borrowed more from their old creditors. Two years after the Peace of Paris, Carolina planters had added $4.9 million to their old debts. When Henry Laurens lamented that "debtors are here the great majority," he spoke without exaggeration.[16]

For planters in the lower South, the obvious solution was to somehow obtain more black bodies. Early on, slaveholders scoured the countryside in search of cheap slaves, but the few masters who were willing to sell demanded exorbitant prices. In 1776, traders rarely sold a "seasoned Negro" for less than £40, but wartime losses drove the price up to between £70 and £100 (or $333) by 1784. (For several decades after the war, Americans used both pounds and dollars, usually at an exchange rate of £1 to $3.33.) The disruption of the British traffic in humans explains why traders such as Joseph Vesey were anxious to sell the living cargoes they acquired in the Caribbean, but the one hundred "Prime Slaves" that he advertised for sale in September 1783 could not begin to replace the tens of thousands lost to the South Carolina economy. A consensus in Charleston quickly emerged, as Henry Laurens admitted, that economic recovery "will in a considerable degree depend upon future importation of Negroes." A "great supply" of young Africans was necessary to rebuild the region, one Georgia firm argued, given "the Numbers we lost by the War, and the large bodies of fertile lands we have cultivated." So far removed were these planters from the world of Quok Walker, who at that moment was winning his freedom in a Massachusetts court, that coastal South Carolina and Georgia might as well have been in a separate country.[17]

Despite the growing clamor in the lowcountry for more slaves, the decision to resume the African trade was not an easy one. White Carolinians told themselves that small traders like Vesey merely imported bondpeople already enslaved in the Caribbean; previously free African captives were harder to rationalize. Even the most determined supporter of unfree labor could not defend the conditions of the Middle Passage. A few conceded the paradox of professing liberty and equality while becoming involved in a traffic that would deny young Africans their freedom. "Will it be righteous just and virtuous to enslave hundreds of thousands of free born Men and Women," wondered Henry Laurens in early 1783, "to sell them under the most arbitrary power of their fellow Mortals?" Still others, more pragmatic, believed white security required a reduction in the dangerously high percentage of black Carolinians. Those planters who had somehow held on to their enslaved labor force during the war also recognized that an influx of new Africans would reduce the value of their current holdings, and like those planters in the Chesapeake who opposed a renewal of the international trade, they hoped to sell the next generation of their surplus workers to their upcountry brethren.[18]

No longer under British imperial control, American shippers were free to market their wheat, lumber, tobacco, and rice in a number of far-flung ports, not just within the empire. France consistently failed to live up to the trading provisions in the 1778 Franco-American treaty of commerce, but American vessels just as consistently bought and sold a variety of goods—including slaves—in French and Danish Caribbean harbors. As lowcountry merchants and planters attempted to recover from the devastation of war, many began to adjust their former aversion to the traffic in humans. Writing to one of his London contacts, Laurens "recommended" the services of James Bloy, whose ship *Betsey* purchased slaves along the African coast as early as 1782. "I have told him candidly my wish that the further importation of Negroes may be prohibited," the increasingly flexible Laurens observed, but should "that Branch [of trade] be continued there will be no Evil in your receiving Consignments." By 1784, English-born trader Josiah Collins, who had been shipping small numbers of slaves between the Caribbean and North Carolina, fitted out his *Camden* for the longer voyage to West Africa. His ship, rebuilt and insured in Boston, returned to the Carolinas bearing eighty African captives.[19]

The swiftness with which the lowcountry's white minority abandoned their scruples suggests that earlier denunciations of the Middle Passage hardly reflected deeply held convictions. For all of their talk about the patriarchal duties of masters to their African American retainers, residents of slave societies could not afford to be particular about where they found the next generation of unwaged laborers. As John Rutledge instructed South Carolina's delegates to Congress, "the recovery of our Country" in the wake of having "lost our Slaves" meant that whites "found it necessary to help ourselves," and he did not wish to hear the slightest "reproach or even reproof." Savannah merchant Joseph Clay agreed. The "Negro business is a great object with us," he admitted in 1784. "[I]t is to the Trade of this Country, as the Soul to the body, and without it no House gain a proper Station, [so] the Planter will as far in his power sacrifice every thing to attain Negroes." British, Dutch, Danish, and French traders rushed to fill the market, and together with American traders, slavers transported roughly eleven thousand bondpeople from Africa and the Caribbean into Georgia and South Carolina between 1783 and 1785. Not without justification, Henry Laurens fumed that the country of Lord Mansfield was also "the fountain from whence we have been supplied with Slaves upwards of a Century."[20]

As had been the case just prior to the war, the largest ships—typically those operating out of Liverpool—purchased their human cargoes in the heart of the trade region in the Gulf of Guinea. Smaller vessels obtained Africans in Angola or the Gambia region. Regardless of their origins, however, those men involved in the Carolina trade deposited their captives just outside Charleston Harbor on Sullivan's Island, where they were quarantined and observed for signs of disease. Within a month of arrival, most were resold into South Carolina, although a smaller number were destined for resale into Georgia and North Carolina. The harsh realities of the African trade were never far from Charleston's view; Africans sometimes mutinied within sight of land, and dead bodies thrown from slave ships often washed into the harbor. Visitors found the sight ghastly, but locals learned to ignore the problem except when the bobbing corpses became so numerous that "nobody [could] eat any fish."[21]

As lowcountry planters hurried to purchase captives, they borrowed from city merchants, who granted loans only in exchange for promises to grow export staple crops. This cycle tied the lowcountry further to the commercialized economy of the Atlantic basin. The great estates along the Cooper continued to produce rice, although some diversified and turned to the increasingly popular staple of Sea Island cotton. For upcountry agriculturists, who bought a few young bondmen before moving westward, tobacco replaced indigo as the new cash crop. The move inland meant that even as the Chesapeake abandoned tobacco for wheat, southern tobacco production actually increased by 36 percent in the decade prior to 1790. Black workers, most of them Africans, increased in the Carolina and Georgia upcountry as well, by nearly 68 percent. Inspired by the large number of Africans tramping across Charleston docks, the state assembly imposed an import duty on the slave trade.[22]

In 1785, however, the South Carolina economy began to stumble. Assemblyman David Ramsay argued that the frenetic pace of human purchases aggravated the state's unfavorable balance of trade. His critics, notably Congressman John Rutledge and Governor Thomas Pinckney, argued that the state's depression was merely part of the larger national depression, and that as Charleston ceased to import Africans, the trade would simply move south to Savannah, which would then monopolize the profitable business. Their arguments carried the day, but by 1787, with the rice market still grim, the state voted to suspend the African trade for three years as a depression countermeasure. Not a single voice in the assembly spoke to the question of the trade's cruelties, although South Carolina politicians were acutely aware of the howls of protest heard in Richmond and Baltimore when Charleston opened its port to African captives. The economy remained stagnant, but as the glut of Africans imported after 1783 had served to slash the price of bondpeople— from nearly $500 to an affordable $250 by 1787—upcountry agriculturalists saw little reason to demand that the trade be reopened. When the price of black bodies began to creep back up, the assembly voted to resume the traffic as of December 17, 1803. By that Christmas, as Carolina whites flocked to churches to celebrate Christian fellowship, "vessels were fitted out in numbers for the coast of Africa," as one merchant described the frenzy, "and as fast as they returned, their cargoes were bought up with avidity."[23]

From that date until January 1, 1808, when the Republic's involvement in the Atlantic slave trade was banned by federal law, another 56,000 Africans were dragged into Carolina harbors. Altogether, European and American shippers brought a staggering 86,121 Africans into Georgia and the Carolinas between 1783 and 1808, which meant that slightly less than one-fifth of all the black captives ever carried into what became the thirteen British mainland colonies arrived in just three states *after* American independence was won at Yorktown. The enormous influx served to preserve unwaged labor in the lowcountry and expand it into the backcountry and even into the Kentucky territory and the lower Mississippi Valley. For those in search of historical turning points, the decisions made in Charleston in 1783 meant there could be no turning back for the lower South, and the journey toward secession and Fort Sumter was well under way.[24]

The fervent desire of the planter class to rebuild their shattered empire forced white Carolinians not merely to crack down on the black guerrillas in the backcountry but also to reimpose those labor controls that had fallen into disuse during the British invasion. For urban slaves such as young Telemaque, the most visible sign of white authority was the Workhouse, formally known as the House of Correction. Built on Magazine Street, the imposing brick structure, two stories tall and bristling with battlements, fulfilled the role that overseers played on rural plantations. If discipline on the rice and cotton plantations was a private affair, the Workhouse warden symbolized public control in the postwar city. Night watchmen sent the slaves they rounded up each evening to the Workhouse, while individual masters, one resident noted, frequently ordered their "refractory slaves" into its spacious chambers "with a note from the owners directing a specified number of lashes to be given." One visitor to Charleston discovered "about forty individuals of both sexes" awaiting "correction." The "whipping-room," constructed of double walls filled with sand to muffle the screams of inmates, housed a crane, "on which a cord with two nooses runs over pullies." The warden chained the feet of slaves to the floor, then hoisted the crane until their bodies were "stretched out as much as possible." Slaves took the beatings, but masters paid a price for their squeamishness: each visit to the Workhouse cost twenty-five cents.[25]

A few voices, white as well as black, spoke out against this increasingly proslavery course, contrary as it was to the program of liberty being slowly adopted by the rest of the nation. Such antislavery views met with little success. A number of North Carolina politicians, representing the lower South state most ambivalent about retaining slavery, urged the federal government to prohibit unwaged labor in the frontier lands they ceded to the national government in 1790. (The request was met with the sort of saber rattling that would become common among southern politicians in later years, and in 1796 the region became the slave state of Tennessee.) When local assemblies did move to free blacks, they did so only for individuals and under unusual circumstances. When Ned Griffin petitioned the North Carolina legislature in 1784, it was on the grounds that his current master, William Kitchen,

Designed to intimidate, the Charleston Workhouse (foreground right) and City Jail symbolized white authority in the Carolina lowcountry. *South Carolina Historical Society.*

had purchased him "for the purpose of Serving in His place" during the war, with the pledge that "he should be a free Man" after victory was achieved. Kitchen then reneged on the promise and Griffin, denouncing his master as a "Desert[er]," appealed to the assembly. Griffin won his freedom, but his victory reflected the legislature's disdain for Kitchen's cowardice rather than any general support for black liberation.[26]

A small band of Quakers and Presbyterian ministers freed individual slaves during the 1780s and early 1790s, but as was the case in the Chesapeake, the few whites who liberated beloved bondpeople typically did so in response to personal acts of service or wartime loyalty. When one community of Quakers manumitted nearly forty slaves, North Carolina legislators denounced such benevolence as "evil and pernicious." Instead of debating a law for gradual emancipation, or at least following Virginia's lead in easing the course of private manumissions, the legislature instead drafted legislation authorizing county sheriffs to seize and sell at auction any bondperson liberated in violation of state law. To ensure that all white residents understood their intent, the assembly renewed the law in 1788 and yet again in 1796.[27]

A far greater number of whites endorsed the course that the region's planter-politicians chose. Of all the new states, South Carolina and Georgia exhibited the least amount of revolutionary idealism in the years after 1776. Instead, the darker side of Lockean theory—and its emphasis on the sanctity of property—held sway. In the northern states, the concept of natural rights and republican optimism helped to dismantle slave codes within a few short decades. But in the lowcountry, the embrace of Lockean notions emphasized the freedom to own and acquire private assets, including the right to retain African chattel. John Locke had argued that all citizens possessed a "property" in both themselves and their possessions. So where Quok Walker argued that his enslavement denied him the just fruits of his labor, Joseph Vesey responded that any interference on the part of the state with his right to profit from the ownership of Telemaque violated the principles for which white Americans had fought. In any case, because white Carolinians, like the Virginia wordsmiths who amended George Mason's Declaration of Rights, rejected the idea that even African Americans born in their state met the definition of citizen, those of African descent existed far beyond the reach of Lockean theory.[28]

Lowcountry politicians not only devoted much of their time to explaining why the promise of the Revolution did not apply to blacks but even began to hint that those ideals enshrined in Jefferson's Declaration were fundamentally unsound. Robert Goodloe Harper, while doubting that Africans were biologically inferior, nonetheless argued that illiterate bondpeople were far too ignorant to be trusted with the responsibilities of citizenship. "Our minds like our bodies," he wrote, "are weak and helpless in their infant state," and black intelligence had not yet "encrease[d] in strength in activity and in hardiness" for African Americans to be included in a free society. But because Harper's theory, whether he recognized it or not, allowed for the possibility of African American improvement if given time enough in liberty, such sentiments were too dangerous for Henry William DeSaussure, who fired back in an angry pamphlet. They lived in a state with a black majority, he reminded Harper, and so if the American ideal that "equality is the natural condition of man" were actually "adopted and reduced to practice, it would instantly free the unfortunate slaves." This counterrevolutionary exchange dismayed observers who prayed that the entire nation might yet live up to its founding ethics. Benjamin Rush urged General Nathanael Greene to exert his "great influence" among white Carolinians to slow this retreat from freedom. "For God's sake, do not exhibit a new spectacle to the world, of men just emerging from a war in favor of liberty," Rush begged, "fitting out vessels to import their fellow creatures from Africa to reduce them afterwards to slavery."[29]

Greene declined to reply, and no wonder. Politicians who failed to endorse the state's course, and loudly, quickly found themselves unemployed. When David Ramsay stood for a seat in the national House of Representatives in 1788, he ran a distant third, the victim of an opponent's proslavery assault. William Loughton Smith, who won the election, placed a broadside in several Charleston newspapers charging that Ramsay was *principled against* the true political interests of this country" on the grounds that he was "*against slavery*." Although the Pennsylvania-born physician had settled in Charleston before the war, he was derided as "a northward man" and lost the election, he believed, because he favored "the abolition of slavery." Ramsay learned his lesson. Shortly after the election, he wrote to his old friend John Eliot, the pastor of the New North Congregational Church of Boston. "You speak feelingly for the poor negroes," Ramsay observed, "but such is our hard case here to the Southward that we cannot do without them." Never again did Ramsay so much as hint about the immorality of slavery.[30]

If lowcountry bondpeople, despite (or because of) their numbers, failed to force politicians to adopt plans for gradual manumission, they were able to achieve a measure of autonomy in the countryside. Long organized according to the task system, coastal work patterns grew even more self-governing after the Revolution. Wartime disruption of the region's economy, together with the long absence of white soldiers, increased the tradition of planter absenteeism, which further handed power to white overseers, black drivers, and the slave community itself. Although the resumption of the African slave trade meant that slavery was more permanently fastened upon Georgia and South Carolina, the influx of thousands of Africans also served to strengthen West African traditions and increase the cultural gulf between the quarters and the big house. This labor and cultural isolation, so different from William Lee's Chesapeake world, even allowed coastal slaves to protect the integrity of family life. Masters might agonize over the way the Revolution had accentuated prewar black autonomy, but they welcomed the prosperity it brought them. One master advertised that he would not purchase "any gang where any of the slaves have been separated from their families." Failure to accept this compromise often had dire economic consequences. When one planter carelessly divided families by ordering some of his bondpeople to another of his properties, an entire gang of thirteen slaves—consisting of three families—attempted to run away.[31]

If the physical separation of slave and master characterized life in the postwar countryside, Savannah, with its carefully planned city squares, and Charleston, with its cramped peninsular geography, did not allow for traditional plantation arrangements. Instead, most urban bondpeople lived in close proximity to their owners, either in nearby slave quarters nestled within an enclosed compound adjacent to the main residence or, in the case of less wealthy masters, in the master's home. In Vesey's narrow house on King Street, Telemaque probably slept in the attic. But if the captain was typical of city dwellers, who retained very few domestic bondpeople, slaveholding in Charleston was all too common. Nearly three-quarters of the population in the Carolina countryside owned not even a single slave, but in postwar Charleston that statistic was reversed, as roughly three-quarters held at least one person in bondage.[32]

Even so, urban bondpeople won a curious form of labor autonomy in the years just after the war. Masters in Charleston and Savannah, whether they owned domestics or skilled bondmen who assisted them in their craft trade, occasionally found themselves with more slaves than they required. At such times masters simply rented them for brief periods, which also allowed white urbanites with short-term labor needs to fill them for a modest cost. Largely peculiar to southern cities—only 6 percent of rural slaves were for hire, compared to 31 percent in Charleston—the practice also allowed slaves to pocket small amounts of cash. Most masters believed that granting their slaves this small amount of control over their day would hardly bring about the downfall of unfree labor. Some penurious whites even encouraged black entrepreneurship, as it meant they could spend less on food and clothing for their human property. Bondwomen from the plantations across the Cooper River, for example, often arrived in the city each Sunday with vegetables grown in small garden plots to sell for their own personal profit. As occasional participants in the urban market economy, South Carolina slaves temporarily enjoyed the same privileges accorded to the white minority, the right to barter their labor—or in this case, the fruits of their labor—for a needed commodity, or even cash.[33]

Bondwomen who sold their vegetables, however, did so in violation of state law. The Negro Act of 1740, which survived the Revolution without revision or amendment, permitted bondpeople into city markets only for the explicit purpose of buying or selling commodities on behalf of their owners, and it prohibited "any shopkeeper, trader, or other person" from dealing in items not "particularly enumerate[ed]" by masters under penalty of a $200 fine. But in the wake of the war, as lowcountry residents struggled to rebuild their state's badly damaged economy, white authorities typically allowed slaves traveling with a "ticket," that is, a pass from their masters, to enter the market house. Few white retailers rejected a modestly priced basket of fresh foodstuffs, regardless of the race of the seller. So long as the slaves who sold goods in the markets on Sunday returned to their master's property by sunup on Monday, white peddlers ignored potential fines and encouraged business with ambitious slave suppliers.[34]

Most rural slaves who ventured into Savannah or Charleston on Sunday mornings tried to conduct their business away from the gaze of white authorities. Others constructed illicit networks along the numerous waterways that poured into the Atlantic so as to avoid the risk of venturing into towns and cities. Plantation slaves often bartered the crops and even livestock they raised to the white boatmen who worked the inland rivers, and one rice planter on the Combahee River observed numerous "ped[d]ling boats which frequent the river [for] the purpose of trading with the Negro Slaves." Despite the obvious dangers involved, however, most enterprising bondpeople chose to hawk their wares in urban centers. According to one white observer, each Sunday morning, an "immense number of canoes of various sizes," some of which "could transport upward of one hundred men," rowed toward Charleston from across the rivers and the coastal islands, bringing "vegetables, [live]stock of every kind and the staple of the country."[35]

If white shopkeepers had every reason to encourage this illegal trade, planter-politicians consistently sought to interdict it. Although some bondmen sold the animals they raised in small pens next to their cabins, others decided that stolen animals provided some compensation for years of unwaged toil. Stolen cattle began to disappear from the countryside, and state legislators responded in 1790 with a statute that required slaves who transported beef to market to "produce the Hides" with brands as evidence of rightful ownership. But black initiative was not so easily denied, particularly among those who sold goods in the markets and quickly came to enjoy the power of cash. A few enterprising upcountry slaves even insisted that their masters obtain goods for them that were unavailable from local shopkeepers. Peter Bacot's bondpeople used the money they earned in the local village market to purchase, through Bacot's intervention, coats, shawls, and even dress patterns from Charleston shops.[36]

Men such as Bacot flattered themselves benevolent masters and saw little harm in placing orders for their bondpeople. But more discerning planters worried about the impact of this unlawful trade on their patriarchal control. Henry Laurens, for one, worried that this underground market's ability to provide slaves with a source of cash or bartered goods did not require them to approach him, cap in hand, and request wares with the expected show of deference. Planters like Laurens correctly perceived the Charleston market-place as an assault on the noncapitalist social order from which they derived their patriarchal authority. So, too, perhaps, did the slaves, who viewed their right to acquire money and property as a challenge to the hegemony of the master class. One bondman, Hercules LeCount, told a surprised visitor to the region that his owner "did not own or even claim a cent worth" of the cash he earned by selling his foodstuffs in the city. Although human property himself, Prince Wilson insisted he was "the only one who has any legal right to the property" he acquired away from his master's fields.[37]

Charleston slaves were particularly adamant on this point. Rural bond-men such as Prince Wilson might cultivate small "provision grounds" beside their cabins for sale of goods in the city, but their actual journeys into the city were infrequent at best. But a good many urban slaves spent at least a portion of each day removed from the watchful eye of the master class. Typical was Telemaque's friend Polydore Faber, "an excellent sawyer of Lumber [and] a Rope Maker." Polydore was the slave to Catherine Faber, an elderly widow, who relied on her "strong [and] intelligent" bondman as her chief source of income. Catherine allowed Polydore to hire his time and even live away from her home on Montague Street, and in exchange he paid her twelve dollars each month. Whatever he could earn beyond that was his to keep. The Work-house might stand as the most visible sign of white authority, but in cities like Charleston, there was no plantation overseer to maintain control over the enslaved population. To the contrary, employers competed with one another for the most skilled slave artisans, and bondmen like Faber, with a reputation for honesty and hard work, shopped around for contractors and even inquired into the reputation of whites who offered them employment.[38]

In southern ports enslaved men and women performed every conceivable task. As in northern cities, slaves worked the docks, loading and unloading merchant vessels. In the lowcountry, slaves also executed tasks carried out by freed blacks or impoverished immigrants to the north. Hotel proprietors often owned a small gang of slaves—sometimes a family—to cook, clean, and handle luggage. Racing enthusiasts bought Africans who exhibited promise as riders or who had experience grooming horses in the country of their birth. Even city governments owned slaves. A small team of three slaves maintained Charleston's sandy streets and kept them free of refuse, an arrangement that in effect made every city taxpayer part of the slave system. By the very nature of their labors, all of these bondpeople spent time away from their masters' homes, and almost all found ample opportunities to earn private incomes.[39]

The vast majority of the lowcountry's urban slaves, however, fell into one of two categories. Most, like Telemaque, served their masters in a domestic capacity. Trained as servants, cooks, butlers, coachmen, valets, and grooms, they labored within their owners' townhouses. But on Sundays or late afternoons when their tasks were complete, they wandered down to the wharves in search of temporary employment as porters and carters. The next largest category was that of enslaved craftsmen. The ownership of slaves by white artisans was common in southern towns, and especially so in Charleston, the largest slave city in the postwar Republic. According to the census of 1790, more than half of all white artisans retained at least a single bondman as a craft apprentice. In some trades, the percentage was higher still. Sixty percent of Charleston carpenters owned bondmen, and some of them ran their entire businesses by maintaining gangs of bond carpenters. A full 25 percent of carpenters possessed more than ten enslaved craftsmen, employed in small groups at construction sites around the city.[40]

On rare occasions, enslaved artisans rose to the top of their profession and essentially managed their masters' companies. One Charleston slave, Adam Robertson, came to serve as foreman at his master's ropemaking business, which twisted nautical cables at the city's South Wharf. Adam's master, John Robertson, was a "merchant and navy agent" with a good many investments, too many, in fact, to manage by himself. Adam early on revealed both an unusual aptitude for his craft as well as the capacity to manage other men, gifts that shrewd observers regarded as inherently dangerous in young bondmen. John Robertson saw only greater efficiency and increased profits and put Adam's talents to use as manager of the other "Rope Walke Negroes," which gave him considerable authority over other slaves.[41]

More commonly, ambitious businessmen such as John Robertson purchased more slaves than they could readily employ, especially as the postwar economy continued to sour throughout the 1780s. When this happened, urban masters routinely rented their slaves to more prosperous but possibly shorthanded white neighbors. The brief employment of enslaved artisans by a temporary master was a recent development in the young Republic, but hardly an illogical one. Since white Georgians or Carolinians owned the very bodies of the Africans they had purchased—as opposed to their labor, which had been the case before the Revolution with white indentured servants—bondpeople had to grow accustomed to the reality that their time could be arbitrarily redirected to suit the needs of their owners and the fluctuating requirements of urban economies. If masters could earn livings by having others toil on their behalf, which was the essence of slavery, it made equal sense for masters to get additional revenues by temporarily transferring that labor power to other whites.[42]

These arrangements soon became every bit as flexible as were the economies of the southern seaports. Some periods of hire stretched to fifty weeks, starting on the first day of January and lasting until seven days before Christmas. Most urban masters, however, rented their human property out for only a few days. Urban businessmen in need of a quick influx of capital usually initiated the process, but skilled slaves learned to bargain with their masters for the right to be hired out. Agreements between masters and slaves varied slightly, but a tradition quickly arose that while masters retained the lion's share of whatever cash their slaves might earn, the bondmen got to pocket roughly one-third of their earnings. Despite the obvious inequities in this division of wages, bond artisans lobbied hard for the right to hire their time. The practice put cash—albeit a paltry amount—in their pockets and removed them from their masters' gaze long enough to visit their wives or purchase goods for their children at the city's markets (which in turn served to strengthen the sales conducted by slaves who sold goods at those markets). Although still slaves in the eyes of the law, bondmen who hired out their time enjoyed a peculiar quasi-independence inconsistent with the maintenance of racial controls.[43]

If lucrative for the owner and welcomed by the bondman, the practice of hiring out was dangerous to social stability. Although skilled slaves encompassed the majority of the rented workforce, city docks also offered untrained bondmen ample opportunities to earn quick wages. Combined, skilled and unskilled slaves comprised roughly 70 percent of all laborers in Charleston. A few whites thought it prudent to accompany the slaves they intended to hire out along the docks each morning, but it was impractical for owners to remain along the wharves to negotiate a new labor agreement every few hours. Instead, after agreeing upon an initial contract, urban masters left trusted bondmen to their own devices, provided that they return home each evening with the agreed-upon sum of money. Typical of those hired along the wharves was Caesar, an "active drayman" who carted goods about Charleston and virtually passed as a free man. Caesar paid his aged owner, Naomi Smith, "two dollars per month" for the privilege of being hiring out. Beyond that, he bought his own "Clothing & Support[ed] himself at his own Expense" and patiently awaited the day he would accrue enough cash to purchase his freedom.[44]

Fewer women than men hired out their time, although the practice was not unheard of for urban bondwomen. Some Savannah slaves hawked fresh bread and cakes on street corners, and a few domestics found themselves rented to white neighbors when an elegant gathering required additional service. But the domestic skills most commonly found in female slaves in southern towns kept enslaved women closely tied their masters' homes. City masters expected six (or more) days of hard labor from their bondwomen. From lighting the morning's fires to washing the evening's dishes, slave women spent virtually every waking moment serving their owners' families. Gender restricted the economic options available to bondwomen just as it did for their white mistresses.[45]

The continuous reallocation of labor through the renting out of surplus bondmen to temporary masters may have rendered unwaged labor—an inefficient, antiquated form of labor organization—more compatible with the requirements of urban economies, but in the process white masters carelessly ignored essential principles of control. White artisans complained about the undercutting of their wages by enslaved craftsmen, and in 1783 white craftsmen petitioned to stop "Jobbing Negroe Tradesm[e]n" who worked on "their own Account." Rural visitors to lowcountry towns and cities discussed the problem not in economic terms but in terms that suggested fear of insubordination. Some pointedly observed that when human chattels were employed as free wage laborers, they generally ceased to behave like human chattels. Charleston city ordinances, for example, forbade slaves from congregating in large numbers, but bondmen in search of work along the docks did so every morning. One astonished visitor to the region, after watching blacks buying wares and selling their time in the Charleston market, blurted out, "[B]ut they are your slaves," as if the cash changing hands put the matter in some doubt.[46]

Masters who garnished the majority of their bondmen's wages or failed to perceive the deceit behind their slaves' benign mask of obedience little understood the liberating power of cash. Nor did they notice that the growing demand for wages on the part of their slaves fueled an illicit trade in stolen wares, as rural bondpeople who carted their produce into city markets each Sunday thought it no sin to supplement their meager earnings by selling items they pinched from their owners' estates. But the more planters railed against the practice of urban slaves hiring out their time, the more the black community was determined to retain this forbidden fruit. Dilapidated alehouses hidden in back alleys so infamous that even night watchmen passed them by housed fences always eager to purchase purloined items, along with men who made a living by hiring slave rivermen to resell stolen goods along the lowcountry's inland waterways.[47]

More troubling still, from the perspective of white control, was the fact that many urban bondmen failed to return to their masters' homes at the end of the evening. Masters often permitted trusted slaves to reside near their places of temporary employment. Working-class white tenants with a spare room to let and a mortgage to pay rarely gave as much attention to the color of the renter as they did to the authenticity of the coin. Although still slaves in the eye of the law, bondmen who lived away from their masters severed the few remaining ties to their owners. Advocates of tighter racial controls found the practice appalling. The ability of hired slaves to rent rooms, observed one group of South Carolina petitioners, had "serious and alarming consequences," the least of which was the "pernicious" model of black autonomy that such living arrangements provided to other slaves more securely tied to their masters.[48]

Both Georgia and South Carolina statutes flatly prohibited slaves from living away from their masters' homes or estates. As early as 1740, in the wake of the slave revolt near the Stono River, colonial legislators forbade slaves "to rent or hire any house, room, [or] store [on] his or her own account." But as with the equally illegal custom of hiring out, living out was difficult to prevent in lowcountry towns and cities, and except in times of alarm few masters saw much danger in allowing trusted servants to live close to their workplaces. Despite the unsanitary conditions of back-alley rentals, no slave wished to exchange the squalor of freedom for a cleaner attic in his owner's home. "The negroes appear to think," noted one Charleston mistress, "that even if they receive wages, [they] are not free as long as they live with their old masters."[49]

For South Carolina legislators, this level of autonomy for men and women the state officially regarded as chattel was intolerable. The endless litany of statutes passed by state and local authorities appeared to have little impact on the habit of hiring out, just as no legislation existed that could retard the countryside's prewar tradition of task labor, which also provided rural bondpeople with a modicum of self-sufficiency. They could, however, clarify their opinion of the northern trend toward gradual emancipation, as well as

Virginia's middle path of private manumissions. On December 20, 1800, South Carolina's planter-politicians passed the Act Respecting Slaves, Free Negroes, Mulattoes, and Mestizoes. Noting that it had become the practice "for persons to emancipate or set free their slaves, in cases where such slaves had been of bad or depraved character, or, from age or infirmity, incapable of gaining their livelihood by honest means," the legislature effectively banned all private manumissions. From this date on, any master wishing to liberate a single slave had to endure the lengthy process of having the transaction approved by a panel of "five indifferent freeholders" who could testify that the bondperson in question would not become a financial burden on the community.[50]

Coming as it did midway between New York's manumission law of 1799 and the last statewide emancipation statute ever to be passed in the Republic, that of New Jersey in 1804, South Carolina's statute was as much a conscious rebuke to most of the nation as it was designed to cap the small number of freed blacks in the state. As a result, by the end of the eighteenth century, the total free African American population for the entire state stood at only 3,185, or 2.1 percent, most of whom were light-skinned Carolinians with ties to the white community. If unfree labor was on the decline in the border South—in that same year, 15.6 percent of Maryland's African American population was free—slavery was ever more firmly entrenched in the lower seacoast states. The law of 1800 served as a reminder both that state-by-state manumission would never be effected in the lower South and of slavery's status as a national issue requiring a federal solution, albeit one that most Founders were too timid to impose.[51]

As for Telemaque, the unusually lucky slave managed to obtain his freedom just prior to the passage of the statute of 1800. On September 30, 1799, he chanced upon a handbill announcing the city's East-Bay Lottery. The approximately thirty-three-year-old manservant purchased ticket number 1884, and on November 9, the Charleston *City Gazette* announced him the winner. The top prize was $1,500, a princely sum that hired slaves might take ten years to earn. Telemaque approached his master, who agreed to sell him his freedom in exchange for $600. On December 31, the last day of the old century, Telemaque handed Vesey more than one-third of his winnings, and Vesey formally "manumitted, released and from the yoke of Servitude set free and discharged a certain negro man named Telemaque." Adopting the name of Denmark Vesey, the former bondman ended his seventeen years as a Charleston slave. To the extent that he would die in 1822 trying to plan an insurrection that would free those still enslaved in the city, his troubled life suggests that for the American Revolution, there was no simple finale.[52]

SEVEN

Mum Bett Takes a Name

The Emergence of Free Black Communities

W HEN THE MASSACHUSETTS COURT of Common Pleas, meeting in Great Barrington in the late summer of 1781, accepted attorney Theodore Sedgwick's argument that the preamble to the state constitution had rendered slavery unconstitutional, his client, Mum Bett, walked out of the courtroom a free woman. In some ways, that was an end to the story. But in so many other ways it was just the beginning. For the thirty-nine-year-old Bett, there was a world of decisions to be made. Like the tens of thousands of black Americans who won their freedom in the last two decades of the eighteenth century, Bett found herself a free person of color in a racist society and a liberated chattel with nothing but the clothes on her back after thirty years as an unwaged domestic. Those in her situation had to choose where to live, how to earn a living, and how to build (or rebuild) a family that had been broken by slavery or ravaged by six years of warfare. To the extent that many bondpeople had only a forename, or, like Telemaque, an absurd pet name chosen by their masters, one of the first things that former slaves had to do was to decide what to call themselves.

Perhaps chastened by the unflattering light the case had shone upon his household (especially his violent, ill-tempered wife, Annetje), Colonel John Ashley, Bett's former master, asked her to return to his employ for wages. But Bett had promised herself never to return to Ashley's home after being struck on the arm, "the scar of which she bore to the day of her death." Instead, she accepted a position as a paid servant in Sedgwick's household, where she remained with the family for a number of years. While there, Bett also helped her female neighbors during the birthing process, earning a reputation as a skilled midwife and nurse. During the first months with the Sedgwick family, Bett began to call herself by the name she deemed more appropriately suited for a liberated woman of the Republic: Elizabeth Freeman.[1]

Freeman never learned to read or write, but according to family oral tradition, she had been married while still a slave. Her husband had fought and died in the Patriot ranks. So it was a war widow and her daughter, then known as Little Bett, who arrived at Sedgwick's door. During the late 1780s, she met Jack Burghardt, a young veteran who had recently lost his wife, Violet. Jack's father, a West African renamed Tom Burghardt after being purchased by Coonrad Borghardt, earned his liberty while fighting for the Patriots at Fort George and then spent his first years of freedom acquiring land around Great Barrington. Jack Burghardt, the father of six young children and the owner of a profitable farm, began to court Freeman, eighteen years his senior. They were married in 1790. Having chosen her cherished name with such care, Elizabeth had no desire to adopt a surname adapted from that of a Dutch slaveholder. She remained Freeman, but she accepted the care of Jack's large family. One of his sons, Othello, would grow old to become the grandfather of William Edward Burghardt Du Bois.[2]

As a reminder that the past is rarely as uncomplicated as one might prefer, the couple did not always identify with others on the bottom rung of society. They refused to support the indebted veterans of central and western Massachusetts who rose in revolt against high taxes and court foreclosures of their farms in 1786. Some of these sentiments grew out of personal loyalty. As insurgents led by Daniel Shays overran the Sedgwick estate, Freeman hid the family silver in her own chest and then, "arming herself with the kitchen shovel," stood her ground. When one group of rebels discovered some bottles in the cellar, Freeman "offered to serve them like gentlemen" but warned "that the next one who uselessly destroyed a vessel, should be instantly leveled by her shovel." Perhaps, having won her freedom through the courts, Elizabeth had more faith in the state government than did Shays's farmers. According to an account later published by Du Bois, Jack Burghardt even marched beside Colonel John Ashley, his fiancée's former master, when they repelled the rebels outside the arsenal at Springfield in February 1787.[3]

Mostly the couple worked quietly at their farm near the village of South Egremont. At the age of fifty-two, Burghardt volunteered yet again, serving in the state militia during the War of 1812, a conflict highly unpopular in Massachusetts. Freeman continued her midwifery, earning the respect of her white neighbors for her "superior experience, energy, skill, and sagacity." She died at the age of eighty-seven, just after Christmas 1829, surrounded by her grandchildren and stepgrandchildren, black Americans born

Elizabeth Freeman was almost seventy when this watercolor-on-ivory portrait
was painted by young Susan Ridley Sedgwick, a writer of juvenile fiction
and the wife of Theodore Sedgwick Jr., the son of Freeman's attorney.
Bridgeman Art Library.

free in part because of the suit she pursued in 1781. "Any time while I was
a slave," she once confided to Catherine Sedgwick, "if one minute's freedom
had been offered to me, and I had been told I must die at the end of that
minute, I would have taken it—just to stand one minute on God's airth a
free woman—I would."[4]

As Elizabeth Freeman's ultimately triumphant life suggests, the gradual
demise of slavery in the northern states created enormous expectations within
the black community. But the egalitarian idealism of the Revolutionary era
proved to be short-lived—and hollow. African Americans quickly discovered
that the struggle to gain freedom was only the first skirmish in a larger battle
for equality and citizenship. As freed communities arose across the North
and in pockets of the South, blacks labored to forge the institutional foundations necessary for collective success, from schools to churches to self-help

associations and politicized assemblies demanding their due as American-born citizens. As the "Free Africans and their descendants of the City of Philadelphia" wrote into the financial rules of the 1787 Free African Society, it was their duty to assist the black needy, provide for "the surviving widow of a deceased member," and place "the children of our deceased members under the care of the society so far as to pay for their schooling" and then find them positions "as apprentices to suitable trades." Whites in northern seaport towns, of course, had been devising such social protections almost since the arrival of the first European immigrants; black Americans, emerging poor and unlettered from nearly two centuries of enslavement, once again had their work cut out for them.[5]

———

Only in Freeman's Massachusetts did blacks gain their freedom all at one moment, thanks to her case and that filed by Quok Walker. Elsewhere in the Republic, the process was gradual, when it happened at all. The litany of precise dates on which states passed legislation for gradual emancipation masks the fact that those African Americans lucky enough to be born after the passage of manumission laws reached the established year of freedom in stages. A black child, for example, born in Philadelphia on March 2, 1780, the day after the passage of Pennsylvania's gradualist law, would become free on that day in 1808, having reached the age of twenty-eight. Blacks born before 1780 were not covered by the law, and children born in 1781 were not due to be liberated before 1809. This meant that many black parents remained enslaved after their children became free. In most states, black women were freed at a younger age than men, so frequently wives were liberated, only to have to wait several more years before their husbands ceased to be property. As a result, free black communities grew slowly and sporadically. Those occupations already recognized as positions of influence—minister, merchant, and educator—emerged little by little in black society, thanks to the North's gradualist laws. As late as 1790, the year that Freeman and Burghardt were wed, the free African American population in the northern states numbered only 27,000, fewer even than the 32,000 black southerners who found freedom after the war's end.[6]

As enslaved women aged into freedom, however, the free African American population began to develop through natural increase. But because each region followed its own distinctive path to freedom—or, in the case of the lower South, back into slavery—the freed communities were often distinctive as well. In Virginia and Maryland, those freed by state action or private manumissions tended to be veterans or esteemed domestics. In some cases, such as that of James Hemings, Jefferson's enslaved brother-in-law,

Whites, Free Blacks, and Slaves, 1790–1800

1790 New England
Total population: 1,009,522
Slaves: 3,886
Free blacks: 13,101
Total black population: 16,987
Blacks: 1.7 % of total population
Slaves: 22.9% of blacks

1800 New England
Total population: 1,233,011
Slaves: 1,339
Free blacks: 17,323
Total black population: 18,662
Blacks: 1.5% of total population
Slaves: 7.2% of blacks

1790 Middle Atlantic (NY, NJ, PA)
Total population: 958,632
Slaves: 36,484
Free blacks: 13,953
Total black population: 50,437
Blacks: 5.3 % of total population
Slaves: 72.3% of blacks

1800 Middle Atlantic
Total population: 1,399,696
Slaves: 34,741
Free blacks: 29,340
Total black population: 64,081
Blacks: 4.6% of total population
Slaves: 54.2% of blacks

1790 Upper South (MD, VA, DE, KY)
Total population: 1,200,109
Slaves: 416,980
Free blacks: 24,922
Total black population: 441,902
Blacks: 36.8 % of total population
Slaves: 94.4% of blacks

1800 Upper South
Total population: 1,511,942
Slaves: 498,802
Free blacks: 49,089
Total black population: 547,891
Blacks: 36.2% of total population
Slaves: 91.0% of blacks

1790 Lower South (NC, SC, GA, TN)
Total population: 725,372
Slaves: 236,930
Free blacks: 7,174
Total black population: 244,104
Blacks: 33.7% of total population
Slaves: 97.1% of blacks

1800 Lower South
Total population: 1,091,982
Slaves: 352,730
Free blacks: 12,486
Total black population: 365,216
Blacks: 33.4% of total population
Slaves: 96.6% of blacks

Source: U.S. federal census, 1790 and 1800

they had the benefit of blood ties to their white manumitters. Far more commonly they did not, which meant that the emerging free community in the Chesapeake, like that of the North, was predominantly dark-skinned. By comparison, those freed in the Carolina lowcountry were typically the sons and daughters of white planters, making the small freed community of

Charleston overwhelmingly light-skinned. Yet the freed community in the lower South, like that of the North, was increasingly urbanized, while that in the Chesapeake remained rural.[7]

Freed communities also grew or shrank depending on geographical location. Rural freedpeople rarely wished to reside in states or counties where the percentage of enslaved to free remained high, and except when kinship ties to still-enslaved family members chained them to a region—as was often the case in Virginia—newly liberated blacks migrated to nearby towns and cities. Even in New York City, recently freed slaves abandoned those sections of the city where slaveholding remained common; by 1790, there were only four free black families living in the Dock and East Wards, where 37 and 41 percent, respectively, of white families owned at least a single slave. But in general, cities such as Manhattan and Philadelphia, which had been occupied by British troops during the war and so had become early centers of freed communities, provided attractive havens for those emerging out of slavery in New Jersey and Delaware. As early as 1776, black Loyalists in New York staged "Ethiopian Balls," where black musicians and soldiers socialized with British officers. With the end of the war, thousands of blacks evacuated with the British army, but thousands more remained behind to build new lives.[8]

Not only did urbanization allow former bondpeople to reconstruct families shattered by decades of enslavement and forced separation, it also gave young African Americans far greater access to potential marriage partners. Contrary to popular myth, masters did not routinely select partners for their slaves, and the small holdings typical of northern farm slavery limited the romantic options available to rural bondpeople. Jack Burghardt was surely attracted to the strong-willed Freeman; regardless, he had few options in the tiny black community of western Massachusetts. Boston, New York, and Philadelphia were an altogether different matter. Yet even in large urban areas, the process of building a family and starting a household was rarely easy. The 1790 census revealed that in Boston, where slavery had been dead for nearly a decade, one in three blacks resided with whites, and many were the sole African American within the home. Young black men, in particular, often stayed with one another in large, extended households until they were able to set up their own households. When at last financially solvent, northern African Americans wasted little time in starting families. The same census demonstrated that 88 percent of the black households in Philadelphia that contained children below the age of fourteen were headed by both an adult male and female.[9]

If anything, kinship networks among freed people were even more important in the Chesapeake, where freedom did not accompany one's twenty-eighth birthday. Instead, the handful of blacks who gained their liberty after the private manumission act of 1783 frequently labored for years to earn enough to purchase a spouse or child. Slaves with no hopes of freedom often turned to already liberated family members to aid in escapes. When Sam vanished from the Maryland countryside, his master assumed he had fled to Baltimore, where he had "several relations (manumitted Blacks), who will conceal and assist him to make his escape." Young husbands with access to the North were the most likely to risk flight. Tom Turner, a freed waterman whose knowledge of the Chesapeake's rivers increased his odds of success, convinced his enslaved wife, Bet, to leave with him. In opposing plans for gradual emancipation, Jefferson feared that staggered liberation might create problems of racial control in Virginia. Faced with numerous stories such as those of Sam and Bet, Virginia slaveholders petitioned the assembly to restrain the movement of freed blacks, since the "great number of relations and acquaintances they still have among us" motivated men like Turner to liberate their families. The fact that no sooner was Tom Turner freed than he returned to free Bet, of course, suggests the seriousness with which *they* regarded their marriage, even if the state did not.[10]

Upon reaching Baltimore safely, former slaves such as Sam immediately did what Mum Bett had done several years before: they adopted a surname. Although slaves had occasionally taken a family or occupational name for use among themselves, few masters wished to bestow upon their human property the sense of dignity a surname implied. Particularly in the kinship-conscious South, family connections conferred rank and social value, and so slaves were denied both. Kinship among slaves had no standing in the law. The adoption of a surname, therefore, represented a defiant act of personal liberation. For black fathers, it served as a public announcement of patrilineal authority in a country that had long defined the status of black children by the legal condition of the mother. For slaves with comical names, such as Gustavus Vassa, later known as Olaudah Equiano, the adoption of a new name (or in Equiano's case, perhaps, the reclaiming of his birth name) reversed the process of enslavement.[11]

In the urban North, former slaves hurriedly dropped their classical and even biblical forenames in favor of English names or Anglicized versions of African names. Cudjo was changed to Joe, and Kwaku or Quok to Jack. Men more than women transformed diminutive nicknames, so Billy became William rather than Will. When adopting surnames, a few northern freedpeople retained the family names of their masters, but most wished to obliterate any connection to the past. The Dutch, for example, had been significant slaveholders in New York and New Jersey, but the freedman calling himself

Mingo Roosevelt was rare in adopting a Dutch surname. Far more typical were former slaves such as Bett, who selected names in celebration of their new status. Robert Freedom, Landon Freeland, and Robin Justice all chose surnames in commemoration of their societal rise in rank, as did the runaway Tom Toogood. Still others, as had European serfs hundreds of years before, accepted occupational names, some of which had perhaps been previously used within the black community. Jim the drayman became James Carter, Henry Mason was a bricklayer, Charles Green was a talented gardener, and the ambitious clergyman Jake assumed the name of Jacob Bishop.[12]

Naming patterns took a slightly different course in the rural South, where the larger number of African Americans and the cultural isolation of the slave quarters allowed for the greater preservation of West African customs. Few freedpeople adopted the name of their former masters; Denmark Vesey was a notable exception, and the aspiring carpenter surely did so for business reasons. One could also find celebratory surnames. Two black families in Charles County, Maryland, took the name of Wiseman, and during the early 1790s, an Ann Liberty, Thomas Liberty, and Samuel Liberty all appeared in Maryland records. But many of the new surnames, such as Barjona and Featt, were barely Anglicized versions of African family names. Even more common was the practice probably followed by William Lee, who retained his original master's surname even after being sold. This tradition, grounded in the veneration of one's place of origin, was particularly strong, and it may even have been more important to southern freedmen than a blood identification with a larger family network.[13]

Unhappily, life for the vast majority of freed blacks in the postwar North was anything but Toogood. Black migrants relocating to Philadelphia from the Chesapeake typically arrived sick, hungry, and penniless. Out of desperation, some turned to the almshouse in search of shelter and medical assistance. If sojourners from Maryland and Virginia expected to find a welcoming white populace in those states that were abandoning slavery, they were to be sadly disappointed. As white legislators crafted new state constitutions, they deliberately excluded free black voters. (During the next century, most of New England revised its laws to allow blacks to vote, which African Americans would also be able to do in New York provided they met a high property qualification not imposed on white voters.) The emerging public school systems closed their doors to black children, even when their parents earned enough to pay local taxes. In early national cities, and especially seaport towns, white mobs attacked black families who tried to settle in their neighborhoods. Black Virginians fleeing the slave societies of their birth quickly came to grasp the distinction between freedom and equality.[14]

If anything, southern freedmen often discovered that they suffered a decline in occupational status once they relocated to the North. As plantation bondmen, blacks had been trained in a variety of artisanal capacities, but in cities such as Philadelphia and New York, white craftsmen already occupied those trades, and they zealously guarded the keys to membership in craft unions. Consequently, rural refugees found themselves unable to practice the sort of skilled labor they had pursued as slaves. The arrival of Irish immigrants in the 1790s meant free blacks faced competition from equally desperate arrivals in northern cities. Irish workers soon began to reject what they derided as "nigger work" and refused to labor alongside blacks. Most employers preferred to hire white Pennsylvanians over blacks fresh from the Chesapeake; when they did employ blacks they favored the rental of slaves.[15]

As a result, freed blacks were reduced to seeking employment as unskilled domestic laborers. Black women who worked outside of their home—and the majority did—scrubbed the floors of their white neighbors or cooked food in fancy hotels or middle-class boardinghouses. Those who worked inside the home took in washing, while their husbands labored in service occupations as waiters, stewards, and barbers. The small salaries earned from service occupations meant that black children provided an important source of additional income. White children on farms just outside of Philadelphia went into the fields at an early age, but they worked for their parents rather than for strangers, and rarely for long stretches on any given day. By comparison, black children toiled away from their parents' supervision, often as kitchen staff in boardinghouses, or in some cases as domestics to southern visitors to the North. Most children, however, being small and underfed, swept chimneys, a trade they soon came to dominate. Sweeps earned steady wages but were subject to falls, broken bones, and the soot-induced cough known as "chimney sweeper's cancer." Such jobs meant that black children had little time for a formal education, not that many schools admitted black pupils.[16]

Despite these hardships, free blacks, particularly in the northern states, began to forge and name their societies, ones they deemed worthy of their new status. Just as individual African Americans rising out of bondage had to choose a name, this larger community was forced to wrestle with the same question. Since community leaders were determined to gain respectability and prove to the white majority that they were deserving of citizenship as well as freedom, most of this emergent middle class rejected the label "Negro," which they identified with a miserable past. Some spokesmen embraced the term "colored American," emphasizing their American birth and their resolve to play a role in the formation of the new nation. The majority pushed for "African," both as an unabashed reclaiming of their ancestral roots (although whites uniformly derided Africa as the uncivilized continent) and as a frank admission that they would never be recognized as legitimate Americans. Despite having a white father, New York's William Hamilton embraced the term "African" and spoke proudly of the "country of our forefathers." Within a few short years, as black communities constructed the institutional supports of their new life, the term "African" became attached to fraternal orders, schools, and especially churches.[17]

Among the first African institutions to appear was the black Masonic lodge of Boston. Although the lodge's initial roster boasted a number of members, its chief founder was Prince Hall, a veteran of the war and a long-time civil rights advocate. Evidently freed in 1765, he was one of the group of blacks who peppered the colonial assembly with five petitions between 1773 and 1775. In March 1775, Hall and fourteen other black men were inducted into Military Lodge No. 441, an integrated unit attached to the British regiments then stationed in Boston. Despite this, Hall, like most other Massachusetts blacks, sided with the Patriot cause and served in the militia. At war's end, Hall's group of black veterans attempted to merge with white Masonic lodges. When they were rebuffed, Hall turned to the British, and on May 6, 1787, he was granted a charter for African Lodge No. 459, with Hall installed as grand master. As did white lodges, Hall's unit encouraged the need for education and community service, but unlike white lodges, the African Lodge emphasized racial advancement. "Let us lay by our recreations, and all superfluities," he urged in a 1792 address, in hopes of winning over a hostile white world.[18]

When feasible, black activists joined forces with benevolent whites, particularly those whose long years of activism had earned them the trust of the African American community. The Pennsylvania Abolition Society continued to function throughout the 1780s. One of its most important jobs was to retain handwritten copies of the freedom papers given to blacks whose birthdays marked their entrance into freedom. Since the loss or theft of freedom papers meant possible seizure by one of the many slave catchers who roamed the streets of Philadelphia and Baltimore, a permanent copy held by influential whites frequently proved invaluable. One African American, lacking papers to prove himself free, begged "on his knees" not to be separated from his family by "being sent away to the southward." When his pleas failed, the unnamed freedman threw himself from the deck of the ship as it moved down the Delaware River, and he vanished beneath the waters. The very first name inscribed into the society's manumission book was that of Richard, formerly the slave of Philadelphia attorney Benjamin Chew, who also owned three plantations in southern Delaware. The young freedman would adopt the surname of Allen and become the single most influential minister of his era.[19]

Most black activists, however, thought it necessary to create their own self-help societies rather than simply depend upon the goodwill of white abolitionists. Many African Americans believed that only those groups created and run by freedmen as examples of community uplift could dissipate white animosity and create the foundation for a successful black business class. To that end Absalom Jones and Richard Allen, "two men of the African race," announced the formation of the Philadelphia Free African Society on April 12, 1787. Although both were former bondmen, neither wished to be identified as anything but "free Africans." The leadership invited potential members to "advance one shilling" each month, money that would go to assist widows and the education of members' children. Determined to impress white skeptics, the society's preamble announced that "no drunkard or disorderly person [was to] be admitted," and that a white Quaker businessman "is to be chosen to act as Clerk and Treasurer of this useful institution."[20]

If some members of the emerging black working class found the puritanical attitudes of their leaders somewhat patronizing, at least one African American self-help society proved positively detrimental to the needs of the larger black community. In November 1790, five "free brown men" of Charleston founded the Brown Fellowship Society, an exclusive fraternal organization for men of mixed ancestry only. The refusal of these men to be known as "Africans" or "blacks" proved to be the ultimate expression of racial schism. By its charter, the society was open to no more than fifty men, each of whom had to pay a prohibitive initiation fee of $50 in addition to monthly dues. As was the case with northern organizations, the society's general fund supported aged members too ill or infirm to work and provided impressive funerals and burials in the society's private cemetery. But social advancement and economic security for the "brown" elite, not philanthropy for the dark-skinned slave majority, was the goal of the organization. Despite its motto of "Charity and Benevolence," the society existed for the purpose of drawing artificial, biologically based lines of demarcation between the wealthy freedmen and Charleston's sizeable black population.[21]

Ironically, since Charleston's browns enjoyed the patronage of their white fathers, they faced less open animosity than did the black community in the North when it came to education. The vast majority of northern residents, who refused to allow former slaves to practice the same crafts they had while in bondage or to permit them to vote, saw no logic in admitting black children into their schools. But as northern towns and cities, in the wake of the Revolution, began to fund new public school systems, the fact that few admitted African Americans made this neglect far more obvious than it was in the rural South, where education remained the prerogative of the planter class. For Philadelphia's black community, Benjamin Rush's 1786 *Plan for the Establishment of Public Schools* indicated what was at stake. "Freedom," he argued in a lecture before the American Philosophical Society, "can only exist in the society of knowledge." Perhaps it was not surprising, therefore, that one year later, Prince Hall petitioned the Massachusetts legislature that "some provision may be made for the education of our dear children." Hall observed that although the free black community was never "backward in paying our proportionate part of the [tax] burdens," their sons and daughters were banned "from the free schools in the town of Boston." Attracted to Hall's pragmatic warning that all "must fear for our rising offspring to see them in ignorance," the assembly at length responded by funding several segregated schools.[22]

Most of all, newly liberated African Americans began to build churches. Although a few older colonies such as Virginia or New York were home to a small number of black Christians, converted slaves had been a distinct minority throughout the British plantation societies prior to 1776. Where Africans continued to be imported, as in Georgia and South Carolina, the number of black Christians was smaller still. But the return of peace in 1783 brought a religious transformation to the young Republic. In the southern states, the disestablishment of the staid Anglican Church allowed for the dramatic rise of evangelical denominations such as the Methodists and Baptists. Across the North, former bondpeople trying to forge new communities and impress their white neighbors with their earnestness and industry regarded churches, even more than schools or self-help societies, as the doorway to respectability. Families torn apart by war and slavery were searching for spiritual sustenance, just as white evangelicals were searching for souls to convert.[23]

For many white Americans, particularly southern slaveholders, this new and mutual interest on the part of bondpeople and evangelical sects was not a welcome development. Despite their own pious professions of faith, many planters feared that the Christianization of their laborers might produce egalitarian-minded and hence unruly bondpeople. That proved not to be the case with Michael Pascal's slave Equiano, but masters were right to be worried. Virginia newspapers contained advertisements for runaways who "pretend to have a call to preach the gospel." One runaway, forty-year-old Titus, whose back "retain[ed] the mark of the whip," was "fond of preaching and exhorting." No doubt it was the lash rather than the Bible that prompted Titus's escape, but his master was quite certain that the cause was his "Baptist persuasion." Either way, a religion of universal brotherhood posed obvious problems in a slave society. Joseph Ottolenghe of Georgia was hardly alone in believing that "a slave is ten times worse when a Christian, than in his State of Paganism."[24]

Ottolenghe and others also distrusted evangelical sects for the same reason that blacks were drawn to denominations such as the Methodists: their early hostility to slavery. In his *Thoughts upon Slavery*, published in Britain in 1774, John Wesley condemned what he had witnessed as a young man in colonial Georgia as "the vilest [thing] that ever saw the sun." Moreover, the emotional style of Methodist ministers, together with their theological flexibility—which allowed for the retention of African spirituality—won over black converts from New York City to the Carolina lowcountry. Although Methodist leaders frowned on evidence of African "paganisms," their loose structure of organization made strict enforcement of church dogma difficult. Unlike Anglican ministers, whose required training in Britain led to an easy acceptance of class prerogatives, Methodist ministers, many of whom hailed from the middle class, welcomed any convert who shared their spiritual passion. After hearing Manhattan blacks testify about their religious experiences, Methodist Thomas Rankin gushed, "If the rich in this society were as devoted to God as the poor are, we should see wonders done in this city."[25]

Away from the great plantation districts of the South, Baptist ministers were even more successful in winning converts. Although some Baptists in South Carolina owned slaves, the majority of white Baptists in the upcountry did not, and it was those biracial congregations that attracted black congregants. By 1790, perhaps 25 percent of Virginia Baptists were African American, and white ministers even began to proselytize in the predominantly black Sea Islands between Charleston and Savannah. But many recently imported Africans indicated no interest in abandoning the faith of their ancestors. Some captives suspected the deity of the whites "to be a cheat," reported the Reverend John D. Long, since Africans believed "the preachers and the slaveholders to be in a conspiracy against them." Undaunted, Joseph B. Cook set up a Baptist mission in the town of Beaufort, Georgia, where he baptized thirty-two new members, "all poor unlettered negroes excepting one," and led a predominantly black congregation.[26]

Even more than the Methodists, the Baptists quickly earned the reputation among slaveholders as dangerous meddlers in their affairs. Although most white itinerants wanted only to Christianize the slaves, southern churches frequently found themselves drawn into the private relationships between bondpeople and masters. In 1778, the Kehukee Baptist Association of North Carolina threatened to censure masters who divided black families through sale. Few masters of any persuasion cared to be lectured that the unions of any Christians, including enslaved Christians, were "lawful before God," even when not sanctioned by "the laws of the land." Baptist reformers wished primarily to humanize conceptions of bondage, yet many slaveholders worried that aggressive young bondmen would take advantage of "every indulgent master." Georgia trader George Galphin was hardly alone in complaining that "some Ba[ptist] preacher has been the ruin of all our negro[e]s," and when the Cedar Springs Baptist Church of Spartanburg County, South Carolina, debated "whether or not it is agreeable to the gospel to hold Negroes in Slavery," lowcountry politicians found new reason to distrust the evangelical denominations.[27]

Perhaps it is no accident that most of the African Americans who flocked to the new sects and then took the lead in this postwar religious transformation were young men. Because slave captains like Joseph Vesey preferred to ship young males to American buyers, very few religious leaders from West Africa (all of them elderly men) arrived in the British colonies. African rituals and religious ceremonies were remembered imperfectly by younger captives, who were thus more susceptible to fusing their earlier religiosity (or that of their parents) with the teachings of evangelical Christianity. Massachusetts veteran Lemuel Haynes was just twenty-seven when certified to preach his first public sermon in 1780; freedman Harry Hosier, born a slave in North Carolina, was only a few years older when he became an itinerant Methodist preacher; Peter Spence and Daniel Coker, both born into slavery in Maryland, had just reached the age of twenty-three when they gave their first sermons. Coker's scathing abolitionist pamphlet appeared on the eve of his twenty-sixth birthday. Like his contemporary Equiano, Haynes exhibited a pride in Africa (a place he never visited) in his writings, but also like Equiano, he thought it a continent in need of Christ's teachings. "God, that made the World," he wrote, "hath made of *one Blood* all nations of Men."[28]

Most of these ambitious young preachers, like other freedmen in search of a new life, gravitated toward towns and seaport cities. Even small churches required funding, and since black artisans and craftsmen—who constituted what little black middle class then existed—migrated toward urban areas, black ministers followed close behind. An exhorter known only as Moses, together with Gowan Pamphlet, opened the doors to an all-black church in Williamsburg, Virginia, and shortly thereafter African American congregations appeared in Norfolk, Alexandria, and Richmond. The Davenport Baptist Church in Petersburg was "mostly people of color" by 1788, although it did claim "a few white members," presumably artisans who feared God more than they did their neighbors' disapproving glances. But since most southern towns were small by northern standards, membership rosters at congregations such as Pamphlet's indicated that these churches also drew black Baptists from the nearby countryside, many of whom rode or walked for miles to attend Sunday services.[29]

If planters worried about freedpeople and slaves coming together in large numbers without adequate supervision, they were especially unnerved by the fact that some white evangelicals clearly intended to practice what they preached. One Baptist splinter group, calling themselves the "Emancipating Baptists," denounced both slavery and social inequality in no uncertain terms. One of them, David Barrow of Virginia, went so far as to publish a pamphlet with the descriptive title *Involuntary, Unmerited, Perpetual, Absolute, Hereditary Slavery, Examined on the Principles of Nature, Reason, Justice, Policy, and Scripture*. On other occasions Barrow was less explicit, but his sermons typically implied that simple folk were godlier than the smug, ostentatious gentry. Christ himself "had no *slaves*," he thundered on one occasion, emphasizing each point, "but *wrought* for his *livelihood* at the *business* of a carpenter." Indicative of their color-blind fellowship, other evangelicals acquired the word of God from black exhorters. Harry Hosier, better known as "Black Harry," accompanied the Reverend Francis Asbury as he toured the South, but so eloquent was Hosier that most white Methodists "would rather hear him than the bishops."[30]

For white authorities, the social equalitarianism implicit in white artisans or farmers taking religious instruction from former slaves was dangerous enough, but more perilous still was the very existence of men such as Hosier. Denied entrance to the professions and banned from many crafts in the northern states, African American leaders emerged from the pulpits rather than from the courtrooms or statehouses. Black and white congregants alike flocked to hear the eloquent Hosier. As a result, white mobs, state authorities, and even church directors sought to control such men, typically with limited success. After Moses founded his virtually all-black church in Williamsburg, a mob dragged him through the streets before whipping him. His fellow pastor Gowan Pamphlet faced stiff if somewhat less violent opposition. When one Virginia Baptist Association refused to recognize his church, Pamphlet persisted in holding meetings, which led the council to excommunicate him and much of his congregation. Undaunted, Pamphlet then applied to a Delaware association, which finally agreed in 1793 to recognize his congregation, but with the gratuitous insult that they did so only "as they could not have done better under the circumstances." So unnerved were whites by Pamphlet's religious survival that later the same year Virginia authorities alleged that the "Black Preacher Gawin" was one of the leaders of a massive slave conspiracy.[31]

Perhaps the earliest and most successful of all early national black churches was one that emerged out of the lowcountry swamps. Born in Virginia in 1752, George Liele was sold as a young man to Henry Sharp, a Georgia planter but also an early convert to the Baptist faith. In 1773, Liele felt the call to preach, and Sharp not only encouraged him to do so but freed him in 1777. By that time the fighting had begun, and Sharp cast his lot with the Loyalists, only to fall in battle in 1778. Fearing reenslavement by Sharp's heirs, Liele made his way to British-occupied Savannah. Because much of the coast remained in British hands for the duration of the war, Liele was free to travel and preach in the slave quarters of plantations around Savannah and across the border into South Carolina. There, at Silver Bluff, he came into contact with another exhorter, David George, whom he had known "since he was a boy" in Virginia.[32]

With the coming of peace, Liele and George decided to quit Georgia. David George sailed for Nova Scotia, where he founded the second Baptist congregation in the province, while Liele resettled in Kingston, Jamaica. Before his departure, however, Liele baptized and ordained Andrew Bryan, the enslaved coachman of planter Jonathan Bryan. Unlike many African Americans who embraced Christianity during the Revolutionary era, sixty-three-year-old Andrew Bryan was no longer a young man, but his age likely gave him stature in the slave community. Born around 1716 to African parents at Goose Creek, South Carolina, Bryan first heard Liele preach during the war, and with Liele's departure for Jamaica, Bryan fell into the practice of gathering Liele's old supporters about him each morning to pray and sing before going to the fields. Local white patrollers, fearing Bryan's congregation to be contaminated by both Toryism and good fellowship, twice arrested and tortured him. Unrepentant, Bryan "told his persecutors" that he "*would freely suffer death for the cause of Jesus Christ.*"[33]

Bryan was fortunate to have a most unusual master. The Bryan family was among the earliest converts to evangelicalism in Georgia, and years before, Jonathan Bryan had met influential evangelist George White-field during a visit to Charles Town. Planter Bryan and his son William permitted Andrew the use of "his own house or barn" from which to preach to nearby slaves. Jonathan's death in 1788 left the black congregation without a powerful protector, and shortly after the funeral a Georgia grand jury issued a presentment against William Bryan for "permitting Negroes to assemble, in large bodies, at the plantation called Brampton, within this county, in violation of the patrol law." Refusing to abandon what he regarded as his Christian duty to the evangelized black community, William sold Andrew his freedom in 1789 for £50—even charity had its limits during the depression years after the war—and assisted him in purchasing a lot on Savannah's Mill Street. The First African Baptist Church became the oldest continuously functioning black congregation in the United States.[34]

Bryan's church continued to grow steadily to seven hundred souls by 1800, but the congregation faced its share of tribulations. Because most of Bryan's parishioners were bondpeople who resided on plantations just outside of the city, the journey into Savannah was tiring after a week of hard labor. Masters and overseers retained the final say on who might attend services. Still other whites insisted that their slaves could not be baptized without their permission, as they feared spiritual equality was the first step toward freedom. The Reverend Bryan never learned to read or write, so he preached only what he remembered hearing from better-educated ministers. As a result, the First African Baptist Church emphasized spirited singing, extemporaneous responses from the parishioners, and animated sermons from the pulpit during each Sunday's three services. One white visitor wrote of Bryan's homily that his "performances were far beyond expectations," for his "delivery was good and [he was] quite the orator." A more staid guest derided Bryan's "gifts [as] small" but conceded that the freedman was "clear in the grand doctrines of the Gospel." Bryan died in 1812 at the age of ninety-six; over the years, he was able to purchase the freedom of his wife but not his only daughter or his seven grandchildren.[35]

Other evangelical congregations, invariably describing themselves as "African" churches, soon appeared in other parts of the South. Blacks constructed a Methodist church in Wilmington, North Carolina, during the early 1790s. Like other predominantly black congregations, it ostensibly functioned under the control of the Methodist hierarchy, but white control was intermittent at best. The white minister assigned to the Wilmington circuit visited the African church but once a month, leaving it to local exhorters to deliver three Sunday sermons and a Thursday evening discourse. As such, lay class leaders, and especially black women, were free to conduct church affairs as they saw fit. Of the twelve Wilmington leaders, three were women. In the Savannah congregation, freedwomen served as "church mothers," the female counterparts of deacons, who had the responsibility of creating benevolent societies, teaching Sunday school classes, and helping to raise money to keep the chronically underfunded churches afloat. In a society where wages were unusual and want was common, the ability to contribute cash to a congregation empowered black women in ways unheard of among white churchgoers. When the First African Baptist Church of Savannah received a gift of gold and silver plate from its female parishioners, the bequest revealed the extent to which African American women provided crucial support for the emerging black institutions of the early Republic.[36]

Black conversions to Christianity, of course, were not limited to the creation of actual churches in southern towns and cites. Exhorters such as Liele had begun their ministries in the countryside, and as evangelism spread in the years after the Revolution, informal black preaching became familiar to lowcountry plantations. Since Georgia and South Carolina continued to import African captives, it should have come as no surprise to traveling white ministers that plantation sermons contained a creative melding of African and Christian elements. But while white evangelicals tended to emphasize spiritual equality in the next life and pious serenity in this one, enslaved exhorters tended to be far less patient in their sermons. Even more than established black clergymen, who had to temper their messages to accommodate city authorities, plantation preachers were as likely to emphasize the militancy of the children of Israel as they were to concur with compassionate notions of Christian brotherhood. When David Margate preached that "God would send deliverance to the Negroes, from the power of their masters, as he freed the children of Israel from Egyptian bondage," slaveholding Georgians demanded his arrest. Margate's "business," cautioned his white patron, "was to preach a spiritual deliverance to these people [and] not a temporal one."[37]

Faced with what they regarded as Christian insubordination, the planter class began to fight back. In 1795, in an attempt to silence Andrew Bryan, Savannah's city council resolved that no religious gatherings were permitted "unless they have a white preacher." Such restrictions generally failed, but deacons of the African Baptist Church were forced to place the building itself into a trust controlled by four white men, since freed blacks were restricted from owning large amounts of property. In Charleston and elsewhere, night patrollers arrested slaves returning from Thursday night services. The state of Georgia passed legislation in 1792 that imposed a summer curfew of 9:00 P.M. designed to eliminate nightly services, "unless some of the white ministers preached to them." Even this failed to stop bondpeople from congregating in worship. According to one Georgia grand jury report, "between five and six hundred" slaves met just outside of Savannah "under a pretense of Public Worship." Unless properly sanitized by white authorities, black religious services were an "evil" that had to be abolished.[38]

The white ministers who controlled the church associations, with a few vocal exceptions, proved susceptible to gentry pressure. White evangelicals continued to reside in the same communities and do business with their wealthier neighbors. Still proclaiming their belief in spiritual equality, church leaders began to quietly emphasize amelioration over emancipation.

Their primary duty, white Baptists increasingly argued, was to save souls and persuade their slaveholding congregants to obey St. Paul's injunction to be kind and loving masters. In 1793, the General Association of the Baptist Church in Virginia voted by "a large majority" to cease all debate on abolition, "believing it belongs to the [gentry-controlled] legislative body." By 1800, the General Association went so far as to ban all blacks, even if freed, from voting in church meetings. Only one decade after the Virginia leadership had denounced slavery as a "violent deprivation of the rights of nature," southern Baptists began to institute assigned, segregated seating, so that white Christians would not have to sit beside their black brothers and sisters in Christ.[39]

To the north, independent African churches with predominantly black congregations, ironically, were slower to develop. Although black churches in southern towns were invariably led by freed ministers, the number of available congregants to help create and fund the churches—even when the majority of the parishioners remained enslaved—was far larger than in most regions of the North. The type of men who received the call to preach the gospel, however, varied little across the Republic. In Massachusetts, minuteman and activist Lemuel Haynes became the first black clergyman formally ordained to preach when he received his license toward the end of the war in November 1780. While preaching in Middle Granville, he met Elizabeth Babbitt, an evangelical who shared his religious passions but not his color. Undaunted, they wed and started a family. Perhaps that fact, even more than his uncompromising determination to preach abolitionism from his pulpit, cost Haynes his first position, as minister in Torrington, Connecticut. Finally in 1788 he became the pastor of a mostly white church in Rutland, Vermont, where he remained for thirty years. Like Andrew Bryan, Haynes preached with "no notes but spoke with freedom and correctness," though not for lack of literacy; when not crafting sermons, Haynes published numerous essays on the necessity of a republic to grant liberty to all.[40]

Given its sizeable black population, New York City was surprisingly slow to create African churches, but when they did emerge, they were also far less integrated than Haynes's Vermont congregation. After disestablishment, the Anglican Church, long renowned in the colony for its early interest in black conversion, continued its benevolence as the Episcopal Church. But its efforts were hampered by the fact that many church members resisted the leadership's sermons on liberation, and so a good number of the black Episcopalians who appeared on church rolls were also the slaves of white parishioners. As a result, Methodists made more headway, as they did elsewhere, by fusing African folkways with Christian theology. Because the Methodist hierarchy balked at accepting black preachers as equals, potential Andrew Bryans found it difficult to obtain pulpits. Former slave George White, raised on a Chesapeake plantation, converted to Methodism in 1795 during a "memorable watch-night" service in the Bowery but was unable to find a pulpit. Instead, he spent the next twenty-five years as a wandering itinerant, preaching from the streets of New York City and the fields of northern New Jersey. Even so, by the time White found his calling, 154 black residents of the city had become Methodists.[41]

Faced with such unabashed racism within Christian denominations—the state had yet to pass its act of gradual manumission—black New Yorkers began to consider forming a truly independent African church. When in 1795 the John Street Church refused to reconsider its policy of forcing African American parishioners to sit in segregated "black pews," former slave Peter Williams Sr., who had purchased his freedom with his extra earnings as a cigar maker, marched out of the building, followed by the rest of the black congregation. Williams's son, also named Peter, then only sixteen, would go on to become the leading black minister at Harlem's St. Philip's African Church. Between 1796 and 1826, blacks in Manhattan founded four Methodist Episcopal congregations, three Protestant Episcopal ones, two Baptist churches, and even a Presbyterian congregation. Although these principally black churches generally followed the pattern established by their white parent organizations and catered to their members' spiritual needs, these African congregations focused also on their parishioners' economic and political aspirations, unlike the white churches they had left behind. In the process, black entrepreneurs such as Williams and black preachers developed the critical leadership skills their white counterparts learned in the professions prohibited to African Americans.[42]

The African church that was to have the greatest impact across the young Republic, however, was also one of the last to be founded during the Revolutionary era. Its leader, Richard Allen, had helped Absalom Jones begin Philadelphia's Free African Society in 1787. At the age of seventeen, just as the war was breaking out, Richard heard an itinerant Methodist preacher and became "born again." Regarding his owner, Stokely Sturgis, as both a decent man yet also one badly in need of a lesson in Christian egalitarianism, Richard invited the revivalist to his master's home. Swiftly converted as well, Sturgis agreed to liberate Richard and his brothers, but as he was "much in debt," they would have to purchase their freedom. Determined to put an end to the "bitter pill" of bondage, Richard set to work in a Delaware brickyard, hauling bricks and chopping wood for $50 per month. Following six years of backbreaking toil, Richard amassed the agreed-upon $2,000, and became a free man on August

27, 1783. He promptly adopted the surname of Allen, perhaps in honor of the progressive Pennsylvania jurist who had been Chew's neighbor.[43]

Even before making his final payment to Sturgis, Allen began his ministry. When Francis Asbury traveled through Delaware in 1779—perhaps with Harry Hosier in tow—he ordained Allen as a Methodist preacher. With his freedom papers in hand, Allen took to the road. He first used Wilmington as a base of operations, but a host of white Methodists offered him rooms in nearby states, and 1784 and 1785 found Allen walking the circuit from Delaware to Burlington, New Jersey, and from Baltimore to Pennsylvania. "I walked until my feet became so sore I blistered," he remembered in later years. "I could scarcely bear them to the ground." By early 1786, Allen finished his itinerancy and settled permanently in Philadelphia. There he fell in with fellow Delaware freedman Absalom Jones, and together the two men turned to activism. Like Jones, Allen attended the integrated St. George's Methodist Church, and each Sunday at daybreak he preached to blacks at the sunrise service. "I soon saw a large field open in seeking and instructing my African brethren," he wrote.[44]

When not preaching at St. George's, Allen gave sermons at the nondenominational Free African Society or even on street corners, "wherever [he] could find an opening." Within the year, the number of black congregants at St. George's, many of whom had been Anglicans or Quakers, rose to forty-two. Allen's enormous success in attracting Philadelphia blacks led to friction with the church's white elders. They reproached him for exhorting in a euphoric manner and urged him to deliver his sermons in a calm, unemotional fashion. Other congregants balked at any black presence in the church and regarded the rising number of African American members—some of whom remained enslaved—"as a nuisance." As a result, Allen and Jones began to consider the prospect of finding a more hospitable "place of worship for the colored people," or perhaps even building an independent African church. A few well-do-to black parishioners, however, worried about the possibility of offending their white benefactors, and with good reason; when Allen and Jones broached the possibility with white churchmen, their patrons angrily responded with "very degrading and insulting language."[45]

The inevitable explosion came in late 1792 or early 1793. As St. George's grew in membership, church elders began construction of an upstairs gallery so as to segregate their black parishioners while keeping their weekly tithes. Allen and Jones had no intention of enduring such humiliation and planned a protest. Although the leaders later insisted that black parishioners received word of the newly implemented segregation only after they took their seats, that can hardly be true, since Allen spent so many hours at St. George's.

As they prayed, Allen heard "considerable scuffling and low talking." Opening his eyes, Allen saw several white trustees attempting to drag a kneeling Jones to his feet, saying, "[Y]ou must get up—you must not kneel here." Jones asked them to wait until the prayer was concluded, but the official insisted that he "must get up now or I will call for aid and force you away." With that, in a clearly prearranged act, Jones, Allen, and the entire black congregation swept out the doors "in a body," and the whites, Allen wrote, "were no more plagued by us in the church."[46]

Faced with a need for funding, Jones believed their best recourse was to turn to the Episcopalians, particularly since so many black Christians in the city had initially converted to Anglicanism. But Allen could not imagine leaving Methodism behind. There "was no religious sect or denomination that would suit the capacity of the colored people as well as the Methodists," he argued, "for the plain and simple gospel suits best for any people." And so the protesters splintered. In 1794 Jones founded the St. Thomas African Episcopal Church. The two men remained close, and Allen left Jones and his flock "in peace and love," but the split also revealed emerging class divisions, not just theological ones. The more "respectable" black members of St. George's followed Jones, while the enslaved and members of the free black working class went with Allen. Out of desperation, Allen turned to his old patron Francis Asbury for support. The bishop interceded with the Methodist leadership, who grudgingly acquiesced in the building of an all-black church. With conference funds, Allen purchased a shuttered blacksmith shop and had it dragged to a lot on the corner of Sixth and Lombard streets. On June 29, 1794, Bishop Asbury dedicated the African Methodist Episcopal (AME) Church, commonly known as Bethel. At the age of thirty-four, the Reverend Allen had his own congregation and a permanent pulpit.[47]

Despite the religious split within the black community, Allen and Jones remained close and continued to work together. In the same way that their various congregations were the logical next step after the formation of the Free African Society, it followed that their third project was the creation of a school for Philadelphia's black community. Despite his irritation with independent black churches, Rush remained the most vocal supporter of black education among influential whites. When pressed in early 1793, Rush agreed to help, but his efforts were hampered by the inclination of Pennsylvania's white churchgoers to instead donate funds for French refugees escaping the slave revolt in Saint-Domingue. An underfinanced school for black children opened in 1797 survived only a few months. Absalom Jones tried again two years later, but an inspection committee from the Pennsylvania Abolition Society judged him too lenient with his students and reported

Constructed out of a blacksmith's shop, Philadelphia's Bethel African Methodist Episcopal Church, shown here in 1829, became the cornerstone of the city's free black population. *Library Company of Philadelphia.*

it "not practicable at present to have the black children taught by a black person." Richard Allen fared little better. In 1795 his Bethel Church opened a Sunday school, and evidence suggests that he launched a short-lived night school the following year.[48]

The triumph of the city's African churches, however, was an altogether different story. By 1800, roughly 40 percent of Philadelphia's growing black community belonged to one of the two congregations. Within several years, interracial churches in other parts of the nation experienced secessions, and the Bethel Church became the hub of a quickly expanding series of African Methodist Episcopal churches. Satellite congregations sprang up in Baltimore, Wilmington, Richmond, Norfolk, and New York City. While affluent patrons such as Rush quietly prayed that these congregations would become mirror images of white congregations, the black congregations had waged their own revolution against an oppressive hierarchy, and it was inevitable that they would evolve in a separate direction. White visitors to African churches or black funerals consistently remarked on the striking difference between staid white services and the ecstatic nature of black exhorters, but then AME churches, particularly in the Chesapeake, embodied a black culture that was nearly two centuries in the making. To the extent that separate Virginia congregations sprang to life only after it was clear that the legislature had no intention of passing a law for gradual emancipation, African churches in Richmond or Norfolk stood as eloquent testimony to the failure of the American Revolution to create an integrated, egalitarian society.[49]

Since Charleston was demographically the blackest city in the early Republic, it followed that South Carolina's leading port was soon home to an AME congregation second only in size to that of Bethel. Here too the prelude was a mass exodus from the white-run Methodist fold. But as the Carolina lowcountry was manifestly not Pennsylvania, the potential leaders, at least initially, preached Christian humility as much as they urged community activism. Interested in the possibility of founding a black congregation, two South Carolina Methodists, Morris Brown, a free man of color born around 1770, and Henry Drayton, a former slave, journeyed north to confer with Allen about the formation of a branch of the Philadelphia church in Charleston. Both Brown, a pious bootmaker who once served twelve months in the city Workhouse for using his earnings to help slaves purchase their freedom, and Drayton were already ordained. Brown in particular was a pragmatist who believed that his first responsibility was to the spiritual life of the city's black community rather than its political betterment in this world. In hopes of conciliating Charleston authorities, Brown encouraged his son Malcolm to join the accommodationist Brown Fellowship Society.[50]

Morris Brown's Bethel worried Charleston's Methodist hierarchy, who were nervous about their potential loss of theological control. Brown and Drayton returned south to discover that Anthony Senter, an influential Methodist leader, was attempting to reassert authority over the black Methodist majority and the disbursement of the funds from their collection plates and other revenues. In a show of force—as well as a calculated act of sacrilege—white trustees voted to construct a carriage house atop a small black cemetery. In response, 4,376 slaves and free blacks quit the church in protest and began construction of an independent African Methodist church. The "Whites wanted nothing," a suddenly less than pacific Henry Drayton remarked, "but a good spanking with a sword."[51]

Built on Anson Street near the corner of Boundary, the church found its congregation growing so quickly that the city's black community soon began work on a second church in the predominantly black Hampstead neighborhood along the town's northern edge. The African churches, as both white and black Charlestonians dubbed the congregations, drew their leadership from free craftsmen such as Morris Brown. Of the twenty-six freedmen who boldly affixed their signatures to the petition sent to the state legislature for the purpose of incorporating the African Methodist Church, at least ten were artisans. The two churches housed the largest black Methodist congregations in the South, and Charleston's membership was second only in size to the parent body in Philadelphia. Although briefly a practicing Presbyterian, free carpenter Denmark Vesey promptly became both a member and a lay preacher in the Cow Alley congregation, as did his sons Robert and Sandy Vesey.[52]

Like Allen's Philadelphia church, Brown's emerging Charleston congregations implicitly challenged not merely white religious domination but white social and political control as well. The black community's struggle to create autonomous sacred institutions by seceding from white governance was, in the context of a slave society, a decidedly radical act. In the process of managing their own churches, slaves and free blacks defied established theories on African intellectual inferiority. As individuals, even the shrewdest slaves could amass little property, but collectively, impoverished freedpeople and enslaved congregants purchased burial grounds, raised and disbursed charity funds for care of the aged and indigent, maintained church buildings, and in the North attempted to create schools for their children. Because both white ministers and secular authorities regarded the African churches as dangerous bastions of slave autonomy, Charleston's city government would make it a routine practice to disrupt these services of "Gullah tribe Mechanic's and draymen."[53]

From Mum Bett's individual choice of a new name to the black community's collective debate over what label to embrace, and from Jones's formation of the Free African Society to the creation of black churches by Andrew Bryan, Richard Allen, and Morris Brown, these actions reflected the needs and aspirations of a free people. Many of those who attended these congregations or requested the assistance of black mutual aid societies, of course, remained enslaved, or had a family member who had not yet reached the legal age required by the state for manumission. Even the decision to adopt the group term "African" suggests that newly freed Americans recognized that the nation, for all of its discourse of republicanism and individual rights, at best tolerated their presence. If the architects of these emerging communities regarded their schools and churches as institutions of self-help (and also self-defense), even white abolitionists typically saw their creation as acts of defiance. Little wonder that even as ministers like Andrew Bryan sought only to protect their flocks, other black men and women, such as Bryan's spiritual mentor George Liele, turned their backs on the United States and joined the thousands of black Loyalists who fled American shores.

EIGHT

Harry Washington's Atlantic Crossings

The Migrations of Black Loyalists

FOR EIGHT YEARS, Harry Washington resided on the same plantation as William Lee, but in many ways their lives were worlds apart. Although young "Mulatto Will" adopted the surname of Lee as an adult, William was undoubtedly the forename given to him at birth. By contrast, the man who came to be known as Harry carried names bestowed upon him by a series of masters, the last of whom was George Washington. Lee was a light-skinned Virginian, whereas Harry Washington was born near the Gambia River in West Africa. They must have known one another, but they spent little time in each other's company. Harry, acquired by planter Washington in 1763 at a Virginia estate sale, labored first in the Great Dismal Swamp, where his master hoped to drain enough land to create a rice plantation. By 1766, Harry was moved to Mount Vernon, where he worked "upon [the] Mill Race" and in the fields around the big house. Two years later, Washington purchased William Lee, who dwelled beside his master. One remained loyal to his master—even in Philadelphia, where he might have slipped quietly away—while the other eventually pledged loyalty to a distant king.[1]

In at least one respect, however, they followed similar trajectories, ending their lives near where they began. William was born on the Lee estate around 1750, and despite his travels about America, he died not far away, in his cabin at Mount Vernon in 1828. Harry Washington's travels were greater still, for he crossed the Atlantic twice. Like so many slaves, Washington lacks precise birth and death dates, but British records indicate that he was born around 1740, so he was roughly sixty years old when he vanished from the sight of history in 1800. By then he was living on the Bullom Shore, just north of Freetown in the colony of Sierra Leone, approximately five hundred miles from where he was sold into slavery near the Gambia River. William Lee was born a slave; Harry became one while still very young. But both lived long enough to die as free men, separated though they were by a vast ocean and even wider political loyalties.[2]

Harry Washington's first marriage was torn asunder both by the demands of the plantation regime and by the dislocation of war. Although Harry evidently lived with a woman named Nan while laboring in the Swamp, the two were separated in 1766, when his master sent Harry to work on the main plantation, while Nan was assigned to the distant farm of Muddy Hole. Perhaps that separation cost planter Washington the loyalty of the African, but more likely Harry simply wished to be free. He ran away in July 1771, but Washington placed "Letters & Advertisements of Harry," who was captured and returned to Mount Vernon. When Dunmore's flotilla sailed up the river during the summer of 1776, Harry was one of the slaves who scrambled aboard a British craft. When the governor abandoned Virginia for New York City in late August, Harry sailed north with him, but no bondwoman by the name of Nan appeared in British records.[3]

Still fit at age thirty-six, Harry Washington joined the newly formed Black Pioneers, a Loyalist band attached to the Royal Artillery Department. He rose quickly through the ranks, and soon Corporal Washington was nearly as famous among the blacks who carried the Union Jack as General Washington was among the white soldiers who followed the Stars and Stripes into battle. In 1780, the Black Pioneers were ordered south, where they faced Francis Marion's guerrilla band in the Carolina lowcountry. The end of fighting found Washington in occupied Charles Town, and in December 1782 he boarded the last British warship to evacuate the harbor. Once more, Harry Washington sailed with the British for New York City.[4]

For the better part of the next year, Washington remained in Manhattan. Few black Loyalists believed that their commanders would hand them back to their masters to face beatings and resale or, paradoxically, even a traitor's noose for fighting against a nation that refused to recognize them as citizens. Yet veterans of the Black Pioneers experienced more than their share of racism at the hands of their liberators, and the realists among them understood that Dunmore's proclamation was born of wartime considerations rather than of egalitarian benevolence. Disquieting rumors reached Corporal Washington that his old master was just up the Hudson River in Newburgh, negotiating with the British and pressing the new commander, Sir Guy Carleton, to return all stolen property, "especially the Negroes." Harry might have been more worried still had he been aware that the general evidently knew he was in the city. "Several of my own [slaves] are with the Enemy but I scarce ever bestowed a thought on them," Washington informed Virginia governor Benjamin Harrison. In fact, General Washington intended to press the point of human property hard when he met with Carleton.[5]

The British general stubbornly refused to yield, however, and so on July 31, 1783, Harry Washington boarded the *L'Abondance*, bound for Port Roseway, Nova Scotia. Sailing with him were 276 other black men, women, and children of all ages. Many hailed from Virginia, but there were refugees from every state in the new nation. David Edwards, age twenty-seven and described as a "stout fellow," claimed he was born free in Boston, where he served as a coachman. Jenny Toney, "worn out" from hard labor at fifty-two, had lived in both Connecticut and Rhode Island, and Becky Seabrook had escaped from South Carolina. Dinah Weeks had been owned by Robert Bruce of New York, and James Jones was "of the Island of Bermuda." Prior to the chaos of war, roughly 90 percent of runaways had been young men, but nearly half of those who boarded the *L'Abondance* were women and children. Jane Thompson, who thought herself about seventy, traveled with her five-year-old grandchild. Like a good many of the black Virginians on board, Thompson swore to British authorities that she "was born free." One of those who saw no reason to prevaricate was the self-liberated Sarah Jones of South Carolina, a "stout wench" of thirty-three, who appears to have married Harry Washington upon arrival in Canada.[6]

Runaway Harry Washington, having risen to the rank of corporal in the Black Pioneers, boarded the *L'Abondance* on July 31, 1783, bound for Nova Scotia. *British National Archives.*

Washington's Atlantic crossings were a part of the black Loyalist diaspora that would transform the British Atlantic empire. Countless thousands of Africans and black Americans abandoned the United States after 1782 in search of liberty. Sometimes they put down roots where they landed, but more often they relocated numerous times as European powers reshuffled their colonial holdings or as they discovered that British promises of freedom rarely translated into prosperity or political equality. Some washed ashore in East Florida, while others landed in Jamaica or the Bahamas. A few reached Britain and settled into a life of poverty in London. Most, like Harry Washington, evacuated to the windswept coast of Nova Scotia before setting sail a final time for West Africa. In the process, they carried with them their culture, their religious faith, and their firm belief in revolutionary struggle. In the same way that black Patriots who returned to New England after fighting in the war were determined to impose abolition on their communities, battle-hardened black Loyalists like Corporal Washington were not about to accept second-class citizenship within the empire. But their flight from the United States also serves as a tragic reminder that for most former slaves, the pursuit of happiness and freedom, ironically, was available only in British colonies such as Canada, and not in the Republic that trumpeted its support of natural rights.[7]

————

Even as British troops stacked their muskets at Yorktown on the afternoon of October 19, 1781, weary Patriots had every cause to believe that the fighting would continue. General Cornwallis had surrendered nearly one-quarter of the British army in North America, but that meant that approximately 21,000 redcoats remained at arms. King George's forces occupied New York City, Savannah, Charles Town, Wilmington, North Carolina, and Penobscot, and there was no reason to believe that Parliament would not reassign regulars stationed in Canada, East Florida, or the Caribbean. Huddled within those mainland enclaves were somewhere between fifteen thousand and twenty thousand African Americans. Some had fled to British lines as early as 1775, although most refugees escaped Patriot masters only after the 1778 invasion of the southern states. Black residents of Manhattan, Savannah, and Charles Town, of course, simply came within British protection following the capture of those ports. Should Lord North fall from power and Parliament vote to discontinue hostilities, the fate of this large refugee group—roughly four times the number of Connecticut's prewar black population—would have to be resolved.[8]

The issue of the refugees, unsurprisingly, became a major point of contention between the United States and Britain even before the formal surrender ceremony. To reach final terms, Cornwallis and Washington each appointed two commissioners. The American general chose the viscount de Noailles, the marquis de Lafayette's brother-in-law, and John Laurens. Neither of the two young officers was shy about his antislavery sentiments, so it was only with difficulty that the commissioners informed their counterparts of a key American demand: all "property" within the British garrison, including runaway slaves, was subject to recovery. Since sick or starving black refugees were already attempting to slip away under the cover of darkness, General George Weedon of the Virginia militia stationed sentinels "all along the Beach" to recapture runaways. Hiding in a grotto and desperately short of provisions for his eight thousand soldiers, Cornwallis was in no position to bargain. General Washington recovered two young bondwomen, Lucy, age twenty, and eighteen-year-old Esther. In the process, the victorious American army, which boasted a number of black Patriots from New England, established an unfortunate precedent of demanding and obtaining wayward human property.[9]

For British officers stationed in more secure locations, Cornwallis's inability to protect civilians within his lines was nothing short of dishonorable. If Dunmore's proclamation was born of military necessity, a good many officers had come to respect their black allies. For every aristocratic British soldier who believed that black refugees existed only to polish their boots or cook their meals, there was another who valued the courage of a Harry Washington. Among the latter was Colonel James Moncrief, who had constructed fortifications for Charles Town before volunteering to lead the Black Pioneers. When word of Cornwallis's capitulation reached the Carolinas, Moncrief wrote directly to General Henry Clinton in New York, boldly informing his commander that he had no intention of betraying those "who look to me for protection in this part of the country." Fearing that Cornwallis's surrender agreement might develop into a uniform policy, Moncrief reminded Clinton of "the many advantages which his Majesty's service has derived from their labor in carrying on the different works in this and the province of Georgia." So devoutly did Moncrief believe in the ability of black troops that he raised the prospect of fighting on at the head of "a Brigade of the Negroes of this country." But even as Moncrief wrote these words, the humiliated Cornwallis was drafting his resignation, and across the Atlantic the Marquis of Rockingham, a vocal advocate of peace, was replacing Lord North.[10]

Rockingham merely wanted the conflict done with, but one of his appointees was openly sympathetic to the American position. Seventy-five-year-old Scottish merchant Richard Oswald, named as one of the British peace negotiators, had made his fortune buying Africans at Bunce Island in the mouth of the Sierra Leone River, and before the war his leading agent in the Carolinas was Henry Laurens. At the conclusion of the Yorktown campaign, Laurens was imprisoned in the Tower of London, having been captured by the Royal Navy after obtaining Dutch support for the American cause. Oswald posted £2,000 bail for his old business partner's release (before Lord Mansfield's court), and the two sailed for Paris, where they joined the remainder of the American delegates, Benjamin Franklin, John Jay, and John Adams. Despite the fact that his son John was then advocating the use of black troops against the British, Laurens insisted that the treaty include the "stipulation that the British troops should carry off no Negroes or other American property." Adams and Jay expressed surprise that Oswald agreed to the demand, but only because they were unaware of Oswald's plans to purchase a plantation in South Carolina. Despite their increasingly antislavery sensibilities, Jay and Franklin raised no objection to Laurens's insertion, which became Article VII of the preliminary Peace of Paris, inked by the delegates on November 29, 1782. Shortly thereafter, word arrived in France that John Laurens had been shot and killed on August 27, most likely by black Loyalists, in one of the final skirmishes of the war.[11]

Henry Laurens, however, was quite unable to control the behavior of his French allies. As the conflict wound down, Chesapeake slaves tended to flee toward any ship in American waters flying a foreign flag. The problem became so acute that George Washington drafted a personal appeal to the comte de Grasse, whose fleet was harboring "forty of [the] most valuable Slaves" belonging to a single Maryland planter. "I will take it as a great favor," Washington begged, "if your Excellency will direct them to be sent back." Governor Harrison even beseeched the comte de Rochambeau to order a return of "the slaves supposed to be with the French army," but with little luck. Some of their enslaved domestics, the French general explained, were purchased in Rhode Island, and other blacks in their employ had sworn they were free. Still others had accompanied their masters from the French Caribbean. One of the latter was André Rigaud, who fought beside his French master at the siege of Savannah. Rigaud returned to Saint-Domingue with military experience and radical notions of liberty and fraternity, both of which he would put to good use in 1791 when Haitian slaves rose for their freedom.[12]

Further complicating matters for those expected to sort out the meaning of Article VII was the fact that a good many of the blacks behind British lines in South Carolina were not runaways but the legal property of white Loyalists. Some Tory refugees had arrived in Charles Town with their slaves in tow, while others had purchased "abandoned" blacks after reaching the occupied city. A few masters even encountered their lost property on the streets of the cramped port town. When one startled master "spoke to several" of the runaways, they replied "with an air of insolence [that] they were not coming back." Disgruntled Loyalists suspected that sympathetic British officers were coaching runaways to insist that they had been born free, and given the implausibly large number of black Virginians who later advanced the same claim before boarding the *L'Abondance,* such suspicions were undoubtedly true. One Carolina master swore that his slave was "Secreted away by her friends" before they were to "embark the next morning." With some runaways crossing the Ashley and Cooper rivers *into* Charles Town while the chattel of white Loyalists paddled *away* from the city, harried British administrators might be forgiven for thinking that an orderly evacuation of the mainland took precedence over sorting out questions of slave ownership.[13]

Although Harry Washington and his regiment were evacuated north to Manhattan, the vast majority of Carolina freedpeople and slaves planned to sail south toward British East Florida. Much of the colony remained swampy and sparsely populated. A small town had emerged under the protective shadow of massive Fort Augustine, and during the two decades after 1763, Carolina and Georgia planters had begun to establish estates along the St. Johns River. As early as 1776, the crown settled some blacks there, most likely Virginia slaves who escaped with Dunmore's flotilla, and with the British invasion of the southern states in 1779 the influx of Loyalists and black runaways became so pronounced that the African American population quickly quadrupled in size. Given this fact, together with its close proximity to Savannah, it was sound logic for Lord North, as one of his final official acts as prime minister in January 1782, to designate Florida an asylum for Loyalists. Within eight months of the surrender at Yorktown, roughly three hundred evacuees had arrived from Georgia, three-fifths of whom were black.[14]

To hasten the moment of final departure, American troops surrounding Charles Town imposed a trade embargo on the city, particularly regarding foodstuffs. "The more scanty we can render their supplies of provisions," observed General Nathanael Greene, "the sooner it will happen, and the fewer negroes they will have in their power to take with them." By early December 1782, a virtual armada was assembled in Charles Town harbor. Because British authorities in the South did not keep precise records of Loyalist evacuees, the exact number of refugees abandoning the lowcountry remains uncertain. Fragmentary documents, however, suggest that between seven thousand and eight thousand blacks sailed away from the city on December 14, the vast majority of whom were yet-enslaved Carolinians who belonged to white Loyalists. But at least fifteen hundred of these women and men, including Harry Washington, left Charles Town as freedpeople. Although few African

Americans believed a future as Tory refugees would be anything but bleak, no black Carolinian wished to remain behind to face the wrath of former masters, and as the ships slowly pulled away from the docks, blacks not authorized to board clung to the sides or tried to paddle along in small craft. Six months before, the British had abandoned Savannah in similar fashion, taking with them nearly 4,000 blacks, including 150 African American soldiers.[15]

No sooner had the British ships begun to discharge their human cargo in Florida than they had to reload them. On January 20, 1783, exactly one year to the month after North's ministry designated East Florida a "commodious asylum" for Loyalists, the Rockingham government retroceded the colony to Spain. Still determined to reclaim its lost human property, the state of South Carolina, having received word of the November 1782 preliminary treaty of peace, dispatched a commissioner to East Florida to hold the evacuated blacks under Article VII. Faced with yet another logistical nightmare as they planned a second evacuation, British officials in St. Augustine were in no mood to hear more demands from Carolina Patriots. According to British embarkation records, by the time the last ship, the *Cyrus*, cast off on August 29, 1785, 3,398 white Loyalists and 6,540 blacks had vacated Florida for various ports around the British Atlantic. In the twenty-two months between June 1783 and April 1785, the population of the British Bahamas increased by nearly seven thousand people. Since many of the blacks shipped to Florida had been transported as the chattel of white Tories, it was probably not surprising that most of the black refugees were put to work in the cane fields. Late in 1784, however, one enterprising Bahaman planter, James Grant, sold twenty-six of his slaves—ten men, five women, and eleven children—back into servitude in South Carolina. One of the children was an infant girl, newly christened with the name of Providence.[16]

At least 714 slaves evacuated from East Florida arrived in Jamaica. Since the outbreak of war in 1775, Loyalists from the mainland had been relocating to Kingston. According to one church registry in St. Elizabeth's parish, 183 white families from Georgia alone had settled on the island, bringing with them nearly five thousand slaves. Certainly the greatly diminished number of blacks in South Carolina by war's end largely explains the dramatic increase in the island's black population, which rose from 166,914 in 1768 to 240,000 in 1785. So many black Americans arrived in Jamaica that professional traders imported almost no Africans in the decade before 1785. But in that year a series of hurricanes flattened the island and washed away the plantain crop, which served as the principal source of food for slaves. Then in 1788, a ship from Philadelphia brought yellow fever to the island, and the black newcomers to Jamaica, overworked and underfed, were the first to fall victim. Between the hurricanes and the fever, fifteen thousand slaves perished on the island within a period of two years.[17]

Initially, those Tories emigrating from the mainland were welcomed in the British islands. Caribbean planters had long regarded British authority as the best guardian against slave rebelliousness, and colonial administrators who had served on the mainland before 1776 were especially eager to assist white refugees who left North America "on account of troubles in their own country." But when trade with the mainland failed to revive with the end of hostilities, Caribbean masters worried that shortages of foodstuffs might lead to famine, which typically resulted in slave rebellions. As whites overheard enslaved refugees whispering about liberty and natural rights, they began to fear that the spread of black Americans throughout the empire meant the dissemination of radical ideas. These fears nearly became reality in 1787 when John Murray, the Earl of Dunmore, was appointed governor of the Bahamas. Wishing to clarify which black refugees were free and which remained legitimate Tory property, Dunmore, still enjoying his somewhat undeserved fame as the Virginia liberator, empaneled a "Negro Court" to adjudicate property claims. A number of "rebel property Negroes" tried to reach the court but were prevented from doing so by armed whites. Some of the blacks fled inland, while others armed themselves for battle. Fearing widespread "insurrection of their Slaves," terrified planters appealed to the governor to disband his court. Faced with rebellion from whites and blacks alike, Dunmore retreated, inviting only those blacks who could document their freedom to attend his tribunal. Of the thirty slaves naive enough to do so, the court found only one of them to be free. A delegation of planters appeared before the governor to thank him for his "fair, candid and impartial Trials which have been afforded our runaway Slaves," and black refugees in the island returned to a life of unwaged toil.[18]

Of the three large enclaves of black Loyalists and refugees in North America in the months after Yorktown, that left only British-occupied Manhattan to be evacuated. Just as the debacle in Virginia meant a political change at the highest levels, the surrender of eight thousand British soldiers also necessitated a military alteration. The ignominy of that submission rested with Cornwallis, but the larger strategy was Henry Clinton's. When word of Yorktown reached London in November 1781, Lord North recognized that the humiliated Clinton would wish to be replaced, which in any event the mood of Parliament demanded. To succeed Clinton and negotiate the retreat from New York, North chose Sir Guy Carleton, the former governor of Quebec.[19]

Upon his arrival in May 1782, Carleton discovered more than three thousand black Loyalists living in the city. Although some white Tories continued to own domestics, most black refugees were runaways who had fled into Manhattan from farms on Long Island and estates along the banks of the Hudson. Although there is no indication that Carleton had long possessed antislavery convictions, he was well aware of his predecessor's Phillipsburg proclamation of 1779, which had guaranteed liberty to "every Negro who shall desert the Rebel Standard." The preliminary treaty of peace and its troubling Article VII lay seven months into the future, but Carleton was well aware of the American demands placed on Cornwallis. As he pondered the situation, he came to believe that Lord Mansfield's 1772 decision perhaps applied to British-held sections of the Americas and not merely to the British isles. As "the British Constitution not allowing of slavery but holding out freedom and protection to all who came within," he concluded in a slightly strained interpretation of the Somerset ruling, promises made to black dependents by Clinton should be "universally deemed equal to Emancipation." For Carleton, national honor, even more than morality, permitted no compromise on this point.[20]

As it became clear that Carleton had no intention of expelling them from the city, and especially after the December 1782 arrival of the Black Pioneers in Manhattan, runaways from the countryside increased their attempts to reach the island. Although sentinels captured a number of runaways, others, such as South Carolina runaway Boston King, who swam two rivers and stole a boat from Staten Island, were successful. In New York City, Carleton had fourteen months to protect Loyalists like King, and he dealt harshly with white residents who hindered the process of black liberty. When Thomas Willis, a city employee, accepted a bribe to return Caesar, "who came to New York City under [Clinton's] proclamation," Carleton fined Willis fifty guineas and ordered him exiled from the city. Nor did the British general reserve freedom only for those blacks who arrived during Clinton's tenure. When Jacob Duryea of Dutchess County entered the city to make a delivery of foodstuffs, Duryea's slave announced he intended to remain in Manhattan. Duryea lashed the slave to his boat and prepared to shove off into the Hudson, only to be stopped by a Hessian patrol. The Germans turned the matter over to Carleton, who freed the bondman.[21]

By the spring of 1783, seventeen months had passed since the surrender at Yorktown, but General Washington, comfortably ensconced in a large stone house thirty miles up the Hudson in Newburgh, New York, was in no hurry to press for negotiations. Far across the Atlantic, the diplomats were laboring over the treaty, and given his headaches near at hand—many of his white soldiers, ironically, were in open revolt over unpaid wages—the American commander's inclination was to await word from Paris. On April 5,

Thomas Townshend, the new secretary of state for the colonies, apprised Carleton of the contents in the preliminary peace agreement, and at about the same time, word reached Newburgh of the November 29 agreement, including Laurens's inclusion of Article VII. Both Carleton and Washington issued the order for an immediate cessation of all hostilities, and on April 21, the American general wrote Carleton to request "a Personal interview" so that they might coordinate the release of British prisoners in America, the evacuation of Manhattan, and the restoration of all American property. Several of Carleton's aides argued against a face-to-face meeting, but after considering the matter, the British general agreed to it.[22]

On May 6, the two delegations—those of Sir Carleton and George Washington, their senior staffs, and Governor George Clinton—met at a farmhouse in Tappan, some twenty-five miles up the Hudson. Following nearly an hour of pleasantries and congratulations, they faced one another across a parlor table. With "great Slowness, and [in] a low Tone of Voice," Washington explained the American demands. Topping the list was "the Preservation of Property from being carried off, and especially the Negroes." Carleton had already informed Parliament that he regarded Oswald's capitulation on this to be "a disgrace," and now he coolly informed his American counterpart that since the independent republic desired the removal of British forces as quickly as possible, several ships had already sailed for Nova Scotia, ferrying with them "a large number of Negroes." The normally unflappable Washington was surprised and even angry, shouting: "Already embarked!" Carleton calmly replied that national honor required keeping promises made by Henry Clinton, to which Washington responded that such conduct was "totally different from the Letter and Spirit of the [November 29] Treaty."[23]

According to one of Carleton's aides, the meeting continued contentious for some time. "The Rebels bluster about this Matter and declare it a Violation of the Provisional Treaty," one reported, but Carleton blandly insisted that Article VII was only meant to apply to runaways and other forms of property removed *after* the 1782 accord was signed. As a representative of the British government, Carleton observed, Oswald surely did not intend to deliver to their former masters blacks who had been liberated by the Phillipsburg proclamation, since that "would be a disagreeable violation of the public faith." Former slaves who arrived within British lines prior to the previous November were "permitted to go wherever they please." Should they "chuse to go [back] to their Masters, it is well," Carleton added, sensitive of the fact that he was speaking to a slaveowner, "if not, they are transported to Nova Scotia or else where as they desire." The "Altercation" ended when an exasperated Washington suddenly stood and called for wine and food. Preparing dinner in the farmhouse kitchen, and undoubtedly hanging on every word, was "Black Sam" Fraunces, the Jamaican freeman who ran the Queen's Head Tavern.[24]

Late that night, Washington drafted a lengthy rebuttal, in which he again ventured his "private opinion" that Carleton's reading of the treaty was incorrect. Carleton, of course, secretly shared the opinion that Oswald and Laurens meant for every last runaway to be returned, and he was painfully aware that Parliament was prepared to ratify this betrayal. So little confidence did Carleton have in Rockingham's ministry that months before, he had begun to issue passports to black Loyalists. Known as "Birch Certificates," after Samuel Birch, the officer in charge of the paperwork, the documents guaranteed passage "to Nova-Scotia, or wherever else [the bearer] may think proper [in] consequence of the Proclamations of Sir William Howe, and Sir Henry Clinton." Whatever his private misgivings, however, Carlton continued to publicly insist that no treaty could "disannul those Proclamations." When pressed, Carlton hinted "that Compensation may be made to the Masters of Negroes if judged necessary" by future negotiators, and he remained baffled by Washington's insistence on recovering the slaves themselves. Not being a Virginian, Carleton, as historian Henry Wiencek has perceptively observed, failed to "grasp a fundamental point of plantation economics: the value of slaves lay not only in their productivity but in their fertility."[25]

Four days later, Washington confided to the marquis de Lafayette that he "could extract nothing more" from Carleton than "that it was his wish to withdraw the Troops as soon as possible." That was not the complete truth. In hopes of appeasing the Americans, Carleton created a Board of Inquiry to resolve individual slaveholders' claims. Although the tribunal, following Carleton's lead, evidently refused to turn over any runaways who had arrived in Manhattan prior to late November, its weekly deliberations cast an air of unease over the sluggish preparations for evacuation. With good reason, black refugees wondered whether beleaguered British forces would stand by them if Washington persisted in his demands that they be returned to their masters. These concerns explain why so many black Loyalists solemnly informed the officers who conducted the embarkation interviews—which came to be known as the "Book of Negroes"—that they had been born free. The officer who interviewed Harry Washington and Ralph Henry surely enjoyed noting that the former once belonged to "General Washington; left him 7" years before, while the latter was "Formerly slave to Patrick Henry."[26]

Carleton remained as good as his word, however, and a churlish Washington arrived at the unhappy conclusion "that the Slaves which have absconded from their Masters will never be returned to them." Between April 23 and late July, the British assembled a small armada of eighty-one ships, and at last the black Loyalists began to board. By the time the last vessel cleared the harbor on November 30, 1783, exactly 3,000 African Americans had departed New York. Of that number, 1,336 were men, 914 were women, and the remainder were children. Roughly half of the refugees had fled the coastal areas between Maryland and South Carolina, while 21 percent hailed from New York and New Jersey. The number of females on board the vessels indicated how the war years allowed for the flight of women and children, since one-third of those who traveled to Canada sailed as family units. Most of the ships reached Nova Scotia within ten days, but the *Joseph*, one of the last ships out, was hit by a gale and blown south. The ship finally made landfall in Bermuda, where the captain decided to remain for the winter. But the freedpeople on board could see slaves sweating along the docks, so most refused to disembark and spent the next few months camped below decks. Finally in May 1784, the refugees reached Nova Scotia.[27]

The African Americans who landed in Nova Scotia were not the first blacks in the province. When British forces evacuated Boston in 1776, they took a "Company of Negroes" with them. But the arrival of the Manhattan flotilla meant that the tiny black communities scattered along Canada's rocky coast suddenly mushroomed in size. Just under 1,500 refugees, including Harry and Sarah Washington, settled in Birchtown, while another 1,269 landed in Shelburne, a small port on Nova Scotia's southeastern shore.

Loyalist settlements in Nova Scotia and Canada.

To aid the "pioneers," Anglican missionaries landed barrels of flour and pork, and surveyor Benjamin Marsden, a Massachusetts Tory, began his surveys while black men felled trees for the construction of crude huts. As with most colonial ventures, the settlement did not start well. Only five hundred of the veterans received the promised land grants, and the plots turned out to be substantially smaller than the parcels awarded to white Loyalists. Despite his long service in King George's army, Washington was not among the lucky grantees. Perhaps thinking it dangerous to retain the Black Pioneers as a military unit, Carleton ordered the regiment disbanded as soon as the ships left New York. The result was that the veterans were not entitled to pay or clothing upon arrival, and valuable lines of military command, which had proved useful in other colonial schemes, were lost. By the time the refugees disembarked, the Canadian air was already turning cold. Carleton shipped north what foodstuffs he could obtain, but by the late fall there was little to be had, and once the general sailed for Britain, no administrator remained to oversee the task.[28]

Secure in their freedom, the settlers, accustomed to hard labor, set to work with a diligence that surprised even the British officials, who had known them only as underemployed refugees in an occupied port. Determination and long hours, however, went only so far during that first, long winter in Canada. Former slaves accustomed to fertile tobacco fields in the Chesapeake or lowland rice plantations in South Carolina had no experience in producing the cereal crops necessary for the survival of a new colony. Nor did they know how to force the thin, rocky soil of Nova Scotia and its far shorter growing season to generate respectable harvests, a problem compounded by the failure of promised seed and rations to arrive with the spring. White Nova Scotians, who had watched their coastal hamlets double in size with the arrival of the black Loyalists, were too poor to provide much assistance. As historian Robert McColley has aptly observed, the former slaves "were at pains to decide which was chillier, the climate or the white Nova Scotians."[29]

The black Americans could scarcely fail to note that there were slave-owners among the wealthier Canadians. (What would become Lower Canada passed a gradual emancipation act only in 1793.) The American refugees had quit one slave country only to arrive in another. The existence of a small number of slaves in the province served as yet one more painful reminder that for His Majesty's government, their liberation had been but a means to a military end, not a moral goal in itself. So determined were whites in the region to maintain slavery that in 1781, the colonial legislature of Prince Edward Island declared that Christian baptism would not alter the legal status of African captives. Veterans such as Harry Washington were also aware that some white Tories arrived in Canada with slaves brought from the United States. Matthew Elliott, a retired British officer, brought sixty American slaves, spoils of war, when he relocated to Amherstburg in 1784. On his eight-hundred-acre government grant, Elliott kept an iron ring hanging over a branch on a large elm, which his slaves dubbed "the bloody whipping tree."[30]

Life proved especially hard for the freedmen who expected to use previous training as craftsmen to build a new life in Canada. According to a January 1784 census, forty-six of the fifteen hundred Birchtown settlers gave their occupations as carpenters, with another thirty-seven describing themselves as sawyers or coopers. Skilled artisans such as Boston King expected to thrive in their rapidly growing province. White Nova Scotians saw it differently. Later the same year, a disbanded British regiment rioted in Shelburne and "pulled down" about twenty houses owned by black settlers. In nearby Birchtown, whites organized a protest against black workers, who they insisted devalued white labor; here too the protest descended into an "Extraordinary mob" and set more fires. When rioters failed to drive African Americans out of the province, Shelburne authorities added official sanction to the intolerance by banning "Negro Dances and Negro Frolicks in the town." Local courts responded to minor infractions with ferocity. Magistrates ordered David Anderson confined to jail for thirty days and then striped with thirty-nine lashes for selling a borrowed watch "to equip him for a negro dance." By 1790, a report circulating within Parliament described the black communities in Canada as "unimproved and destitute." For white Americans below the St. Lawrence who eagerly publicized every scrap of ill news as evidence that African Americans were better off as slaves, the rising tide of racial intolerance in Nova Scotia made for perfect propaganda.[31]

Between the unforgiving climate and the hostility of white colonials, many blacks were forced to retreat into domestic service. By the end of the decade, 138 white families in or near Birchtown employed 386 servants. One wealthy merchant, Oliver Brueff, hired sixteen black Americans. Most employed only a single servant. Although some African Americans returned to their homes following the day's labor, others did not, repeating earlier employment patterns in which blacks did not reside with spouses or children. Thanks to the large number of black refugees, Shelburne emerged as the largest and most prosperous town in Nova Scotia by 1785. Yet as skilled craftsmen increasingly toiled for their white neighbors, wages for African Americans fell to about one-fourth of those paid to white workers. For the majority of black veterans denied the land bonuses promised while in New York, plowing the fields of white landlords in sharecropping arrangements became the principal method of survival. Denied the right to vote and segregated into the meanest sections of Birchtown and Shelburne, black refugees must have begun to wonder what the precise distinction was between freedom in Nova Scotia and enslavement in New York.[32]

Even African American attempts to erect churches drew the ire of white Canadians. During his travels, carpenter Boston King had undergone a profound religious experience, and upon arriving in Birchtown he "began to exhort both in families [homes] and prayer meetings." In his endeavors, King was assisted by David George, the former Virginia bondman who had preached along the Carolina coast during the British occupation. After his evacuation from Charles Town, George first landed in Shelburne. "Numbers of my own color were there," he discovered, but "the white people were against" his ministry. George continued to preach, and his followers constructed a crude log church on his quarter-acre lot. "The Black people came far and near, it was so new to them," he remembered. Just as George's flock began to prosper, nearly fifty "disbanded soldiers" marched on the village. They arrived armed "with the tackle of ships, and turned [George's] dwelling house, and every one of their houses, quite over, and the meeting house they would have burned down, had not the ringleader of the mob himself prevented it."[33]

When threatened a second time and finally "beaten with sticks," George lost heart. He and his family joined King in Birchtown, where he remained until December 1784. Since Birchtown lacked an actual church, George, like King, preached "from house to house" and "baptized about twenty three" people. The fiery George, however, appeared suspect to more sedate black Methodists such as Moses Wilkinson, a blind and lame minister who was also attracting a large flock. Before the spring thaw, the George family returned to Shelburne. The water near the shore froze, and they moved their boat along only by using saws to "cut away the ice." Upon reaching Shelburne, George discovered that his former meetinghouse had turned into a pub. "The old Negro wanted to make a heaven of this place," laughed the tavern keeper, "but I'll make a hell of it." Undaunted, George somehow retained control of the building and "preached in it as before."[34]

At the same time that any realistic hopes of building a new life in Canada were fading, black Loyalists across the Atlantic were reaching similar conclusions about their situation in Britain. Between Yorktown and the final evacuation of Manhattan, somewhere between six hundred and a thousand black Loyalists, most of whom had arrived in small groups as mariners with the Royal Navy, had been resettled in London. The sprawling metropolis, already burdened with a desperately impoverished and starving underclass, offered these refugees little in the way of employment opportunities unless they wished to return to the sea. But conditions in what British sailors dubbed "floating hells" were usually worse than those previously faced by enslaved watermen who had worked the rivers of Virginia or the Carolinas, and they were subject to discipline by the lash and the cat-o'-nine-tails. A few found work in domestic service. George Peters "attended at a gentleman's house," and William Snow and John Robinson, both evacuees from Charles Town, earned decent salaries as a tailor and as a cook, respectively, in Newmarket Street. But most begged in the streets. Shadrach Furman, who lost his sight while fighting as a Loyalist, supplemented his meager pension by fiddling on street corners. As far as Lord Rockingham was concerned, Britain had done these men a favor by removing them from the land of their enslavement. If they could not find employment in London, that was hardly the government's concern.[35]

Exactly how many African Americans arrived in London after 1781 will never be known, due in part to the already large black community existing in Britain by the eve of the war. British records, unlike American documents, rarely mentioned ethnicity, and when they did, they lumped together immigrants from the Indian subcontinent and even Native Americans as "black." Whatever their exact number, one of the factors making life difficult for African American refugees in Britain was gender inequality. Arriving as mariners or domestic servants to British officers, the vast majority of this group were men, whereas nearly half of the Loyalists evacuated to Nova Scotia were women or children. In some areas of London, there were four black men for every woman, and in the riverfront suburb of Deptford, the gender imbalance may have been sixteen to one. Most of these watermen had liberated themselves by paddling to freedom when a royal vessel floated into view, which meant that their wives and families remained enslaved away from British-occupied cities such as Savannah or Charles Town. Peter Anderson had left behind a wife and three children in Virginia, as had Walter Harris, whose family remained the property of the Byrd estate in Westover. Some freedmen recognized this grim reality by marrying again, this time to white Englishwomen. At least within the working class, these interracial unions raised few eyebrows. But in the same way that Virginia planters publicized the bleak conditions in Nova Scotia so as to raise doubts about the abilities of freed blacks, British investors in the Caribbean sugar plantations drew attention to the plight of black Loyalists in London in hopes of quieting reform voices demanding emancipation in the West Indies, or at least an end to the Atlantic slave trade.[36]

Recognizing the need to assist veterans who had served their adopted country, as well as the necessity of responding to the proslavery propaganda being spread by West Indian investors, a "Committee of Gentlemen" placed an advertisement in the January 6, 1786, edition of the *Public Advertiser* announcing the creation of the Committee for the Relief of the Black Poor. Consisting mostly of wealthy Quaker and Anglican reformers, including Thomas Clarkson and Granville Sharp, the group planned to raise money to alleviate the "extreme Distress" of the black sailors who "came over in his Majesty's Ships, having served in the late War." Leading abolitionists such as William Wilberforce, the country's chief advocate of banning the Atlantic traffic in humans, hastened to add their donations. But some very public contributions arrived from unexpected quarters. William Pitt, the new prime minister, donated £5, and George Rose, one of the two administrators of Parliament's Board of Treasury, donated another £30. By the end of April, the committee had raised the considerable sum of £890.[37]

However, even Britain's staunchest reformers doubted that black veterans enjoyed any real future in London. Given the enormous number of impoverished soldiers and former slaves residing in the city, the fund would assist only a small number of refugees, and then only for a short time. The committee doled out £69 for patients in London hospitals, £135 for food for "above 300 Persons," and another £55 for clothes. But even with Pitt's implicit endorsement, the group could only raise money for so long. The long-term answer, a number of white reformers believed, was to transport the black Loyalists to a permanent and more welcoming home. Several committee members briefly considered Bermuda, while others suggested Nova Scotia. But by 1787, disquieting rumors of the appalling conditions in Canada had begun to reach London. Thomas Johnson, one of the lucky soldiers smuggled out of Yorktown in defiance of Cornwallis's order, spent only one bitter winter there before taking his family and sailing for London. While committee members provided the Johnsons with food and clothing, they received a first-hand account of conditions in Canada.[38]

One of those advocating a settlement far to the south was a contributor to the committee, naturalist Henry Smeathman, whose hunt for rare insects once carried him to Bunce Island in West Africa, where he had encountered Richard Oswald's slave-trading operation. Having wandered the Sierra Leone coast, where he took two wives, Smeathman believed that West Africa posed the best solution for the black poor. In his 1786 pamphlet, *Plan of Settlement to Be Made Near Sierra Leone*, he argued that the climate, unlike that of Nova Scotia, was "congenial to [the] constitution" of black veterans. As the land was inhabited only by Africans, Smeathman's logic went, each settler could "possess as much land as he or she could cultivate." As most members of the committee had amassed their fortunes through trade and almost all were well-intentioned evangelicals, Smeathman's proposal appeared to resolve a number of interconnected problems. A thriving colony could generate commerce and wealth for both black settlers and London shippers, while the very existence of the outpost would hinder the purchase of Africans by men like Oswald. Since the majority of black Loyalists were born in North America rather than in Africa, they might bring the Bible as well as the plow. A better entomologist than a mathematician, perhaps, Smeathman calculated that this "retreat from former suffering" could be financed for a modest £14 per capita.[39]

To better win the support of black Americans and Africans residing in London, committee members approached Olaudah Equiano about the position of colonial commissary. Although his *Interesting Narrative* had not yet been published, Equiano was already a well-known essayist, and his experience in the Royal Navy qualified him for the post. He initially expressed grave doubts about the undertaking, particularly the dangers of placing recently liberated blacks near the clutches of professional "slave-dealers," but Equiano finally agreed. He promptly butted administrative heads with Joseph Irwin, Smeathman's clerk and close friend, who was promoted to company agent after Smeathman died suddenly. Despite Irwin's lack of African experience, the committee sided with him and dismissed Equiano in March 1787. In the process, the organization lost the sole person of African descent in their administration, a foolish step in an era when most black Britons distrusted their government. African Americans, Equiano's friend Quobna Ottobah Cugoano editorialized in the *Public Advertiser*, were wiser to "preserve their lives and liberties in Britain, than to hazard themselves at Sea with such enemies to their welfare, and the peril of settling at Sierra Leone."[40]

Faced with continuing poverty in London, most refugees nonetheless believed they had little choice. That spring, 411 settlers (including nearly seventy white women married to black men) boarded the *Nautilus* and began their voyage down the Thames toward Africa. After one month at sea, the ship settled on the southern edge of the Sierra Leone River at an inlet known as Frenchman's Bay. Captain Thomas Thompson fired a thirteen-gun announcement to the Africans onshore, and a delegation marched to the crest of a nearby hill to plant the British flag. Thompson and Irving met with the local ruler of the Temne, dubbed "King Tom," who was willing to grant the settlers and "their heirs and successors" a ten-mile stretch of coast. Speaking in the mixture of pidgin English and Portuguese that was common to traders along the river, Tom demanded eight muskets, thirty-six swords, thirty-four pounds of tobacco, ten yards of scarlet cloth, twenty-five iron bars, and 120 gallons of rum. He also swore his protection over "the said free settlers" against "the insurrections and attacks of all Nations and people whatsoever."

The blacks named their latest home Granville Town, in honor of abolitionist Granville Sharp.[41]

As settlers began to clear the land to farm under the direction of their newly elected governor, Richard Weaver, a runaway from Philadelphia, the rainy season began. The canvas tarps purchased from the navy tore as the winds rose, drenching the colonists. No covering could protect the rice seedlings carefully planted by former Carolina agriculturalists, and the fields washed down the river. Hungry, wet, and assaulted by red ants and spitting cobras, whose venom blinded their prey, the settlers began to die. Joseph Irwin died in mid-July, and by the end of another week, thirty blacks and

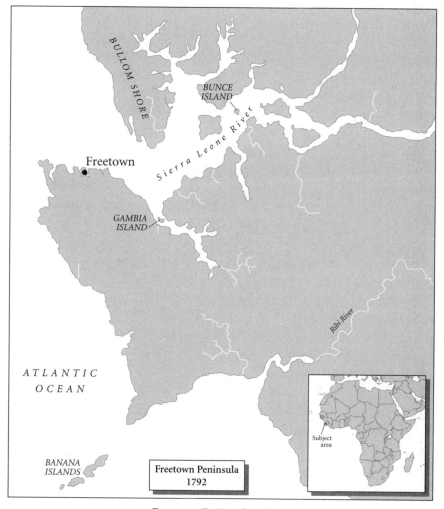

Freetown Peninsula, 1792.

twenty-four whites had been buried. Sick with malaria, most settlers gave up and refused to work. Captain Thompson railed at their "obstinacy and laziness" and had two of them flogged for "misbehavior," but to no avail. By the time the *Nautilus* hauled anchor to return to Britain on September 16, 122 of the men and women who had waded ashore the previous May were gone. At the point of starvation, a few of the former slaves accepted jobs at Oswald's slave-trading station on Bunce Island.[42]

Just as it appeared that Granville Town would simply vanish off the map, assistance arrived from an unexpected quarter. Across the Atlantic in Nova Scotia, black settlers knew nothing of the disastrous months in Sierra Leone, but they had read Smeathman's pamphlet, which Sharp had disseminated as widely as possible. According to committee member Thomas Clarkson, as London reformers discussed the Sierra Leone venture one evening over dinner, a black domestic "who waited at the table" promptly wrote to refugees he knew in Canada. One of them, evidently, was African-born Thomas Peters, who had served with the Black Pioneers in North Carolina. At the war's end, Peters joined the exodus to Nova Scotia, where he discovered that few of the promises made by men such as Dunmore were honored. "When We first Inlisted & swore [an oath of loyalty to Britain,] we was promised that we should have land & provisions the same as the [white] Disbanded Soldiers," he complained, "Which We have not Received." Unable to purchase land, Peters found work as a mechanic in a flour mill, so that in freedom he continued to perform the tasks he had formerly done as a Carolina slave, albeit for modest wages.[43]

Peters's fellow settlers hoped that as a former sergeant, he might have some small influence in London. Armed with a petition signed by the heads of two hundred black families demanding that old promises be honored, Peters sailed for Britain in the fall of 1790. Either the families who wished to leave Canada pooled their meager resources to raise the required £17 or Peters paid his passage by working his way across the Atlantic. When at last he reached London, Peters looked up his old commanding officer, who took him to meet General Henry Clinton, Guy Carleton's predecessor as commander in chief in America. Clinton, in turn, gave the black veteran a small contribution before putting him in touch with Granville Sharp and John Clarkson, a naval officer and younger brother of Thomas Clarkson and an avid promoter of the Sierra Leone venture. All that the black Loyalists desired, Peters insisted, was either the land they had been promised in Nova Scotia or resettlement "wherever the wisdom of Government may think proper to provide for [them] as free subjects of the British Empire."[44]

Within the year, Peters was back in Canada. Although the Sierra Leone colony remained a privately funded venture, it enjoyed the implicit backing of the government, which always endorsed the idea of yet another trading outpost, and a few members of Parliament still wished to do right by the black veterans. Peters returned with word that any settler who desired to relocate to Sierra Leone could obtain free passage to Africa and twenty acres of land if male, ten if female. Accompanying Peters as a sign of official support was John Clarkson. The two traversed the length of eastern Canada, contacting black ministers and speaking in churches. In Birchtown in October 1791, 350 parishioners traveled through a pouring rain to hear them speak in Moses Wilkinson's church. Clarkson's speech was interrupted frequently by applause, and the next morning 514 African Americans signed on as prospective emigrants. Within the month, 700 other black settlers from nearby towns announced their desire to leave as well.[45]

Although Clarkson's promises of land came as welcome news to those former Chesapeake bondpeople who had abandoned hope of ever acquiring their own farms in Nova Scotia, a good many of those who signed the 1790 petition were Canadian landowners. Of the 151 men from Shelburne and Birchtown who were accepted by Clarkson as essential immigrants—since they had done well for themselves as refugees—roughly two-thirds owned at least a small plot. Even if those who wished to relocate yet again believed that the soil of West Africa would be richer than that of Nova Scotia, there were risks involved in another long ocean voyage. For the black Loyalists, Canada had failed to be a prosperous home or provide political independence. Denied the right to cast a vote, settlers understood that they and their sons were doomed to remain second-class citizens within the decidedly inegalitarian British Empire. Nova Scotia offered them a tiny haven, but West Africa held out the opportunity to build a new country. And for Harry Washington, the Gambia River had been the start of a very long journey.[46]

To better organize what was rapidly becoming a tricoastal operation, the London benefactors decided to formally reorganize. On June 6, 1791, Parliament agreed to the incorporation of the Sierra Leone Company, which gave an eight-man board of white directors the power to govern the colony for black refugees and their descendants. Yet to the extent that the original settlement had foundered upon the lack of a stable and permanent government, this provision initially worried few potential emigrants in Nova Scotia, particularly since they had every reason to trust the committee. Black refugees, however, might have been less sanguine had they known that when Granville Sharp objected to this "humiliating change" to his plan, under which African Americans were to elect their governor and other officials, he was forced out as chairman of the enterprise. His replacement was businessman Henry Thornton, who was far more interested in making the colony turn a profit than he was in assisting black veterans and their families.[47]

During the winter of 1791, Clarkson and Peters made final preparations for the voyage. The company, together with Parliament, sent fifteen ships for what they expected to be the first wave of emigrants from Canada. Clarkson and Peters inspected each vessel, removing lower decks and carving windows and ventilation holes into the cramped vessels so that Africans such as Washington would suffer no terrifying reminders of the Middle Passage. Finally, on January 15, 1792, 1,196 colonists sailed out of Halifax Harbor. As in the exodus out of Charles Town and Manhattan, the ships carried young and old, men and women. Among those aboard were Thomas Peters, Harry and Sarah Washington, Boston King, and competing ministers David George and Moses Wilkinson. Washington was approximately fifty-two years old, and in an era when people died young, starting life anew in yet another colony was a daunting undertaking. But Harry was far from the oldest emigrant. According to Clarkson, an unnamed African "woman of 104 years of age" marched up the gangplank and demanded that they "take her [so] that she might lay her bones in her native country."[48]

Sixty-five colonists perished during the midwinter voyage across the North Atlantic. "We met with a dreadful storm which continued sixteen days," remembered one black Loyalist. But the first ships in the fleet anchored six miles downriver from Granville Town at the new port of Freetown on February 26, and the other twelve arrived within the next two weeks. A delegation of town leaders, all "very neatly dressed," welcomed the voyagers and "expressed the general joy of themselves & comrades at [their] safe arrival." Apart from erecting a large house sided with canvas, however, the original settlers had done nothing to prepare for the landing of more than one thousand weary immigrants. Even so, a very sick Thomas Peters stumbled ashore singing, "The day of jubilee is come; return ye ransomed sinners home." Having resided in North Carolina, New York, Nova Scotia, and London, and having crossed the Atlantic four times, Peters prayed that at long last, his struggle for freedom and equality was nearing its end.[49]

Unhappily, it was far from over. Having approached the British philanthropists, and then having personally recruited more than one-third of all the migrants, Peters anticipated a leadership post upon arrival. Instead, awaiting the fleet was a letter from the London directors naming John Clarkson as the colony's superintendent. For black refugees desperately in search of political autonomy, the news that Peters, a former sergeant in the Black Pioneers, would answer to a white Englishman half his age was more than disappointing. Other black veterans, such as Harry Washington, continued to look to Peters for leadership, and more than one hundred colonists signed a petition demanding Peters be named governor. Yet even Superintendent Clarkson wielded little authority in Sierra Leone, with the eight white directors in London deciding policy. As a result, the sudden death of Peters in June did nothing to resolve the problem of an undemocratic governmental structure. The colony's distant management, the superintendent complained to his brother, company director Thomas Clarkson, "is one of the most absurd kind and calculated to make [the settlers] miserable."[50]

Adding to the confusion, Lieutenant William Dawes arrived from Britain three months later carrying orders from the London directors that Clarkson was to be governor, while he was to serve as councilor and help govern the colony. The black settlers, mourning the loss of Peters, were faced with two white leaders, neither of whom they had much use for. As a former soldier turned evangelical, Dawes accepted the position because he was anxious to bring the word of Jesus to the Africans. While he shared the Christian faith of most African American settlers, he looked askance at the theological "ignorance" of black preachers such as Moses Wilkinson. Clarkson took the opportunity to abandon the colony for London in December so that he might marry. Traveling with him to London was David George, who wished to study with the Baptist clergy in Britain. George also carried with him a petition for the company directors, which urged the speedy removal of Dawes and the return of Clarkson. Dawes "may be a very good man," one settler told George, "but he does not show it." Dawes himself returned to London in March 1794, taking with him King Tom's son for schooling and Boston King for further training as a teacher. In his absence, yet another white man became acting governor, twenty-four-year-old Zachary Macaulay.[51]

No governor, however, was able to fulfill the company's goal of using Sierra Leone as a bulwark against the slave trade. Slavers routinely docked at Freetown, and although the settlers earned welcome money selling their foodstuffs to the ships' masters, they despised the traffic and the white captains who ran it. On June 13, 1794, while the colonists were loading goods into the *Thomas*, its captain laughed at "what manner he would use them if he had them in the West Indies." One of the dock workers, Robert Keeling, swung at him with a hammer. When Keeling proudly confirmed the attack, Macauley had him fired "on account of disrespectful conduct." So outraged were the colonists that their governor would take the side of a slave trader that they ransacked the company's offices and threatened to burn the governor's house. A terrified Macaulay begged David George and other leading Baptists to speak to their congregations, but the obtuse governor only made matters worse by distributing a statement warning settlers that if they did not support his administration, they might return to Nova Scotia. A cannon mounted at Macaulay's gate maintained peace, if not harmony.[52]

The governor's small cannon intimidated the men and women he governed, but it was little use against the French navy, which arrived in September 1794. With the outbreak of war between the British and the French on February 1, 1793, the black Loyalists became pawns in the Atlantic wars. Despite the Clarkson brothers' endorsement of the revolutionary government in Paris, the French, who had recently abolished slavery in their Caribbean empire, regarded the blacks as nothing more than British colonists. Without warning, a squadron of French warships sailed up the Sierra Leone River and poured cannon fire into Freetown for nearly ninety minutes. Most of the African Americans managed to flee into the mountains before French sailors landed to better demolish what remained. They looted the town, destroyed a printing press, burned the company's warehouses and office, and slaughtered the settlers' livestock and pets. At last, the French commander, Citizen Armaud, demanded that Macaulay run up the tricolor. He had none, so instead the governor hoisted a white tablecloth in surrender.[53]

For the embattled colonists, the final blow arrived not from Paris but from London. The directors, in hopes of improving the financial standing of their company, demanded a quitrent—a payment from landholders in lieu of services—of two shillings per acre from each settler. Years before, John Clarkson had promised the Nova Scotians free land, but investments based upon these collections quietly became the basis of the company's financial strategy. After all they had endured, the blacks responded with fury. "Who could say now they were not slaves?" one wondered. Macaulay, as ever, sided against those he governed, warning critics that "the smallest degree of clamour" would cost them the support of the company. Regarding Britain's protection as worthless, one settler retorted that had they been told of the quitrent while in Canada, they "never [would have] come here." Another threatened to negotiate with the local Temne people for land. Denied the right to govern themselves, the freedmen regarded land ownership as the antithesis of their former condition. Denied even that, they remained chattel. After a heated debate, David George and his Baptist followers reluctantly agreed to pay the quitrent, but Methodist leaders announced that any parishioner who paid the fee would be banished from the congregation.[54]

When a delegation of blacks fired off a petition to King George, reminding him of their "good behavior in the last war," Macaulay resigned his position and abandoned Sierra Leone in April 1799. Macaulay did not sail alone, but he took only Temne children with him, Africans he regarded as the future of the mutinous colony. For the colonists, this was at last their chance. In the absence of company authority, they elected the Methodist preacher Mingo Jordan as a judge and appointed Isaac Anderson, an Angolan sold into South Carolina, and John Cuthbert, a runaway from Savannah, as justices of the peace. They then created a bicameral assembly and began to pass legislation. In an act of quasi-independence, the assembly resolved that the true "proprietors" of Sierra Leone were the settlers who had arrived with Clarkson, together with the original London poor who founded Granville Town. (No mention was made of the rights of the region's indigenous Africans.) As had their former masters who met at the First Continental Congress, the delegates announced that the distant directors were entitled only to regulate external trade. What the settlers did not know was that at that very moment, Macaulay and the company were applying to Parliament for a "royal charter," which would put a halt to the colonists' demands for popular democracy and elections.[55]

Sailing into this tempest was Thomas Ludham, a printer's apprentice who at twenty-three was the newest white governor of Sierra Leone. As a peace offering, Ludham carried news that the directors were willing to abandon the quitrent, but, as he informed a meeting of colonists on December 5, 1799, no black judges or elected leaders would be permitted. The blacks responded that they were "resolved to persist in their appointment of judges [and] to make and execute laws themselves," as they could not "get justice from the White people." Ludham called yet another meeting to explain why he was unable to agree to their demands. Utterly out of patience, approximately 150 heads of black households, representing half of all families in Freetown, gathered in Charleston runaway Cato Perkins's chapel on September 3, 1800, to announce that Ludham governed only the company's business; they themselves ran Sierra Leone. Every black settler was to agree to their "paper of laws" or "quit the place."[56]

The black Tories, although still professing loyalty to a distant monarch, were in rebellion against the company's (and Parliament's) legal governor. David George remained true to the company, but the elected black officials, together with former corporal Harry Washington, cast his lot with the rebels—as had Harry Washington's master twenty-five years before. On September 27, the insurgents elected Isaac Anderson as their new governor and began to fortify Buckle's Bridge, which lay between Freetown and Granville Town, with fifty armed men. Those loyal to Ludham gathered on Thornton Hill. Among their number were about thirty black Baptists, a dozen white employees, and nearly forty African mariners who sailed with the company's fleet. King Tom, who claimed to govern the region, let it be known that if Ludham and the rebels could not resolve the dispute, he would do it for them.[57]

Unexpectedly on Sunday, September 28, reinforcements arrived. The *Asia* brought Alexander Macaulay (Zachary's brother), forty-seven British soldiers from the Twenty-Fourth Regiment, and 550 exiled Jamaican Maroons (the descendants of runaway slaves who had made their peace with Britain in exchange for land in Sierra Leone, provided they paid their quitrent). When Ludham informed Montague James, the aged Maroon leader, that the rebellion endangered "the allocation of their land," he extended "an unanimous & hearty offer" to fight for the company. Ludham promptly demanded the unconditional surrender of the rebels. If not, the Maroons, renowned for their refusal to give quarter, would have free rein. With that, the rebel forces began to melt away, and by early October Ludham's men had captured thirty-one prisoners, with rewards posted for another fourteen still at large.[58]

By then, the colony's new royal charter had arrived; freshly empowered by crown and Parliament, Governor Ludham convened a military tribunal. Fifty-five rebels appeared before the court, and the two leading members of the failed revolution, Isaac Anderson and Frank Patrick, were hanged, their bodies left swinging from the gibbet for several days. Thirty-three more, including Harry Washington, were banished across the Sierra Leone River to the Bullom Shore; their property was given to the Maroons, and they might return on penalty of three hundred lashes. With that, Harry Washington, the second man with that surname to defy the British Empire, vanished from history. Perhaps, at the age of sixty, he began life anew just north of Sierra Leone, or perhaps he began the dangerous five-hundred-mile trek back to the Gambia River, the site of his sale into slavery and perhaps also the place of his birth.[59]

Under its new charter as a royal colony, all authority returned to the distant company directors. The black judges, justices, and legislators were replaced by a white mayor, three white aldermen, and a white sheriff. Any movement toward popular democracy was reversed. The rebellion soured even British philanthropists and reformers on the experiment. African Americans made "the worst possible subjects," abolitionist William Wilberforce complained, while the London directors marveled at "the crude notions [the blacks] had formed of their own rights." Even William Dawes returned in January 1801, to replace the habitually unwell Governor Ludham. One of his first acts was to announce that all settlers, rebels and Loyalists alike, had to reapply for new farm grants and pay the quitrent, since during the transfer of charters, all land reverted to company ownership.[60]

As Harry Washington's numerous journeys and as many struggles reveal, the pursuit of life, liberty, land, and autonomy did not reside only with

North America's master class. Historians today, and properly so, empha-size the enormous risks wealthy landlords like George Washington took in banding together against British authority. Had white Americans lost their bid for independence, General Washington might have ended his days as did Isaac Anderson, kicking at the end of a rope, rather than serving as his nation's first president. To the extent that he was a slave and not the owner of a grand estate such as Mount Vernon, Harry Washington perhaps had less to lose. Yet in the end he had to travel much farther, and over a longer period, in search of his democratic dream, first to Nova Scotia, and then back across the ocean to West Africa. And like the majority of Africans and African Americans who were betrayed by the failings of the American Revolution, he never found it.

NINE

A Suspicion Only

Racism in the Early Republic

R ICHARD, THE HIRED SLAVE who served him his tea during the summer of 1776, had long vanished from his account book by the fall day in November 1780 when Thomas Jefferson again picked up his quill pen, this time with the intention of answering a series of questions posed about Virginia by François Barbé-Marbois, secretary to the French minister in Philadelphia. The Frenchman inquired as to the state's geography, natural resources, educational system, commerce, and agriculture, and most of all its people. As the governor of Virginia as well as one of the Republic's leading philosophes, who better than Jefferson to respond to a young diplomat "Constantly in Search of knowledge"? So when Barbé-Marbois approached Joseph Jones, a Virginia delegate to Congress and uncle to Jefferson's young protégé James Monroe, Jones forwarded the list to the governor, who set aside his wartime duties long enough to begin work on what would become his only book, *Notes on the State of Virginia*.[1]

Shortly thereafter, turncoat general Benedict Arnold's army invaded Virginia, and Jefferson was forced to flee Monticello (which allowed a number of his slaves to flee as well). Jefferson returned to the project in the fall of 1781, and that December he posted his answers to the Frenchman. But regarding his brief responses as "very imperfect," Jefferson at once began to revise and expand his draft "to nearly treble bulk." The unsatisfied author continued to rework and amend his manuscript well into 1784. It was finally published in Paris on May 10, 1785, by which time the widowed Jefferson had replaced Franklin as minister to France. Intended initially for foreign publication only, Jefferson finally consented to an American edition after a pirated, poorly translated English language edition appeared in Philadelphia.[2]

In responding to Barbé-Marbois's queries, Jefferson reordered the questions so that his framework resembled that of Denis Diderot's celebrated *Encyclopédie*. In Query XVIII, a very brief meditation on "manners," the Virginian turned to slavery, conceding that the practice defied the spirit of the Revolution. Like George Mason, Jefferson fretted over the tendency of such raw class power to debauch the morals of the state's young men. "The whole commerce between master and slave," he admitted, "is a perpetual exercise of the most boisterous passions, the most unremitting despotism." Jefferson worried far less about the effects of slavery on black Virginians, but in the wake of Dunmore's regiment he had little doubt that slaves might rise for their freedom. "And can the liberties of a nation be thought secure when we have removed their only firm basis," he wondered, "a conviction in the minds of the people that these liberties are the gift of God?" The answer was a resounding no. "Indeed I tremble for my country when I reflect that God is just: that his justice cannot sleep forever." Some of his readers were shocked, but John Adams applauded the honesty: "The Passages upon slavery, are worth Diamonds."[3]

Such an admission appearing in a book read on both sides of the Atlantic begged the obvious question. If slavery was "an evil of great magnitude," why had the state with the largest population of African Americans done so little to erase it? The answer, Jefferson insisted, lay in the complications inherent in the forced colonization of those liberated through state manumission. That in turn led to the next question. "It will probably be asked, Why not retain and incorporate the blacks into the state," Jefferson wrote. The answer to this was the physiology of people of African descent. "The first difference which strikes us is that of colour," Jefferson observed, warming to his subject of the "physical and moral" differences between "the two races." Whites enjoyed "the superior beauty" of appearance, while slaves wore "that immoveable veil of black which covers all the emotions." This was a point upon which whites and blacks might agree, Jefferson insisted, since African American men "declared [a] preference" for white women, "as uniformly as is the preference of the Oranootan for the black women over those of his own species." Perhaps, he mused, that was due to the fact that their secretions gave off "a very strong and disagreeable odour."[4]

Jefferson hastened to add that these distinctions were more than skin deep, which was itself possibly darkened by "the colour of the blood." Long observation of enslaved workers, together with the science of physiognomy (in which physical characteristics reflected moral inclinations), suggested that African Americans were poor candidates for citizenship. Their utter illogic, Jefferson insisted, was all too apparent. "A black, after hard labour through the day, will be induced by the slightest amusements to sit up till midnight, or later, though knowing he must be out with the first dawn of the morning." The former governor, who had good reason to know, conceded that black soldiers "are at least as brave" as whites, but that, he suspected, "perhaps proceeds from a want of forethought." Most of all, their "griefs are transient." Jefferson had lost his beloved wife, Martha, in September 1782, and it made him wonder "whether heaven has given life to us in mercy or in wrath." But as "love seems with them to be more an eager desire, than a delicate mixture of sentiment," the dissolution of black families through death or sale is "sooner forgotten with them."[5]

"Add to these" factors, Jefferson concluded, empirical evidence that African Americans were "in reason much inferior" to whites, so much so that they could never hope to become informed voters. "I think one could scarcely be found capable of tracing and comprehending the investigations of Euclid," Jefferson maintained, despite the fact that "[s]ome have been liberally educated." (When later approached by mathematician Benjamin Banneker, a Maryland freeman, Jefferson responded that Banneker possessed "a mind of a very common stature indeed" and suspected that white neighbors had assisted Banneker in writing his almanac.) Admittedly, most slaves were "confined to tillage," yet never could he "find that a black had uttered a thought above the level of plain narration; never see even an elementary trait of painting or sculpture." Whether "originally [created as] a distinct race, or made distinct by time and circumstances," blacks were "inferior to the whites in the endowments both of body and mind," and this "unfortunate difference of colour, and perhaps of faculty," was a "powerful obstacle to the emancipation of these people."[6]

Writing as he initially was for a French audience, Jefferson was anxious to note that his ruminations on the biological inferiority of those whose veins flowed with "negro blood" were "a suspicion only," and biographers anxious to absolve the Virginian of the charge of scientific racism have been quick to trumpet that caveat. That Jefferson clearly harbored few doubts about his conclusions in what one scholar has called "the most important American book published before 1800" is, however, hardly the point.[7] Rather more serious was the fact that Jefferson's determination to invoke science as a method of explaining racial inferiority—and hence to defend slavery—was new to the 1780s and appeared only *after* the Revolution. Before 1776, as inhabitants of a monarchical, class-based empire, colonists might safely own slaves, since bondpeople, like women, indentured servants, and the laboring poor, lay quite outside of the system of governance. But Jefferson's Declaration exploded ancient hierarchical notions of society, for under the new Republic lines of authority were horizontal. Power rested with individuals, who granted their mutual consent to an elected government. How then to explain the persistence of such raw class power? Race and biology could be advanced as reasons why some Americans were not endowed with certain natural and inalienable rights, such as liberty and equality. *Notes on the State of Virginia* was very much a book of the post-Yorktown era, its tortured explication of racial dissimilarity as novel as it was retrograde.[8]

———

Racism was nothing new to North America, of course. From the first moment captive Africans were sold into Western colonies, masters emphasized differences of one kind or another to justify their enslavement (as had master classes in slave societies around the globe). West Africa was barbaric and uncivilized, British traders argued, its people heathen. Even so, until the ownership of one person by another became ideologically problematical, few intellectuals felt the need to expend so much paper and ink on the topic of racial differences. Especially since earlier distinctions largely ceased to exist by the last quarter of the eighteenth century—Chesapeake blacks, as the offspring of creoles born in the colonies, spoke English and practiced Christianity—pigmentation, as well as the unique "negro blood" that coursed beneath it, became central to the defense of slavery in a nation of equality. As color was not as easily altered as was language or religion or culture, for white Americans ill at ease with their failure to eradicate slavery, race served as the best argument for the innate inferiority of men and women of African descent and explained why they could not participate in a democratized republic.[9]

If Jefferson has come to be regarded as the preeminent racial theorist of his day, the sad truth remains that the pseudoscience on display in *Notes* and in his private missives mirrored what other American intellectuals—and not all of them residents of the southern states—were suggesting about the connection between skin color and intelligence. But as Jefferson, like the older Franklin, was regarded as one of the leading American philosophes of the age, his words carried more weight, and so did more damage, than did the writings of other politicians and scientists. But the fact that a writer as determined to impress as was Jefferson felt comfortable in his racially based speculations, knowing that his book would be purchased by highly educated readers on both sides of the Atlantic, indicates that most of his comments were within the mainstream of Western thought. If white southerners were anxious to explain why slaves, as biological descendants of "savage ancestors" who once stalked "the wilds of Africa like wild beasts," should not be freed, northern intellectuals were every bit ready to embrace findings that justified their slow pace of gradual emancipation, or rationalized why black men, even when manumitted, were denied the ballot.[10]

No less desirous of expunging the role their nations had played in shipping millions of Africans to the Americas were European writers and intellectuals, some of them friends and correspondents of American revolutionaries. Franklin's close friend David Hume argued as early as the 1740s that the enslavement of North Africans had helped to destroy ancient republics, in part because of the incorporation of inferior people into classical societies. Swedish botanist Carolus Linnaeus, in his 1758 *Systema Naturae*, a set of standard reference volumes that appeared in Jefferson's library, described both Europeans and Africans in cultural and physical terms, rather than in scientific ones. *Homo sapiens europaeus*, white and blue-eyed, was gentle and innovative, while *H. sapiens afer*, ranked well below *H. sapiens europaeus* on Linnaeus's vertical chart, featured flat noses and "tumid" lips. Africans were indolent and negligent, yet governed "by caprice." Even Jefferson's friend Benjamin Rush, a respected physician and abolitionist, speculated that African pigmentation was the result of widespread leprosy, for only a primeval disease could explain such "unnatural" coloring.[11]

Nor even were such racialist conjectures limited to nations that bragged of egalitarian political systems. Edward Long was a resident of the British Caribbean and a proud member of the empire when his 1774 *History of Jamaica* first appeared in London. Long's theories that Africans probably constituted a separate species of humankind and that they were certainly "allied" with the "ourang-outang"—neither of which originated with him, and which predated similar speculations in Jefferson's *Notes* by a decade—were hardly the product of republican ideology. Yet Long admitted writing his tome in reply to British abolitionism in general and Lord Mansfield in particular. To that extent, Long's scientific racism was like Jefferson's, in that both were a response to antislavery activity. Yet if Long's rejoinder was intended to silence progressive voices in Parliament, Jefferson's ruminations, to a curious extent, were directed at himself. As the Patriot increasingly dubbed "the pen of the Revolution," Jefferson had to find a way to assuage his embattled conscience, and in doing so, his *Notes* gave voice to those republicans who sought to limit earlier claims that "all men are by nature equally free." As historian Sylvia Frey observes, the "idea that blackness was itself prima facie evidence of inferiority" was articulated in new ways during the two decades after Yorktown. If writers such as Jefferson based their pseudoscience on earlier publications, the fact remains that "until the Revolution there had been little need to constitutionally deny rights of citizenship to blacks."[12]

If Jefferson raised eyebrows among the white reading public, it was largely because his assertion that Africans were of a different origin than Europeans raised troubling questions about the biblical version of creation, which was still widely believed by the transatlantic scientific community. So where Rush turned to his medical texts in search of an explanation for pigmentation, more orthodox Americans looked to the Bible. Many theorists insisted that black skin originated with Noah's curse of Canaan. "May not the difference between Europeans, Asiatics, and Africans," wondered Virginia's John Page, "be attributable to the Punishment of Ham as to the blacks?" Since Noah's blight doomed the descendants of Ham to perpetual servitude, this explanation had the virtue of hinting that God planned a different, and degraded, destiny for blacks than for whites, an arrangement that could not be contravened by human agency. As the pseudonymous Camillus insisted in the September 1789 *Delaware Gazette*, since God proclaimed blacks to be the "servants of servants," abolitionist hopes were by definition heretical.[13]

Although Jefferson's willingness to entertain the possibility of polygenesis put him at odds with more conventional writers such as Camillus, whose use of Old Testament genealogy revealed a belief that all humankind, black and white alike, were descendants of Adam and Eve, at least one passage in his *Notes* implied that theology played a role in determining black physiology. Speculation on this point was futile, he cautioned, yet it was possible that Africans owed their "rank in the scale of being" to the low status "which the Creator may perhaps have given them." Certainly Jefferson and his fellow southern Patriots had a powerful psychological compulsion to believe this. Were he to concede that Africans possessed brains and abilities equal to Europeans, Jefferson would have to reject the underlying assumptions of his Revolutionary Republic, that rational men might govern themselves without resort to unelected monarchs. But by assuring himself that they were lesser beings, consigned to a biological rank below his by the hand of the Creator, Jefferson was able to flatter himself a benevolent and humane protector of his inferior black wards until that day when slaves might somehow be colonized elsewhere.[14]

By the age of revolution, however, the logic of republicanism demanded a flexibility in nature, and increasingly men of science theorized that it was not a "Creator" who assigned groups of humans to fixed rankings, but rather "accidental causes," that is, the environment. Influenced by the optimism of the Enlightenment, as well as by the success of the Revolution, some American intellectuals began to argue that the natural order mandated few fixed categories. By altering the cultural environment, society might transform what Jefferson and others referred to as "the chain of being" into a ladder that humankind might ascend. Indeed, when discussing Native Americans, Jefferson found this idea most attractive. "Before we condemn the Indians of this continent as wanting genius," he lectured in his *Notes*, "we must consider that letters have not yet been introduced among them." Natives, Jefferson suspected, were comparable to northern Europeans prior to the advancement of Roman law and culture. All that was required to "place [Native Americans] on a level with the Whites" was time and technology. There was little doubt that "in body and mind" Native Americans were fully "equal to the Whiteman."[15]

A good number of Jefferson's correspondents promptly applied the same standards to African Americans, insisting that the inability of slaves to comprehend Euclid was due only to the fact that black Bostonians had yet to be allowed into the halls of Harvard College. Northern intellectuals, whose science did not have to be twisted to suit their labor needs, were far more likely to embrace environmental explanations for human nature. Speaking before the Pennsylvania Abolition Society in early 1795, Benjamin Rush argued that enslavement alone kept African Americans from producing a black Isaac Newton. By educating blacks "in all the useful parts of learning," he suggested, scientists might prove "that the unhappy sons of Africa, in spite of the degrading influence of slavery, are in no wise inferior to the more fortunate sons of Europe and America." A few influential southerners accepted the logical of environmentalism, but it was no accident that those who did desired an end to slavery. Virginia's St. George Tucker publicly dissented from the theory, "as Mr. Jefferson seems to suppose, that the Africans are really an inferior race of mankind." South Carolina physician David Ramsay wrote Jefferson to express satisfaction at the "generous indignation at slavery" revealed in his *Notes*, but added that he believed Jefferson "depressed the negroes too low" in the scale of being. Like Rush, Ramsay attributed the lack of black advancement to their environment, and particularly to climate. If freed and allowed to remain in the United States, most of which was cooler than West Africa, "in a few centuries the negroes will lose their black color" and resemble Europeans. "I think now they are less black in Jersey than Carolina," he added.[16]

To that, Jefferson would never agree. When it came to African Americans, Jefferson consistently refused to adopt the same environmental reasoning that he applied to Native Americans. Instead, Jefferson recognized only one method by which black Virginians might climb the natural ranking the Creator had afforded them: the body itself had to be transformed. When a young correspondent bravely challenged Jefferson to explain how blacks might advance in society, provided that altering their legal condition was

...of their compound in some cases, may become in the case, it becomes a Mathematical problem of the same class with those on the mixtures of different liquors or different metals, as in these therefore, the algebraical notation is the most convenient & intelligible.

let us express the pure blood of the white in the capital letters of the printed alphabet, the pure blood of the negro in the small letters of the printed alphabet, and any given mixture of either, by way of abridgment in MS. letters.

let the 1st crossing be of a, pure negro, with A pure white. the Unit of blood of the issue being composed of the half of that of each parent, will be $\frac{a}{2} + \frac{A}{2}$ call it, for abbreviation. h (half-blood)

let the 2nd crossing be of h and B. the blood of the issue will be $\frac{h}{2} + \frac{B}{2}$. or substituting for $\frac{h}{2}$ it's equivalent, it will be $\frac{a}{4} + \frac{A}{4} + \frac{B}{2}$. call it q (quarteroon) being $\frac{1}{4}$ negro blood

let the 3rd crossing be of q. and C. their offspring will be

$$\frac{q}{2} + \frac{C}{2} = \frac{a}{8} + \frac{A}{8} + \frac{B}{4} + \frac{C}{2}.$$ call this e. (eighth) who having less than $\frac{1}{4}$ of a. or of pure negro blood, to wit $\frac{1}{8}$ only, is no longer a mulatto. so that a 3rd cross clears the blood.

from these elements let us examine other compounds.

for example, let h. and q. cohabit. their issue will be

$$\frac{h}{2} + \frac{q}{2} = \frac{a}{4} + \frac{A}{4} + \frac{a}{8} + \frac{A}{8} + \frac{B}{4} = \frac{3a}{8} + \frac{3A}{8} + \frac{B}{4}$$ wherein we find $\frac{3}{8}$ of a. or of negro blood.

let h. and e. cohabit. their issue will be

$$\frac{h}{2} + \frac{e}{2} = \frac{a}{2} + \frac{A}{4} + \frac{a}{16} + \frac{A}{16} + \frac{B}{8} + \frac{C}{2} = \frac{5a}{16} + \frac{5A}{16} + \frac{B}{8} + \frac{C}{2}$$ wherein $\frac{1}{16}$ a. makes still a mulatto.

let q. and e. cohabit. the half of the blood of each will be

$$\frac{q}{2} + \frac{e}{2} = \frac{a}{8} + \frac{A}{8} + \frac{B}{4} + \frac{a}{16} + \frac{A}{16} + \frac{B}{8} + \frac{C}{2} = \frac{3a}{16} + \frac{3A}{16} + \frac{2B}{8} + \frac{C}{2}$$ wherein $\frac{3}{16}$ of a is no longer mulatto.

and thus may every compound be noted & summed, the sum of the fractions composing the blood of the issue being always equal to Unit. It is understood in Natural history that a 4th cross of one race of animals with another gives an issue equivalent for all sensible purposes to the original blood. thus a Merino ram being crossed 1st with a country ewe, 2nd with this daughter, 3rd with this grandaughter, and 4th with the great grandaughter, the last issue is deemed pure Merino, having in fact but $\frac{1}{16}$ of the country blood. our Canon considers 2. crosses with the pure white, and a 3rd with any degree of mixture, however small. as clearing the issue of the negro blood. but observe that this does not reestablish freedom, which depends on the condition of the mother, the principle of the civil law, partus sequitur ventrem, being adopted here. but if a be emancipated, he becomes a free white man, and a citizen of the US. to all intents and purposes. — so much for this trifle, by way of correction.

By the time Jefferson wrote this letter in 1815, his speculations were more than abstract theories, since his six "octoroon" children by "quarteroon" Sally Heming were biologically "white" according to his calculations. *Library of Congress.*

not an option, Jefferson turned to mathematics. Following several pages of calculations, he concluded that when a "quarteroon" (three-quarters white) and a Euro-American produced children, "their offspring [containing] less than 1/4 pure negro blood, to wit 1/8 only, is no longer a mulatto" (borrowed from the word "mule," in that the person was half black and half white).

This "third" introduction of white genes "clears the blood." Octoroons, being seven-eighths white, were purged of "negro blood" and hence had improved their biological ranking. Should such a child "be emancipated," Jefferson added, "he becomes a free *white* man, and a citizen of the United States." In fact, by the time that Jefferson devised these calculations, he had evidence of a human variety for observation, since in October 1795, Sally Hemings, Jefferson's enslaved quadroon sister-in-law, gave birth to Harriet, the first of his six octoroon children.[17]

Precisely how many intellectuals and statesmen took the side of Rush, Tucker, and Ramsay in this debate can never be known. Perhaps unfairly, Jefferson has earned the opprobrium of later generations for committing to print opinions shared by untold thousands of his countrymen. Yet as a writer widely recognized as one of the Republic's leading intellectuals, and as a politician on whom voters repeatedly heaped the nation's highest honors, Jefferson's public ruminations on race and pigmentation were bound to have enormous influence. As more than a few biographers have insisted by way of defense, the theories advanced in *Notes on the State of Virginia* reflected the biases of many of his neighbors. But there can be little doubt that his words hardened already unfeeling hearts. By an odd coincidence, on the day in March 1790 that Jefferson arrived in Manhattan to assume his position as the country's first secretary of state, Congressmen James Jackson of Georgia and William Loughton Smith of South Carolina were putting the *Notes* to good use in denouncing northern interference in the Atlantic slave trade. In explaining why black Americans could never be citizens, Jackson summarized Jefferson's "physical and moral objections, as the difference in colour, and so forth." As these were "the observations of this learned gentleman," they were "not merely theoretical" but simply "the truth." Joining the debate, Smith then read directly from the volume by "that respectable author," Jefferson's *Notes* "proving that negroes were by nature an inferior race; and that the whites would always feel a repugnance at mixing their blood with that of the blacks."[18]

A shocked Elias Boudinot of New Jersey spoke in reply and encouraged those who sought to "prove the lawfulness of slavery" to recall "the genius of our government and the principles of the revolution." Boudinot too quoted Jefferson, but this time by citing the Declaration of Independence as "the language of America." The very fact that both proslavery and antislavery politicians could quote contradictory phrases crafted by the same author served as a reminder that white Americans were of two minds when it came to the thorny question of black rights. The "principles of the revolution," as Boudinot reminded, had indeed transferred the lines of authority from King

George to the people, but in the wake of Yorktown, American policy makers rarely agreed on exactly how much power the people should have, or even who the people were. The creation of a republic hardly implied the formation of an egalitarian utopia, and most states left untouched old colonial laws that denied voting rights to the laboring poor, women, Native Americans, and blacks. Moreover, classical republican theory, which emphasized responsibilities over rights, demanded a great deal of its citizens, on whom the burden of government now rested. Pamphleteers of the 1780s consistently described ideal voters as disciplined, virtuous, self-sacrificing, hardworking, and wise, all traits essayists attributed to European civilization—and so to Euro-American males. Whiteness, as a result, was an important component of republican ideology.[19]

Concerns over what role, if any, freed slaves might play in the American polity surfaced the moment northern states passed legislation for gradual emancipation. For state assemblies, what next to do with former bondpeople became the question, and the lack of answers reflected a growing national unease with the presence of a large population allowed to play no role in the emerging political order. To the extent that the majority of African Americans remained enslaved in the decades after 1781, even the very term "free black" represented a political anomaly. Black Americans recognized this and understood that freedom represented only part of the equation; in state after state, emancipation was but the first step toward equality and citizenship.[20]

Since emancipation had erased one form of social demarcation, the same legislators who grudgingly agreed to manumission hastened to craft new laws codifying the legally degraded status of free blacks. For the first time, to better illustrate what former slaves were *not*, politicians began to adopt the word "white" as synonymous with "citizenship." Colonial statutes, of course, had rarely been color-blind, but typically definitions of blackness had been used to signify enslavement. Now that many northern blacks were free, whiteness, rather than freedom itself, was used to denote the highest category of political involvement. Pennsylvania, for example, the first state to pass an act for gradual manumission, was also the first to have its courts rule that black Philadelphians were not citizens eligible to vote. Three years after passing its 1804 law for abolition, New Jersey banned free blacks from voting. In Quok Walker's Massachusetts, legislators approved the 1786 Act for the Solemnization of Marriage, which made it illegal for whites to marry outside their race, and thirteen years later, Rhode Island adopted a similar law that prohibited the union of "any white person with any Negro, Indian, or mulatto." So determined were they to separate the races sexually—or at least to hide the offspring of such relationships—that when a Rhode Island freedwoman sued a prominent white judge for paternity support, the assembly responded in 1800 by outlawing the right of black women to prosecute white men for child support. "Thus it is," observed a foreign visitor, "that the prejudice which repels Negroes seems to increase in proportion as they are emancipated."[21]

The designation "white" moved to the national level when the word appeared in the Articles of Confederation of 1777. (Since the Second Continental Congress was empowered only to act in response to external British threats, the need for Congress to govern the nation after independence required the creation of an internal constitution of sorts as well.) Drafted by a committee chaired by John Dickinson, the earliest version struggled with cost "incurred for the common Defence." Since the national government was in debt from financing the war, Congress had to devise a system under which the debt might be discharged, and also to obtain day-to-day expenditures should independence be won on the battlefield. Although still a large slaveholder, Dickinson believed the most equitable means of taxation was to requisition "the several Colonies in Proportion to the Number of Inhabitants of every Age, Sex and Quality, except Indians not paying Taxes, in each Colony, a true Account of which, distinguishing the white Inhabitants." Perhaps forgetting that he had added the word "white," Dickinson first wrote "white Inhabitants who are not slaves," then crossed out the last four words.[22]

As copies of early drafts of the articles began to circulate throughout state assemblies, the obvious criticism immediately arose. At one New Haven town meeting, Patriots protested the clause on the grounds that "the time may be when the black man may be a freeman." Connecticut had yet to move against slavery, and the complaint, although couched in the progressive language of abolition, obscured a deeper concern. If slaves remained uncounted in states such as South Carolina, northern taxpayers would shoulder a disproportionate share of the burden. In Congress, Samuel Chase of Maryland promptly retorted that slaves were clearly property and no more "population" than "cows or horses." In hopes of resolving the issue, Congress opted instead to use the value of land for the basis of assessment, a compromise that ultimately proved unworkable due to an inability to appraise land uniformly. But southern men won a related fight when another revision established a quota on soldiers due the national government "in proportion to the number of white inhabitants." Under this clause, Massachusetts, with a population of 378,787, owed Washington's army the same number of soldiers as Virginia, whose population stood at 691,737 when its 293,427 slaves were counted.[23]

As it became increasingly clear that attempts to discern a consistent value on land were impractical, Congress returned to the proposition that

taxation should be proportionate to prosperity, and that "wealth principally arises from the labour of men." Since small children performed little
valuable labor in any corner of the Republic, northern delegates offered to
exclude "all [slaves] under ten years old." But having revealed themselves
"willing to do as appears equitable [regarding] the negros," as Connecticut's
Roger Sherman admitted, northern men opened the door to further southern demands. Instead of not counting black children, Virginia's Benjamin
Harrison proposed, why not have "two blacks be rated as equal to one freeman?" James Madison rose to offer "proof of the sincerity of his professions
of liberality" by suggesting instead that five African Americans be counted
as three people. On April 18, 1781, nine states voted to approve this ratio in
Article 8, with only Rhode Island opposed. Although this version of Article 8 later failed to achieve ratification by four states, the idea, as historian
Donald Fehrenbacher observed, "remained in men's minds as an example
of successful sectional accommodation." Contrary to later assertions, however, the "three-fifths compromise," known also as the "federal ratio," was not
intended to indicate a slave's dual position as both human being and property. No other method appeared workable, and the idea of a fraction, Madison
explained, was merely "a compromise between the wide opinions & demands
of the Southern & other States."[24]

If nothing else, the readiness of northern politicians to give way in the face
of a united southern onslaught set as unfortunate a precedent as the three-
fifths compromise itself. So when the issue returned at war's end, southern
delegates had learned the virtue of a confrontational stand. In March 1783
Congress once again turned to taxation, this time in the guise of relative eval-
uations of state property. Since Samuel Chase had argued that bondpeople
were material goods rather than people to be counted, Connecticut's delegation proposed to count all slaves at full value. Southern members insisted
upon the three-fifths ratio, which was hardly a concession as they proposed
to fully tax northern property. As the debate in Congress grew acrimonious, cracks in the northern bloc began to appear. Even New Englanders once
again proposed various fractions—and then steadily retreated from them.
Connecticut's Oliver Ellsworth, the principal author of the bill, conceded
defeat and agreed to the three-fifths ratio. The result was that Massachusetts
owed the government $373,000, while slave-heavy South Carolina paid a far
smaller $165,000.[25]

Raised in 1781 and again in 1783, the three-fifths proportion took hold
among politicians as the logical solution to national questions dealing with
people who were also property. As yet, the "federal ratio" had been considered
only regarding taxation. Since each state, irrespective of population, received

but one vote in the Articles Congress (a continuation of the policy established by the Continental Congress) the number of enslaved Americans who resided within every state was a moot point. But as the 1780s wore on, and increasing numbers of politicians concluded that the highly decentralized framework of the Articles of Confederation required revision, one amendment bandied about was to give the larger states greater representation in Congress. In an about-face from Chase's 1777 position, Carolinians insisted that should such a change come to pass, every last slave must be counted for purposes of apportionment. At the same time, however, they hinted at a willingness to accept the "federal ratio." In short, long before delegates met in Philadelphia in 1787 to draft the new constitution, the three-fifths figure was an established compromise. The fraction had become, as Rufus King of New York acknowledged, "the language of all America."[26]

A second troublesome precedent buried deeply within the Articles of Confederation, vaguely worded but acknowledged by all contemporaries to pertain to slaves, was Article IV. One of the final changes made to the articles, this clause emerged out of a committee chaired by Richard Henry Lee of Virginia. As it became clear that one or more northern states intended to pass bills for manumission, southern legislators worried that runaways crossing state borders might liberate themselves simply by passing into free states. Other delegates expressed concerns about bringing enslaved domestics with them as they crafted the nation's laws, since the capital might remain in Philadelphia or relocate to New York. The committee responded by changing one word in the passage that dealt with the "privileges and immunities" that Americans enjoyed even after crossing state lines (since state laws might vary from region to region). The "privileges" applied only to "free citizens," Lee proposed, and not "inhabitants" of a given state, which had been the wording of an earlier draft. Since no state considered even freed blacks to be citizens, African Americans could scarcely claim the "privileges" reserved to white Americans. With the change of a single word, Lee helped lay the legal foundation for the notion that runaways could not free themselves by moving within the United States, hiding beneath phrasing that all understood applied to slavery. The troublesome word itself need not be put to paper.[27]

The question of slaveholders' rights in states and territories beyond their borders took on greater urgency in 1784, when Congress addressed the question of the western territories. The Peace of Paris, ratified during the previous year, brought the trans-Appalachian territories—the lands to the Mississippi in the south, and the Ohio Valley in the north—under congressional jurisdiction. The necessity of settling and selling the frontier was a pressing one, since the United States needed to repay foreign nations for their wartime loans, and most of all, the government wished to raise revenue to reimburse Continental soldiers for years of uncompensated service. As the army had the greatest claim on the land, it fell to Quartermaster General Timothy Pickering of Massachusetts to devise a plan for the settlement of the western lands. The son of a Presbyterian deacon and antislavery activist, Pickering was a second-generation abolitionist, and as Congress had proclaimed the "great truths" that "all men are created equal," he regarded any expansion of slavery into the frontier as "a violation of these truths." His draft of a governing ordinance thus mandated "the total exclusion of slavery" from any new territory, south or north.[28]

Pickering sent his rough proposal along to Alexander Hamilton, who expanded on the draft. It was then submitted to a committee chaired by Thomas Jefferson, at that time a congressman. The committee retained Pickering's ban on slavery along the entire frontier, but with a significant modification. Under Jefferson's pen, Pickering's immediate prohibition was revised so that "after the year 1800 of the Christian era there shall be neither slavery nor involuntary servitude" in the western areas. By softening Pickering's immediate ban, Jefferson's bill legalized bondage for sixteen years, which would have allowed proslavery settlers a solid foothold along the frontier. After the region began to fill with emigrants from the Chesapeake, western slaveholders would have petitioned to have the ban removed, and faced with an united South, northern congressmen would just as surely have yielded the point. A furious Timothy Pickering, who in later years became one of Jefferson's staunchest critics, believed Jefferson wished to have it both ways and satisfy his troubled conscience while quietly allowing for the expansion of slave soil. "I should indeed have objected to the period proposed (the year 1800) for the exclusion of slavery, for the admission of it for a day or an hour ought to have been forbidden," Pickering reflected.[29]

Since voting under the Articles was by state, delegations had to caucus in advance to decide how to cast their single ballot. Among the Virginians, only Jefferson argued for the antislavery clause, and in fact, only one other southern congressman, Hugh Williamson of North Carolina, supported the ban in caucus. In the final vote, a congressman from New Jersey who was known to support the prohibition was too ill to leave his bed, and the vote of New Jersey was lost. The ban failed to pass, and with it, support for the larger Ordinance of 1784 collapsed. "Thus," Jefferson observed, "we see the fate of millions unborn hanging on the tongue of one man, and heaven was silent in that awful moment."[30]

With that, the proposal for western settlement and political incorporation was divided into two plans, so that the subsequent 1785 Land Ordinance dealt only with the survey and sale of public lands. Several of Pickering's allies, including Rufus King, attempted to include his instantaneous prohibition on slavery. In hopes of winning southern moderates to their cause, King also drafted a fugitive slave clause, in which the vague phrases introduced into the Articles by Richard Henry Lee were made more explicit. Although King's passage also avoided using the term "slave," his reference to those held in "labor or service" allowed for no other construction. For the first time, a national law was to unequivocally state that runaways escaping their masters remained slaves so long as they resided in any federal territory, and that they were liable to "be lawfully reclaimed" by their owners. Southern congressmen, however, refused to support King's immediate ban on slavery, leading him to withdraw his sentence regarding fugitives. Still, since King's clause, slightly modified, eventually became Article IV, Section 2 of the 1787 Constitution, which empowered Congress to pass the Fugitive Slave Act of 1793, there is no little irony in the fact that the words were first supplied by an antislavery New Yorker.[31]

The first national prohibition on slavery, together with King's fugitive slave clause, finally made it into federal legislation with the passage of the Northwest Ordinance of 1787. A greatly modified version of the failed Ordinance of 1784, the bill carved the northwest country into five territories and established the method by which those territories were to become states. Initially, the bill contained no mention of slavery, as the statute's principal author, Nathan Dane of Massachusetts, believed southern delegates would reject the entire measure if it did. But on July 13, on the eve of a final vote on the measure, Dane included what became Article VI at the request of Manasseh Cutler, a speculator who had already invested more than a million dollars to develop the Ohio Valley. Since Cutler regarded Pickering's soldiers as his principal customers, he urged Dane to "move the article [banning slavery], which was agreed to without opposition." The brief article, which melded portions of Jefferson's 1784 ordinance with King's wording from two years before, announced: "There shall be neither Slavery nor involuntary Servitude in the said Territory," but added, "Provided always, that any person escaping into the same, from whom labor or service is lawfully claimed in any one of the original states such fugitive may be lawfully reclaimed and conveyed to the person claiming his or her labor or service as aforesaid."[32]

Given the southern wall of opposition to almost identical clauses in 1784 and 1785, why this time were proslavery voices so silent? The answer undoubtedly lies in the fact that the Northwest Ordinance, as its name indicates, pertained only to the lands north of the Ohio River, while Jefferson's 1784 bill (and King's failed 1785 amendment) restricted slavery in all western territories. Dane's statute said nothing about the lands below the Ohio, and the inescapable implication was that the act constituted a quiet compromise. Northern congressmen surreptitiously permitted slavery to expand into America's southwestern regions in exchange for restriction in the northwestern portions, lands that few southerners coveted in any case. As Dane's last-minute addition included King's 1785 sentence allowing them to recover their footloose property, southerners might actually have regarded the bill as a victory. Richard Henry Lee, who voted against Jefferson's bill three years before, openly endorsed the 1787 measure. So confident was North Carolina about the right to carry slaves into the West that when in 1789 it ceded to the federal government what would become Tennessee, the stipulation that "no regulations made by Congress shall tend to emancipate slaves" was regarded as being perfectly consistent with federal law.[33]

Although the northern frontier hardly constituted a slave society, settlers from western Virginia had already begun to move across the Ohio River. The region was also home to a number of slaveholding French nationals who had arrived in the region prior to 1763. Both groups angrily petitioned Congress to repeal the ban, arguing the prohibition violated the Revolution's promise to protect private property. When that failed, some Frenchmen accepted Spain's offer to relocate "from Illinois to the Spanish Side" of the Mississippi River, "in consequence of a resolve in Congress respecting negroes, who were to be free." Congress ignored the petitions, yet neither did they trouble themselves about the small number of slaves already living in the southern parts of the Illinois Territory. Even so, if the Northwest Ordinance allowed slavery into what would become five slave states, it immediately banned it from another five. In the process, Dane established the critical precedent that Congress possessed the legal authority to ban slavery in the western territories.[34]

Two months before passage of the Northwest Ordinance, and only two blocks away from where it would be passed, fifty-five men gathered at the old statehouse in Philadelphia on May 25 for the purpose of "revising" the Articles of Confederation. The result was to be not the few modifications grudgingly requested by Congress, but a completely new constitution. At least fifteen of the delegates, such as Virginia's Edmund Randolph, George Washington, George Mason, and James Madison, were slaveholders; others, such as former slaveholder Benjamin Franklin, were dedicated abolitionists; still others, including Alexander Hamilton, were both. The failure of the Articles of Confederation as a framework had nothing to do with slavery, and none of the men chosen to represent their states rode toward the convention with explicit instructions on the issue. Yet if a small number of powerful men were about to devise a new system of government, no southern state planned to allow northern reformers to tamper with their labor system. So woven into the fabric of American life was unwaged labor that "the institution of slavery and its implications," Madison admitted, "formed the line of discrimination" in virtually all of the summer's debates.[35]

South Carolina was the state with the highest percentage of Africans and enslaved Americans, and its delegation had barely dismounted before they began to express their unease with any alterations that resulted in greater federal power. South Carolinians wished instead to see explicit protections for slavery incorporated into the new document. Early on, Charles Pinckney "reminded the Convention that if [they] should fail to insert some security to the Southern States ag[ain]st an emancipation of slaves," he should "be bound by duty to his State" to vote against the proposed constitution. They were particularly desirous, his cousin General Charles Cotesworth Pinckney warned, that the convention not include any bill of rights. "[S]uch bills generally begin with declaring that all men are by nature born free." In the sort of blunt admission permitted behind closed doors—delegates also swore an oath not to reveal during any member's lifetime what was said—Pinckney conceded that "we should make that declaration with a very bad grace, when a large part of our property consists in men who are actually born slaves."[36]

As the delegates began their deliberations, it quickly became clear that slavery was not just a veiled topic that lurked beneath almost every issue, but rather *the* issue. The first instance dealt with state representation, since only the small-state delegates wished to retain the Articles' one-state, one-vote feature. On May 29, Virginia governor Randolph presented the Virginia Plan, which featured a bicameral national legislature. Both chambers were to contain the number of representatives equal to their "quotas of [tax] contribution" to the federal budget, "or to the number of free inhabitants." James Wilson of Pennsylvania offered a clarifying amendment, under which apportionment would be based on a count of all "white and other free citizens," together with "three-fifths of all other persons not comprehended in the foregoing description." Since that proportion had been debated in Congress in 1781 as the "federal ratio," Wilson's amendment meant that the three-fifths formulation, previously discussed only in the context of taxation, was now to be extended to representation. Wilson was careful not to actually use the word "slave," and he disingenuously insisted that slaves were "indirectly only an ingredient in the rule."[37]

The fact that it was a Pennsylvania delegate who revived the three-fifths precedent was ironic, since Madison had counseled his fellow Virginians to abandon the thorny issue of counting slaves for representation. As the leading spokesman of the populous states, Madison thought it critical not to be distracted from the larger goal of replacing equal state voting with proportional representation, upon which "every thing depended." But now the issue was on the floor, and Gouverneur Morris rose in response. Morris had labored, unsuccessfully, to abolish slavery in New York's state constitution, and together with John Jay had co-founded the New York Manumission Society. In a blistering reply, Morris announced he could never "concur in upholding domestic slavery," which invited "the curse of heaven on the states where it prevailed." The old "federal ratio" was a failure, he argued, since more taxes might be collected on "the bohea tea used by a Northern freeman [than] the whole consumption of a miserable slave." Far from being a compromise, the three-fifths formula was nothing more than a slaveholders' plot to gain more seats in Congress. Given their persistent determination to obtain greater representation than their numbers warranted—South Carolina ranked ninth in free population according to the 1790 census—perhaps it was best, Morris thundered, banging his iron-capped peg leg on the wood floor for emphasis, for the free and slave states to "at once take friendly leave of each other."[38]

With that the convention grew increasingly bitter and contentious. Although South Carolina's delegation originally swore they could accept nothing less than a complete counting of their slaves for purposes of apportionment—which would elevate the state to seventh in total population—they had always been prepared to accept what they depicted as the "compromise" of three-fifths. The South Carolina state constitution based representation on a combination of wealth and population, a formula that resulted in lowcountry dominance of state politics, and since the alternative in Philadelphia was Morris's demand that only free individuals be counted, the "federal ratio" was where they drew the line. North Carolina's William Davie thought it "high time now to speak out." His state "would never confederate on any terms that did not rate them at least as 3/5," and if the northern delegates intended "to exclude them altogether the business was at an end." Pierce Butler of South Carolina agreed: "The security the South[e]rn States want is that their negroes may not be taken from them which some gentlemen within or without [the convention] doors, have a very good mind to do." Despite his eloquent denunciation of slavery, Morris's only object was to base apportionment on the number of free Americans. Yet Butler's reply that any criticism of their political positions was tantamount to abolition was to become a Carolina staple over the next decades.[39]

Whether northern delegates put much faith in Butler's hints of sectional conflict is unclear, but certainly Davie's assurance that his state, South Carolina, and Georgia were prepared to bolt the convention terrified moderates who regarded the conference as the last hope of keeping the Union together. Edmund Randolph, ever the Virginian, "lamented" the very existence of "such a species of property," but added that since slavery "did exist the holders of it would require this security" of the federal ratio. Other delegates observed that the apportionment question had no real impact on slaves themselves and argued that denying southern demands would not improve the status of bondpeople. Still others, such as Virginia's George Mason, doggedly promoted the idea that the three-fifths ratio amounted to a national compromise. In July, Mason rose to announce that he "could not agree" with South Carolina's demands that slaves be counted equal to whites, "notwithstanding it was favorable to Virg[ini]a because he thought it was unjust." By adopting the pose of a reasonable statesman, Mason provided political cover for northern moderates who did not wish to appear to be giving ground to Carolina extremism.[40]

Even Franklin, despite his increasingly antislavery sensibilities, eventually endorsed the ratio as the final tinkering necessary to win the convention's approval of Sherman's so-called Connecticut Compromise, in which the Senate represented the states while the seats in the House of Representatives were to be based on populations. Few delegates, apart from Rufus King, shared Morris's belief that if the North united behind apportionment based only on free individuals, the lower South might accept the defeat and remain at the conference. So following weeks of debate, a weary convention voted to return to James Wilson's amendment but revised his wording so that the phrase "the whole number of free persons" replaced "white and other free citizens." The final version of Article I, Section 2, however, maintained Wilson's use of "all other Persons," so that they might abstain from using the terms "black" or "slaves." This ratio, used for both apportionment and taxation, remained part of the Constitution until ratification of the Fourteenth Amendment after the Civil War.[41]

By the conclusion of this debate, Madison decided that conflicts separating the North and the South had replaced the earlier divisions between large and small states, which was virtually the only opinion Madison shared with Morris and King. Perhaps because of this realization, northern delegates were less inclined to contest a second demand made by southern politicians: the inclusion of a federal fugitive slave clause. Chesapeake delegates proved most determined on this point, and since Madison and Randolph, unlike the Pinckney cousins, had not arrived in Philadelphia armed with threats, northern moderates were willing to listen to their arguments. Since Pennsylvania's manumission act lay seven years in the past, delegates who represented nearby Virginia, Maryland, and Delaware hoped to include wording regarding fugitive slaves similar to that then being written into the Northwest Ordinance. For once, Georgia and South Carolina politicians sat silent. Philadelphia was too far from Charleston and Savannah for safe escape, and most Georgia runaways raced for Spanish Florida, which placed them beyond the reach of federal authority. The record is unclear on who drafted what became Article IV, Section 2, but the clause denying freedom to those who escaped into northern states was lifted verbatim from the 1787 Northwest Ordinance, which was itself modified from King's 1785 phrase. Even then, Virginian George Mason denounced the clause as too weak, for it provided "no security."[42]

Madison was wrong on one point, however. The third question to involve slavery, which was also far and away the most contentious, did not pit the North against the South, but rather placed the Chesapeake and northern border states in opposition to a coalition of Lower South and New England delegates. As one of the last topics to be considered, the issue of the Atlantic slave trade drew the most heat. Since one of the leading political topics during the 1780s was the inability of the government under the Articles of Confederation to regulate foreign commerce, the traffic in Africans could hardly be avoided in Philadelphia. By early August, Randolph's notes reveal that some members hoped either to restrict the further importation of Africans or to impose high "duties by way of such prohibition." Since only Georgia and South Carolina reopened the African trade after the Revolution, it surprised nobody that the latter state's John Rutledge promptly renewed threats to quit the meeting. If the convention expected lowcountry planters to remain in a Union that banned the slave trade, Rutledge swore, "the expectation is in vain. The people of those states would never be such fools as to give up so important an interest."[43]

This time, it was not a northern man who rose in rebuttal, but the same Virginia slaveholder who disdained the fugitive slave clause as too ineffective. In an irate tirade that summarized several decades of Virginia's antislavery rhetoric, George Mason denounced "this infernal traffic," which "originated in the avarice of British Merchants." Virginia, he insisted with more anger than accuracy, had attempted to abolish the traffic before the Revolution but was "constantly checked" by crown and Parliament. Counting off the list of standard complaints, Mason argued that "Slavery discourages arts & manufactures" and led "poor [whites to] despise labor when performed by slaves." Mason was clearly familiar with Jefferson's *Notes*, as he endorsed the assertion that slavery exerted "an unhappy influence on the manners of our people." As a result, eleven states already had banned the trade, but now the "Western people are already calling out for slaves for their new lands, and will fill that

Country with slaves if they can be got thro' S. Carolina & Georgia." Noting that most African Americans fought on the side of King George or were increasingly inclined to rise for their freedom, Mason thought the "present question concerns not the importing of Slaves alone but the [security of] the whole Union."[44]

Mason, however, was not the man to condemn slavery on humanitarian grounds. As a planter and neighbor to George Washington, Mason hardly delivered the sort of speech that might have been given by a Richard Allen or an Elizabeth Freeman. Moreover, as a representative of a state in the midst of an economic transition from tobacco to wheat, Mason was suspected of wishing to close South Carolina ports to less expensive Africans so that his constituents might sell their costlier "surplus" African Americans into the fresh lands of Kentucky and Tennessee. Because Mason had failed to mention the emerging internal slave trade during his lengthy oration, his lowcountry critics thought him more guilty of hypocrisy and economic self-interest than of error.[45]

It helped little that the next voice to endorse Mason was another delegate from a slave exporting state, Luther Martin of Maryland. Martin too denounced the Atlantic trade as "inconsistent with the principles of the revolution" and added that it was "dishonorable to the American character to have such a feature in the Constitution." But following this brief expression of dismay over slavery, Martin demonstrated how Carolinian demands for more Africans raised new concerns about the just-resolved three-fifths compromise on representation. If slaves were taxed as free individuals, Martin observed, that might tend to "discourage slavery." But "to take them into account in giving representation tended to encourage the slave trade, and to make it the interest of the States to continue that infamous traffic."[46]

Suspecting that Mason and Luther spoke for the Chesapeake slave trader as much as they safeguarded the innocent African captive, or perhaps because of these suspicions, South Carolinians again leapt to their feet in reply. John Rutledge expressed shock that anybody thought "Religion & humanity" to have any bearing on "this question." Unlike the timid Mason, Rutledge added "he was not apprehensive of insurrections and would readily exempt the other States from the obligation" to help protect them. The only "true question at present" was whether South Carolina and Georgia "shall or shall not be parties to the Union." But having allowed his colleague to again rattle the saber of secession, Charles Pinckney next attempted compromise. Perhaps, Pinckney suggested, the convention might place no prohibition on the importation of Africans before 1800, or better yet, grant the lower South a twenty-year window, until 1808. He even went so far as to hint that the best solution was for the federal government to completely reject any "med-dling with the importation of negroes." Unless the convention forced the issue, Pinckney added, and "the States be all left at liberty on this subject, S. Carolina may perhaps by degrees do herself what is wished, as Virginia & Maryland have already done."[47]

Since Charles Cotesworth Pinckney had previously contradicted his younger cousin by bluntly stating that "S. Carolina & Georgia cannot do without slaves," the absurdly optimistic idea that these states might simply decide to import no more Africans drew Gouverneur Morris back into the fray. It was crime enough, Morris shouted, that the delegates expressed no desire to eradicate slavery through the Constitution, but to actually assist its growth by allowing for new captives was worse yet. Echoing Martin, Morris denounced "the inhabitants of Georgia and S.C. who goes to the Coast of Africa, and in defiance of the most sacred laws of humanity tears away his fellow creatures from their dearest connections & dam[n]s them to the most cruel bondages," so that they "shall have more votes in a Govt. instituted for protection of the rights of mankind, than the Citizens of Pa or N. Jersey who view with laudable horror, so nefarious a practice." Then, having grown weary of the polite euphemisms convention word-smiths adopted so that they might avoid using the term "slavery," Morris concluded by suggesting that the relevant clause should read: "The impor-tation of slaves into North Carolina, South Carolina, and Georgia shall not be prohibited." This honesty "would be most fair and would avoid the ambiguity." After two northern delegates sitting at a nearby table shushed him, Morris took his seat.[48]

Morris waited for other northern delegates to add their words of outrage, but instead a curious series of speeches ensued from New England men. Oliver Ellsworth of Connecticut blandly observed that as "he had never owned a slave [he] could not judge of the effects of slavery on character." In a barb clearly intended for Mason, Ellsworth added that since slaves "multiply so fast in Virginia & Maryland that it is cheaper to raise than import them," it was "unjust" to deny the lowcountry fresh Africans, as "in the sickly rice swamps foreign supplies are necessary." Having conceded that new captives were likely to perish upon arrival, Ellsworth considered his job done and resumed his chair with the final comment, "Let us not intermeddle."[49]

Ellsworth was seconded by Roger Sherman, a fellow Connecticut dele-gate, who noted that "as the States were now possessed of the right to import slaves, [and] as the public good did not require" any national provision for emancipation, "he thought it best to leave the matter" alone. As outraged middle-state delegates began to suspect that a deal had been reached over this issue between New England and the lower South, Sherman insisted that in principle he opposed the slave trade. Because of that, paradoxically, he believed imported Africans should not be taxed, since he "could not reconcile himself to the insertion of human beings as an article of duty, among goods, wares, and merchandise." Pointing to South Carolina's unyielding demands for the traffic while hinting that Virginians such as Madison were so desirous of a new constitution that they would swallow their anger at this provision, Sherman reasoned that prohibiting the African trade was the more imprudent position. Besides, he added, the delegates had been in session for nearly three months, and he wished to return home.[50]

Watching all of this was James Madison, who correctly guessed that Ellsworth and Sherman had an "understanding" with Pinckney and Butler. To a degree, the Constitution was a series of negotiations, and this one, as Mason grumbled, which came at the cost of tens of thousands of African captives, was "a Compromise between the [North] Eastern & the two Southern States, to permit the latter to continue the Importation of Slaves." New England was determined to obtain a commerce clause, which had been lacking under the Articles of Confederation government and which the export-minded planters were not inclined to endorse unless they obtained what Mason dubbed their "favourite Object." Moreover, Rhode Island was the sole state to boycott the convention; as its merchants owned many of the ships that carried Africans to the tidewater, Sherman possibly hoped to win the Rhode Island delegates' support during what all assumed would be a bruising ratification fight. But since the slaveholding states had already obtained major concessions on the three-fifths ratio and the fugitive slave clause, Mason believed this compromise to be unnecessary, and probably with considerable justification. New England was firmly committed to the new constitution, and planter delegates had achieved most of their demands. Now it was Randolph's turn to announce that this clause was "so odious" that he "doubted whether he should ever be able" to endorse the complete document.[51]

On this matter, however, as on so many others, Randolph turned irresolute. On August 22 he pled "that some middle ground might, if possible, be found," and since so much of the negotiations in Philadelphia revolved around finances, it was no surprise that revenue soothed many a tender conscience. James Wilson of Pennsylvania noted that as "all articles imported are to be taxed," it made little sense that "Slaves alone are exempt." North Carolina's Hugh Williamson, one of two southern congressmen to endorse territorial restriction of slavery in 1784, added that his state did not currently ban the trade, but it "imposed a duty of £5 on each slave imported from Africa," £10 on blacks sold down from the Chesapeake states, and £50 "on each from a

State licensing manumission." As always, South Carolina's extreme position proved to be a bargaining tactic, and Charles Cotesworth Pinckney announced he could support a duty on slave equal to a "tax with other imports." With that, what became Article I, Section 9—which here too avoided the troublesome words "Africans" or "slaves"—permitted the "migration or importation of such persons as any of the States shall think proper to admit" and protected the traffic until "the year one thousand eight hundred and eight."[52]

Why did the delegates, who almost unanimously expressed a desire to frame a stronger and more lasting federal government, agree to what one historian has termed a series of "dirty compromises"? The most obvious answer is that they converged upon Philadelphia to cement a dangerously decentralized Union, not to abolish slavery. Several key delegates also professed to believe that since slavery was disappearing across the North, fighting over a dying system at the possible cost of disunion appeared the height of folly. "The abolition of slavery seemed to be going on in the United States," Roger Sherman observed, and Oliver Ellsworth agreed: "Slavery in time will not be a speck in our country." But as these optimistic assessments were delivered by two New Englanders deep in consultation with South Carolina delegates, their sanguinity may be regarded as a rhetorical ploy. Did the Connecticut delegates honestly believe that South Carolina, with its black majority, shared "the good sense of the several states" that had begun "by degrees" to eradicate it? Perhaps the truth is that the wealthy delegates cared little about the plight of faraway Africans, particularly when their importation provided the bankrupt federal government with a useful tax. As Ellsworth admitted, "what enriches a part enriches the whole."[53]

Certainly the endless threats of secession on the parts of Georgia and South Carolina delegates, or at least a refusal to ratify the finished document, cowed a number of northern moderates into concessions regarding slavery. Within a few weeks of debate, many of those in Philadelphia had come to regard Pinckney's proud assertion that his state would "never receive the plan if it prohibits the slave trade" as a bluff. James Wilson, for one, noticed the obvious. Since Pinckney agreed "to get rid of the importation of slaves in a short time," that is, after twenty years, this implied "they would never refuse to Unite because the importation might be prohibited." Washington kept his counsel to himself, but privately he was certain that South Carolina's threats to bolt the convention were hollow. The delegates needed nine states to ratify, and if enough states did so, what would then be the lowcountry's options? Could they actually form a two-state confederacy, or rejoin the British Empire, or even turn to Madrid for protection? Washington thought not. Georgia in particular was "a weak State with [Creek and Cherokee] Indians on its back and the Spaniards on its flank." Yet the fact that no Virginian cared enough about the Atlantic slave trade to call Pinckney's bluff is telling.[54]

At the same time, many if not most delegates were profoundly uneasy with these compromises, as their determination to apply a variety of euphemisms in place of the term "slave" suggests. Nobody could doubt whom the framers meant by "person[s] held in labor" or "the importation of such persons," yet the fact that these normally precise men—the vast majority of whom were attorneys—held back reveals the extent of their embarrassment. New Jersey's William Paterson admitted the delegates "had been ashamed to use the term 'Slaves' & had substituted a description" when it came to apportionment, and another referred to the "particular scruples" of "northern delegates" in explaining the vague wording of the fugitive slave clause.[55]

Not even Gouverneur Morris seriously expected the delegates to include a provision in the Constitution for gradual manumission on a nationwide basis. Ultimately the question is not what the Philadelphia delegates did *not* do but rather what they *did*. A number of witnesses, including John Jay, then in New York City, were aware that during that same summer the Congress banned slavery in the Old Northwest, and he believed that northern delegates in Philadelphia had made far too many concessions to the slave states. Under the three-fifths agreement, its critics calculated, slaveholders were allowed to count 60 percent of their bondpeople in the population that was to decide apportionment in the House of Representatives and, more ominously, votes in the Electoral College. Certainly Edmund Randolph, who refused to sign the final document in Philadelphia before advocating its ratification in Richmond, mocked those who feared that the new government could tamper with slavery. "[E]ven South Carolina herself," he promised, "conceived this property to be secure," and that "there was not a member of the Virginia delegation who had the smallest suspicion of the abolition of slavery." Indeed, at that moment in South Carolina, Charles Cotesworth Pinckney encouraged ratification on the grounds that slaveholders "have a right to recover our slaves in whatever part of America they might take refuge."[56]

As if to prove the point, the Congress, newly empowered by the stronger and "more perfect" Constitution, promptly set about to equate whiteness with citizenship. In 1790, while drafting the nation's first naturalization act, Congress permitted all "free white persons who have, or shall, migrate into the United States" to take the "oath of citizenship," provided they remained in the country for two years. So unthinking was the correlation of light pigmentation to political rights that during the debates over the bill, no congressman or senator noted the irony of boasting that the nation "opened an asylum for the oppressed of all nations" while allowing enslaved Africans to be imported into the lower South. Congress also restricted militia service to "every free able-bodied white male citizen" but, perhaps remembering black military service during the war, allowed African Americans into the army and navy. As the elite branch of the nation's armed forces, however, the Marine Corps was restricted to whites. Responding to southern concerns about the transmission of information, Congress also banned free blacks from carrying the U.S. mails.[57]

Legislators across the Republic wrote whiteness into their franchise requirements, which under the Constitution was a state prerogative. As early as 1777, Georgia restricted voting rights to "male white inhabitants," and South Carolina followed suit by insisting that both voters and officeholders be "free white male[s]." Virginia incorporated whiteness into its laws in a unique way, doing so on Jeffersonian grounds. Rather than taking whiteness for granted, in 1792 the assembly devised a special legal category for residents who were free but carried "black blood"; for the first time Virginia used genetic percentages to provide a scientific rationale for separating the races. Having announced Virginians with "black blood" to be inferior to whites, the Assembly in 1805 took steps to ensure that blacks would never comprehend Euclid. Colonial statutes had banned teaching slaves to read, but the prohibition on "mental improvement" was now extended to free African American children. Theories of black biological inferiority were thus employed to explain subsequent political inferiority, but this linkage quickly became a cruel cycle as legislators then used the power of the state to further consign blacks to a degraded legal status. Unable to vote in any state, blacks from Boston to Charleston were powerless to halt this downward spiral.[58]

For blacks who had expected the struggle for American rights to culminate in a government based upon the principles once championed by essayists, ministers, and politicians, the counterrevolution of the 1780s proved a bitter disappointment. State by state, legislators denied the vote to native-born black Patriots who had served their country, even as the federal government opened the doors of residency to foreign immigrants. The fifty-five men who rode toward Philadelphia—home to Absalom Jones and Richard Allen—to "secure the blessings of liberty" to themselves and their posterity crafted a constitution that made it all too clear that black Americans were not intended to be citizens of the country of their birth.

Faced with this wall of hostility, Jones and Allen spent the hot summer of 1787 creating their own kind of political order in the Free African Society. To their south, where most African Americans remained enslaved, other young men arrived at the conclusion that if the framers of the Constitution did not intend to grant them liberty, they would seize it for themselves.

TEN

Eli Whitney's Cotton Engine

Expansion and Rebellion

T HE VOYAGE DOWN THE COAST did not begin well, and the tempests Eli Whitney encountered between Connecticut and Savannah were portents of the ill winds shortly to batter African Americans. Nearly twenty-eight years of age, Whitney had finally graduated from Yale College. He wished to read law, but his father, a farmer in Westboro, Massachusetts, struggled just to settle his final tuition bills. Requiring money "to furnish himself for his future employment," Whitney accepted a position as tutor for a Major Dupont in South Carolina. While sailing for Manhattan, Whitney met Catherine Greene, the widow of General Nathanael Greene. But the seas were choppy and the ship ran aground on rocks, and when Whitney stumbled ashore, alarmed passengers noticed he "was broke out full with the small-Pox." Greene helped nurse Whitney, and she invited him to stop at Mulberry Grove, her Georgia plantation, before he rode on for the Carolina lowcountry.[1]

When he finally arrived in Savannah in October 1792, Whitney discovered that Dupont intended to pay him less than originally promised. As he sought new employment, Whitney resided with the Greene family, where he became friendly with Phineas Miller, another Yale graduate who had served as the children's tutor before becoming the estate's manager. "During this time," Whitney wrote his father, "I heard much said of the extreme difficulty of ginning Cotton, that is, separating it from the seeds." The problem, as Greene and Miller explained it, was the difficulty in prying the tightly clinging green seeds from short-staple cotton. Long-staple cotton, also known as black seed cotton, had a larger boll and fewer seeds, but its requirement of low-lying terrain and considerable water limited its production to coastal areas. Catherine Greene, who noticed Whitney's facility at repairing clocks and farm equipment, encouraged him to try his hand at "a machine [that] would clean the cotton with expedition."[2]

The production of cotton, of course, was hardly new to the American South. Almost since the dawn of the colonial era, farmers from southern Virginia through the lowcountry planted small amounts of cotton for domestic use. But neither of the two common varieties of cotton suited commercial production. South Carolinians who wished to market their products abroad devoted most of their acreage to rice and indigo. The odd agriculturalist who bothered with cotton, one admitted, "plants no more than just what serves their Plantations in some few trifling articles to employ some old Superannuated Negroe Wenches." But as tensions between Britain and its mainland colonies grew, Patriots who complied with congressional nonimportation pacts found it necessary to produce their own textiles.[3]

Recognizing the potential for commercial expansion, particularly given the emergence of cotton mills in Britain and Samuel Slater's new "spinning factory" in Rhode Island, a number of Americans tried to improve upon the *charkha*, devised centuries before in India. Similar to a clothes wringer, the *charkha* featured a pair of rollers that almost touched; as the cylinders were turned by a crank, the machine squeezed out some seeds, but rarely green seeds, to which the cotton's short fibers clung obstinately. As early as 1725, Count Belleisle near French New Orleans tried to alter the *charkha*, but although it cleaned long-staple cotton from Saint-Domingue "very easily," his attempts to "purge [short-staple cotton] of its seed [were] not successful." Twenty years later, James Marion of South Carolina devised a machine that cleaned "eighty Pounds Weight of Cotton" within the span of twelve hours, and in 1790 Joseph Eve, a resident of the Bahamas, attempted to resolve the problem by constructing a much larger series of rollers. A machine nearly five feet high, Eve's complicated system involved three metal rollers, each nearly four feet long, and when it was cranked, the seeds of black seed cotton flew off "like sparks." Eve's contraption, however, was so large and heavy that it required water power or horses to make it run, and those who could afford it were disappointed with the results. Word of Eve's invention arrived in Savannah in February 1791, just ahead of Eli Whitney, when the *Georgia Gazette* carried a story claiming that Eve's machine was effective with both types of cotton.[4]

Whitney's hosts were not alone in praying for a technological breakthrough. Nine years after the British evacuation of Charleston, the lowcountry remained ravaged by the war. Throughout the 1780s, production of rice, indigo, and tobacco in Georgia and the Carolinas remained far below prewar levels, and Whitney observed the ramshackle farms and unplowed fields on his journey inland. He was told that planters expected each adult bondman and his family to painstakingly clean four pounds of cotton each week—in addition to their main labors—which "would amount to one bale in two years." Although a number of planters wished to diversify and add cotton to their list of commercial crops, they might do so only if they could effectively farm green seed cotton away from the coast.[5]

"In about ten days," Whitney explained later, he had "made a little model." As he studied drawings of a *charkha*, he thought to affix metal teeth to one roller, while adding a third roller with small brushes to separate the cotton lint from the wire teeth. He initially planned to use iron plates for the teeth, but with none at hand, he substituted a coil of wire the Greene children planned to use to build a birdhouse. A hand crank turned a series of belts, so that the cylinder with wire teeth turned at a different speed than the cylinder that cleaned it. Greene's overseer offered Whitney "fifty Guineas a Year" in exchange "for all right and title to it," but the Connecticut Yankee instead chose to return "Northward for the purpose of having a machine made on a larger scale and obtaining a Patent for the invention."[6]

Back in New Haven, Whitney spent several months perfecting his system. Manufacturing a number of the "cotton engines," as he called them, or "gins" for short, was expected to cost thousands of dollars. Phineas Miller recognized that fortunes stood to be made, and in exchange for a share of future profits, he funded the development of the machine and the rental of a factory. Taking advantage of the new federal patent law, Whitney wrote to Secretary of State Thomas Jefferson. Using his invention, Whitney insisted, "one negro [could] clean fifty weight [pounds] of the green seed cotton per day." Jefferson replied immediately. The state of Virginia, Jefferson observed, "carries on household manufactures of cotton to a great extent, as I also do myself, and one of our greatest embarrassments is the cleaning of the cotton of the seed." Jefferson peppered the young inventor with questions. Could a single slave really operate the engine? "What will be the cost of one of them made?" Since Jefferson wished to purchase one "for family use," he felt "a considerable interest in the success of your invention." Pleased with Whitney's response, the government approved the patent on March 14, 1794, retroactive to November 6, 1793, the day on which Jefferson had received Whitney's first missive.[7]

Unhappily for Whitney, the genius of his invention lay in its simplicity, and almost anybody who saw it was able to construct one. A series of competitors sued Whitney and Miller, claiming the two had infringed upon their inventions. The pair lost one suit in 1797, despite the fact that Miller invited "the Judge with a Party to dine with us twice before the trial." But after considerable lobbying, in 1801 a grateful South Carolina legislature paid Whitney's company a princely $50,000 to purchase the "patent right for the Machine for Cleaning Cotton." Whitney, who was in Columbia to witness the triumph, assured a former classmate that it "may without exaggeration be said to have raised the value of seven eights of all the three Southern States from 50 to 100 pr. Cent." Whitney's brag was supported by evidence. In the year he invented his gin, South Carolina produced 94,000 pounds of cotton, most of it long-staple cotton grown in the lowcountry. Only seven years later, the South Carolina upcountry was exporting 6.5 million pounds of cotton, all of it of the short-staple variety. In 1810, the figure rose again, to 50 million pounds. Cotton was about to become king.[8]

For lowcountry whites attempting to plant their way out of the postwar recession of the 1780s, cotton promised a number of advantages. While sugar and rice production required tremendous capital outlays for equipment and terracing, cotton production required only land and simple tools. Even when closely monitored, Caribbean bondpeople vanished into the tall cane fields, and more than a few overseers fell victim to the machetes used for harvesting. Green seed cotton, by comparison, grew to only three feet, so overseers could always monitor the progress of bondpeople across the fields. For upcountry yeomen, the purchase of uncleared acres, a family of slaves, a plow, and a handful of hoes allowed for an easy entrance into the planter class. Even tenant farmers could become landowners and staple crop producers. With the Republic stretching all the way to the Mississippi, all that limited the expansion of cotton was labor.[9]

The remarkable expansion of cotton production provides the misleading impression that Whitney's invention gave new life to a dying institution. The admission of slaveholding Kentucky as the fifteenth state in June 1792, four months before Whitney arrived at Mulberry Grove, demonstrates that slavery's expansion westward was already under way. Even as St. George Tucker drafted his *Dissertation on Slavery*, unfree labor grew ever more entrenched in central Virginia. But if slavery was hardly moribund in 1793, it remains true that cotton reinvigorated large-scale plantation slavery, driving it toward the Mississippi at a furious rate. This quickly led to an organized internal traffic in humans, tearing apart black family structures that had just begun to stabilize after the war. Black activists responded with a new wave of petitions and demands, and when that failed, aggressive young men reacted as had Colonel Tye, by hammering farm scythes into swords.[10]

Chesapeake traders had yet to organize a formal traffic into the frontier, but many of the young Virginians who crossed the Appalachians in search of richer lands brought slaves with them. The slaves who were initially marched or sold south into the Carolina upcountry came from the tidewater, but so rapidly did whites purchase undeveloped lands in central Georgia and the Alabama Territory that prospective planters had to look elsewhere for laborers. The same Chesapeake planters who demanded an end to the African slave trade in 1787 proved more than willing to sell their surplus bondpeople into the lower South. According to the 1790 census, whites in Virginia and Maryland owned 56 percent of all American slaves, far more than those states could effectively employ, and their sales brought in cash needed for the transition to new cereal crops. Within a decade, the terminus of the domestic slave trade shifted south. During the 1780s, Chesapeake masters sold their excess slaves west into the fresher lands of central Virginia or the Kentucky Territory, but by the dawn of the nineteenth century roughly 60 percent of Chesapeake blacks for sale were marched south toward Mississippi and Alabama. Since the percentage of blacks owned by Virginians steadily declined by comparison to the rest of the southern states, upper South slaveowners were able to maintain their pose as caring masters who continued to pray for an early end to unfree labor.[11]

Slaves had always been commodities, but in earlier decades Chesapeake masters valued a bondman's worth by his ability to labor in the fields. By the mid-1790s, however, white Virginians began to regard slaves as valuable investments in themselves, or as some put it, as "goods" to be sold. In Charleston, where cramped urban geography limited the space available to enslaved domestics, buyers continued to advertise for house servants "without a Child." But rural masters interested in selling their surplus laborers recognized the value of a young woman's reproductive capacity. Although there is no evidence that masters bred their slaves for sale, Chesapeake sellers increasingly understood the value of healthy young women. "I consider the labor of a breeding woman as no object," Jefferson explained, "and that a child raised every 2 years is of more profit than the crop of the best laboring man." On the eve of the Revolution, when Chesapeake planters had a surfeit of labor, some sellers used a bondwoman's sterility as a selling point. But by the end of the century, sellers advertised "likely young breeding NEGRO WOMEN" for sale.[12]

As the Chesapeake region turned to the exporting of black Americans, professional domestic traders emerged to help facilitate the internal traffic.

Like any astute businessmen, buyers developed regular circuits so that prospective sellers knew them by sight. In states such as Virginia, where transactions were traditionally conducted on paper or through barter, traders paid cash for young bondpeople and encouraged masters to sell their most troublesome slaves. In his 1787 *Richmond Gazette* advertisement seeking "One hundred Negroes, from 20 to 30 years old," Moses Austin wanted it known that his goods were "to be sent out of state, therefore we shall not be particular respecting the character of any of them," provided they were "Hearty and well made." Despite the promise of profits, slave trading came with its dangers. Young bondmen sold away from their families had little to lose, and in 1799 a man named Speers, who traded between Virginia and Georgia, was murdered by his coffle.[13]

Before the onset of the Civil War, approximately one million black Americans would be resold into the southwestern states and territories, a figure roughly twice the number of Africans sold into the British mainland colonies (and then the young Republic) prior to 1808. But this organized internal traffic was slow to develop, and by the late 1780s, some Carolinians began to discuss reopening the trade with West Africa, which the Constitution permitted them to do. Determined to preempt such a development, the Pennsylvania Abolition Society decided to raise the issue with Congress. James Pemberton, the society's vice president and a prosperous Quaker merchant, drafted two petitions. The first called upon Congress to pass a national law for gradual emancipation, and the second requested an immediate federal ban on the importation of Africans. Realizing that the first Congress, already burdened by contentious fights over the funding and assumption of state debts, was likely to ignore the petitions, Pemberton approached Benjamin Franklin for sponsorship. Almost to the society's surprise, Franklin, then eighty-four and at the end of his career, agreed to endorse the second petition. Pemberton was thrilled, yet it remained a sad commentary on the founding generation that only a statesman so near the shades was willing to affix his signature to a petition denouncing the traffic in humans.[14]

Dated February 3, 1790, and signed by Franklin as honorary president of the society, the petition, presented to the House by Congressman Frederick A. C. Muhlenberg of Pennsylvania, consisted of three brief paragraphs. It refrained from making any specific requests for legislative action, apart from noting that Congress enjoyed the power of "promoting the welfare and securing the blessings of liberty to the people." Sensitive to the fact that a good many legislators owned slaves, the society adopted a respectful tone and merely observed that "mankind are all formed by the same Almighty Being" and were "equally designed for the enjoyment of happiness." No earlier version of the petition exists, and quite possibly the politically astute Franklin softened its specific demands into a vague request that Congress devote "serious attention to the subject of slavery" and "step to the very verge of the power vested in you for discouraging every species of traffic in the persons of our fellow-men."[15]

Despite its obsequious tone and the endorsement of the Republic's most eminent statesman, the response of the lower South was both immediate and fierce. Congressman Thomas Tucker of South Carolina leapt to his feet, shouting that the document be "thrown aside." As had Carolinians at the Philadelphia convention, Tucker raised the specter of disunion. "Do these men expect a general emancipation of slaves by law," he wondered. "This would never be submitted to by the Southern States without a civil war." William Loughton Smith, also of South Carolina, rose to second those sentiments. Choosing to ignore the intentional vagueness of the petition, Smith observed that the Constitution prohibited any federal ban on the Atlantic slave trade, warning that "there is no point on which [white Carolinians] are more jealous and suspicious than on a business with which they think the Government has nothing to do." Three years before, Smith retorted, "we took each other, with our mutual bad habits and respective evils, for better, for worse; the Northern states adopted us with our slaves, and we adopted them with their Quakers."[16]

Later that afternoon, James Jackson of Georgia went further still. In response to a northern colleague who thought the petition "strictly agreeable to the Constitution," Jackson insisted that, far from slavery being an inhumane system, "from Genesis to Revelations [*sic*]," Western "religion is not against it," nor was any government "on the face of the earth." When Jackson finally tired, Smith rose to elaborate. Weary of northern accusations that "the owners of negro property" suffered from "the want of humanity," Smith wished it known that lowcountry planters had "as much humanity as persons in any part of the continent." Although similar claims had been advanced before, most notably at the constitutional convention, this marked the first occasion during which a comprehensive defense of slavery was paraded before a national audience. In a preview of what would become commonplace rhetoric during the antebellum decades, Smith and Jackson treated the Congress to a militant, defiant sectionalism that, as the former presaged, would "never suffer [itself] to be divested of their property without a struggle."[17]

As was ever the case, a Virginian—in this instance, James Madison—adopted the facade of reason and moderation. While privately observing that the "African trade in slaves had long been odious to most of the States," he publicly agreed with Smith's position that "Congress is restricted by the

Constitution from taking measures to abolish the slave trade." The Quaker petition, however, alluded to "every species of traffic," and not exclusively the *external* commerce in Africans. Congress possessed the power to regulate internal commerce and the rising domestic sale of slaves, and Madison reluctantly admitted that there were "a variety of ways by which" Congress might encourage "abolition." What Madison desired was for the whole issue to vanish, and the habitually composed congressman was irate with Smith and Jackson for publicizing what could have been quietly referred to committee. The two congressmen from South Carolina and Georgia, he complained to Benjamin Rush, were "intemperate beyond all example and even all decorum." If buried in committee, the petition would "excite no regret in the patrons of Humanity." But if it was attacked on the floor of the House in "the most virulent language," abolitionist fervor "could hasten more the progress of those reflections & sentiments which are secretly undermining the institution" of slavery.[18]

Equally desirous of allowing the entire affair to vanish from public sight was the president. Although the petition stood little chance of coming "before [him] for an official decision" of signature or veto, Washington endorsed Madison's determination to quietly refer the memorial to a committee for disappearance. Calling the Quakers' submission of their petition to Congress "very mal-apropos," Washington worried that the very existence of the Pennsylvania Abolition Society might have an impact on the concurrent debate over the location of the new federal capital. The South Carolina delegation, according to one presidential confidant, expressed "a most settled antipathy to Pennsylvania, owing" to the "subject of slavery."[19]

As if black Americans needed a further reminder that the national mood was turning against calls for federal manumission, one of those who recommended no action on the petition was Congressman Theodore Sedgwick, Elizabeth Freeman's attorney. Although Sedgwick openly embraced the term "abolitionist" and defended the historic right of petition, he believed the question of the external slave trade had been resolved in 1787. He assured his reform-minded constituents that he wished the Philadelphia convention had never agreed to protect slavery, but since it had, he was now prepared to respect and obey the constitutional compromises. As they had three years before, Virginia politicians suspected collusion between New England slavers and lowcountry buyers. Yet as the domestic slave trade was drawing increasing numbers of African Americans out of the Chesapeake, men such as Madison were in no position to make their suspicions public.[20]

Perhaps not surprisingly, New Hampshire congressman Ariel Foster's committee drafted a seven-point reply to the petition. The first "opinion" pertained to the international trade and upheld the widespread view that the Constitution prohibited Congress from banning human imports before "the year 1808." Perhaps in hopes of demonstrating a willingness to compromise, however, the fourth point reiterated the federal power to tax imported Africans, the fifth and sixth points restricted the trade to American shippers, and the seventh assured the "memorialists" of their desire to promote "the principles of justice, humanity, and good policy." Rather more controversial was the third point, aimed at appeasing the lower South, which disclaimed any authority "to interfere in the internal regulations of particular States, relative to the instruction of slaves in the principles of morality and religion." By abdicating any right to regulate "the separation of children from their parents" or even the "transportation, or sale of free negroes," Foster's committee essentially announced its unwillingness to regulate the internal trade.[21]

The second "opinion" made it all too clear where the federal government stood regarding one-fifth of its population. This point argued that "Congress, by a fair construction of the Constitution," was "restrained from interfering in the emancipation of slaves, who already are, or who may [be] imported into, or born within any of the said States." Although Article 4, Section 2 guaranteed the return of fugitive slaves from free states, there was nothing in the Constitution that prohibited Congress from erasing that clause by passing a law for federally mandated manumission. To impose this construction on the Constitution required the loosest of all readings, yet on other issues raised in 1790, such as the legality of Alexander Hamilton's Bank of the United States, southern politicians demanded strict construction. Even this concession to southern interests brought opposition from the lowcountry. When debate commenced on March 16, Jackson spoke "in opposition to the report," and Smith "lamented much that this subject has been brought before the House." After a week of acrimonious debate, the House voted 29 to 25 to approve the report, but as the statement regarded federal emancipation to be unconstitutional, the minority faction included both enemies and supporters of slavery.[22]

Pennsylvania reformers interpreted the vote to mean that further appeals to revolutionary ideals would only harden the determination of lowcountry politicians to maintain their way of life. Several months after the House debates, the society resolved that the "principal object" of any future petitions "would consist of a request that Congress [only] pass laws to ALLEVIATE as much as possible the horrors of the slave trade," rather than to try to ban it outright. The society hoped that a tactical shift toward specific, piecemeal reform might garner some success, but the next few years were to prove them wrong. In 1791 Madison declined to introduce a Quaker petition against the *domestic* slave trade, confessing, "Those from whom I derive my public station are known by me to be greatly interested in that species of property, and to view the matter in that light." A year later, Congress instructed its clerk to return a mild antislavery petition from Quaker Warner Mifflin after southern politicians denounced it as "mischievous." Although conceding "the right of every citizen to petition" Congress, William Loughton Smith demanded the House reject such "dangerous" memorials, "a mere rant and rhapsody of a meddling fanatic, interlarded with texts of Scripture."[23]

The only victory abolitionists achieved on the federal level was hollow at best. In early 1794, a group of Rhode Island Quakers submitted a petition to Congressman Jonathan Trumbull of Connecticut, who brought it before the House. The Quakers took pains to disclaim any "desire of legislative interference for the purpose of a general emancipation of the slaves already in the United States," nor did they press for a ban on the internal or external trade. Their sole object was to obtain legislation "prohibiting the [Atlantic] trade carried on by citizens of the United States, for the purpose of supplying slaves to foreign nations, and to prevent foreigners from fitting out vessels for the slave trade" in American ports. Since Georgia and South Carolina wished only to import more Africans, the slave-exporting states of the Chesapeake desired to ship their surplus workers into the lower South's cotton fields, and New England slavers wanted an end to foreign competition, no voices from any corner of the Republic were raised in opposition. The measure passed virtually without debate on March 7. It hindered not a single trader in either Africans or black Americans.[24]

As their white allies steadily retreated from demands for national manumission, free black activists responded by increasing their level of agitation and protest. Unwilling to accept the reactionary national mood, African Americans increasingly returned to earlier strategies of petitioning and pamphleteering. In October 1787, Prince Hall, the Methodist minister and founder of Massachusetts's black Masonic Order, arrived at the statehouse with a petition asking either that black children be allowed into the whites-only "free schools in the town of Boston" or that some "provision [be] made for them." Returning to the familiar connection between taxation and political rights, Hall pointedly observed that they had "never been backward in paying [their] proportionate part of the burdens," yet their children "now receive no benefit" of education. In respectful tones, he warned that all Bostonians, regardless of race, "must fear for our rising offspring to see them in ignorance."[25]

Peaceful memorials were not limited to the relative safety of Boston. In January 1791 a group of free blacks in Charleston requested the legislature abolish the state's racially based political caste system. South Carolina's Negro Act of 1740 had drawn no distinction between enslaved and free blacks, in part because virtually none of the latter had existed in the lowcountry. Few enough did by 1791, and although the petition did not reveal the racial composition of the unnamed memorialists, they called themselves "Free Citizens by the Constitution of the United States" and were almost certainly Carolina's self-styled "browns." The 1740 law denied them the right of trial with "the benefit of a Jury" and left them "subject to Prosecution by Testimony of Slaves without Oath." Their petition was immediately rejected. Two years later, after the assembly imposed a tax of twenty-five cents per person on each free black, they returned with a new petition. The state saw no contradiction in denying freed African Americans political rights while taxing them, since the impost was designed to drive them out of the state. Those freedmen less inclined to place their trust in the legislature simply refused to pay their tax, and there is no evidence that Denmark Vesey ever did so.[26]

Particularly in the southern states, however, black Americans picked up not the pen but the sword. Many historians trace the unceasing cycles of black rebelliousness in the 1790s to the 1791 slave revolt in the French Caribbean colony of Saint-Domingue, but the failure of peaceful abolition within the United States was doubtless a central factor. Slaves rarely ventured their lives when safer avenues to freedom existed. As it became clear that southern states would never pass legislation for gradual manumission, and as the emerging cotton kingdom and the resulting domestic slave trade destroyed fragile black families in the upper South, hundreds of young slaves along the Atlantic seaboard (not all of them in the southern states) decided they had little to lose in sharpening a wheat scythe or lighting a torch. Prince Hall had warned of the dangers of rampant ignorance and poverty, but terrified whites from Albany to Savannah were about to discover the perils of enslavement.[27]

If the failure of nonviolent reform within the United States was the cause of widespread slave unrest throughout the 1790s, the revolt that begin in Saint-Domingue in the late summer of 1791 served as the inspiration. Spurred by the ideological currents that washed about the Atlantic basin—at least one of the rebels, Henri Christophe, had served as manservant to a French officer stationed in Georgia during the Revolution—what was later known as the "Night of Fire" began on the northern plain on the evening of August 22, 1791. Led by Boukman, a prominent slave and religious leader originally from Jamaica, bondmen torched the houses and cane fields at the Noé plantation. Within days, as many as ten thousand slaves joined the revolt. As planters fled toward the safety of the port city of Cap Français, slaves burned more than three hundred plantations; refugees reported hearing roaring "fires and the explosions and whistling of cannon." Within the city walls, whites eliminated slaves feared to be complicit in the rebellion. "Above one hundred negro prisoners [were] shot in the burying place" in late August, and authorities erected six gallows in one square, adjacent to a large wooden wheel "to put the poor devils to torture."[28]

Early on in the conflict, Boukman fell in battle; his body was burned, and his decapitated head was displayed on a pike in the central square of Cap Français. Control of the rebel forces fell to forty-eight-year-old François Dominique Toussaint, one of the few Dominguan slaves born on the island and not imported from Africa. Toussaint labored on the Bréda plantation as a coachman and took care of the livestock, but shortly after he reached the age of twenty, Bayon de Libertad, the manager of Bréda, gave him forty acres and thirteen slaves to supervise. At some point in the early 1770s, Toussaint became free, perhaps through self-purchase, and he rented a small coffee plantation. In the fall of 1791, after helping to spirit Libertad's family onto a ship sailing for the United States, Toussaint abandoned Bréda and rode for the camp of the insurgents. As he won battles, his men began to call him Toussaint Louverture, the soldier who always found his opening. By fighting for the principles of liberty that white Americans had embraced in 1776, the Dominguan slaves reminded their mainland brethren that the struggle to fulfill the egalitarian promise of the Revolution was far from over.[29]

With refugees and French planters fleeing in all directions, news of the uprising—thoroughly reported by the American newspapers—spread to mainland bondpeople, especially those in seaport towns and cities. Even before the Franco-American 1778 treaty of commerce, New England merchants in search of sugar, molasses, and coffee quietly slipped into Dominguan ports. Shortly after the trade became legal, Saint-Domingue became the young Republic's second most valuable trading partner, and black mariners kept up an intricate communications network with the slaves and free blacks who labored on American docks. As early as 1792, the first wave of white refugees broke on American shores. One visitor to Virginia reported finding as many as three thousand French immigrants huddled in Norfolk, most of them "from the West Indies, and principally from St. Doming[ue]."[30]

The French refugees brought with them their human property as well as news. By 1795, some twelve thousand Dominguan slaves had entered the United States. Southern authorities regarded them as dangerously infected with the malady of insurrection, and some states promptly enacted laws barring the entry of bondpeople from the rebellious island. In Charleston, Captain Joseph Vesey helped draft a series of resolutions in October 1793 demanding that "negroes and people of colour be on no account suffered to land in any part of the state." Virginia, however, neglected to take this step and so became a popular haven for French planters and their slaves. The colony's bondpeople naturally mixed with urban slaves in Richmond and Norfolk. "Our negro Slaves have become extremely insolent & troublesome," grumbled one Norfolk resident. They "associate with French Negroes from St. Doming[ue] (with whom the place is also over-run)" and appear "to be rife for insurrection."[31]

Other immigrants sailed for Manhattan and Philadelphia. In the former, the arrival of French émigrés on the eve of state manumission served to bolster a declining institution. So many French refugees landed in Manhattan that perhaps one-third of all male New York slaveholders during the 1790s were migrants who brought bondpeople with them or bought American-born slaves upon arrival. Those who found themselves in Philadelphia were stunned to discover that their slaves would become free in six months under the clause in the 1780 manumission law. Some responded by moving across the river into Delaware. Nearly three hundred others freed their slaves days before the deadline but signed them to indentures. Since more than half of the Dominguan slaves brought into Pennsylvania were children and young adults, French masters with resources often took the young men to Charleston for resale into the upcountry cotton fields.[32]

Saint-Domingue, with its overwhelming black majority and largely absentee planter class, posed opportunities for potential rebels that were absent in most parts of the United States outside of South Carolina. The Chesapeake especially lacked the immense plantations that allowed for mass organization, and its geography was inhospitable to the formation of isolated staging grounds from which runaways could besiege the plantation regime. Even so, by the late spring of 1792, slaves around Norfolk and nearby Portsmouth began to "concert a plan" with the bondmen in the Eastern Shore county of Northampton. Norfolk County was home to a white majority, but Northampton and Elizabeth City counties, both just across the Chesapeake Bay, boasted an enslaved majority. The rebels, however, were far from organized. A small number of insurgents, led by Caleb, a plantation driver (a privileged slave who carried out the orders of a white overseer or master), planned to recruit a small army of six hundred rebels who were to cross the bay on a night yet to be appointed and join forces with the Norfolk insurgents. Together they would "blow up the [powder] magazine in Norfolk, and massacre its inhabitants." Because few slaves knew how to use muskets, Caleb began to stockpile "spears [and] clubs," the former manufactured "by a negro blacksmith on the Eastern Shore." As slaves hid "about 300 spears" under cabin floors, some incautious rebels grew dangerously bold. A "favorite servant" of Littleton Savage, upon seeing his master cantering down the road, decided he could wait no longer for the appointed night. The enraged young man demanded his owner's "horse and some money from him, and treated [Savage] in an insolent manner."[33]

Alerted to the fact that the spirit of rebellion had seized blacks in eastern Virginia, Savage questioned a few of his slaves. What he learned worried him enough to hurry off a missive to Colonel Smith Snead of the Northampton militia. "A variety of circumstances hav[e] made it too probable that an Insurrection is intended by the slaves in this County," he warned. Snead, in turn, promptly applied to Governor Henry Lee and Norfolk mayor Thomas Newton for aid. Even before the governor could act, Newton increased the frequency of slave patrols and called upon his town's French refugees to "take up arms as well as the inhabitants, whenever any insurrection Should happen." By mid-May, Northampton patrols apprehended "8 or 10 negroes on suspicion of ploting & conspiring to rebel." Governor Lee, a former cavalry officer, understood all too well the likely tactics of the revolutionaries. The slaves "will begin with firing the town," and "the inhabitants in their zeal to extinguish the fire will fall easy prey to men prepared for their slaughter." With the militia on their side, patrols succeeded in arresting more rebels, including Caleb. Sixteen slaves were put on trial for the capital crime of "insurrection," but the rebels stubbornly refused to confess or implicate their fellows. The court reluctantly found the evidence "insufficient to convict them," so instead the justices of the peace ordered them whipped. Three of the "most dangerous" were transported to Spanish Cuba.[34]

The light sentences, together with the habitual inefficiency of Virginia authorities, only emboldened other bondmen, especially as more refugees poured into American harbors. In June 1793, Dominguans captured Cap Français in a campaign that took the lives of more than ten thousand white colonists, and the following month, French warships ferried several hundred "distressed people" into Norfolk and Hampton Roads. "Our town swarms with strange negroes, foreign & domestick," complained a Portsmouth man. Not far away, a Virginia bondman waved a crude sword forged from a reap hook in his master's face and swore "that he would not serve" a moment longer unless paid wages. When the stunned master refused, the slave stalked away and was not seen again. Rumors circulated that other runaways were observed "armed with pikes fixed on sticks." Some whites feared that these armed runaways were but a small part of a growing army composed "of the people of Colour in this neighborhood."[35]

Confirmation that bondmen throughout the southern seaboard planned to rise for their freedom surfaced in August 1793 when a letter was "found in [the] Streets of Yorktown." Addressed to the "Secret Keeper" of Norfolk, the "Secret Keeper [of] Richmond" instructed his downriver lieutenant to hold himself "in Readiness to strike." The "great Secret that has been so long in being with our Colour" was nearly ready to come to "a head." The rebel leader reported that he "got a Letter from our friend in Charleston" who was also raising a black army. Together they would "appoint a Nite to begin with fire Clubs and shot [and] will kill all before us." Believed to have been dropped by a "Black Preacher" authorities referred to as "Gawin," the letter may have been in the possession of Gowan Pamphlet, the former slave and preacher from the Williamsburg area. Most likely, free black and enslaved mariners carried word of the plot from port to port.[36]

Because the Secret Keeper had mentioned a correspondent in Charleston, Virginia authorities hurried copies of the terrifying letter to South Carolina. Here too, "many of the distressed Inhabitants" of Cap Français had washed ashore, bringing with them their slaves, and thus news of the successful black revolt. As in the Chesapeake, Charleston whites regarded their slaves as increasingly "insolent," a mood they too attributed to the influence of black refugees. A white Virginian warned South Carolina governor William Moultrie that Charleston bondmen planned "to set fire first to the Houses and take the advantage while it is raging," a strategy by which American bondmen "say the Negroes of Cape Francais have obtained their Liberties." At about the same time, news arrived on the governor's desk that slaves along the Charleston docks had been overheard remarking that Charleston "had not many Soldiers [so] we need not be afraid of them." Although it remains unclear how far the Secret Keeper network reached, slaves up and down the James River were talking of revolution. In late July, a resident of Richmond, John Randolph, overheard two slaves talking beneath his window. The "blacks were to kill the white people soon in this place," one slave informed a potential recruit. The revolt was set to begin "between this and the 15th day of October," the rebel explained, "as it would take some time for us to get ready." When the timid recruit replied that such a scheme was not possible, the recruiter reminded him "how the blacks has killed the whites in the French Island and took it a little while ago."[37]

Having won their own liberty by way of a musket, and having watched as impoverished and brutalized refugees sailed into American harbors, white authorities harbored few doubts that black Americans would fight for their freedom if the moment proved auspicious. Certainly none doubted the connection between Louverture's continued victories and the widespread Secret Keeper plot. Richmond dweller Peter Gram shuddered at the peal of every fire bell. The "Negroes of Cap Francais" obtained their freedom using fire, he observed, "and they will proceed here in the same manner." Should Virginia and Carolina bondmen form an army "as is proposed by the Secret Keeper," added James Wood, the lieutenant governor of Virginia, the black refugees from Saint-Domingue "would be ready to operate against us with the others." Wood's fears were only exacerbated when Portsmouth authorities discovered four hanged Dominguan blacks, presumed to have been killed by black rebels. Whites feared that these were "Executions" performed by black rebels upon recruits who either knew too much or had threatened to turn their coats and tell their masters what they knew of the plot.[38]

Governor Lee wasted little time arming Virginia whites. Despite the governor's "best endeavour[s]" to impose order on his terrified state, the town of Petersburg remained "almost without arms," and the Hampton militia was so "very badly armed [that] not more than one-third of the men has guns fitt for duty." But the eventual flashes of sabers in virtually every town along the James soothed the nerves of white Virginians and convinced black rebels that their chances of success were considerably diminished. Lee instructed militia commandant John Marshall to call out "twenty privates of [the] militia" and employ them as long as was "deemed proper." Before the governor's instructions reached them, however, a patrol in Powhatan County stumbled across "a number of negroes from Different parts of this Countrey" assembled in an "Old Schoole house." A few of the slaves were armed, and one of them, a black driver, carried a large sword. Not "knowing at that time anything of [the] Intended Riseing," the patrol confiscated the weapon and "whipped" some of the captives before releasing them. Only too late did the frustrated militiamen realized that the slaves they had encountered were probably part of the Secret Keeper plot. Faced with a massive show of force, Virginia blacks grew quiet, but that was hardly true of African Americans in other sections of the country.[39]

Blacks yet enslaved in northern seaports took heart in late 1793 when word arrived that French commissioners in Saint-Domingue had issued a decree for immediate emancipation, a policy that was extended to the entire French Caribbean on February 4, 1794. For blacks impatient with the sluggish pace of gradual emancipation in the North, news that slavery had collapsed so rapidly in one of the most profitable European empires gave them hope that unfree labor in the Americas was nearing its end. In Philadelphia, where white French émigrés had claimed that their slaves were not subject to the state's 1780 statute, a group of "citizens of color" turned that argument to their benefit by drafting an open letter to Paris that praised the national convention for "breaking our chains [and] wiping out all traces of slavery in the French colonies." Although less common, a few white abolitionists also defended the Haitian Revolution, including Abraham Bishop of Connecticut, whose articles were printed in newspapers across the North. "Freedom is the natural right of all rational beings," Bishop wrote, "and we know that the Blacks have never voluntarily resigned that freedom." Did not the Declaration of Independence, Bishop asked, define a person's rights as "unalienable"? Bishop found it especially significant that Dominguan slaves demanded "Liberty or Death," reminding his readers that revolutionary ideals ignored national boundaries.[40]

Most white Americans, especially in the lowcountry, saw the matter differently. Charleston authorities convened a public meeting in hopes of finding some way to "prevent any evil consequences from that diabolical decree of the national convention." A few politicians argued that the answer was to "expel from the state all Negroes without exception that have within the last three years arrived here from the French West India Islands." That step, however, amounted to state seizure of privately owned human chattel, a precedent most politicians refused to endorse. Instead, white Carolinians responded first by turning against the French Revolution and then by further renouncing the principles of the American Revolution. In April 1794, for instance, congregants in Charleston's prestigious Huguenot Church fired their minister, John Paul Coste, for including French patriotic hymns during the service. That same spring, during a fight over political reform of the state government, Carolina assemblyman Henry William DeSaussure warned advocates of reapportionment to avoid statements such as "equality is the natural condition of man." Should South Carolina actually implement the principles of 1776, the result would be the "ruin of the country, by giving liberty to the slaves, and the desolating [of] the land with fire and sword in the struggles between master and slave." One only had to witness the fate of Saint-Domingue to see the result of "the too hasty adoption of these axioms in all their extent."[41]

Like others in the state assembly, DeSaussure, an attorney and indigo planter, refused to consider the possibility that slave unrest resulted from failure to implement the principles of 1776. In fact, since New York received its share of Dominguan refugees, the capital city of Albany barely escaped its own "Night of Fire." On November 17, 1793, Pomp, a bondman belonging to the estate of Mathew Visscher, encouraged two young bondwomen, Bet and Dean, to set fire to houses along Market Street. As the slave of a deceased master, Pomp, like the remainder of Visscher's property, was in a state of legal limbo, and perhaps he decided to prod New York toward emancipation before he could be transferred to a new owner. After waiting for the night watch to pass, the three placed hot coals in a lantern, which they threw into a nearby stable. The blaze quickly spread, burning twenty-six houses, as well as the offices of the *Albany Gazette*. City authorities placed the damage at $330,000; had a heavy fall of sleet not dampened the fires, the destruction would have been far worse.[42]

Newspaper articles promptly implicated unknown "French Negroes," and General Philip Schuyler—abolitionist Alexander Hamilton's father-in-law—reported that most whites suspected arson. Bet promptly lost her nerve and confided to a freedwoman known as Old Jane that she feared "[s]he would be hanged for it." When a princely reward of $200 was posted, Jane evidently came forward. Hoping that the three might name further accomplices, Governor George Clinton twice stayed the executions. But when their stories held firm, Clinton ordered them hanged. Bet and Dean swung together on March 14; according to one reporter, the unrepentant Bet displayed no concerns "for her immortal welfare" at the end and faced the hangman with courage. Pomp followed in April, his confession printed in a slim pamphlet.[43]

At a time of when elegant wood homes stood adjacent to stables, and lanterns and candles formed the chief source of light, it was often hard to distinguish between an accidental conflagration and slave-produced arson. Yet by late 1796, an unusually large number of fires raged up and down the Atlantic coast. In June, Charleston authorities attributed a series of fires to "French Negroes" who "intended to make a St. Doming[ue] business of it." On November 26, roughly two-thirds of Savannah burned to the ground, and two weeks later a "most terrible fire" in Manhattan consumed "upwards of 60 houses." Diarist Elizabeth Drinker worried that "the many terrible fires that have lately occurred in several different citys and towns" might spread to her Philadelphia, which indeed they did when parts of the city caught fire on December 18. New York's Common Council doubled the patrols and offered a reward of $5,000 in exchange for information about the arsonists, who they suspected were trying to achieve "the freedom of the Negroes."[44]

By the last months of 1796, however, political and international realities coincided to give new hope to antislavery activists and reverse the counterrevolutionary trend under way in much of the Republic since 1783. In that year's presidential contest, New Englander John Adams narrowly bested Jefferson, which meant the federal government was now guided by northern merchant capitalists rather than southern agriculturalists. The victory of the pro-British Adams threatened to lead to a diplomatic breach between the United States and France, which had been at war with Britain since February 1793. As French privateers began to prey on American shipping in the Caribbean, the incoming administration began to cast about for allies, and in the process race—never an important consideration for the president and his secretary of state, the staunchly antislavery Timothy Pickering of Massachusetts—grew less and less significant. If Toussaint Louverture could calm the tempest of servile revolution in the Caribbean and provide support against Paris, his former status as a slave meant nothing to Adams.[45]

At the same time, Louverture discovered he too required allies. Anxious to retain the once prosperous jewel in their empire, Paris followed up their decree of emancipation by showering titles upon Louverture, who rose to the rank of general in the French army. But the shrewd Louverture recognized that European goodwill might not outlast the war on the Continent. The current government in Paris had no intention of reversing the 1794 decree, but as its composition changed annually, France rarely maintained a steady policy on any crucial matter. "The negroes & people of colour of St. Doming[ue]," Pickering advised, "believe with reason that France [intends] to bring them back to Slavery." In preparation for that eventuality, Louverture wrote to Adams in November 1798. Affecting to understand nothing about the so-called Quasi War between the United States and the French nation to which he allegedly remained loyal, the old general did "not pretend to know" why American shippers had "abandoned the ports of St. Domingue," but he assured Adams "that Americans will find protection and security in the ports of Saint Domingue."[46]

Given the growing estrangement between Philadelphia and Paris, military and commercial considerations made it imperative to seduce Saint-Domingue away from the French orbit. The French government turned its Caribbean colonies into bases from which to attack American shipping and even seriously considered sending a black army to "invade both the Southern States of America and the Island of Jamaica [to] excite an insurrection among the negroes." Among those concerned about the very real possibility of a Franco-Dominguan invasion force was former president George Washington. "If the French should be so mad" as to invade the United States, he warned Secretary Pickering, "their operations will commence in the Southern quarter [as] there can be no doubt of their arming our own Negroes against us."[47]

Even those politicians who despised slavery had no wish to see social unrest spread to the southern states. Since the British had made every effort to disrupt the Patriot war effort through the liberation of American slaves during the Revolution, policy makers in Philadelphia had little doubt that the French would apply the same tactics. Pickering cautioned that "France with an army of those black troops might conquer all the British [Caribbean] Isles and put in jeopardy our Southern States." The secretary of state had no worries about the former slaves "if left to themselves," but as "subjects of France" Louverture's legions might become a "military corps of such strength in a future war, as no European or other white force could resist." Writing from his diplomatic post in Berlin, young John Quincy Adams agreed. The "generals of color are decidedly with us," he advised. To a degree, the administration regarded Louverture as an African Bonaparte, the sort of military leader who could restore order to the region, and so President Adams wished to see Saint-Domingue "free and independent" of French control.[48]

Whatever his motivation, Adams soon had the opportunity to demonstrate the utter lack of racial animosity in his statecraft. To better deal with the United States, in December 1798 Louverture sent Joseph Bunel, a trusted advisor, to Philadelphia, where he was greeted by Secretary Pickering. Bunel gave assurances that Louverture would refuse to allow his troops to be used elsewhere to foment slave unrest, a promise he repeated when he dined with Adams, the first-ever breaking of bread between an American president and a man of color. Bunel's promises were all that Adams required. When Congress reconvened in January 1799, Harrison Grey Otis of Massachusetts, chairman of the Committee on Defense, called upon the House to amend a June 1798 embargo with the French Empire to allow a resumption of trade with Saint-Domingue. Adams's willingness to recognize a government led by men of African ancestry infuriated a number of Republicans, even in the North. Swiss-born congressman Albert Gallatin of Pennsylvania rose to complain that Louverture's army had only recently "been initiated to Liberty" through "rapine, pillage, and massacre." Ignoring such warnings, the Federalist majority passed the bill, informally known as "Toussaint's clause." "We may expect therefore black crews, & supercargoes & missionaries" to pour "into the Southern States," fretted Jefferson.[49]

To investigate the situation in the colony and represent American interests, Adams appointed Edward Stevens as consul general to Saint-Domingue. Secretary Pickering made it clear to his envoy that the "Negro general Toussaint now commands" the government in the colony, and Stevens requested and received an audience with the old soldier. The American diplomat emphasized that no trade could resume until all French privateers evacuated the island, and the following day, Louverture replied that he completely accepted "the Justice and Propriety of the President's Demands." Although the general's power was nominally confined to the colony's military administration, he and Stevens signed an agreement in April banning French privateers from the ports under Louverture's control while opening his docks to "the Merchant Vessels and Ships of War of the United States." In this accord—a curious union forged out of military exigency—the New Englander and the former slave advanced the possibility that political fraternity could look beyond color in the name of extending republican liberty to all.[50]

The renewed commerce with the United States was of critical importance to Louverture, as New England merchants were willing to ship guns and ammunition, whereas French and British traders preferred to barter less lethal provisions for Dominguan sugar and coffee. By March 1799, Pickering "confidently" believed that Louverture's appetite for American commerce, together with his concerns over the growing conservative mood in Paris, was but a prelude to "the independence" of Saint-Domingue. To make sure Louverture's shift into the American orbit continued, Adams dispatched warships to help the former slave maintain his hold over the colony. The frigates *Boston*, *Connecticut*, and *General Greene* patrolled the southern shore, while the *Constitution* and the *Norfolk* attacked and captured French vessels. With American warships acting the part of Louverture's navy, the general made short work of those who wished to keep the Dominguan army loyal to Paris. The "black Chiefs," as Stevens dubbed officers Jean-Jacques Dessalines and Paul Louverture (Toussaint's brother), "now talk loudly and openly" in favor of autonomy. For his part, Toussaint Louverture wished to move slowly until forced to act by events in France. But his victory left the general with both military and civil authority on the entire island. "All connection with France will soon be broken off," Stevens informed Pickering.[51]

So deeply invested was the Adams administration in Dominguan liberty that Secretary of State Pickering even thought it worthwhile to advise Louverture on the shape of his emerging government. Having little experience in constitution building, the secretary naturally turned to one who did: Caribbean-born Alexander Hamilton. Although an antislavery politician then pushing, yet again, for gradual manumission in his adopted state, Hamilton's response indicated that Federalist confidence in the black general did not extend to his populace. "The Government if independent must be military," he advised Pickering, "partaking of the feudal system." Echoing, ironically, his enemy Jefferson's doubts about the ability of former slaves to govern themselves, Hamilton preferred a monarchy for the colony but recognized that such an idea was "impracticable." Instead, he recommended a "single Executive to hold his place for life." Land was to be divided among young men following obligatory military service. No hard evidence proves that Hamilton's missive ever reached Louverture's hands, but coincidentally, the general announced shortly thereafter the first-ever constitution for Saint-Domingue (which technically remained a French colony). According to the American consul, it "declared Gen. Toussaint Louverture Governor for life, with the power of naming his successor."[52]

In the end, what altered this promising course in enlightened diplomacy and federal race relations was the presidential election of 1800, again pitting Adams against his 1796 rival and accidental vice president, Thomas Jefferson. Despite Jefferson's fondness for claiming that his narrow victory— the Republicans bested a fractured Federalist ticket by only eight electoral votes—constituted a "revolution of 1800," that simple picture of progress grew murkier when subsequent events are examined from the perspective of blacks in both the Caribbean and the southern parts of the United States. Not only did slavery and sectionalism provide a critical subtext to the two campaigns, but the Constitution's three-fifths rule, as some northerners had feared in 1787, helped to propel Jefferson into the executive mansion. "The absurd policy of representing the negroes of the southern states, who are no better entitled to representation than cattle and horses," fumed the edi-tor of the Hartford *Courant*, "will probably elevate to the presidential chair [Thomas Jefferson] about to ride into the TEMPLE OF LIBERTY, upon the *shoulders of slaves*." Timothy Pickering not only agreed but believed the only solution was for the northern states to secede from the Union. "Without a separation" from the South, he enquired of New York's Rufus King, could free states "ever rid themselves of negro Presidents and negro Congresses?"[53]

Openly fearful of black rebelliousness and determined to limit the influ-ence of Louverture's government on American slaves, the new president immediately changed course regarding the Caribbean. When approached by Louis-André Pichon, the French chargé d'affaires, who wished to know Jefferson's opinion on a possible invasion of Saint-Domingue, the Virginian replied that "nothing would be more simple than to furnish your army and your fleet with everything and to starve out Toussaint." Word of Jefferson's support for a move against black liberty flew across the Atlantic. "France ought to expect from the amity of the United States," Foreign Minister Charles Maurice de Talleyrand advised Napoleon Bonaparte, "that they will interdict every private adventure [that] may be destined to the ports of Saint Doming[ue], occupied by the rebels." Jefferson had once been a rebel him-self, but now he insisted that he "had no reason to be favorable" to antico-lonial patriots such as Louverture. When the new American consul arrived in Cap Français without so much as a perfunctory letter from the president, Louverture "express[ed] his disappointment and disgust." His "Colour was the cause of his being neglected," he insisted, "and not thought worthy of the Usual attentions" once paid by President Adams.[54]

The French invasion force of twenty-five thousand men, led by Gen-eral Victor Leclerc, Bonaparte's brother-in-law, made landfall on January 29, 1802. Seized as a result of treachery, Louverture was shipped to France and imprisoned in an icy underground dungeon at Fort de Joux, near the Swiss border. Denied adequate food and clothing and abused by his jailors,

Louverture died in April 1803. But the former slaves fought on regardless, and when reinforcements from the Continent failed to crush the Dominguan soldiers, Bonaparte abandoned his dreams of a western empire. He instructed his finance minister to sell New Orleans to envoys Robert Livingston and James Monroe, who had just arrived in Paris. As critic Alexander Hamilton archly observed, the Louisiana Purchase came about not through adroit diplomacy or skillful negotiation but because of "the courage and obstinate resistance made by black inhabitants" in Saint-Domingue. In Cap Français, the remaining black generals chose the indigenous Taíno name Haiti (meaning "mountainous") for their independent republic, the second in the Americas. The job of crafting a second Haitian Declaration of Independence—the first version, drafted by "an admirer of the work of Jefferson," was rejected as lacking in "heat and energy"—was given to the fiery young Louis Félix Boisrond-Tonnerre, whose prose style reflected the desire to use "the skin of a white man for parchment, his skull for an inkwell, [and] his blood for ink."[55]

If the acquisition of the vast Louisiana territory was made possible by Haitian intransigence, it nonetheless arrived on Jeffersonian terms. To appease French and Spanish nationals along the Mississippi, Monroe agreed to the protection of slave property in the region. Thanks to the congressional deals made during the creation of the Northwest Ordinance, young planters utilizing Eli Whitney's cotton gin had already begun to carry their slaves into the fresh lands of the Southeast. But the concessions made by American negotiators in Paris allowed for even more slave territory beyond the Mississippi River. Two decades later, as politicians in Washington wrestled with the question of slavery's expansion into Missouri, western settlers loudly embraced it as their Magna Carta, claiming their organic right to hold other people as property under the French Treaty of 1803.[56]

"Now they have felled the trunk of the Negroes' tree of liberty," Louverture had remarked when arrested by the agents of Bonaparte. "However, new shoots will sprout because the roots are deep and many." He was right. Even as cotton slavery began to move into the western territories, tearing apart black families in the Chesapeake and granting unfree labor a new lease on life along the Mississippi, a young Virginia blacksmith named Gabriel began to hatch a plan for making the American Revolution the truly revolutionary, even radical affair some historians depict it to be. His goal, Gabriel assured other bondmen, was to fight not just for black freedom but also "for his Country."[57]

General Gabriel's Flag

Unsuccessful Coda to the Revolution

W HEN DID THE AMERICAN REVOLUTION begin? Was it when the first
shots were fired by Massachusetts militiamen such as Lemuel Haynes
in the spring of 1775, or did the precise moment come four months later on
August 23, 1775, when King George III and his Parliament declared thirteen of his colonies to be in open rebellion? Or was it five years before that,
when runaway slave Crispus Attucks was shot to death by British regulars?
New Jersey's Titus had already abandoned the Corlies farm by that early June
day in 1776 when slaveholder Richard Henry Lee of Virginia introduced
into Congress a resolution for independence. Reflecting on this question in
later years, John Adams concluded that the actual combat "was no part of the
Revolution." The struggle for liberty, Adams suggested to Jefferson, "was in
the Minds of the People, and this was effected, from 1760 to 1775, in the
course of fifteen Years before a drop of blood was drawn at Lexington."[1]

Viewed from this perspective, the American Revolution was not an event
but an idea. And if so, when did it end? If Adams was correct and the war
itself was the least significant aspect of the Revolution, the dream of liberty
did not conclude in October 1781 when Lord Cornwallis struck his colors
or even some ten months later when young John Laurens became one of
the last Patriots to die in combat. Perhaps it ended when white Patriots
utterly and completely crushed any remaining hopes that the first republic in
the Americas would actually put into practice the belief that its inhabitants
were "endowed by their Creator with certain unalienable rights," among
which were "life, liberty, and pursuit of happiness." Some historians believe
that moment came when the aged rabble-rouser Samuel Adams penned

the Massachusetts Riot Act, which helped to subdue Captain Daniel Shays and his agrarian rebels. Others point to 1794, when President Washington ordered thirteen thousand soldiers into central Pennsylvania to crush a frontier tax revolt. But perhaps the ideal of liberty finally ended in the fall of 1800, when the election of Jefferson coincided with the execution of a young Virginia blacksmith who proved willing to die in the cause of democratizing "his Country."[2]

The blacksmith was a slave known only as Gabriel. Born in 1776, Gabriel lived on the Brookfield plantation, a tobacco and wheat estate roughly six miles north of Richmond, owned by Thomas Prosser. Gabriel and his two brothers, Solomon and Martin, were among the fifty-three bondpeople at Brookfield counted by census takers at the war's end in 1783; only three other plantations in the county possessed more slaves. The fact that all three boys bore religious names suggests that their parents had been influenced by the evangelical preachers who tramped Virginia's fields and back roads.[3]

For reasons now unknown, Prosser found himself expelled from the House of Burgesses during its 1765 session and hired attorney Patrick Henry to help win reinstatement to his seat. The two men remained friends, and when Prosser's wife, Ann, gave birth to a son in November 1776 they named the child Thomas Henry Prosser, evidently after the celebrated Patriot. Henry's famous speech demanding "liberty or death," given the previous year in St. John's Church in Richmond, remained legendary for years to come, and both the phrase and its sentiments would come to mean a great deal to Gabriel and other enslaved Virginians.[4]

Every plantation of considerable size, including Brookfield, required a number of highly skilled laborers. Most likely, Gabriel's father was a blacksmith, the craft chosen for both Gabriel and his brother Solomon, since the children of skilled Chesapeake slaves commonly inherited their parents' professions. Perhaps also his father was literate, since somebody taught Gabriel to read. Slaves could not pass down anything more valuable to their offspring than the skill that kept them out of the fields. Status as a craft apprentice provided Gabriel with considerable standing in the slave community, as did his ability to read. As the boy blossomed into an unusually tall young man, even older bondpeople looked to him for leadership. He stood "six feet two or three inches high," and the enormous strength in his chest betrayed long hours spent in the forge. A long and "bony face, well made," was marred by the loss of his two front teeth and "two or three scars on his head," the result, perhaps, of the aggressive young man proving his physical prowess in the quarters. His hair was cut short and was as dark as his complexion. Whites as well as blacks regarded him as a "fellow of courage and intellect above his rank in life."[5]

At some point, probably around 1796, Gabriel fell in love with a young bondwoman called Nanny, most likely one or two years his junior. Enslaved women typically married young; many bore children soon after reaching sexual maturity and settled into permanent relationships by age twenty. Little is known about Nanny, including the identity of her owner and whether she bore Gabriel any children. She probably lived on a nearby farm or tobacco plantation. If Gabriel did take a wife from a neighboring farm, he surely did not "marry abroad" for the usual reason: the desire to be spared the misery of having to watch a spouse being beaten, raped, or overworked. Discipline on Brookfield, at least under the old master, was lax, and Prosser knew Gabriel well enough not to test a slave of his size and worth by openly abusing his wife.[6]

In the fall of 1798, change came to Brookfield with the death of the old planter. At twenty-two Thomas Henry Prosser became the lord and master of the estate. Within months of his father's death, the ambitious young man purchased a rural tavern just north of Richmond, bought into "an extensive auction" and real estate business, and purchased a handsome town home on the corner of K and Fourth streets. So well did Prosser do in his new life that by the summer of 1800, only two men in the county paid more in taxes. But the rural, patriarchal culture of the Chesapeake frowned on those who overly bestirred themselves in the cause of financial advancement. Disquieting rumors held that Prosser, unlike his father, pushed his laborers hard to maximize his profits and "behaved with great barbarity toward his slaves."[7]

If the rumors were true, they explain why the new master did not put a stop to his father's habit of hiring out surplus slaves. Even with all of the work to be performed at Brookfield, Gabriel, and evidently Solomon as well, spent more than a few days each month smithing in and around Richmond. Although still a slave in the eyes of the law, Gabriel enjoyed the quasi freedom common to those slaves who hired their time in the years after the Revolution. As was the case with Denmark Vesey's friend Polydore Faber, the "excellent sawyer" and rope maker, who hired his time around Charleston, young Gabriel came into contact with other young men who shared his quasi freedom. Michael, the property of Prosser's brother-in-law, preferred to be hired into the city so that he could visit his wife, the bondwoman of Joseph Mosby. Another acquaintance was Sam Byrd Jr., a mixed-race slave of the widowed Jane Clarke and the nephew of a Petersburg freedman. But perhaps the most unusual man Gabriel encountered during his travels was Jack Ditcher, a laborer who adopted an occupational surname. If Gabriel was an imposing figure, Ditcher was even more so: six feet five inches tall, "stout made, and perhaps as strong a man as any in the State." His long hair was tied back in a queue, and an ugly scar ran across one eye.[8]

On many occasions, plantation artisans hired themselves out to white artisans and tradesmen in Richmond, particularly those craftsmen who were veterans of the Chesapeake's short-lived abolitionist movement, or those who spent Sundays on the stump preaching about God's fellowship. For modern scholars determined to insist that early national politicians could not have moved more aggressively against slavery, the biracial, Christian fellowship envisioned by David Barrow and "Black" Harry Hosier serves as a reminder that many Virginians prayed for a more egalitarian society. Especially in small shops, black and white artisans labored side by side and in the process often developed strong bonds that cut across racial lines. Unpretentious white craftsmen drew no line of demarcation between the day's labor and the evening's social intercourse and together enjoyed stories and jokes and tankards of grog that made work go more swiftly. Moreover, since both enslaved and free white artisans worked primarily on commission, producing "bespoke goods" for merchants, they were vulnerable to being deceived by unscrupulous merchants, who as importers of raw materials could threaten to shut off the stream of required supplies or take their business elsewhere.[9]

For enslaved artisans such as Gabriel, the power of the merchants could be even more devastating. Businessmen often underpaid or even openly cheated bond hires, since blacks could not take them to court or testify against them. Word would eventually get around that such men were miserly employers, but since the failure to pay one's master a fixed sum could cost the slave the privilege of hiring out, even a single encounter with a dishonest merchant could doom a bondman to a life on the plantation. Evidently Gabriel found himself in this situation at least once and was cheated out of his wages by a wealthy townsman. According to Ben, another of Prosser's slaves, Gabriel wished to pull down "the merchants" who dominated the city's political and economic life, and "possess ourselves of their property."[10]

Why Gabriel was so willing to countenance violence in response to the counterrevolutionary trends of the late 1780s and 1790s involves no simple answer. Perhaps the quarter century that separated his birth from that of William Lee explained Gabriel's lack of patience with the sluggish pace of private manumission in the Chesapeake. Lee had been young and strong at a time when it yet appeared that slavery would perish along with British rule; as the election of Jefferson approached, Gabriel knew better. Perhaps, too, as was the case with Colonel Tye or Corporal Harry Washington, Gabriel regarded himself as a soldier of the Revolution, and while he did not welcome violence, neither did he shrink from bloodshed. The age of revolution had taught the Western world, as Jefferson himself observed, that the "tree of liberty must be refreshed from time to time with the blood of patriots and tyrants." Since the day that James Somerset refused to return to the colonies, or the moment that Crispus Attucks decided to fight for the ideal of liberty, black Americans had shaped political policies as much as they had been shaped by them. Certainly, like Lemuel Haynes, who was twenty-two years old when he marched toward Lexington, Gabriel and his fellows were young radicals, and dangerous beyond their years. When asked if he was "a true-hearted man," the slave known as King replied that he was "ready to join" with Gabriel. "I could slay the white people like sheep."[11]

Gabriel's lack of prejudice against violence was revealed in September 1799, when he lashed out at a white neighbor. Slaves often supplemented their diet with beef or pork taken from their masters' larders, an act of self-payment few bondpeople regarded as theft. But this time the white Virginian in question, Absalom Johnson, was a nearby renter who caught Gabriel, his brother Solomon, and a third slave named Jupiter in the act. Johnson's furious words must have cut deep, for suddenly Gabriel launched himself at Johnson's legs. They fell in a thrashing tangle of limbs, Johnson yelling for help, while Solomon and Jupiter shouted encouragement to their friend. Gabriel got the best of it. Johnson lost his pride and, rather more seriously, the better "part of his left Ear."[12]

Attacking and biting a white man carried a capital penalty. Under Virginia law, slaves were prosecuted by special segregated country tribunals known as courts of oyer and terminer. Composed of five justices of the peace, the court featured no jury and no appeal except to the governor. Accused slaves were supplied with counsel, at a cost of five dollars to their masters. On October 7, Gabriel was "set to the Bar [and] charged with Maiming Absalom Johnson." Gabriel's attorney entered the customary plea of innocent, and Gabriel was examined "in his [own] defense." But the evidence—Johnson's testimony and the absence of his ear—was overwhelming, and the justices found Gabriel guilty. He escaped the gallows, however, due to an odd legal loophole. If Gabriel could recite a verse from the Bible, he could claim "benefit of clergy" and be "burnt in the left hand [by] the Jailor in Open Court." A form of public humiliation as much as a punishment, branding also marked Gabriel as ineligible for a second reprieve if again hauled before the court.[13]

By the fall of 1799, Gabriel, now a branded criminal, stood on the edge of rebellion, and not simply the kind of rebellion that represented the personal victory of stealing a hog or overcoming a white neighbor in a bloody fight. Both before and after his trial, while "remanded to Jail" in Richmond,

Gabriel had leisure to ponder his fate. Had he been born into a different section of the new nation, or had his state instituted gradual manumission— events he certainly heard discussed by white artisans and evangelicals—he would have prospered. His intelligence, his physical size, and his skill all should have marked him as a man on the rise. But he did not live in Quok Walker or Mum Bett's Massachusetts. In a sense, his assault on Johnson was an assault on the system that bound him at every turn, as his punishment was to have the chains of bondage tightened. One option was to run for the North, which meant abandoning his family. The alternative was rebellion, and jail gave him time to plan.[14]

The men Gabriel drew together had been raised amidst the heady talk of liberty and freedom and lived in a region awash with refugees from Saint-Domingue. Hence it was no surprise, as planter John Randolph later observed, that so many of them displayed a proud "sense of their [natural] rights, [and] a contempt of danger." Toussaint Louverture's colony, of course, had benefited from a black majority lacking in the Chesapeake, but had not George Washington's outnumbered Continental Army toppled an empire? Then-governor James Monroe agreed that Gabriel's fellows were "bold adventurers [who were] willing to hazard their lives on the experiment" of freedom. Just as service in the American Revolution had played a role in the later actions of Dominguan rebels such as Henri Christophe and André Rigaud, word of the victory in Saint-Domingue emboldened mainland slaves who yet hoped to make the American republic live up to its stated ideals. Virginia slaves, Randolph worried, "exhibited a spirit, which, if it becomes general, must deluge the Southern country in blood."[15]

Even in Saint-Domingue, with its white minority, potential rebels faced an uncertain future, but that might well be said of any white soldier who served in the Patriot forces. For a young man such as Gabriel, a smart, aggressive slave with so little prejudice against violence or regard for his own welfare that he would bite a white farmer over a stolen hog, leading a popular insurrection was the only solution to the Virginia assembly's failure to implement peaceful reform. His emerging plan, as he explained it to his brother Solomon and to Ben, another of Prosser's slaves, was as simple as Boukman's Night of Fire. The insurgents, including urban slaves, were to meet on Prosser's plantation before marching on Richmond. Fighting in three groups, they would attack the capitol, the powder magazine, and the penitentiary (where arms were stored). His soldiers would then fortify the city as best they could and await word that other towns had been taken or that the slaves from those cities were heading for Richmond. At that juncture, Gabriel expected that embattled whites would "agree to their freedom."

A triumphant Gabriel hoped to "dine and drink with the merchants on the day when it was agreed to."[16]

In the spring of 1800, during his frequent trips into Richmond, Gabriel began to spread word of his plan and recruit followers. He acted cautiously; he first approached other skilled and relatively unsupervised bondmen who hired out their time, especially those who lived apart from their masters. Not surprisingly, his method of recruitment and even his language were influenced by his special status as an artisan. Would they "join a free mason society," Gabriel and his brothers asked, "a society to fight the White people for their freedom"? As slaves around Brookfield joined, they were sworn to a strict oath of secrecy and fidelity. At one early meeting, Gabriel attended a Sunday "barbecue" and casually invited George Smith and Isham to accompany him home. As they walked, Gabriel spoke boldly of liberty. Both eagerly agreed to serve, "and each shaking the other by the hand exclaimed, 'here are our hands and hearts, we will wade to our knees in blood sooner than fail in the attempt.'"[17]

As recruits joined, word of the conspiracy spread beyond Richmond. George Smith "hire[d] his time of his mistress" and journeyed to neighboring counties, and Sam Byrd Jr. hired himself out "for the greater part of the summer" so that he might be able to "engage a number of men in the adjacent counties and in Petersburg," a small port on the falls line of the Appomattox River. There, Byrd persuaded his uncles, Reuben and Jesse Byrd, "two free men of colour," to contact other urban blacks. Reuben, a moderately prosperous carpenter and mason, agreed to serve as coordinator for the Petersburg rebels. Since Sam Byrd Sr., a "free mulatto of Hanover Town[,] enlisted men there," the involvement of freedmen in the plot serves as a reminder that the staggered pace of manumission in Virginia, as in the North, kept the black community bound tightly together even after some members became free.[18]

Inevitably, word began to flow down the James River to Suffolk and Norfolk. Black boatmen around the Chesapeake had long been the carriers of information and runaway slaves as well as goods for merchants; now several became involved as couriers. One of them, Jacob, was a slave but also a ship's captain for hire who regularly "passed between [Petersburg] and Norfolk." As with the Petersburg conspirators, the men of the lower James planned to meet on a yet-to-be-determined date outside of Norfolk and await news of the Richmond uprising. Byrd even prevailed upon a free black mail carrier to maintain contact with Jefferson's Charlottesville, where he had found slaves "very willing to join." By the end of July, word of the revolt had spread to at least six Virginia towns. It was, as Monroe later observed, a secret known "in many and some distant parts of the State."[19]

As late summer arrived, Gabriel decided the time had come to move beyond the recruitment of key lieutenants to enlisting large numbers of soldiers. On August 10, following a child's funeral on a nearby plantation, Gabriel "gave an invitation to some of the Negroes to drink grog down at the Spring." There, he announced, he had a plan to fight not just for black freedom but also "for his Country." Wielding the weapons he and Solomon had forged—swords "made of [wheat] scythes cut in two"—Gabriel talked of storming the capitol after a diversionary fire at Rockett's warehouse landing had drawn most whites down to the James. Governor Monroe was to be taken hostage but not harmed, and the friends of liberty, "Quakers, Methodists, and French people," would be spared, together with "poor white women who had no slaves."[20]

Having outlined his plan, Gabriel shouted that all who wished to join him should "stand up—and those who would not [to] set down." As one by one the slaves rose to their feet, Gabriel's men worked their way through the crowd "and enlisted a considerable number who signed a paper [with their names or] their marks." At that moment, Jack Ditcher, who had been involved in the conspiracy for as long as Byrd had been, challenged Gabriel's leadership by asking those there "to give him the voice for General." Only a few years older than Gabriel, Ditcher had also learned a few lessons from the Revolutionary years. "We have as much right to fight for our liberty as any men," he shouted. The bondmen decided to resolve the question as did white Americans that fall: they held an election. Preparing to march into a potentially suicidal battle, the men at the spring evidently preferred Gabriel's brains to Ditcher's brawn. "[U]pon the votes being taken, Gabriel had by far the greater number."[21]

Ditcher's challenge had introduced disharmony into the ranks of the rebels. To quell divisions within the movement that might lead the cautious to back away, Gabriel raised the doctrine of political equality. He "expected the poor white people would also join him," for the Revolution had failed them as much as it had Chesapeake bondpeople. Gabriel also revealed a secret previously known only to the rebel leadership. "Two [white] Frenchmen," Charles Quersey and Alexander Beddenhurst (perhaps a member of the German-speaking Fourth Regiment), both Revolutionary War veterans, "had actually joined," he told the crowd. Gabriel understood that the age of revolution was less an event than it was a process. When the fighting began, poor whites and rural slaves would be immediately forced to choose sides. Typical of those expected to throw in against the merchants was an unskilled white laborer known only as Lucas; he promised George Smith that he would join once the uprising was under way and if there was money to be had. There was good reason, as one horrified journalist later wrote, to believe that "the most redoubtable democrats in the state" might join Gabriel's revolutionary army. To make his point clearer still, Gabriel concluded by announcing that he planned to march into battle carrying a crude flag emblazoned with the words "death or Liberty."[22]

The fact that Gabriel turned the words of Patrick Henry upside down suggests that his hope was to do the same with Chesapeake society. Not only had the Revolution failed to fulfill its egalitarian promise, but the counter-revolution under way in the South was spreading slavery farther across the new country. He knew that Virginia had refused to consider serious reform following its 1782 act permitting private manumission; perhaps only a con-flagration like that in Saint-Domingue and high-visibility hostages such as Governor Monroe were necessary to force the state into action. No American alive in the late eighteenth century could forget that their nation was con-ceived in violence, and Gabriel's flag was to be a visible reminder that white Virginians once claimed to believe in liberty.[23]

The rebels decided on Saturday, August 30, for the night of the assault. Acting in concert with the Richmond soldiers, nearly 150 slaves, "mulat-toes," and "some whites" from Suffolk and Norfolk gathered at Whitlock's mill outside of Norfolk to await word from Richmond. But then the skies opened and a torrential rain poured down on the Richmond area, washing away bridges and cutting communications between Brookfield and the city. Whites noticed slaves "going [away] from the town," whereas it was normal to see rural slaves entering Richmond on Saturday night, but due to the ris-ing waters they were unable to reach the plantation. In desperation, Gabriel and his wife, Nanny, passed the word as best they could for the rebels "to meet at the tobacco house of Mr. Prosser the ensuing night."[24]

The chaos of the storm and the now likely failure of the revolt convinced two minor recruits, Pharoah and Tom, to save their lives by revealing the plot to their master, Mosby Sheppard. After several tries, Sheppard succeeded in reaching the city and informing Monroe, who called out the militia. Gabriel managed to flee the county and Jack Ditcher went into hiding in Richmond, but patrols captured Solomon and Martin, who were tried and hanged on September 15. Gabriel was arrested eight days later in Norfolk, where an enslaved boatman for hire named Billy, who had known Gabriel in Richmond, turned him in for the reward. Monroe, however, had offered a reward of $300 and a full pardon to one of Gabriel's accomplices. Because Billy was uninvolved in the plot, as well as the property of another man, the state paid him only $50 for his information, far from the sum required to purchase his own freedom. Ironically, Billy would have fared better had he been a conspirator.[25]

Finally, on October 6, "the property of Thomas Henry Prosser" was brought before the Richmond court and "charged with Conspiracy and Insurrection." Several of Gabriel's lieutenants had turned state's evidence in exchange for pardon, but while their testimony was damning for the black general, it also served to indict the aged Patriots serving as the tribunal's justices. One witness repeated Gabriel's egalitarian dream that "the poor White people would also join him," while another revealed his promise not to harm "Quakers, Methodists, [or] French people." One way to halt the agony was to pass sentence, which Justice Miles Selden did. "It is the unanimous Opinion of the Court," he snapped, "that the said Negro man Slave Gabriel is Guilty of the Crime with which he stands accused and for the same that he be hanged by the neck until he be dead." The court valued the condemned man at an impressive $500, an inadvertent admission of his intellect and ability. When asked if he had anything to add, Gabriel requested only that the date of his execution be delayed so that he might die beside fellow revolutionaries George Smith and Sam Byrd Jr.[26]

As dawn broke on October 10, one wagon carried two of the insurgents to the crossroads at Four Mile Creek; by hanging the men near the plantation quarters, the executions would be witnessed by their families and so serve as warnings for other revolutionaries. It was most likely one of these two men—William and Sam Graham—whose courtroom bravado provided the most eloquent comment on the alleged radicalism of the American Revolution. Upon being charged, the accused slave made the political nature of the conspiracy all too evident. "I have nothing more to offer than what General Washington would have had to offer, had he been taken by the British and put to trial," the young revolutionary patiently explained. "I have adventured my life in endeavouring to obtain the liberty of my countrymen, and am a willing sacrifice in their cause."[27]

Four more slaves, including Smith and Byrd, were carried to a large tree near Brookfield, where four ropes were thrown over a high branch. The last tumbrel was reserved for the black general alone, who was driven to the city gallows near Fifteenth and Broad streets. Since slave wives were not allowed to collect their husbands' bodies, the executed were buried within feet of the scaffold. "I do hereby certify," scribbled Mosby Sheppard, "that the within mentioned Slave [Gabriel] was executed agreeably to the within Centance of the Court." In all, twenty-seven men, including Gabriel, paid for their dream of liberty with their lives. Eight more rebels, including Ditcher, were pardoned but transported to Spanish New Orleans.[28]

In becoming part of the forced migration of Chesapeake slaves to the lower South, Ditcher and the other condemned black Patriots exemplified an

American Revolution that in the end proved to be far from radical, and which failed to fulfill its promise of freedom to one-fifth of the republic's population. It is true that by the day Gabriel swung from the gallows, unfree labor had been eradicated in parts of the North. But the gradual end of slavery in the northern states masked the movement of far larger numbers of black men and women into the fresh lands of the frontier South and allowed too many founders to trumpet the success of a Revolution that abolished slavery only in that half of the republic that was home to few African Americans. Condemning the generation that broke with Britain, won their war, and then crafted the world's oldest continually functioning constitution is not unproblematic, and it is far easier to dismiss their failures by observing that their egalitarian ideals laid the basis for the eventual end of slavery. Gabriel, of course, knew better. He was sentenced to die by white men who had once been revolutionaries and still spoke in the language of natural rights. The failure of these men—and those throughout the new nation—to act during their lifetimes not only led to the death of Gabriel and his soldiers but also allowed slavery to flourish for another half century and led to the death of approximately 600,000 young Americans in the four years after 1861.

Two sections of modern-day Richmond, both monuments of sorts, say much about how Americans now remember the Revolutionary era. The first is an enormous bronze equestrian statue of George Washington, erected on the capitol grounds atop a forty-foot granite pedestal; the planter who freed his slaves only in death gazes down at the bustling city as cars speed along Broad. If those drivers are heading east, roughly a mile away, just as Broad crosses Interstate 95, they can glance to their left and see a parking lot partly hidden by tall trees. Beneath the worn pavement lies the old "Negro Burial Ground," where Gabriel and many of his soldiers were interred after being cut down from the gibbet. In October 2004, the state erected a historical marker to commemorate the graveyard, but the marker is located on a busy overpass, and so few drivers can read the description of Gabriel's final resting place as they race by. Below the bridge and behind the trees, rusty cars leak oil onto the blacktop just above Gabriel's bones.[29]

NOTES

Prologue: The Trials of William Lee

1. Fritz Hirschfeld, *George Washington and Slavery: A Documentary Portrayal* (Columbia, MO, 1997), 98, 110.

2. Henry Wiencek, *An Imperfect God: George Washington, His Slaves, and the Creation of America* (New York, 2003), 130–31; Robert F. Dalzell Jr. and Lee Baldwin Dalzell, *George Washington's Mount Vernon: At Home in Revolutionary America* (New York, 1998), 136.

3. Douglas R. Egerton, "George Washington and Blacks," in *Oxford Encyclopedia of Black History*, ed. Graham Russell Hodges (New York, forthcoming); Dorothy Twohig, "'That Species of Property': Washington's Role in the Controversy Over Slavery," in *George Washington Reconsidered*, ed. Donald Higginbotham (Charlottesville, VA, 2001), 116–17; George Washington to Daniel Jenifer Adams, July 20, 1772, in *The Writings of George Washington*, ed. John C. Fitzpatrick (Washington, DC, 1931–44), 3:98.

4. Bruce Chadwick, *The General and Mrs. Washington: The Untold Story of a Marriage and a Revolution* (Naperville, IL, 2006), 150; Hirschfeld, *Washington and Slavery*, 98–99.

5. Entry of September 6, 1774, in *The Diaries of George Washington*, ed. Donald Jackson and Dorothy Twohig (Charlottesville, VA, 1976–79), 3:276; Helen Bryan, *First Lady of Liberty: Martha Washington* (New York, 2002), 184.

6. Ira Berlin, *Many Thousands Gone: The First Two Centuries of Slavery in North America* (Cambridge, MA, 1998), 257.

7. Sylvia R. Frey, *Water from the Rock: Black Resistance in a Revolutionary Age* (Princeton, NJ, 1991), 120–24; George W. P. Custis, *Recollections and Private Memoirs of Washington* (New York, 1860), 224; Joseph J. Ellis, *His Excellency: George Washington* (New York, 2005), 119.

8. Hirschfeld, *Washington and Slavery*, 98–99; Wiencek, *An Imperfect God*, 356. On the taking of names, see Gary B. Nash, *Forging Freedom: The Formation of Philadelphia's Black Community, 1720–1840* (Cambridge, MA, 1989), 80; James Thomas Flexner, *George Washington: Anguish and Farewell, 1793–1799* (Boston, 1969), 441.

9. George Washington to Clement Biddle, July 28, 1784, in *The Papers of George Washington: Confederation Series*, ed. W. W. Abbot (Charlottesville, VA, 1983–), 2:14. On Lee's family life, still useful is Mary Beth Norton, Herbert Gutman, and Ira Berlin, "The Afro-American Family in the Age of Revolution," in *Slavery and Freedom in the Age of the American Revolution*, ed. Ira Berlin and Ronald Hoffman (Charlottesville, VA, 1983), 175–92.

10. Although somewhat dated and focused on the antebellum era, Thomas L. Webber, *Deep Like the Rivers: Education in the Slave Quarter Community, 1831–1865* (New York, 1978), remains the standard study of African American literacy.

11. Hirschfeld, *Washington and Slavery*, 101; Chadwick, *General and Mrs. Washington*, 172; Thomas Slaughter, *The Whiskey Rebellion: Frontier Epilogue to the American Revolution* (New York, 1986), 82; Entry of April 22, 1785, in Jackson and Twohig, *Diaries*, 4:125.

12. James Thomas Flexner, *George Washington and the New Nation, 1783–1793* (Boston, 1969), 42; Hirschfeld, *Washington and Slavery*, 105.

13. Flexner, *Washington and the New Nation*, 42; W. J. Rorabaugh, *The Alcoholic Republic: An American Tradition* (New York, 1979), 13–14. On the self-treatment of slaves, see Todd L. Savitt, *Medicine and Slavery: The Diseases and Health Care of Blacks in Antebellum Virginia* (Urbana, IL, 1978), 171–86, and Rhys Isaac, *Landon Carter's Uneasy Kingdom: Revolution and Rebellion on a Virginia Plantation* (New York, 2004), 219–22.

14. Entry of March 1, 1788, in Jackson and Twohig, *Diaries*, 5:281; George Washington to William Pearce, May 18, 1794, in Washington Papers, Library of Congress (hereafter LC).

15. Flexner, *Washington and the New Nation*, 173; Bryan, *Martha Washington*, 287.

16. Donald R. Wright, *African Americans in the Early Republic, 1789–1831* (Arlington Heights, IL, 1993), 1; Clement Biddle to George Washington, April 27, 1789, and note 1 in Abbot, *Papers of George Washington: Presidential Series*, 2:133–34.

17. George Washington to Tobias Lear, November 8, 1793, and George Washington to William Pearce, May 18, 1794, both in Washington Papers, LC.

18. Ellis, *His Excellency*, 263; John Ferling, *The First of Men: A Life of George Washington* (Knoxville, TN, 1988), 502; Richard Norton Smith, *Patriarch: George Washington and the New American Nation* (Boston, 1993), 346.

19. Wiencek, *An Imperfect God*, 357; the best analysis of black life in the big house remains Eugene D. Genovese, *Roll, Jordan, Roll: The World the Slaves Made* (New York, 1972), 327–65.

20. Custis, *Recollections*, 157.

21. Benjamin Quarles, *The Negro in the American Revolution*, 2nd ed. (Chapel Hill, NC, 1996), viii–ix, 79; Gordon S. Wood, *The Radicalism of the American Revolution* (New York, 1991), 7.

22. Steven Deyle, *Carry Me Back: The Domestic Slave Trade in American Life* (New York, 2005), 26.

23. Testimony of Prosser's Sam at trial of Jack Ditcher, October 29, 1800, in Negro Insurrection Files, Executive Papers, Library of Virginia (hereafter LV).

24. Ira Berlin, *Generations of Captivity: A History of African-American Slaves* (Cambridge, MA, 2003), 272–74; Ira Berlin, *Slaves Without Masters: The Free Negro in the Antebellum South* (New York, 1974), 396; Robert McColley, *Slavery and Jeffersonian Virginia* (Urbana, IL, 1964), 141; Gordon S. Wood, *Revolutionary Characters: What Made the Founders Different* (New York, 2006), 27.

Chapter 1: Equiano's World

1. Marie Jenkins Schwartz, *Born in Bondage: Growing Up Enslaved in the Antebellum South* (Cambridge, MA, 2000), 99; Wilma King, *Stolen Childhood: Slave Youth in Nineteenth-Century America* (Bloomington, IN, 1995), 71.

2. Olaudah Equiano, *The Interesting Narrative and Other Writings*, ed. Vincent Carretta (New York, 2003), 47–63.

3. Equiano, *Interesting Narrative*, 72–76; James Walvin, *An African's Life: The Life and Times of Olaudah Equiano, 1745–1797* (London, 1998), 40; Fred Anderson, *Crucible of War: The Seven Years' War and the Fate of Empire in British North America, 1754–1766* (New York, 2000), 362.

4. Vincent Carretta, "Olaudah Equiano or Gustavas Vassa? New Light on an Eighteenth-Century Question of Identity," *Slavery and Abolition* 20 (1999): 102–3; Vincent Carretta, *Equiano the African: Biography of a Self-Made Man* (Athens, GA, 2005), 147.

5. Equiano, *Interesting Narrative*, Appendix B. Initially titled *Portrait of a Negro Man*, the Royal Albert Memorial Museum now dates the painting to the 1780s—although it seems unlikely the painting preceded the publication of the autobiography—and calls it *Portrait of Olaudah Equiano*. Equiano was first suggested as the sitter only in 1961, and the portrait bears but a cursory resemblance to the man depicted on the *Narrative*'s frontispiece.

6. Walvin, *An African's Life*, 34, 46–49, 99, 135; James Green, "The Publishing History of Olaudah Equiano's *Interesting Narrative*," *Slavery and Abolition* 16 (December 1995): 364; Equiano, *Interesting Narrative*, xvii.

7. Equiano, *Interesting Narrative*, 74; Daniel G. Hill, *The Freedom Seekers: Blacks in Early Canada* (Toronto, 1992), 6; Maureen G. Elgersman, *Unyielding Spirits: Black Women and Slavery in Early Canada and Jamaica* (New York, 1999), 15; Berlin draws this critical distinction in *Many Thousands Gone*, 8.

8. Sue Peabody, *"There Are No Slaves in France": The Political Culture of Race and Slavery in the Ancien Régime* (New York, 1996), 11–15; B. Singh Bolaria, *Racial*

Oppression in Canada, 2nd ed. (Toronto, 1988), 189; Hill, *Freedom Seekers*, 8–9; Afua Cooper, *The Hanging of Angélique: The Untold Story of Canadian Slavery and the Burning of Old Montreal* (Athens, GA, 2007), 75.

9. Baron of Montesquieu, *The Spirit of the Laws*, trans. Thomas Nugent (New York, 1949), 1:235; Elgersman, *Unyielding Spirits*, 15.

10. Robin W. Winks, *The Blacks in Canada*, 2nd ed. (Montreal, 1997), 16; Kenneth Donovan, "A Nominal List of Slaves and Their Owners in Ile Royale, 1713–1760," *Nova Scotia Historical Review* 16 (1996): 156–59.

11. Lorenzo J. Greene, *The Negro in Colonial New England*, 2nd ed. (New York, 1971), 74; Berlin, *Generations of Captivity*, 83; David Hackett Fischer, *Albion's Seed: Four British Folkways in America* (New York, 1989), 52–53.

12. John Ferling, *John Adams: A Life* (Knoxville, TN, 1992), 172; Joanne Pope Melish, *Disowning Slavery: Gradual Emancipation and "Race" in New England, 1770–1860* (Ithaca, NY, 1998), 16; Greene, *Negro in Colonial New England*, 81.

13. William M. Wiecek, "The Statutory Law of Slavery and Race in the Thirteen Mainland Colonies of British America," *William and Mary Quarterly* (hereafter *WMQ*) 34 (1977): 261; Leviticus 25:45; Jill Lepore, *The Name of War: King Philip's War and the Origin of American Identity* (New York, 1998), 154; Gary B. Nash, *The Unknown American Revolution: The Unruly Birth of Democracy and the Struggle to Create America* (New York, 2005), 35.

14. Jackson Turner Main, *The Social Structure of Revolutionary America* (Princeton, NJ, 1956), 41; Christopher Collier, *Roger Sherman's Connecticut: Yankee Politics and the American Revolution* (Middletown, CT, 1971), 123; Mark J. Sammons and Valerie Cunningham, *Black Portsmouth: Three Centuries of African-American Heritage* (Durham, NH, 2004), 19; Melish, *Disowning Slavery*, 16–17; Greene, *Negro in Colonial New England*, 103–8.

15. Greene, *Negro in Colonial New England*, 86; Hugh Thomas, *The Slave Trade: The Story of the Atlantic Slave Trade, 1440–1870* (New York, 1997), 260–61; Jack P. Greene, *Pursuits of Happiness: The Social Development of Early Modern British Colonies and the Formation of American Culture* (Chapel Hill, NC, 1998), 72; Fergus M. Bordewich, *Bound for Canaan: The Underground Railroad and the War for the Soul of America* (New York, 2005), 18; Charles Rappleye, *Sons of Providence: The Brown Brothers, the Slave Trade, and the American Revolution* (New York, 2006), 84–88; "Slavery, the Brown Family of Providence and Brown University," Brown University News Service, July 2001.

16. Greene, *Pursuits of Happiness*, 71–73; Melish, *Disowning Slavery*, 17–23.

17. Robert K. Fitts, *Inventing New England's Slave Paradise: Master/Slave Relations in Eighteenth-Century Narragansett, Rhode Island* (New York, 1998), 143; William D. Piersen, *Black Yankees: The Development of an Afro-American Subculture in Eighteenth-Century New England* (Amherst, MA, 1988), 130–31; Shane White, "'It Was a Proud Day': African Americans, Festivals, and Parades in the North, 1741–1834," *Journal of American History* 81 (1994): 17; Joseph P. Reidy, "'Negro Election Day' and Black Community Life in New England,

1750–1860," *Marxist Perspectives* 1 (1978): 104–5; Sterling Stuckey, *Slave Culture: Nationalist Theory and the Foundations of Black America* (New York, 1987), 74; Melish, *Disowning Slavery*, 46.

18. Graham Russell Hodges, *Root and Branch: African Americans in New York and East Jersey, 1613–1863* (Chapel Hill, NC, 1999), 106; Walter Stahr, *John Jay: Founding Father* (New York and London, 2005), 236; Shane White, *Somewhat More Independent: The End of Slavery in New York City, 1770–1810* (Athens, GA, 1991), xx.

19. Hodges, *Root and Branch*, 6–7, 106; Leslie M. Harris, *In the Shadow of Slavery: African Americans in New York City, 1626–1863* (Chicago, 2003), 46–47; Berlin, *Many Thousands Gone*, 185; James G. Lydon, "New York and the Slave Trade, 1700 to 1774," *WMQ* 35 (1978): 379.

20. Alan Watson, *Slave Law in the Americas* (Athens, GA, 1989), 94; Edgar J. McManus, *A History of Negro Slavery in New York* (Syracuse, NY, 1966), 23–24; Wiecek, "Statutory Law of Slavery," 261; Carl Nordstrom, "The New York Slave Code," *Afro-Americans in New York Life and History* 4 (1980): 8–10.

21. Berlin, *Many Thousands Gone*, 185–86. This popular assumption was first challenged by White, *Somewhat More Independent*, 88–89.

22. Berlin, *Generations of Captivity*, 87; White, *Somewhat More Independent*, 95–96; James O. Horton and Lois E. Horton, *In Hope of Liberty: Culture, Community and Protest Among Northern Free Blacks, 1700–1860* (New York, 1997), 31.

23. Carretta, *Equiano the African*, 95, 111; Equiano, *Interesting Narrative*, 131; Walter Isaacson, *Benjamin Franklin: An American Life* (New York, 2003), 463; Gary B. Nash and Jean R. Soderlund, *Freedom by Degrees: Emancipation in Pennsylvania and Its Aftermath* (New York, 1991), 5; Walvin, *An African's Life*, 70–71.

24. Nash and Soderlund, *Freedom by Degrees*, 7; Donald Wright et al., *African Americans in the Colonial Era* (Wheeling, IL, 1990), 93–94; White, *Somewhat More Independent*, 22; Nash, *Unknown American Revolution*, 32.

25. Nash and Soderlund, *Freedom by Degrees*, 12–13; "An Act for the Better Regulating of Negroes in This Province," March 5, 1726, in *The Statutes at Large of Pennsylvania from 1682–1801*, ed. Clarence M. Busch (Philadelphia, 1897), 2:59–64.

26. Nash, *Forging Freedom*, 26–29; Graham Russell Hodges, *Slavery and Freedom in the Rural North: African Americans in Monmouth County, New Jersey, 1665–1865* (Lanham, MD, 1997), 72; Equiano, *Interesting Narrative*, 132.

27. Nash, *Forging Freedom*, 26; Hodges, *Slavery and Freedom*, 74–75; Jean R. Soderlund, *Quakers and Slavery: A Divided Spirit* (Princeton, NJ, 1985), 158–62; *Pennsylvania Gazette*, January 18, 1770, in *Blacks Who Stole Themselves: Advertisements for Runaways in the Pennsylvania Gazette, 1728–1790*, ed. Billy G. Smith and Richard Wojtowicz (Philadelphia, 1989), 97.

28. Paul A. Gilje, *Liberty on the Waterfront: American Maritime Culture in the Age of Revolution* (Philadelphia, 2004), 25–26; Quarles, *Negro in the American Revolution*, 83; W. Jeffrey Bolster, *Black Jacks: African American Seamen in the Age of Sail* (Cambridge, MA, 1997), 38; *Pennsylvania Gazette*, June 23, 1763, in Smith and Wojtowicz, *Blacks Who Stole Themselves*, 62.

29. Patience Essah, *A House Divided: Slavery and Emancipation in Delaware, 1638–1865* (Charlottesville, VA, 1996), 22; William H. Williams, *Slavery and Freedom in Delaware, 1639–1865* (Lanham, MD, 1996), 42–43.

30. Peter Kolchin, *American Slavery, 1619–1877* (New York, 1993), 24; Williams, *Slavery and Freedom in Delaware*, 46–47, 110.

31. Christopher Phillips, *Freedom's Port: The African American Community of Baltimore, 1790–1860* (Urbana, IL, 1997), 10–14; Ronald Hoffman and Sally D. Mason, *Princes of Ireland, Planters of Maryland: A Carroll Saga, 1500–1782* (Chapel Hill, NC, 2000), 120–21; T. Stephen Whitman, *The Price of Freedom: Slavery and Manumission in Baltimore and Early National Maryland* (Lexington, KY, 1997), 10–11; Alan Taylor, *American Colonies* (New York, 2001), 336; Gerald W. Mullin, *Flight and Rebellion: Slave Resistance in Eighteenth-Century Virginia* (New York, 1972), 16.

32. Allan Kulikoff, *Tobacco and Slaves: The Development of Southern Cultures in the Chesapeake, 1680–1800* (Chapel Hill, NC, 1986), 335; "Advertisement for Runaway Slaves," August 11, 1761, in *Papers of George Washington: Colonial Series*, 7: 65–67; Equiano, *Interesting Narrative*, 62; Wiencek, *An Imperfect God*, 84–86.

33. Jackson Turner Main, *The Antifederalists: Critics of the Constitution, 1781–1788* (Chapel Hill, NC, 1961), 2–3; Wiencek, *An Imperfect God*, 27–28, 45.

34. Sally E. Hadden, *Slave Patrols: Law and Violence in Virginia and the Carolinas* (Cambridge, MA, 2001), 28–29; Thomas D. Morris, *Southern Slavery and the Law, 1619–1860* (Chapel Hill, NC, 1996), 22–23; Philip J. Schwarz, *Twice Condemned: Slaves and the Criminal Laws of Virginia, 1705–1865* (Baton Rouge, LA, 1988), 16–20.

35. This irreconcilable feature of slave law was first suggested by Genovese, *Roll, Jordan, Roll*, 28; Anthony S. Parent Jr., *Foul Means: The Formation of a Slave Society in Virginia, 1660–1740* (Chapel Hill, NC, 2003), 124; Philip Vickers Fithian, *Journals and Letters: A Plantation Tutor of the Old Dominion*, ed. Hunter Farish (Charlottesville, VA, 1957), 38.

36. Lorena S. Walsh, *From Calibar to Carter's Grove: The History of a Virginia Slave Community* (Charlottesville, VA, 1997), 61–65; Thomas Jefferson, *Thomas Jefferson's Farm Book*, ed. Edwin M. Betts (Charlottesville, VA, 1987), 77; Mullin, *Flight and Rebellion*, 48–52.

37. Equiano, *Interesting Narrative*, 36; Norman Risjord, *Jefferson's America, 1760–1815*, 2nd ed. (Lanham, MD, 2002), 25; Rhys Isaac, *The Transformation of Virginia, 1740–1790* (Chapel Hill, NC, 1982), 33; Mechal Sobel, *The World They Made Together: Black and White Values in Eighteenth-Century Virginia* (Princeton, NJ, 1987), 71–73, 166.

38. Frey, *Water from the Rock*, 22–23; Mechal Sobel, *Trabelin' On: The Slave Journey to an Afro-Baptist Faith* (Princeton, NJ, 1988), 80–87; Hodges, *Slavery and Freedom*, 77.

39. Betty Wood, *Slavery in Colonial America, 1619–1776* (Lanham, MD, 2005), 58; Parent, *Foul Means*, 160–62.

40. Equiano, *Interesting Narrative*, 128; Taylor, *American Colonies*, 335; Walter J. Fraser Jr., *Charleston! Charleston! The History of a Southern City* (Columbia, SC, 1989), 110–11.

41. Margaret Washington, *"A Peculiar People": Slave Religion and Community Culture Among the Gullahs* (New York, 1988), 35; Thomas, *Slave Trade*, 268–70; Michael Gomez, *Exchanging Our Country Marks: The Transformation of African Identities in the Colonial and Antebellum South* (Chapel Hill, NC, 1998), 45; Wright, *African Americans in the Colonial Era*, 104–5; Donald R. Wright, *The World and a Very Small Place in Africa*, 2nd ed. (Armonk, NY, 2004), 95.

42. Washington, *"A Peculiar People,"* 3; Janet Duitsman Cornelius, *When I Can Read My Title Clear: Literacy, Slavery, and Religion in the Antebellum South* (Columbia, SC, 1991), 40–41; Norrece T. Jones Jr., *Born a Child of Freedom, Yet a Slave: Mechanisms of Control and Strategies of Resistance in Antebellum South Carolina* (Hanover, NH, 1990), 139.

43. Taylor, *American Colonies*, 335; Judith A. Carney, *Black Rice: The African Origins of Rice Cultivation in the Americas* (Cambridge, MA, 2001), 63–68; Frey, *Water from the Rock*, 6; Peter Wood, *Black Majority: Negroes in Colonial South Carolina from 1670 Through the Stono Rebellion* (New York, 1974), 225–26, 324–25; Philip D. Morgan, *Slave Counterpoint: Black Culture in the Eighteenth-Century Chesapeake and Lowcountry* (Chapel Hill, NC, 1998), 179–80.

44. Wiecek, "Statutory Law of Slavery," 263; Barry Gaspar, "With a Rod of Iron: Barbados Slave Laws as a Model for Jamaica, South Carolina, and Antigua, 1661–1697," in *Crossing Boundaries: Comparative History of Black People in Diaspora*, ed. Darlene Clark Hine and Jacqueline McLeod (Bloomington, IN, 1999), 344; Robert Olwell, *Masters, Slaves, and Subjects: The Culture of Power in the South Carolina Low Country, 1740–1790* (Ithaca, NY, 1998), 62–71; "Negro Act," 1740, in *An Alphabetical Digest of the Public Statute Law of South Carolina*, ed. Joseph Brevard (Charleston, SC, 1814), 2:202.

45. Olwell, *Masters, Slaves, and Subjects*, 91; J. Hector St. John de Crèvecoeur, *Letters from an American Farmer and Sketches of Eighteenth-Century America*, ed. Albert E. Stone (New York, 1981), 177–79. Some scholars have suggested that the author never actually visited the Americas, but Stone demonstrates that the twenty-four-year-old Frenchman, having served briefly in New France, arrived in New York City for his tour of the English colonies in 1759.

46. Betty Wood, *Slavery in Colonial Georgia, 1730–1775* (Athens, GA, 1984), 89, 98–99; Carretta, *Equiano the African*, 109; Equiano, *Interesting Narrative*, 128–30.

47. Jane Landers, *Black Society in Spanish Florida* (Urbana, IL, 1999), 158–59.

48. Walvin, *An African's Life*, 23. On the emergence of sugar slavery in the British Empire, the standard account remains Richard S. Dunn, *Sugar and Slaves: The Rise of the Planter Class in the English West Indies, 1624–1713* (Chapel Hill, NC, 1972).

49. Equiano, *Interesting Narrative*, 171; Trevor Burnard, *Mastery, Tyranny, and Desire: Thomas Thistlewood and His Slaves in the Anglo-Jamaican World* (Chapel Hill, NC, 2004), 15–17.

50. Burnard, *Mastery, Tyranny, and Desire*, 15–18.

51. Equiano, *Interesting Narrative*, 171–72; Taylor, *American Colonies*, 330; Burnard, *Mastery, Tyranny, and Desire*, 158–78.

52. Genovese, *Roll, Jordan, Roll*, 10–12; Jefferson, *Thomas Jefferson's Farm Book*, 5; Andrew Jackson O'Shaughnessy, *An Empire Divided: The American Revolution and The British Caribbean* (Philadelphia, 2000), 4.

53. Richard S. Dunn, "Sugar Production and Slave Women in Jamaica," in *Cultivation and Culture: Labor and the Shaping of Slave Life in the Americas*, eds. Ira Berlin and Philip D. Morgan (Charlottesville, VA, 1993), 49–58.

54. Equiano, *Interesting Narrative*, 104–7; Peter Linebaugh, *The London Hanged: Crime and Civil Society in the Eighteenth Century* (Cambridge, UK, 1992), 280; Jones, *Born a Child of Freedom*, 91; Betty Wood, "'Until He Shall Be Dead, Dead, Dead': The Judicial Treatment of Slaves in Eighteenth-Century Georgia," *Georgia Historical Quarterly* 71 (Fall 1987): 395.

55. Equiano, *Interesting Narrative*, 60; Larry Gragg, *Englishmen Transplanted: The English Colonization of Barbados, 1627–1660* (New York, 2003), 1; O'Shaughnessy, *An Empire Divided*, 165; Gragg, *Englishmen Transplanted*, 127; Equiano, *Interesting Narrative*, 109; Liza Picard, *Dr. Johnson's London: Coffee-Houses and Climbing Boys, Medicine, Toothpaste and Gin, Poverty and Press-Gangs, Freakshows and Female Education* (New York, 2001), 295–96.

56. Walvin, *An African's Life*, 133; Simon Schama, *Rough Crossings: Britain, the Slaves and the American Revolution* (New York, 2006), 23; James Walvin, *England, Slaves and Freedom 1776–1838* (Jackson, MS, 1986), 43.

57. James O. Horton and Lois E. Horton, *Slavery and the Making of America* (New York, 2005), 41; Frey, *Water from the Rock*, 27–28; Wright, *African Americans in the Colonial Era*, 156–57.

Chapter 2: Richard's Cup

1. The phrase is taken from Garry Wills, *Inventing America: Jefferson's Declaration of Independence* (New York, 1978). I am grateful to Anna Berkes and Lucia C. Stanton of the Thomas Jefferson Foundation for their investigation into who might have owned Richard; no evidence remains, unfortunately, to indicate who his master was.

2. Dumas Malone, *Jefferson the Virginian* (Boston, 1948), 202; Marie Kimball, *Jefferson: The Road to Glory, 1743–1776* (New York, 1943), 265.

3. James A. Bear and Lucia C. Stanton, eds., *Jefferson's Memorandum Books: Accounts, with Legal Records and Miscellany, 1767–1826* (Princeton, NJ, 1997), 1:397–403.

4. Lucia C. Stanton, "'Those Who Labor for My Happiness': Thomas Jefferson and His Slaves," in *Jeffersonian Legacies*, ed. Peter S. Onuf (Charlottesville, VA, 1993), 148.

5. Noble E. Cunningham Jr., *In Pursuit of Reason: The Life of Thomas Jefferson* (Baton Rouge, LA, 1987), 42–45.

6. Herbert Aptheker, *The American Revolution, 1763–1783* (New York, 1960), 108.

7. Berlin, *Many Thousands Gone*, 220.

8. Carretta, *Equiano the African*, 114; Gary B. Nash, *Race and Revolution* (Lanham, MD, 1990), 58.

9. John Wood Sweet, *Bodies Politic: Negotiating Race in the Early American North, 1730–1830* (Baltimore, 2003), 186; Winthrop D. Jordan, *White over Black: American Attitudes Toward the Negro, 1550–1812* (Chapel Hill, NC 1968), 270.

10. Alfred W. Blumrosen and Ruth G. Blumrosen, *Slave Nation: How Slavery United the Colonies and Sparked the American Revolution* (New York, 2005), 37; Horton and Horton, *In Hope of Liberty*, 56. The theory that this connection grew slowly and began in the southern colonies was first made by Bernard Bailyn, *The Ideological Origins of the American Revolution* (Cambridge, MA 1967), 235, but F. Nwabueze Okoye, "Chattel Slavery as the Nightmare of the American Revolutionaries," *WMQ* 37 (January 1980): 5, persuasively argues that Bailyn was wrong in claiming that slavery "was initially not a part of the American controversy with Great Britain." David Waldstreicher, *Runaway America: Benjamin Franklin, Slavery, and the American Revolution* (New York, 2004), 177, agrees.

11. James Otis, *The Rights of the British Colonies Asserted and Proved* (Boston, 1764), 29.

12. Nash, *Unknown American Revolution*, 62–63; Baron de Montesquieu, *The Spirit of the Laws*, trans. and ed. Anne Cohler et al. (New York, 1989), 249–50; Adam Smith, *The Theory of Moral Sentiments* (New York, 1999), 281.

13. Waldstreicher, *Runaway America*, 176–77; Duncan J. MacLeod, *Slavery, Race, and the American Revolution* (New York, 1974), 15.

14. Quarles, *Negro in the American Revolution*, 38; "Slew v. Whipple," 1766, in *Am I Not a Man and a Brother: The Antislavery Crusade of Revolutionary America, 1688–1788*, ed. Roger Bruns (New York, 1977), 105–7; Nash, *Unknown American Revolution*, 124–25; John Adams to Jeremy Belknap, March 21, 1795, in Adams Papers, Massachusetts Historical Society (hereafter MHS).

15. Eric Foner, *The Story of American Freedom* (New York, 2001), 31–33; Horton and Horton, *Slavery and the Making of America*, 54.

16. Alyn Brodsky, *Benjamin Rush: Patriot and Physician* (New York, 2004), 86–87; David Brion Davis, *Inhuman Bondage: The Rise and Fall of Slavery in the New World* (New York, 2006), 145; Benjamin Rush, *An Address to the Inhabitants of the British Settlements in America, upon Slave-Keeping*, in Wood, *Slavery in Colonial America*, 119.

17. Jordan, *White over Black*, 298; Nash first made this point in *Race and Revolution*, 10.

18. Jack P. Greene, "Slavery or Independence: Some Reflections on the Relationship Among Liberty, Black Bondage, and Equality in Revolutionary South Carolina," *South Carolina Historical Magazine* 80 (July 1979): 202–3; Williamsburg *Virginia Gazette*, October 1, 1767.

19. George Washington to George William Fairfax, June 10, 1774, and George Washington to Bryan Fairfax, July 4, 1774, and July 20, 1774, in *Writings*

of George Washington, 3:221–26, 227–34; Ellis, *His Excellency*, 62; Richard Brookhiser, *Founding Father: Rediscovering George Washington* (New York, 1996), 178.

20. Louis W. Potts, *Arthur Lee: A Virtuous Revolutionary* (Baton Rouge, LA 1981), 28–30; Richard Henry Lee to unknown, May 31, 1764, in *The Letters of Richard Henry Lee*, ed. James Curtis Ballagh (New York, 1914), 1:5–7; Arthur Lee, "Address on Slavery," in Williamsburg *Virginia Gazette*, March 19, 1767.

21. Henry Mayer, *A Son of Thunder: Patrick Henry and the American Republic* (New York, 1986), 168–69; Patrick Henry to Robert Pleasants, January 18, 1773, in *The Spirit of 'Seventy-Six: The Story of the American Revolution as Told by Participants*, ed. Henry Steele Commager and Richard B. Morris (New York, 1975), 402.

22. Potts, *Lee*, 28; Donald L. Robinson, *Slavery in the Structure of American Politics, 1765–1820* (New York, 1970), 83; Lawrence Goldstone, *Dark Bargain: Slavery, Profits, and the Struggle for the Constitution* (New York, 2005), 63; Jeff Broadwater, *George Mason: Forgotten Founder* (Chapel Hill, NC, 2006), 35; George Mason, "Scheme for Replevying Goods and Distress for Rent," December 23, 1765; "Virginia Nonimportation Association," June 22, 1770; "The Nonimportation Association as Corrected," April 23, 1769, all in *The Papers of George Mason, 1725–1792*, ed. Robert A. Rutland (Chapel Hill, NC, 1970), 1:61, 120, 103.

23. Eric R. Papenfuse, *Evils of Necessity: Robert Goodloe Harper and the Moral Dilemma of Slavery* (Philadelphia, 1997), 13; Greene, "Slavery or Independence," 201; Equiano, *Interesting Narrative*, 128; Peter Linebaugh and Marcus Rediker, *The Many-Headed Hydra: The Hidden History of the Revolutionary Atlantic* (Boston, 2001), 245.

24. Peter Wood, "'The Dream Deferred': Black Freedom Struggles on the Eve of White Independence," in *In Resistance: Studies in African, Caribbean, and Afro-American History*, ed. Gary Y. Okihiro (Amherst, MA, 1986), 169; Peter Wood, "'Liberty Is Sweet': African American Freedom Struggles in the Years Before White Independence," in *Beyond the American Revolution: Explorations in the History of American Radicalism*, ed. Alfred Young (DeKalb, IL 1993), 157; Charles Johnson, *Africans in America: America's Journey Through Slavery* (New York, 1998), 156; Olwell, *Masters, Slaves, and Subjects*, 225.

25. Wood, "Liberty Is Sweet," 159; Fraser, *Charleston*, 113; Nash, *Unknown American Revolution*, 60, 117. On the way in which whites attempted to terrify blacks through threats of mutilation after death, see my "A Peculiar Mark of Infamy: Dismemberment, Burial, and Rebelliousness in Slave Societies," in *Mortal Remains: Death in Early America*, ed. Nancy Isenberg and Andrew Burstein (Philadelphia, 2003), 149–60.

26. Linebaugh and Rediker, *Many-Headed Hydra*, 228–29.

27. Nash, *Forging Freedom*, 42; Kolchin, *American Slavery*, 76–77; Davis, *Inhuman Bondage*, 144.

28. David Brion Davis, *The Problem of Slavery in the Age of Revolution, 1770–1823* (Ithaca, NY, 1975), 480–81. The most recent account of proceedings is Steven M. Wise, *Though the Heavens May Fall: The Landmark Trial That Led to the End of Human Slavery* (New York, 2005), but see also Mark Weiner, "New Biographical Evidence on Somerset's Case," *Slavery and Abolition* 23 (April 2002): 121.

29. Adam Hochschild, *Bury the Chains: Prophets and Rebels in the Fight to Free an Empire's Slaves* (Boston, 2005), 48–50; E. C. P. Lascelles, *Granville Sharp and the Freedom of Slaves in England* (London, 1928), 3–32; Granville Sharp to Anthony Benezet, August 21, 1772, in *Am I Not a Man and a Brother*, 196–99; Walvin, *An African's Life*, 48–49.

30. Edmund Heward, *Lord Mansfield* (London, 1979), 145–46; William R. Cotter, "The Somerset Case and the Abolition of Slavery in England," *History* 79 (1994): 34–35; Wise, *Though the Heavens May Fall*, 180–82; Carretta, *Equiano the African*, 206–7; Blumrosen and Blumrosen, *Slave Nation*, 10–11.

31. Nash, *Unknown American Revolution*, 120; Carretta, *Equiano the African*, 212; Blumrosen and Blumrosen, *Slave Nation*, 24–25.

32. Hochschild, *Bury the Chains*, 50–51; Granville Sharp to Anthony Benezet, August 21, 1772, in Bruns, *Am I Not a Man and a Brother*, 197; Wise, *Though the Heavens May Fall*, 194–95. Not until 1778, when the case of Joseph Knight made slavery illegal in Scotland, was slavery abolished everywhere in the British Isles. See Frey, *Water from the Rock*, 75.

33. Christopher L. Brown, "The Politics of Slavery," in *The British Atlantic World, 1500–1800*, ed. David Armitage and Michael Braddick (New York, 2002), 226; Andrew Jackson O'Shaughnessy, "Redcoats and Slaves in the British Caribbean," in *The Lesser Antilles in the Age of European Expansion*, ed. Robert L. Paquette and Stanley Engerman (Gainesville, FL, 1996), 122–23.

34. Linebaugh and Rediker, *Many-Headed Hydra*, 222–24; Waldstreicher, *Runaway America*, 211; O'Shaughnessy, *An Empire Divided*, 36–38, 56.

35. O'Shaughnessy, *An Empire Divided*, 101.

36. *Diary and Autobiography of John Adams*, January 2, 1766, ed. L. H. Butterfield (Cambridge, MA 1962), 1:285; Lowell J. Ragatz, *The Rise and Fall of the Planter Class in the British Caribbean, 1763–1833* (New York, 1928), 142; O'Shaughnessy, *An Empire Divided*, 98–99; O'Shaughnessy, "Redcoats and Slaves in the British Caribbean," 120–21.

37. Alfred F. Young, *The Shoemaker and the Tea Party: Memory and the American Revolution* (Boston, 1999), 38; James O. Horton and Lois E. Horton, *Hard Road to Freedom: The Story of African America* (New Brunswick, NJ, 2001), 60.

38. Ferling, *John Adams*, 65; Horton and Horton, *Slavery and the Making of America*, 47–48; Linebaugh and Rediker, *Many-Headed Hydra*, 240.

39. Linebaugh and Rediker, *Many-Headed Hydra*, 237; Lynne Withey, *Dearest Friend: A Life of Abigail Adams* (New York, 1981), 60; Wiencek, *An Imperfect God*, 41.

40. John K. Alexander, *Samuel Adams: America's Revolutionary Politician* (Lanham, MD, 2004), 45–46; Samuel Adams, *Boston Gazette*, February 27, 1769, in *The Writings of Samuel Adams*, ed. Harry Alonzo Cushing (New York, 1904–8), 1:316.

41. Horton and Horton, *In Hope of Liberty*, 59; Louis Birnbaum, *Red Dawn at Lexington* (Boston, 1986), 249; John Saillant, *Black Puritan, Black Republican: The Life and Thought of Lemuel Haynes, 1753–1833* (New York, 2003), 51–52; Richard D. Brown, "'Not Only Extreme Poverty, but the Worst Kind of Orphanage': Lemuel Haynes and the Boundaries of Racial Tolerance on the Yankee Frontier, 1770–1820," *New England Quarterly* 61 (March 1988): 508.

42. James J. Allegro, "'Increasing and Strengthening the Country': Law, Politics, and the Antislavery Movement in Early-Eighteenth-Century Massachusetts Bay," *New England Quarterly* 75 (March 2002): 20; Alexander, *Samuel Adams*, 46; Nash, *Unknown American Revolution*, 151.

43. John R. Alden, *The South in the Revolution, 1763–1789* (Baton Rouge, LA, 1957), 347; Quarles, *Negro in the American Revolution*, 41; Davis, *Problem of Slavery*, 121–22; William Cohen, "Thomas Jefferson and the Problem of Slavery," *Journal of American History* 56 (1969): 507; Joseph Ellis, *American Sphinx: The Character of Thomas Jefferson* (New York, 1997), 52; Woody Holton, *Forced Founders: Indians, Debtors, Slaves, and the Making of the American Revolution in Virginia* (Chapel Hill, NC, 1997), 68–69.

44. Davis, *Inhuman Bondage*, 149; Kolchin, *American Slavery*, 79; Joseph Ellis, *Founding Brothers: The Revolutionary Generation* (New York, 2000), 89; Alden, *South in the Revolution*, 347.

45. Foner, *American Freedom*, 34; Nash, *Forging Freedom*, 49; Stanley Harrold, *The American Abolitionists* (New York, 2000), 19; Quarles, *Negro in the American Revolution*, 39.

46. Davis, *Inhuman Bondage*, 147; Thomas J. Davis, "Emancipation Rhetoric, Natural Rights, and Revolutionary New England: A Note on Four Black Petitions in Massachusetts, 1773–1777," *New England Quarterly* 62 (June 1989): 253; Felix Holbrook, Petition of January 6, 1773, in Nash, *Race and Revolution*, 171–73.

47. Harlow G. Unger, *John Hancock: Merchant King and American Patriot* (New York, 2000), 185; Patricia Bradley, *Slavery, Propaganda, and the American Revolution* (Jackson, MS, 1998), 61–64; Quarles, *Negro in the American Revolution*, 39.

48. Davis, "Emancipation Rhetoric," 254–55; Manisha Sinha, "To 'Cast Just Obliquy' on Oppressors: Black Radicalism in the Age of Revolution," *WMQ* 64 (January 2007): 152; Peter Bestes, Sambo Freeman, Felix Holbrook, and Chester Joie, Petition of April 20, 1773, in Nash, *Race and Revolution*, 173–74.

49. Frey, *Water from the Rock*, 53; Berlin, *Many Thousands Gone*, 193; Petition of May 25, 1774, in *The Founders' Constitution*, ed. Philip P. Kurland and Ralph Lerner (Chicago, 1987), 1: Chapter 14, Document 9.

50. Norman K. Risjord, *Jefferson's America, 1760–1815*, 2nd ed. (Lanham, 2002), 181; Petition of May 1779, in *Race and Revolution*, 174–76; Petition of New Hampshire Slaves, November 12, 1799, in "Slavery in New Hampshire," ed. Isaac W. Hammond, *Magazine of American History* 21 (January 1889): 63–64; Lemuel Haynes, "Liberty

Further Extended," in *Major Problems in the Era of the American Revolution, 1760–1791: Documents and Essays*, ed. Richard D. Brown (Lexington, KY, 1992), 309–10; Caesar Sarter, "Essay on Slavery," in Nash, *Race and Revolution*, 167–70.

51. Petition of May 1779, in Nash, *Race and Revolution*, 175; Berlin, *Many Thousands Gone*, 291; Sidney Kaplan, "The 'Domestic Insurrections' of the Declaration of Independence," *Journal of Negro History* 61 (1976): 249.

52. James Madison to William Bradford, November 26, 1774, in *The Papers of James Madison*, ed. William T. Hutchinson et al. (Chicago, 1962–1977), 1:129–30; Nash, *Forging Freedom*, 44; Nash, *Unknown American Revolution*, 158–59; Holton, *Forced Founders*, 141.

53. Berlin, *Many Thousands Gone*, 293; Fraser, *Charleston*, 144–46; Wood, "Liberty Is Sweet," 167; Isaac, *Landon Carter's Uneasy Kingdom*, 35.

54. Eric Foner, *Tom Paine and Revolutionary America* (New York, 1976), 73; Craig Nelson, *Thomas Paine: Enlightenment, Revolution, and the Birth of Modern Nations* (New York, 2006), 64–65; Wood, "Liberty Is Sweet," 160; Linebaugh and Rediker, *Many-Headed Hydra*, 227; Thomas Paine, "African Slavery in America," in *Common Sense and Related Writings*, ed. Thomas P. Slaughter (Boston, 2001), 57–59; John Keane, *Tom Paine: A Political Life* (Boston, 1995), 99; Paine, "African Slavery," 59–60.

55. McManus, *Negro Slavery in New York*, 152; David Brion Davis, *Revolutions: Reflections on American Equality and Foreign Liberations* (Cambridge, MA, 1990), 18; Wood, "Liberty is Sweet," 172.

56. Cunningham, *In Pursuit of Reason*, 46; Malone, *Jefferson the Virginian*, 216.

57. R. B. Bernstein, *Thomas Jefferson* (New York, 2003), 33–34; Allen Jayne, *Jefferson's Declaration of Independence* (Lexington, KY, 1998), 124; John C. Miller, *The Wolf by the Ears: Thomas Jefferson and Slavery* (New York, 1977), 8; Waldstreicher, *Runaway America*, 213.

58. Paul Finkelman, "Jefferson and Slavery: 'Treason Against the Hopes of the World,'" in Onuf, *Jeffersonian Legacies*, 191; Bailyn, *Ideological Origins of the American Revolution*, 239–45; Wiencek, *An Imperfect God*, 192; Isaac, *Landon Carter's Uneasy Kingdom*, 3–7.

59. Main, *The Antifederalists*, 2–3. Rhys Isaac makes this point in *Transformation of Virginia*, 308–9.

60. Berlin, *Many Thousands Gone*, 232; Benjamin Quarles, "The Revolutionary War as a Black Declaration of Independence," in Berlin and Hoffman, *Slavery and Freedom in the Age of the American Revolution*, 301; Saillant, *Black Puritan, Black Republican*, 50; John Ferling, *A Leap in the Dark: The Struggle to Create the American Republic* (New York, 2003), 260.

Chapter 3: The Transformation of Colonel Tye

1. Giles R. Wright, "Moving Toward Breaking the Chains: Black New Jerseyans and the American Revolution," in *New Jersey and the American Revolution*, ed. Barbara J. Mitnick (New Brunswick, NJ, 2005), 116; Hodges, *Slavery and Freedom*, 92.

2. Hodges, *Slavery and Freedom*, 92–94; Schama, *Rough Crossings*, 111.

3. Nash, *Unknown American Revolution*, 231; Hodges, *Slavery and Freedom*, 92.

4. Horton and Horton, *Slavery and the Making of America*, 58; Hodges, *Slavery and Freedom*, 97.

5. Wright, "Moving Toward Breaking the Chains," 128; David Hackett Fischer, *Washington's Crossing* (New York, 2004), 169; Hodges, *Slavery and Freedom*, 96–98; Nash, *Unknown American Revolution*, 231.

6. Hodges, *Slavery and Freedom*, 102–4; Nash, *Unknown American Revolution*, 232.

7. Benjamin Quarles, *The Negro in the American Revolution* (Chapel Hill, NC, 1961), viii–ix.

8. James Madison to William Bradford, November 26, 1774, in *Papers of James Madison*, 1:129–30; Pete Maslowski, "National Policy Towards the Use of Black Troops in the Revolution," *South Carolina Historical Magazine* 73 (1972): 4.

9. Wood, "The Dream Deferred," 170; Alan D. Watson, "Impulse Toward Independence: Resistance and Rebellion Among North Carolina Slaves, 1770–1775," *Journal of Negro History* 63 (1978): 324–25.

10. Frey, *Water from the Rock*, 55; Kaplan, "The 'Domestic Insurrections,'" 250.

11. Benjamin Quarles, "Lord Dunmore as Liberator," *WMQ* 15 (1958): 496–97.

12. Wood, "The Dream Deferred," 174; Frey, *Water from the Rock*, 60–61; Sylvia R. Frey, "Between Slavery and Freedom: Virginia Blacks in the American Revolution," *Journal of Southern History* 49 (1983): 377; Philip D. Morgan and Andrew Jackson O'Shaughnessy, "Arming Slaves in the American Revolution," in *Arming Slaves: From Classical Times to the Modern Age*, ed. Christopher L. Brown and Philip D. Morgan (New Haven, CT, 2006), 188.

13. Williamsburg *Virginia Gazette*, September 23, 1775; Frey, *Water from the Rock*, 66–67.

14. Berlin, *Slaves Without Masters*, 16; Broadside, [November 7,] 1775, in John Murray (Earl of Dunmore) Papers, Alderman Library, University of Virginia.

15. Robert Carter Nicholas to the Virginia Delegates in Congress, November 25, 1775, in Jefferson Papers, LC; William Woodford to Edmund Pendleton, December 5, 1775, in *The American Revolution: Writings from the War of Independence*, ed. John Rhodehamel (New York, 2004), 89.

16. Williamsburg *Virginia Gazette*, November 16, 1775; John B. Boles, *Black Southerners, 1619–1869* (Lexington, KY, 1983), 54; Quarles, *Negro in the American Revolution*, 28.

17. Berlin, *Many Thousands Gone*, 257; James Sidbury, *Ploughshares into Swords: Race, Rebellion, and Identity in Gabriel's Virginia, 1730–1810* (New York, 1997), 27.

18. Horton and Horton, *Hard Road*, 67–68; Wood, "The Dream Deferred," 178; Williamsburg *Virginia Herald*, January 6, 1776, March 29, 1776, November 24, 1775.

19. Wood, "Liberty Is Sweet," 169; Wiencek, *An Imperfect God*, 113; "Harry Washington" and "Ralph Henry," both in *The Black Loyalist Directory: African Americans in Exile After the American Revolution*, ed. Graham Russell Hodges (New York, 1996), 196, 112.

20. Quarles, "Lord Dunmore as Liberator," 505; Kolchin, *American Slavery*, 72; Merrill Jensen, *The Founding of a Nation: A History of the American Revolution, 1763–1776* (New York, 1968), 645; Cassandra Pybus, *Epic Journeys of Freedom: Runaway Slaves of the American Revolution and Their Global Quest for Liberty* (Boston, 2006), 19.

21. Gary B. Nash, *First City: Philadelphia and the Forging of Historical Memory* (Philadelphia, 2001), 91; Nash, *Forging Freedom*, 45; Olwell, *Masters, Slaves, and Subjects*, 239, 229; Holton, *Forced Founders*, 153.

22. Judith Van Buskirk, "Crossing the Lines: African Americans in the New York City Region During the British Occupation, 1776–1783," *Pennsylvania History* 65 (1998): 82; Frey, "Virginia Blacks in the American Revolution," 567; Holton, *Forced Founders*, 158–59; Robinson, *Slavery in the Structure of American Politics*, 105; Charles Patrick Neimeyer, *America Goes to War: A Social History of the Continental Army* (New York, 1997), 81.

23. Risjord, *Jefferson's America*, 132–33.

24. Quarles, *Negro in the American Revolution*, viii; Saillant, *Black Puritan, Black Republican*, 57.

25. Quarles, *Negro in the American Revolution*, 79; Neimeyer, *America Goes to War*, 73.

26. Ellis, *His Excellency*, 84; Wiencek, *An Imperfect God*, 201; George Washington to Continental Congress, December 31, 1775, in Washington Papers, LC; Quarles, *Negro in the American Revolution*, 16.

27. Ferling, *John Adams*, 173; Horton and Horton, *Slavery and the Making of America*, 57.

28. Robin Blackburn, *The Overthrow of Colonial Slavery, 1776–1848* (New York, 1988), 114; Horton and Horton, *Slavery and the Making of America*, 63; Lorenzo J. Greene, "Some Observations on the Black Regiment of Rhode Island," *Journal of Negro History* 37 (1952): 149, 167; Quarles, *Negro in the American Revolution*, 60; Fischer, *Washington's Crossing*, 22.

29. Neimeyer, *America Goes to War*, 85.

30. Quarles, *Negro in the American Revolution*, 73; Greene, *Negro in Colonial New England*, 190; Nash, *Unknown American Revolution*, 223.

31. John Shy, *A People Numerous and Armed*, rev. ed. (Ann Arbor, MI, 1990), 238; Melish, *Disowning Slavery*, 67; Neimeyer, *America Goes to War*, 76–77.

32. Horton and Horton, *Hard Road to Freedom*, 69–70; Neimeyer, *America Goes to War*, 32; Greene, "Black Regiment of Rhode Island," 161.

33. Gary B. Nash, *The Forgotten Fifth: African Americans in the Age of Revolution* (Cambridge, MA, 2006), 8; Nash, *Unknown American Revolution*, 229.

34. Thelma Wills Foote, *Black and White Manhattan: The History of Racial Formation in Colonial New York City* (New York, 2004), 213; Harris, *In the Shadow of Slavery*, 54–55.

35. Nash, *Forging Freedom*, 51; Bolster, *Black Jacks*, 153–54; Julie Winch, *A Gentleman of Color: The Life of James Forten* (New York, 2002), 36–37.

36. L. Scott Philyaw, "A Slave for Every Soldier: The Strange History of Virginia's Recruitment Act," *Virginia Magazine of History and Biography* 109 (2001): 376; Tommy L. Bogger, *Free Blacks in Norfolk, Virginia, 1790–1860: The Darker Side of Freedom* (Charlottesville, VA, 1997), 10; Hodges, *Root and Branch*, 144; Miller, *Wolf by the Ears*, 24–25; Malone, *Jefferson the Virginian*, 342–43.

37. Davis, *Problem of Slavery*, 79; Hodges, *Root and Branch*, 144; L. P. Jackson, "Virginia Negro Soldiers and Seamen in the American Revolution," *Journal of Negro History* 27 (1948): 254.

38. Jordan, *White over Black*, 302–3; Horton and Horton, *In Hope of Liberty*, 67.

39. Neimeyer, *America Goes to War*, 71; O'Shaughnessy, *An Empire Divided*, 152–53. Deane was here quoting Dante's *De Monarchia* (*On Monarchy*), 9.3. I am grateful to Professor John McMahon of Le Moyne College for this translation.

40. Ferling, *A Leap in the Dark*, 213; Ira D. Gruber, "Britain's Southern Strategy," in *The Revolutionary War in the South: Power, Conflict, and Leadership: Essays in Honor of John Richard Alden*, ed. W. Robert Higgins (Durham, NC, 1979), 220–21; John Shy, "British Strategy for Pacifying the Southern Colonies, 1778–1781," in *The Southern Experience in the American Revolution*, ed. Jeffrey J. Crow and Larry E. Tise (Chapel Hill, NC, 1978), 160–61; Boles, *Black Southerners*, 55; Frey, *Water from the Rock*, 79–80; Whittington B. Johnson, *Black Savannah, 1788–1864* (Fayetteville, AR, 1996), 7.

41. James Haw, *John and Edward Rutledge of South Carolina* (Athens, GA, 1997), 132; David B. Mattern, *Benjamin Lincoln and the American Revolution* (Columbia, SC, 1995), 97; Fraser, *Charleston*, 158–59.

42. Edward Ball, *Slaves in the Family* (New York, 1998), 222–23; Schama, *Rough Crossings*, 56; James T. Flexner, *George Washington in the American Revolution* (Boston, 1967), 341; Richard J. Hargrove, "Portrait of a Southern Patriot: The Life and Death of John Laurens," in Higgins, *Revolutionary War in the South*, 197; Gregory D. Massey, *John Laurens and the American Revolution* (Columbia, SC, 2000), 93–94.

43. Nash, *Forgotten Fifth*, 174; "Antibiastes," in *Observations on the Slaves and the Indented Servants, Inlisted in the Army, and in the Navy of the United States* (Philadelphia, 1777), n.p.; John Laurens to Henry Laurens, January 14, 1778, in *The Army Correspondence of Colonel John Laurens*, ed. William Gilmore Simms (reprint, New York, 1969), 108–9; John Laurens to Henry Laurens, February 2, 1778, ibid.

44. John Laurens to Henry Laurens, February 17, 1779, in *The Papers of Henry Laurens*, ed. David R. Chesnutt and C. James Taylor (Columbia, SC, 2000), 15:59–60; John Laurens to Henry Laurens, March 10, 1779, ibid., 64–65.

45. Henry Laurens to George Washington, March 16, 1778, in Washington, SC, Papers, LC.

46. George Washington to Henry Laurens, March 20, 1778, in Washington Papers, LC.

47. Massey, *John Laurens*, 132; Wiencek, *An Imperfect God*, 232; Neimeyer, *America Goes to War*, 78.

48. Massey, *John Laurens*, 132–33; Stahr, *John Jay*, 94; Alexander Hamilton to John Laurens, April, 1779, in *The Papers of Alexander Hamilton*, ed. Harold C. Syrett (New York, 1961), 2:35; Alexander Hamilton to John Laurens, May 22, 1779, ibid., 2:52.

49. Quarles, *Negro in the American Revolution*, viii, 63–64; Henry Laurens to John Laurens, August 14, 1776, in Bruns, *Am I Not a Man and a Brother*, 427; Haw, *John and Edward Rutledge*, 165; Fraser, *Charleston*, 154; Arthur H. Shaffer, "Between Two Worlds: David Ramsay and the Politics of Slavery," *Journal of Southern History* 50 (1984): 181; John Laurens to Alexander Hamilton, July 14, 1779, in Syrett, *Papers of Alexander Hamilton*, 2:102–3; Alexander Hamilton to John Laurens, September 11, 1779, ibid.

50. Frey, *Water from the Rock*, 99; Van Buskirk, "Crossing the Lines," 84.

51. Frey, *Water from the Rock*, 113–14; Foote, *Black and White Manhattan*, 215; James W. St. G. Walker, "Blacks as American Loyalists: The Slaves' War for Independence," *Historical Reflections* 2 (1975): 54–55.

52. Henry Clinton, *The American Rebellion*, ed. William B. Willcox (New Haven, CT, 1954), 170–71; Ball, *Slaves in the Family*, 225; Haw, *John and Edward Rutledge*, 132; John Laurens to Henry Laurens, January 27, 1780, and Note 11 in Chesnutt and Taylor, *Papers of Henry Laurens*, 15:232–33; Walter Edgar, *South Carolina: A History* (Columbia, SC, 1998), 235.

53. Nash, *Unknown American Revolution*, 330–31; David Brion Davis, "American Slavery and the American Revolution," in Berlin and Hoffman, *Slavery and Freedom in the Age of the American Revolution*, 271; Charles Cornwallis, Proclamation, July 22, 1780, in Banastre Tarleton, *A History of the Campaigns of 1780 and 1781 in the Southern Provinces of North America* (reprint, New York, 1968), 124–25; Rachel N. Klein, *Unification of a Slave State: The Rise of the Planter Class in the South Carolina Backcountry, 1760–1808* (Chapel Hill, 1990), 105; Wright, *African Americans in the Colonial Era*, 180–81.

54. Van Buskirk, "Crossing the Lines," 83; Pybus, *Epic Journeys of Freedom*, 41.

55. Berlin, *Many Thousands Gone*, 298; Olwell, *Masters, Slaves, and Subjects*, 255; Johann Ewald, *Diary of the American War: A Hessian Journal*, ed. Joseph P. Tustin (New Haven, CT, 1979), 305.

56. Pybus, *Epic Journeys of Freedom*, 24; Nash, *Forging Freedom*, 49; McManus, *Negro Slavery in New York*, 154–55.

57. Jeffrey J. Crow, "Slave Rebelliousness and Social Conflict in North Carolina, 1775 to 1802," *WMQ* 37 (January 1980): 88–89; Horton and Horton, *Slavery and the Making of America*, 58; Blackburn, *Overthrow of Colonial Slavery*, 115; Olwell, *Masters, Slaves, and Subjects*, 248; *Letters of Eliza Wilkinson*, ed. Caroline

Gilman (New York, 1839), 67. Tarleton was demonized as William Tavington in screenwriter Robert Rodat's racist fantasy film *The Patriot*.

58. Quarles, *Negro in the American Revolution*, 152–53; Ewald, *Diary of the American War*, 58, 203; Tarleton, *History of the Campaigns*, 26–27, 353.

59. Olwell, *Masters, Slaves, and Subjects*, 249; Neimeyer, *America Goes to War*, 82; Fraser, *Charleston*, 161; Frey, *Water from the Rock*, 141.

60. Wood, "The Dream Deferred," 173; Frey, *Water from the Rock*, 45; Philip D. Morgan, "Black Society in the Lowcountry, 1760–1810," in Berlin and Hoffman, *Slavery and Freedom in the Age of the American Revolution*, 109; Robert A. Olwell, "'Domestick Enemies': Slavery and Political Independence in South Carolina, May 1775–March 1776," *Journal of Southern History* 55 (1988): 21–48.

61. Berlin, *Many Thousands Gone*, 258–61; Ira Berlin, "Revolution in Black Life," in *The American Revolution: Explorations in the History of American Radicalism*, ed. Alfred F. Young (DeKalb, IL 1984), 355; Mullin, *Flight and Rebellion*, 108.

62. Berlin, *Many Thousands Gone*, 231; Nash, *Forging Freedom*, 47–48; Harris, *In the Shadow of Slavery*, 55; Hodges, *Black Loyalist Directory*, xiv; Hodges, *Root and Branch*, 152.

63. Richard Henry Lee to William Lee, July 15, 1781, in *The Letters of Richard Henry Lee*, ed. James C. Ballagh (reprint, New York, 1970), 242–43; Joseph Atkins, Diary, June 5–July 7, 1781, in Rhodehamel, *American Revolution*, 690; Pybus, *Epic Journeys of Freedom*, 53.

64. Flexner, *George Washington in the American Revolution*, 428–29; Tarleton, *History of the Campaigns*, 302–3; Wiencek, *An Imperfect God*, 243.

65. Frey, *Water from the Rock*, 170–71; Brookhiser, *Founding Father*, 179; Ewald, *Diary of the American War*, 335–36; Ellis, *His Excellency*, 136–37.

66. Hirschfeld, ed., *Washington and Slavery*, 101; Quarles, *Negro in the American Revolution*, 150; Boles, *Black Southerners*, 56; Berlin, *Many Thousands Gone*, 296.

67. Hargrove, "John Laurens," 200; John W. Gordon, *South Carolina and the American Revolution: A Battlefield History* (Columbia, SC, 2003), 172; Massey, *John Laurens*, 226–27; Robinson, *Slavery in the Structure of American Politics*, 109.

68. Willie Lee Rose, "Impact of the American Revolution on the Black Population," in *Legacies of the American Revolution*, ed. Larry R. Gerlach (Logan, UT, 1978), 186.

Chapter 4: Quok Walker's Suit

1. William O'Brien, "Did the Jennison Case Outlaw Slavery in Massachusetts?" *WMQ* 17 (1960): 223; Robert M. Spector, "The Quock Walker Cases: Slavery, Its Abolition, and Negro Citizenship in Early Massachusetts," *Journal of Negro*

History 53 (1968): 12. In various court documents, Quok's forename appears as Cuarco, Quack, Quork, Quaco, Quarko, but most commonly as Quok, which is the spelling I have adopted. I am grateful to Donald R. Wright for his insight into Quok's Akan day-name.

2. William Cushing to the Jury, 1783, in "Commonwealth v. Jennison," in Bruns, *Am I Not a Man and a Brother*, 474; T. H. Breen, "Making History: The Force of Public Opinion and the Last Years of Slavery in Revolutionary Massachusetts," in *Through a Glass Darkly: Reflections on Personal Identity in Early America*, ed. Ronald Hoffman, Mechal Sobel, and Fredrika J. Teute (Chapel Hill, NC, 1997), 94; O'Brien, "Jennison Case," 226.

3. Spector, "Quock Walker Cases," 12; O'Brien, "Jennison Case," 225, 237.

4. Arthur Zilversmit, "Quok Walker, Mumbet, and the Abolition of Slavery in Massachusetts," *WMQ* 25 (1968): 614; Emily Blanck, "Seventeen Eighty-Three: The Turning Point in the Law of Slavery and Freedom in Massachusetts," *New England Quarterly* 75 (2002): 26; O'Brien, "Jennison Case," 225; A. Leon Higginbotham, *In the Matter of Color: Race and the Legal Process, the Colonial Period* (New York, 1978), 91; John D. Cushing, "The Cushing Court and the Abolition of Slavery in Massachusetts: More Notes on the 'Quock Walker Case,'" *American Journal of Legal History* 5 (1961): 119.

5. Leon Litwack, *North of Slavery: The Negro in the Free States* (Chicago, 1961), 6–7; Arthur Zilversmit, *The First Emancipation: The Abolition of Slavery in the North* (Chicago, 1967), 226–29; Nash and Soderlund, *Freedom by Degrees*, 79; Neimeyer, *America Goes to War*, 86.

6. Davis, *Inhuman Bondage*, 156; Melish, *Disowning Slavery*, 82; Horton and Horton, *Hard Road to Freedom*, 73–74.

7. Hodges, *Root and Branch*, 168; Saillant, *Black Puritan, Black Republican*, 50; Davis, *Inhuman Bondage*, 144.

8. Eugene D. Genovese, *The Political Economy of Slavery: Studies in the Economy and Society of the Slave South* (New York, 1961), 10, suggests that it is "a fruitless pursuit" to "weigh economic against ideological factors" in this debate.

9. Vermont Constitution, July 4, 1777, in *Laws of Vermont*, ed. Allen Soule (Montpelier, VT, 1964), 5–8; Nash, *Unknown American Revolution*, 282; Blackburn, *Overthrow of Colonial Slavery*, 117.

10. Higginbotham, *In the Matter of Color*, 302; Nash and Soderlund, *Freedom by Degrees*, 138.

11. Preamble, Constitution of the Society for the Relief of Free Negroes Unlawfully Held in Bondage, April 14, 1775, in Bruns, *Am I Not a Man and a Brother*, 384–85; Nash, *Forging Freedom*, 64–65.

12. *Pennsylvania Gazette*, June 21, 1779, May 31, 1780, in Smith and Wojtowicz, *Blacks Who Stole Themselves*, 135, 137; Billy G. Smith, "Runaway Slaves in the Mid-Atlantic Region During the Revolutionary Era," in *The Transforming*

Hand of Revolution: Reconsidering the American Revolution as a Social Movement, ed. Ronald Hoffman and Peter J. Albert (Charlottesville, VA, 1995), 228–29.

13. Winch, *A Gentleman of Color*, 28–29; Brodsky, *Benjamin Rush*, 298.

14. Nash and Soderlund, *Freedom by Degrees*, 156, 102–3.

15. Nash, *Unknown American Revolution*, 322–23; Zilversmit, *First Emancipation*, 128–29; Bordewich, *Bound for Canaan*, 49.

16. Keane, *Tom Paine*, 194; Francis S. Fox, *Sweet Land of Liberty: The Ordeal of the American Revolution in Northampton County, Pennsylvania* (Philadelphia, 2000), 127.

17. An Act for the Gradual Abolition of Slavery, March 1, 1780, in *The Statutes at Large of Pennsylvania*, ed. William Stanley Ray (Philadelphia, 1904), 10:67–73; Jack Ericson Eblen, "New Estimates of the Vital Rates of the United States Black Population During the Nineteenth Century," *Demography* 11 (May 1974): 306.

18. Nash and Soderlund, *Freedom by Degrees*, 111.

19. Ibid., 110; Nash, *Forging Freedom*, 63; Higginbotham, *In the Matter of Color*, 306.

20. Nash and Soderlund, *Freedom by Degrees*, 115–16; Quaker Petition to the Congress, October 4, 1783, in Bruns, *Am I Not a Man and a Brother*, 501–2.

21. Nash and Soderlund, *Freedom by Degrees*, 124–25; Tench Coxe to David Barclay, March 6, 1787, in Bruns, *Am I Not a Man and a Brother*, 510–12; Edward Needles, *An Historical Memoir of the Pennsylvania Society, for Promoting the Abolition of Slavery* (Philadelphia, 1848), 28–33; Isaacson, *Benjamin Franklin*, 464; Waldstreicher, *Runaway America*, 225.

22. Higginbotham, *In the Matter of Color*, 304–5.

23. Ibid., 99; John Adams to Thomas Jefferson, February 3, 1821, in *The Adams-Jefferson Letters: The Complete Correspondence Between Thomas Jefferson and Abigail and John Adams*, ed. Lester Cappon (Chapel Hill, NC, 1959), 571; John Adams to Jeremy Belknap, March 21, 1795, in Adams Papers, MHS.

24. Petition of Prince Hall, January 13, 1777, in Bruns, *Am I Not a Man and a Brother*, 428–29; Melish, *Disowning Slavery*, 65 (Melish, however, dates this petition as 1771, *before* the Somerset decision); Peter P. Hinks, "John Marrant and the Meaning of Early Black Freemasonry," *WMQ* 64 (January 2007): 106; Lamont D. Thomas, *Paul Cuffe: Black Entrepreneur and Pan-Africanist* (Urbana, 1986), 10; Petition of Paul Cuffe, February 10, 1780, in Bruns, *Am I Not a Man and a Brother*, 454–56.

25. Nash, *Unknown American Revolution*, 290; "Response of Sutton, Massachusetts," May 18, 1778, in *The Popular Sources of Political Authority: Documents on the Massachusetts Constitution of 1780*, ed. Oscar Handlin and Mary Handlin (Cambridge, MA, 1966), 231–32.

26. Greene, *Negro in Colonial New England*, 293–94; Theodore Sedgwick Jr., *The Practicability of the Abolition of Slavery* (New York, 1831), 14; Bethany K.

Dumas, "Elizabeth Freeman," in *American National Biography*, ed. John A. Garraty and Mark Carnes (New York, 1999), 8: 439; Nash, *Forgotten Fifth*, 20–21; Zilversmit, "Abolition of Slavery in Massachusetts," 619.

27. Elaine MacEacheren, "Emancipation in Massachusetts, 1770–1790," *Journal of Negro History* 55 (1970): 291; Zilversmit, "Abolition of Slavery in Massachusetts," 619; Mum Bett Case, Court Decision, August 1781, in Bruns, *Am I Not a Man and a Brother*, 468–70; Sedgwick, *Practicability of the Abolition of Slavery*, 16.

28. Zilversmit, "Abolition of Slavery in Massachusetts," 621–22; Richard E. Welch, *Theodore Sedgwick, Federalist: A Political Biography* (Middletown, CT, 1965), 51.

29. Blanck, "Seventeen Eighty-Three," 26; O'Brien, "Jennison Case," 222, 225–26, 229–30.

30. Higginbotham, *In the Matter of Color*, 92; Cushing, "Cushing Court," 121; Sedgwick, *Practicability of the Abolition of Slavery*, 15; Spector, "Quock Walker Cases," 14–15.

31. Cushing, "Cushing Court," 127 n. 11; Blanck, "Seventeen Eighty-Three," 43–44; O'Brien, "Jennison Case," 233–34.

32. Blanck, "Seventeen Eighty-Three," 44 n. 48; Spector, "Quock Walker Cases," 23, 17.

33. Davis, *Problem of Slavery*, 508 n. 70; Commonwealth v. Jennison, Chief Justice William Cushing to the Jury, April 1783, in Bruns, *Am I Not a Man and a Brother*, 474–75.

34. Blanck, "Seventeen Eighty-Three," 29; MacEacheren, "Emancipation in Massachusetts," 303; Piersen, *Black Yankees*, 30–31.

35. Higginbotham, *In the Matter of Color*, 91, 96–97; Cushing, "Cushing Court," 138; John Adams to Jeremy Belknap, March 21, 1795, in Adams Papers, MHS.

36. Roy Finkenbine, "Belinda's Petition: Reparations for Slavery in Revolutionary Massachusetts," *WMQ* 64 (January 2007): 95–102.

37. Sweet, *Bodies Politic*, 79; Zilversmit, *First Emancipation*, 120–21; Rappleye, *Sons of Providence*, 226.

38. Zilversmit, *First Emancipation*, 122–23; Melish, *Disowning Slavery*, 68–69; Collier, *Roger Sherman's Connecticut*, 194 and n. 2; Roger S. Boardman, *Roger Sherman: Signer and Statesman* (New York, 1971), 200.

39. Melish, *Disowning Slavery*, 66, 76; Quarles, *Negro in the American Revolution*, 48–49; Lawrence Shaw Mayo, *John Langdon of New Hampshire* (Port Washington, NY, 1937), 189–90.

40. Shane White, *Stories of Freedom in Black New York* (Cambridge, MA, 2002), 12–13; Daniel C. Littlefield, "John Jay, the Revolutionary Generation, and Slavery," *New York History* 87 (January 2000): 992; Hodges, *Root and Branch*, 164–65; McManus, *Negro Slavery in New York*, 199–200.

41. Higginbotham, *In the Matter of Color*, 139; William Howard Adams, *Gouverneur Morris: An Independent Life* (New Haven, CT, 2003), 84; Quarles, *Negro in the American Revolution*, 184–85.

42. Littlefield, "John Jay," 93 n. 5; McManus, *Negro Slavery in New York*, 162; Milton Lomask, *Aaron Burr: The Years from Princeton to Vice President, 1756–1805* (New York, 1979), 119–20; David N. Gellman, *Emancipating New York: The Politics of Slavery and Freedom, 1777–1827* (Baton Rouge, LA, 2006), 48; Nancy Isenberg, *Fallen Founder: The Life of Aaron Burr* (New York, 2007), 90.

43. Patrick Rael, "The Long Death of Slavery," in *Slavery in New York*, ed. Ira Berlin and Leslie Harris (New York, 2005), 123; McManus, *Negro Slavery in New York*, 162; Gellman, *Emancipating New York*, 48–49.

44. Joyce Appleby, *Inheriting the Revolution: The First Generation of Americans* (Cambridge, MA, 2000), 45; Gellman, *Emancipating New York*, 50; John Kaminski, *George Clinton: Yeoman Politician of the New Republic* (Lanham, MD, 1993), 206, 320–21 n. 54.

45. Higginbotham, *In the Matter of Color*, 140; McManus, *Negro Slavery in New York*, 168–69.

46. Harris, *In the Shadow of Slavery*, 56; Paul A. Gilje and Howard B. Rock, "Sweep O! Sweep O!: African American Chimney Sweeps and Citizenship in the New Nation," *WMQ* 51 (July 1994): 518–19; Rules of the New York Manumission Society, 1785, in Bruns, *Am I Not a Man and a Brother*, 504–6.

47. Stahr, *John Jay*, 236–39; John Jay to the President of the English Society for Promoting the Manumission of Slaves, June 1788, in *The Correspondence and Public Papers of John Jay*, ed. Henry P. Johnston (New York, 1893), 3: 340–44; White, *Somewhat More Independent*, 81; Littlefield, "John Jay and Slavery," 103.

48. Ron Chernow, *Alexander Hamilton* (New York, 2004), 210–14; Rob Weston, "Alexander Hamilton and the Abolition of Slavery in New York," *Afro-Americans in New York Life and History* 18 (1994): 31–45; Alexander Hamilton to John Jay, March 14, 1779, in Syrett, *Papers of Alexander Hamilton*, 2:17–18; Alexander Hamilton to George Clinton, May 22, 1781, ibid., 2:642–43.

49. Chernow, *Hamilton*, 215.

50. Littlefield, "John Jay and Slavery," 91; Stahr, *John Jay*, 346; Hodges, *Root and Branch*, 188; John H. Hewitt, "Peter Williams, Jr.: New York's First African-American Episcopal Priest," *New York History* 79 (April 1998): 102–3; Chernow, *Hamilton*, 735, argues that the "paucity of evidence" regarding William Hamilton's paternity makes the "matter too tenuous to merit inclusion in the text," but in the wake of the Jefferson-Hemings DNA test, historians might not wish to be as quick in discounting the oral traditions of black American families.

51. Harris, *In the Shadow of Slavery*, 68; Judith Van Buskirk, "Crossing the Lines," 83; Gellman, *Emancipating New York*, 160; *New Jersey Gazette*,

August 28, 1782, *New York Gazette*, July 17, 1782, in *Pretends to be Free: Runaway Slave Advertisements from Colonial and Revolutionary New York and New Jersey*, ed. Graham Russell Hodges and Alan Brown (New York, 1994), 274, 270.

52. Gellman, *Emancipating New York*, 70–71; White, *Somewhat More Independent*, 46, 27; Davis, *Inhuman Bondage*, 153, McManus, *Negro Slavery in New York*, 200.

53. Higginbotham, *In the Matter of Color*, 141; Zilversmit, *First Emancipation*, 150–51.

54. Rael, "Long Death of Slavery," 124; Kaminski, *George Clinton*, 204–5; Stahr, *John Jay*, 370–71.

55. Lomask, *Burr*, 209; Chernow, *Hamilton*, 581.

56. McManus, *Negro Slavery in New York*, 174–75; Gellman, *Emancipating New York*, 185; Hodges, *Root and Branch*, 170; Stahr, *John Jay*, 347.

57. White, *Somewhat More Independent*, 38; Hodges, *Root and Branch*, 191; Rael, "Long Death of Slavery," 133.

58. Horton and Horton, *In Hope of Liberty*, 73; William Livingston to Samuel Allinson, July 25, 1778, in Bruns, *Am I Not a Man and a Brother*, 442–43; Zilversmit, *First Emancipation*, 152–53.

59. Wright, "Moving Toward Breaking the Chains," 131; David Cooper, *A Serious Address to the Rulers of America*, in Nash, *Race and Revolution*, 117–18; Zilversmit, *First Emancipation*, 152, 145.

60. Hodges, *Slavery and Freedom*, 135–36, 148–49.

61. Matthew Mason, *Slavery and Politics in the Early American Republic* (Chapel Hill, NC, 2006), 14; John Adams to George Churchman, January 24, 1801, in Adams Papers, MHS; Melish, *Disowning Slavery*, 76–77; Berlin, *Many Thousands Gone*, 228; Alfred F. Young, "Afterward: How Radical Was the American Revolution?" in Young, *Beyond the American Revolution*, 339.

62. Mason, *Slavery and Politics*, 26; Jordan, *White over Black*, 282.

63. Melish, *Disowning Slavery*, 75; Spector, "Quock Walker Cases," 29; Greene, *Negro in Colonial New England*, 301.

64. Horton and Horton, *Hard Road to Freedom*, 74; Davis, *Inhuman Bondage*, 152.

Chapter 5: Absalom's "Meritorious Service"

1. Nash, *Forging Freedom*, 67; Anne B. Allen, "A Voice to Counter Public Opinion: Absalom Jones, 1746–1818," *The Living Church*, February 11, 1990, 8.

2. Nash, *Forging Freedom*, 68; Ann C. Lammers, "The Rev. Absalom Jones and the Episcopal Church: Christian Theology and Black Consciousness in a New Alliance," *Historical Magazine of the Protestant Episcopal Church* 51 (1982): 163.

3. Nash, *Forging Freedom*, 68; Donald S. Armentrout, "Absalom Jones," in Garraty and Carnes, *American National Biography*, 12:176; Williams, *Slavery and Freedom in Delaware*, 220.

4. Armentrout, "Absalom Jones," 12:176; Nash, *Forging Freedom*, 68; Allen, "Absalom Jones," 8.

5. Nash, *Forging Freedom*, 68; Kolchin, *American Slavery*, 87–89; Thomas Jefferson to John Holmes, April 22, 1820, in Jefferson Papers, LC.

6. Essah, *House Divided*, 25, 39–41.

7. Ibid., 40–41, 48.

8. Williams, *Slavery and Freedom in Delaware*, 145; Milton E. Flower, *John Dickinson: Conservative Revolutionary* (Charlottesville, VA, 1983), 200–201.

9. Essah, *House Divided*, 102–3, 7.

10. Berlin, *Many Thousands Gone*, 264; Whitman, *The Price of Freedom*, 10–13.

11. Phillips, *Freedom's Port*, 16; Kolchin, *American Slavery*, 74; Barbara Jeanne Fields, *Slavery and Freedom on the Middle Ground: Maryland During the Nineteenth Century* (New Haven, CT, 1985), 5; Robert J. Brugger, *Maryland, A Middle Temperament: 1634–1980* (Baltimore, 1988), 159.

12. Matthew Frye Jacobson, *Whiteness of a Different Color: European Immigrants and the Alchemy of Race* (Cambridge, MA, 1998), 27; Nash, *Race and Revolution*, 19; Paul S. Clarkson and R. Samuel Jett, *Luther Baldwin of Maryland* (Baltimore, 1970), 164–65.

13. Fields, *Slavery and Freedom on the Middle Ground*, 5; Phillips, *Freedom's Port*, 16; Whitman, *Price of Freedom*, 67.

14. Jean B. Lee, *The Price of Nationhood: The American Revolution in Charles County* (New York, 1994), 208–9.

15. Richard S. Dunn, "Black Society in the Chesapeake, 1776–1810," in Berlin and Hoffman, *Slavery and Freedom in the Age of the American Revolution*, 62–63; Berlin, *Slaves Without Masters*, 46–47; Fields, *Slavery and Freedom on the Middle Ground*, 1; Nash, *Unknown American Revolution*, 416–17.

16. Frey, *Water from the Rock*, 218–19; Edmund S. Morgan, *Challenge of the American Revolution* (New York, 1976), 142; Jeff Broadwater, *George Mason, Forgotten Founder* (Chapel Hill, 2006), 36; Mullin, *Flight and Rebellion*, 126; Dunn, "Black Society in the Chesapeake," 79.

17. Allen Kulikoff, "Uprooted Peoples: Black Migrants in the Age of the American Revolution, 1790–1820," in Berlin and Hoffman, *Slavery and Freedom in the Age of the American Revolution*, 145; Cassandra Pybus, "Jefferson's Faulty Math: The Question of Slave Defections in the American Revolution," *WMQ* 62 (April 2005): 263–64; McColley, *Slavery and Jeffersonian Virginia*, 80–83; Frey, *Water from the Rock*, 210–11.

18. Berlin, *Generations of Captivity*, 112; Berlin, "Revolution in Black Life," 358–59; Wright, *African Americans in the Colonial Era*, 187; Deyle, *Carry Me Back*, 21.

19. Edmund S. Morgan, *American Slavery, American Freedom: The Ordeal of Colonial Virginia* (New York, 1975), 385.

20. Melvin Patrick Ely, *Israel on the Appomattox: A Southern Experiment in Black Freedom from the 1790s Through the Civil War* (New York, 2004), 23; Saillant, *Black Puritan, Black Republican*, 57; Kulikoff, *Tobacco and Slaves: The Development of Southern Cultures in the Chesapeake*, 419; Richard Henry Lee to James Monroe, January 5, 1784, in Ballagh, *The Letters of Richard Henry Lee*, 2:286.

21. Robert D. Meade, *Patrick Henry: Patriot in the Making* (Philadelphia, 1957), 299–300; Eva Sheppard Wolf, *Race and Liberty in the New Nation: Emancipation in Virginia from the Revolution to Nat Turner's Rebellion* (Baton Rouge, LA, 2006), 18.

22. Berlin, *Many Thousands Gone*, 259; Ralph Ketcham, *James Madison: A Biography* (New York, 1971), 148–49; Littlefield, "John Jay and Slavery," 125–26.

23. Ellis, *Founding Brothers*, 114; Mason, *Slavery and Politics*, 19; François Furstenberg, *In the Name of the Father: Washington's Legacy, Slavery, and the Making of a Nation* (New York, 2006), 90.

24. Broadwater, *George Mason, Forgotten Father*, 36; Larry E. Tise, *The American Counterrevolution: A Retreat from Liberty, 1783–1800* (Mechanicsburg, PA, 1998), 449; Thomas Jefferson, *Notes on the State of Virginia*, in *Jefferson: Writings*, ed. Merrill Peterson (New York, 1984), 265; McColley, *Slavery and Jeffersonian Virginia*, 120.

25. Wolf, *Race and Liberty*, 9, 32; Andrew Levy, *The First Emancipator: The Forgotten Story of Robert Carter, the Founding Father Who Freed His Slaves* (New York, 2005), 117–18; Kolchin, *American Slavery*, 89.

26. Wolf, *Race and Liberty*, 56–57; Nash, *Unknown American Revolution*, 433; Frederick County Petition, November 8, 1785, in Bruns, *Am I Not a Man and a Brother*, 506–7; James Madison to George Washington, November 11, 1785, in Washington Papers, LC.

27. Williamsburg *Virginia Gazette*, May 13, 1780, August 19, 1780, August 21, 1778, January 29, 1780, December 18, 1784.

28. Herbert Aptheker, *American Negro Slave Revolts*, 50th Anniversary Ed. (New York, 1993) 206; Petitions of a Court of Oyer and Terminer, May 8, 1781, in Legislative Petitions, Prince William County, Record Group 78, LV.

29. Robert Rutland, *George Mason: Reluctant Statesman* (New York, 1961), 53–54; George Mason, "Virginia Declaration of Rights, 1776," in Rutland, *Papers of George Mason*, 1:274–76; Broadwater, *George Mason, Forgotten Father*, 84.

30. Thomas Jefferson, "Bill to Prevent the Importation of Slaves," June 16, 1777, in *The Papers of Thomas Jefferson*, ed. Julian P. Boyd (Princeton, NJ, 1950), 2:22–23; Deyle, *Carry Me Back*, 25.

31. Robin L. Einhorn, *American Taxation, American Slavery* (Chicago, 2006), 47; Richard Henry Lee to George Washington, September 17, 1781, Washington Papers, LC; George Mason, "A Bill to Compensate Citizens for Enemy Damage," May 19, 1779, in *Papers of Mason*, 2:502.

32. Quarles, *Negro in the American Revolution*, 108; Kulikoff, *Tobacco and Slaves*; Richard Henry Lee to Henry Laurens, July 10, 1780, in Ballagh, *The Letters of Richard Henry Lee*, 2:187.

33. Wolf, *Race and Liberty*, 28.

34. Levy, *First Emancipator*, 101; "An Act to Authorize the Manumission of Slaves," May 1782, in *The Statutes at Large; Being a Collection of All the Laws of Virginia*, ed. William Waller Hening (Richmond, VA, 1823), 11:39–40.

35. Bogger, *Free Blacks in Norfolk*, 10; Quarles, Negro *in the American Revolution*, 185, 194.

36. Bernstein, *Thomas Jefferson*, 40; Jordan, *White over Black*, 347; Jefferson, *Notes on the State of Virginia*, in Peterson, *Jefferson: Writings*, 264; Finkelman, "Jefferson and Slavery: 'Treason Against the Hopes of the World," in Onuf, *Jeffersonian Legacies*, 196; John R. Alden, *The South in the Revolution, 1763–1789* (Baton Rouge, 1962), 334; Robinson, *Slavery in the Structure of American Politics*, 94; John Ferling, *Setting the World Ablaze: Washington, Adams, Jefferson, and the American Revolution* (New York, 2000), 162.

37. Levy, *First Emancipator*, 118, suggests the 1783 proposal was "another," that is, a second "emancipation plan"; Jefferson, *Notes on the State of Virginia*, in Peterson, *Jefferson: Writings*, 264; Thomas Jefferson, "Draft for a Constitution for Virginia," 1783, in Boyd, *Papers of Thomas Jefferson*, 6:298.

38. James Madison, "Memorandum on an African Colony for Freed Slaves," October 20, 1789, in *Papers of James Madison*, 12:437–38; William Freehling, *Road to Disunion*, 126–27; Ellis, *American Sphinx*, 148.

39. The historian in question was C. Vann Woodward, "A Few Words About Jefferson and Madison on Slavery," *Journal of Blacks in Higher Education* 9 (1995): 50; Davis, *Problem of Slavery*, 89; Wolf, *Race and Liberty*, 54–55.

40. Wolf, *Race and Liberty*, 72–75; Eric Burin, "Manumission," in *Encyclopedia of Antislavery and Abolition*, ed. Peter Hinks and John McKivigan (Westport, CT, 2007), 456–61; Sidbury, *Ploughshares Into Swords*, 224; Bogger, *Free Blacks in Norfolk*, 12–13.

41. Bogger, *Free Blacks in Norfolk*, 14; Michael L. Nichols, "Strangers Among Us: The Sources and Challenge of the Urban Free Black Population of Early Virginia," *Virginia Magazine of History and Biography* 108 (2000): 165; Wolf, *Race and Liberty*, 48–49.

42. Wolf, *Race and Liberty*, 44; Morgan, *Slave Counterpoint*, 665; McColley, *Slavery and Jeffersonian Virginia*, 147.

43. Levy, *First Emancipator*, 144–45, 150–51.

44. Madison, "Memorandum on an African Colony," 437; Jefferson, *Notes on the State of Virginia*, in Peterson, *Jefferson: Writings*, 264; Levy, *First Emancipator*, 144, 147, 150.

45. Kolchin, *American Slavery*, 81; Berlin, *Slaves Without Masters*, 46–47.

46. Ellis, *Founding Brothers*, 105; Fernando Fairfax, "Plan for Liberating the Negroes within the United States," *American Museum* (December 1790): 285–87.

47. McColley, *Slavery and Jeffersonian Virginia*, 132–33; Charles T. Cullen, *St. George Tucker and Law in Virginia, 1772–1804* (New York, 1987), 150.

48. St. George Tucker to Jeremy Belknap, January 24, 1795, in *Massachusetts Historical Society Collections, Fifth Series* (reprint, Boston, 1835), 3:379–81; James Sullivan to Jeremy Belknap, July 30, 1795, ibid., 3:412–15.

49. St. George Tucker to Jeremy Belknap, June 29, 1795, in *Massachusetts Historical Society Collections, Fifth Series*, 3:407–10; St. George Tucker, *A Dissertation on Slavery: With a Proposal for the Gradual Abolition of It, in the State of Virginia* (Philadelphia, 1796), 91–94.

50. Tucker, *Dissertation on Slavery*, 82–83, 93–103; McColley, *Slavery and Jeffersonian Virginia*, 54, first made the point about the connection between abundant lands in the West and the inability of planters to replace slaves with white tenants.

51. *Journal of the House of Delegates of Virginia* (Richmond, VA, 1797), 52; St. George Tucker to Thomas Jefferson, August 2, 1797, in Jefferson Papers, LC; Thomas Jefferson to St. George Tucker, August 28, 1797, ibid.

52. *Minutes of the Proceedings of the Fourth Convention of Delegates from the Abolition Societies* (Philadelphia, 1797), 39; Richard S. Newman, *The Transformation of American Abolitionism: Fighting Slavery in the Early Republic* (Chapel Hill, NC, 2001), 34; Jordan, *White over Black*, 348; Ely, *Israel on the Appomattox*, 35.

53. Mason, *Slavery and Politics*, 20; Philip Hamilton, "Revolutionary Principles and Family Loyalties: Slavery's Transformation in the St. George Tucker Household of Early National Virginia," *WMQ* 58 (1998): 537.

54. Davis, "American Slavery and the American Revolution," 273; Frey, *Water from the Rock*, 223; Levy, *First Emancipator*, 121; Roger G. Kennedy, *Mr. Jefferson's Lost Cause: Land, Farmers, Slavery, and the Louisiana Purchase* (New York, 2003), 77; David Meade to Joseph Prentis, July 23, 1801, in Prentis Family Papers, University of Virginia.

55. Wiencek, *An Imperfect God*, 5; Berlin, *Generations of Captivity*, 116–17; Berlin, *Many Thousands Gone*, 263.

56. Genovese, *Roll, Jordan, Roll*, 5; Philip Morgan, "Three Planters and Their Slaves: Perspectives on Slavery in Virginia, South Carolina, and Jamaica, 1750–1790," in *Race and Family in the Colonial South*, ed. Winthrop Jordan and Sheila Skemp (Jackson, MS, 1987), 39–40; Frey, *Water from the Rock*, 264–66; Thomas Jefferson to Edward Bancroft, January 26, 1789, Jefferson Papers, LC.

57. Miller, *Wolf by the Ears*, 14; Morgan, *Slave Counterpoint*, 662–63; Morgan, *American Slavery, American Freedom*, 376, 380–81.

58. Wood, *The Radicalism of the American Revolution*, 7–8, 186; Alfred F. Young, "Historians Confront 'The Transforming Hand of Revolution,'" in Hoffman and Albert, *The Transforming Hand of Revolution*, 488.

59. Ferling, *Setting the World Ablaze*, 275; Brookhiser, *Founding Father*, 180; Ellis, *His Excellency*, 257–63; Ferling, *The First of Men*, 502; Smith, *Patriarch*, 346.

60. Brookhiser, *Founding Father*, 180; Ellis, *His Excellency*, 166; Nash, *Forgotten Fifth*, 70.

61. Ellis, *His Excellency*, xii; Blackburn, *American Revolution*, 121; Thomas Jefferson to Richard Price, August 7, 1785, in Jefferson Papers, LC.

Chapter 6: Captain Vesey's Cargo

1. Stephen C. Crane to John Lofton, January 27, 1983, in Denmark Vesey File, South Carolina Historical Society; Levinus Clarkson to David Van Horne, March 1, 1775, in *Naval Documents of the American Revolution*, ed. William J. Morgan (Washington, DC, 1964–80), 1:118–19; Land Deed, February 1774, JM Plats, #6346, South Carolina Department of Archives and History (hereafter SCDAH).

2. Fraser, *Charleston*, 139–41; William Henry Drayton to Joseph Vesey, November 4, 1775, in Morgan, *Naval Documents*, 2:889.

3. Henry Laurens to Joseph Vesey, January 5, 1776, in Morgan, *Naval Documents*, 3:647–48; John Paul Jones to Robert Morris, January 21, 1777, in *The Life and Letters of John Paul Jones*, ed. Anna DeKoven (New York, 1913), 131–32; Sloop *Adriana*, in *Naval Records of the American Revolution, 1775–1788* (Washington, DC, 1906), 220.

4. Brig *Prospect*, in *Naval Records*, 421; James Hamilton, *An Account of the Late Intended Insurrection Among a Portion of the Blacks of the City* (Charleston, SC, 1822), 17; Lydia Maria Child to Thomas Wentworth Higginson, March 17, 1860, in William Palmer Collection, Western Reserve Historical Society. Philip D. Morgan, "Conspiracy Scares," *WMQ* 59 (January 2002): 161–62, incorrectly describes Vesey as a mulatto; the source he cites, Archibald H. Grimké, *Right on the Scaffold, or, The Martyrs of 1822* (Washington, DC, 1901), 3, describes Vesey only as "black."

5. Schooner *Active*, December 11, 1786, Duties on Trade at Charleston, Manifests and Entries, December 11, 1786, SCDAH.

6. Berlin, *Many Thousands Gone*, 304.

7. Frey, *Water from the Rock*, 207; Rawlins Lowndes to John Laurens, December 24, 1778, in Chesnutt and Taylor, *Papers of Henry Laurens*, 15:10–11; Henry Laurens to William Read, February 9, 1779, ibid., 15:55; Henry Laurens to William Manning, February 22, 1783, ibid., 16:153.

8. John Lewis Gervais to Henry Laurens, September 27, 1782, in Chesnutt and Taylor, *Papers of Henry Laurens*, 16:30–31; Jeffrey R. Young, *Domesticating Slavery: The Master Class in Georgia and South Carolina, 1670–1837* (Chapel Hill, NC, 1999), 73, 78; Aptheker, *American Negro Slave Revolts*, 204; Wood, "The Dream Deferred," 175–79.

9. Darold D. Wax, "'New Negroes Are Always in Demand': The Slave Trade in Eighteenth Century Georgia," *Georgia Historical Quarterly* 68 (Summer 1984): 214; Schama, *Rough Crossings*, 97; Frey, *Water from the Rock*, 174.

10. Berlin, *Many Thousands Gone*, 304; Frey, *Water from the Rock*, 174, 207; Schama, *Rough Crossings*, 105.

11. Eldon Jones, "The British Withdrawal from the South, 1781–1785," in Higgins, *Revolutionary War in the South*, 268; Kolchin, *American Slavery*, 73.

12. Nash, *Forgotten Fifth*, 44–45; Robert G. Mitchell, "The Losses and Compensation of Georgia Loyalists," *Georgia Historical Quarterly* 68 (Summer 1984): 239; Landers, *Black Society in Spanish Florida*, 66–67.

13. Klein, *Unification of a Slave State*, 118–19; Hugh F. Rankin, *Francis Marion: The Swamp Fox* (New York, 1973), 287; Sue Montes, "Post-Revolutionary Recognition: Slave Honored as 'African American Patriot' at Capitol," *Washington Post*, December 16, 2006, A01.

14. Olwell, *Masters, Slaves, and Subjects*, 276–77; Ben Marsh, "Women and the American Revolution in Georgia," *Georgia Historical Quarterly* 88 (Summer 2004): 161; David S. Cecelski, "The Shores of Freedom: The Maritime Underground Railroad in North Carolina, 1800–1861," *North Carolina Historical Review* 71 (April 1994): 178.

15. Morgan, *Slave Counterpoint*, 666.

16. Walter Edgar, *South Carolina: A History* (Columbia, 1998), 244–46; Fraser, *Charleston*, 173; Klein, *Unification of a Slave State*, 114–15; Wood, *Slavery in Colonial Georgia*, 203.

17. *South Carolina Gazette*, September 16, September 27, 1783; Henry Laurens to William Drayton, February 23, 1783, in Chesnutt and Taylor, *Papers of Henry Laurens*, 16:156; Wax, "New Negroes Are Always in Demand," 214–15; James A. McMillin, *The Final Victims: Foreign Slave Trade to North America, 1783–1810* (Columbia, SC, 2004), 8–9.

18. Deyle, *Carry Me Back*, 18; Henry Laurens to James Bourdieu, February 6, 1783, in Chesnutt and Taylor, *Papers of Henry Laurens*, 16:143–44; Haw, *John and Edward Rutledge*, 192.

19. McMillin, *Final Victims*, 91–92; Henry Laurens to John Owen, August 9, 1783, in Chesnutt and Taylor, *Papers of Henry Laurens*, 16:259.

20. Governor John Rutledge to Delegates in Congress, May 14, 1780, in *Papers of Laurens*, 15:295; McMillin, *Final Victims*, 76–77; Henry Laurens to Richard Price, February 1, 1785, in Chesnutt and Taylor, *Papers of Henry Laurens*, 16:533.

21. Daniel C. Littlefield, *Rice and Slaves: Ethnicity and the Slave Trade in Colonial South Carolina* (reprint, Urbana, IL, 1991), 110; Walter E. Minchinton, "The Seaborne Slave Trade of North Carolina," *North Carolina Historical Review* 71 (January 1994): 17; Jordan, *White over Black*, 366–76.

22. McMillin, *Final Victims*, 10; Shaffer, "Between Two Worlds," 185.

23. Shaffer, "Between Two Worlds," 186; Jordan, *White over Black*, 373; McMillin, *Final Victims*, 12–13; Fraser, *Charleston*, 188.

24. Frey, *Water from the Rock*, 213; McMillin, *Final Victims*, 31–32.

25. Wood, "Until He Shall Be Dead, Dead, Dead," 397; Jones, *Born a Child of Freedom*, 76–77; William Hasell Wilson, *Reminiscences of William Hasell Wilson*, ed. Elizabeth B. Pharo (Philadelphia, 1937), 8; Karl Bernhard, *Travels Through North America* (Philadelphia, 1828), 2:10.

26. Nash, *Forgotten Fifth*, 72; Petition of Ned Griffin, April 4, 1784, in *A Documentary History of the Negro People in the United States*, ed. Herbert Aptheker (New York, 1951), 5.

27. Crow, "Slave Rebelliousness," *WMQ* 37 (January 1980): 90–91; Klein, *Unification of a Slave State*, 273.

28. Horton and Horton, *Hard Road to Freedom*, 74; Jordan, *White over Black*, 350–51.

29. Greene, "Slavery or Independence," 206; Papenfuse, *Evils of Necessity*, 14; Brodsky, *Benjamin Rush*, 266.

30. Shaffer, "Between Two Worlds," 191–92; Arthur H. Shaffer, "David Ramsay and the Limits of Revolutionary Nationalism," in *Intellectual Life in Antebellum Charleston*, ed. Michael O'Brien and David Moltke-Hansen (Knoxville, TN, 1986), 71.

31. Kolchin, *American Slavery*, 75; Wright, *African Americans in the Colonial Era*, 184; Morgan, "Black Society in the Lowcountry," 124–25.

32. Goldstone, *Dark Bargain*, 69; Alex Bontemps, *The Punished Self: Surviving Slavery in the Colonial South* (Ithaca, NY, 2001), 71; Richard C. Wade, *Slavery in the Cities: The South, 1820–1860* (New York, 1964), 20.

33. Kolchin, *American Slavery*, 110; John Campbell, "As 'A Kind of Freeman'?: Slaves' Market-Related Activities in the South Carolina Up Country, 1800–1860," in *Labor and the Shaping of Slave Life in the Americas*, ed. Ira Berlin and Philip D. Morgan (Charlottesville, VA, 1993), 243; Robert Olwell, " 'Loose, Idle, and Disorderly': Slave Women in the Eighteenth Century Charleston Marketplace," in *More Than Chattel: Black Women and Slavery in the Americas*, ed. David Barry Gaspar and Darlene Clark Hine (Bloomington, IN, 1996), 99–100.

34. Negro Act, 1740, in Brevard, *An Alphabetical Digest*, 2:248–49; Wade, *Slavery in the Cities*, 143.

35. Loren Schweninger, "Slave Independence and Enterprise in South Carolina, 1780–1865," *South Carolina Historical Magazine* 93 (April 1992): 105; "A Narrative of the Conspiracy," in *An Official Report of the Trial of Sundry Negroes*, ed. Lionel Kennedy and Thomas Parker (Charleston, SC, 1822), 38–39.

36. Schweninger, "Slave Independence and Enterprise," 106; Campbell, "As 'A Kind of Freeman,' " 271.

37. Robert Olwell, "'A Reckoning of Accounts': Patriarchy, Market Relations, and Control on Henry Laurens's Lowcountry Plantations, 1762–1785," in *Working Toward Freedom: Slave Society and Domestic Economy in the American South*, ed. Larry E. Hudson Jr. (Rochester, NY, 1994), 38; Philip D. Morgan, "The Ownership of Property by Slaves in Mid-Nineteenth Century Low Country," *Journal of Southern History* 49 (August 1983): 410.

38. Petition of Catherine Faber, November 18, 1822, General Assembly Petitions, 1822, SCDAH; Wade, *Slavery in the Cities*, 148; Boles, *Black Southerners*, 129.

39. Betty Wood, *Women's Work, Men's Work: The Informal Slave Economies of Lowcountry Georgia* (Athens, GA, 1995), 107; Wade, *Slavery in the Cities*, 33, 37–38, 45; Boles, *Black Southerners*, 126.

40. Wood, *Women's Work, Men's Work*, 118; Ira Berlin and Herbert G. Gutman, "Natives and Immigrants, Free Men and Slaves: Urban Workingmen in the Antebellum American South," *American Historical Review* 88 (December 1983): 1185–86.

41. *Charleston Directory and Stranger's Guide* (Charleston, SC, 1819), 47, 49; John Potter to Langdon Cheves, July 15, 1822, Cheves Papers, South Carolina Historical Society.

42. Wood, *Black Majority*, 205; Wade, *Slavery in the Cities*, 38.

43. Clement Eaton, "Slave-Hiring in the Upper South: A Step Toward Freedom," *Mississippi Valley Historical Review* 46 (March 1960): 677–78; Mary Beth Corrigan, "'It's a Family Affair': Buying Freedom in the District of Columbia, 1850–1860," in Hudson, *Working Toward Freedom*, 168.

44. Berlin and Gutman, "Natives and Immigrants," 1187; Wood, *Women's Work, Men's Work*, 107; Petition of Naomi Smith, November 16, 1822, General Assembly Petitions, 1822, SCDAH.

45. Morgan, *Slave Counterpoint*, 250; Wood, *Women's Work, Men's Work*, 117; Corrigan, "It's a Family Affair," 168.

46. Schweninger, "Slave Independence and Enterprise," 114; Loren Schweninger, *Black Property Owners in the South, 1790–1915* (Urbana, IL, 1990), 48–49; Bernard E. Powers Jr., *Black Charlestonians: A Social History, 1822–1885* (Fayetteville, AR, 1994), 14; Olwell, "Loose, Idle, and Disorderly," 103.

47. Wood, *Black Majority*, 216–17; Schweninger, "Slave Independence and Enterprise," 107.

48. Wood, *Women's Work, Men's Work*, 129; Schweninger, "Slave Independence and Enterprise," 114–15.

49. "Negro Act," 1740, in Brevard, *An Alphabetical Digest*, 2:243; Wade, *Slavery in the Cities*, 74–75.

50. Klein, *Unification of a Slave State*, 273; "An Act Respecting Slaves, Free Negroes, Mulattoes, and Mestizoes," December 20, 1800, in *Statutes at Large*, 7:440–43.

51. Berlin, *Slaves Without Masters*, 47; W. Augustus Low, ed., *Encyclopedia of Black America* (New York, 1981), 764.

52. Charleston *City Gazette*, October 1, 1799, November 9, 1799; Emancipation Deed, December 31, 1799, in Miscellaneous Records, Vol. 3M, pages 427–28, SCDAH; for Vesey's conspiracy and execution, see Egerton, *He Shall Go Out Free: The Lives of Denmark Vesey*, 2nd ed. (Lanham, MD, 2004), ch. 6–8.

Chapter 7: *Mum Bett Takes a Name*

1. Welch, *Theodore Sedgwick*, 51; Nash, *Unknown American Revolution*, 409. On the way that the process of "social childbirth" worked as a prelude to professional midwifery, see Laurel Thatcher Ulrich, *A Midwife's Tale: The Life of Martha Ballard, Based on Her Diary, 1785–1812* (New York, 1990), 11, 46–49.

2. David Levering Lewis, *W. E. B. Du Bois: Biography of a Race, 1868–1919* (New York, 1993), 13–14; W. E. B. Du Bois, *Dusk of Dawn*, in *W. E. B. Du Bois: Writings*, ed. Nathan Huggins (New York, 1986), 561.

3. Welch, *Theodore Sedgwick*, 51; Gary B. Nash and Graham Russell Gao Hodges, *Friends of Liberty: Thomas Jefferson, Tadeusz Kościuszko, and Agrippa Hull* (New York, 2008), 92; Lewis, *Du Bois,* 14.

4. Nash, *Unknown American Revolution*, 409.

5. "Preamble," Philadelphia Free African Society, April 12, 1787, in R. R. Wright, *The Negro in Pennsylvania* (Philadelphia, 1918), 31.

6. Litwack, *North of Slavery*, 12–13; Risjord, *Jefferson's America*, 182.

7. Berlin, *Slaves Without Masters*, 48–50; Kolchin, *American Slavery*, 82–83.

8. White, *Somewhat More Independent*, 173; Van Buskirk, "Crossing the Lines," 75; Barnet Schecter, *The Battle for New York* (New York, 2002), 276.

9. Horton and Horton, *In Hope of Liberty*, 84; Nash, "Emancipation in Northern Seaport Cities," in Berlin and Hoffman, *Slavery and Freedom in the Age of the American Revolution*, 30–31, 35.

10. Thomas Jefferson to Jared Sparks, February 4, 1824, in Jefferson Papers, LC; Norton, Gutman, and Berlin, "Afro-American Family," in Berlin and Hoffman, *Slavery and Freedom in the Age of the American Revolution*, 190.

11. Hirschfeld, *Washington and Slavery*, 108; Charles Joyner, *Down by the Riverside: A South Carolina Slave Community* (Urbana, IL, 1984), 221; Berlin, "Revolution in Black Life," 80.

12. Kathryn Grover, *The Fugitive's Gibraltar: Escaping Slaves and Abolitionism in New Bedford, Massachusetts* (Amherst, MA, 2001), 48–49; Schwartz, *Born in Bondage*, 168–70; Van Buskirk, "Crossing the Lines," 93; White, *Somewhat More Independent*, 193; Berlin, "Revolution in Black Life," 363–64.

13. Nash, "Emancipation in Northern Seaport Cities," 21; Lee, *Price of Nationhood*, 208–10; John C. Inscoe, "Generation and Gender as Reflected in Carolina

Slave Naming Practices: A Challenge to the Gutman Thesis," *South Carolina Historical Magazine* 94 (October 1993): 262–63.

14. Nash and Soderlund, *Freedom by Degrees*, 172; Marc W. Kruman, *Between Authority and Liberty: State Constitution Making in Revolutionary America* (Chapel Hill, NC, 1997), 106; Kolchin, *American Slavery*, 82.

15. Patrick Rael, *Black Identity and Black Protest in the Antebellum North* (Chapel Hill, NC, 2002), 19; Litwack, *North of Slavery*, 154–60; Berlin, "Revolution in Black Life," 368–69.

16. Harris, *In the Shadow of Slavery*, 80; Hodges, *Root and Branch*, 178–79, 201–3; Gilje and Rock, "Sweep O! Sweep O!" 507–19.

17. Berlin, *Generations of Captivity*, 122–23; Rael, *Black Identity*, 84; Stuckey, *Slave Culture*, 200–1.

18. Quarles, "Revolutionary War as Black Declaration of Independence," 298; Nash, *Race and Revolution*, 65.

19. Nash, *Unknown American Revolution*, 411–14; Richard S. Newman, *Freedom's Prophet: Bishop Richard Allen, the AME Church, and the Black Founding Fathers* (New York, 2008), 28–31.

20. Wright, *Negro in Pennsylvania*, 31; Newman, *Freedom's Prophet*, 15.

21. Robert L. Harris Jr., "Charleston's Free Afro-American Elite: The Brown Fellowship Society and the Humane Brotherhood," *South Carolina Historical Magazine* 82 (October 1981): 304; Larry Koger, *Black Slaveholders: Free Black Slave Masters in South Carolina, 1790–1860* (reprint, Columbia, SC, 1995), 173; Powers, *Black Charlestonians*, 50.

22. Papenfuse, *Evils of Necessity*, 15; Petition of October 17, 1787, in Aptheker, *A Documentary History*, 19–20.

23. Frey, *Water from the Rock*, 37; Sylvia R. Frey and Betty Wood, *Come Shouting to Zion: African American Protestantism in the American South and British Caribbean to 1830* (Chapel Hill, NC, 1998), 118–19.

24. Frey and Wood, *Come Shouting*, 114; Mullin, *Flight and Rebellion*, 130; Marvin L. Michael Kay and Lorin Lee Cary, *Slavery in South Carolina, 1748–1775*, 194; Alan Gallay, *The Formation of a Planter Elite: Jonathan Bryan and the Southern Colonial Frontier* (Athens, 1989), 41–42.

25. Frey and Wood, *Come Shouting*, 110–11; Hodges, *Slavery and Freedom*, 77; Graham R. Hodges, *Black Itinerants of the Gospel: The Narratives of John Jea and George White* (New York, 1998), 5.

26. Klein, *Unification of a Slave State*, 277; Jordan, *White over Black*, 419; Jones, *Born a Child of Freedom*, 139; Washington, *"A Peculiar People,"* 3; Frey, *Water from the Rock*, 291.

27. Charlotte A. Haller, "'And Made Us to Be a Kingdom': Race, Antislavery, and Black Evangelicals in North Carolina's Early Republic," *North Carolina Historical Review* 80 (April 2003): 128; Young, *Domesticating Slavery*, 83; Fraser, *South Carolina*, 259.

28. Nathan O. Hatch, *The Democratization of American Christianity* (New Haven, CT, 1989), 106; Boles, *Black Southerners*, 37; Nash, *Forgotten Fifth*, 51–52; Saillant, *Black Puritan, Black Republican*, 17.

29. Frey, *Water from the Rock*, 30; Berlin, *Generations of Captivity*, 118–19; Sobel, *The World They Made Together*, 189.

30. Gayraud S. Wilmore, *Black Religion and Black Radicalism: An Interpretation of the Religious History of African Americans* (New York, 1998), 34; James D. Essig, "A Very Wintry Season: Virginia Baptists and Slavery, 1785–1797," *Virginia Magazine of History and Biography* 88 (April 1980): 174–75; Christine L. Heyrman, *Southern Cross: The Beginnings of the Bible Belt* (New York, 1997), 218.

31. Morgan, *Slave Counterpoint*, 656; Berlin, "Revolution in Black Life," 373; William Nelson to Thomas Newton, August 8, 1793, in Records of the General Assembly, Governor's Messages, SCDAH.

32. Thomas J. Little, "George Liele and the Rise of Independent Black Baptist Churches in the Lower South and Jamaica," *Slavery and Abolition* 16 (1995): 188–90; Johnson, *Black Savannah*, 8–9. John W. Davis, "George Liele and Andrew Bryan, Pioneer Negro Baptist Preachers," *Journal of Negro History* 3 (April 1918): 119–20; Schama, *Rough Crossings*, 96, 98; "An Account of the Life of Mr. David George from S. L. A. Given by Himself," *Annual Baptist Register*, 1793, 4.

33. Johnson, *Black Savannah*, 9–10; Gallay, *Formation of a Planter Elite*, 52.

34. Johnson, *Black Savannah*, 11; Davis, "George Liele and Andrew Bryan," 123–26; Gallay, *Formation of a Planter Elite*, 52–53.

35. Johnson, *Black Savannah*, 17–18; Edgar G. Thomas, *The First African Baptist Church of North America* (Savannah, GA, 1925), 34–37; Whittington B. Johnson, "Andrew C. Marshall: A Black Religious Leader of Antebellum Savannah," *Georgia Historical Quarterly* 69 (Summer 1985): 175.

36. Haller, "Black Evangelicals in North Carolina," 139; Whittington B. Johnson, "Free African-American Women in Savannah, 1800–1816: Affluence and Autonomy Amid Adversity," *Georgia Historical Quarterly* 76 (Summer 1992): 262–63; Wood, *Women's Work, Men's Work*, 171.

37. Timothy J. Lockley, *Lines in the Sand: Race and Class in Lowcountry Georgia, 1750–1860* (Athens, GA, 2001), 134; Charles Joyner, "'If You Ain't Got Education': Slave Language and Slave Thought in Antebellum Charleston," in O'Brien and Moltke-Hansen, *Intellectual Life*, 273.

38. Lockley, *Lines in the Sand*, 136; Wood, *Women's Work, Men's Work*, 164.

39. Levy, *First Emancipator*, 132; Albert J. Raboteau, "The Slave Church in the Era of the American Revolution," in *Slavery and Freedom*, 198–200; W. Harrison Daniel, "Virginia Baptists and the Negro in the Early Republic," *Virginia Magazine of History* 80 (1972): 66.

40. Saillant, *Black Puritan, Black Republican*, 84–85; Nash, *Unknown American Revolution*, 414–15.

41. Hodges, *Black Itinerants of the Gospel*, 3–7.
42. Hodges, *Root and Branch*, 183; Craig Steven Wilder, "Black Life in Freedom: Creating a Civic Culture," in Berlin and Harris, *Slavery in New York*, 221; John Stauffer, *The Black Hearts of Men: Radical Abolitionists and the Transformation of Race* (Cambridge, MA, 2004), 88; Harris, *In the Shadow of Slavery*, 82.
43. Gary Nash, "New Light on Richard Allen: The Early Years of Freedom," *WMQ* 46 (April 1989): 332–40; Nash, *Unknown American Revolution*, 413; Newman, *Freedom's Prophet,* 44–50.
44. Wilmore, *Black Religion*, 81–83; Wright, *African Americans in the Colonial Era*, 190; Newman, *Freedom's Prophet,* 47; Lammers, "Absalom Jones," 164.
45. Newman, *Freedom's Prophet*, ch. 2; James T. Campbell, *Songs of Zion: The African Methodist Episcopal Church in the United States and South Africa* (New York, 1995), 9.
46. Johnson, *Africans in America*, 234–35; Julie Winch, *Philadelphia's Black Elite: Activism, Accommodation, and the Struggle for Autonomy, 1787–1848* (Philadelphia, 1988), 9; Newman, *Freedom's Prophet*, 63–68. Although Allen himself later dated the protest as 1787, Milton C. Sernett, *Black Religion and American Evangelicalism: White Protestants, Plantation Missions and the Flowering of Negro Christianity, 1787–1865* (Metuchen, NJ, 1975), 117–18, demonstrates that St. George's did not begin construction of a gallery until 1792.
47. Hatch, *Democratization of American Christianity*, 104; Winch, *Philadelphia's Black Elite*, 11–12; Campbell, *Songs of Zion*, 10–11; Vincent Harding, *There Is a River: The Black Struggle for Freedom in America* (New York, 1981), 67.
48. Allen, "Absalom Jones," 9; Winch, *Philadelphia's Black Elite*, 10; Nash, *Forging Freedom*, 202–4.
49. Raboteau, "The Slave Church," 212; Berlin, "Revolution in Black Life," 376.
50. Harding, *There Is a River*, 67; "Morris Brown" and "Henry Drayton," in *The Black Abolitionist Papers: The United States, 1830–1860*, ed. C. Peter Ripley (Chapel Hill, NC, 1992), 3:134 n. 3, 196 n. 14; Harris, "Charleston's Free Afro-American Elite," 292.
51. Campbell, *Songs of Zion*, 35; Frey, *Water from the Rock*, 322; William Colcock's Confession, July 12, 1822, in Records of the General Assembly, Governor's Messages, SCDAH.
52. Peter P. Hinks, *To Awaken My Afflicted Brethren: David Walker and the Problem of Antebellum Slave Resistance* (University Park, MO, 1996), 27; Testimony of Monday Gell, July 16, 1822, in Records of the General Assembly, Governor's Messages, SCDAH.
53. Harding, *There Is a River*, 67; Powers, *Black Charlestonians*, 19; Martha Proctor Richardson to James Screven, September 16, 1822, in Arnold and Screven Papers, Southern Historical Collection, University of North Carolina.

Chapter 8: Harry Washington's Atlantic Crossings

1. Pybus, *Epic Journeys of Freedom*, 3, 218; Entry of September 14, 1770, in Jackson and Twohig, *Diaries of George Washington*, 2:275.

2. Pybus, *Epic Journeys of Freedom*, 218; Embarkation records for the *L'Abondance*, July 31, 1783, in Hodges, *Black Loyalist Directory*, 111–12.

3. Pybus, *Epic Journeys of Freedom*, 3; Entry of August 2, 1771, in Jackson and Twohig, *Diaries of George Washington*, 3:45; Wiencek, *An Imperfect God*, 259; Hodges, *Black Loyalist Directory*, 16, 112.

4. Schama, *Rough Crossings*, 9; Wiencek, *An Imperfect God*, 259.

5. Quarles, *Negro in the American Revolution*, 167–68; George Washington to Benjamin Harrison, April 30, 1783, in Washington Papers, LC.

6. Embarkation records for the *L'Abondance*, July 31, 1783, in Hodges, *Black Loyalist Directory*, 103–17.

7. Frey, *Water from the Rock*, 204–5; Linebaugh and Rediker, *Many-Headed Hydra*, 247; Bordewich, *Bound for Canaan*, 244.

8. Flexner, *George Washington in the American Revolution*, 467–69; Schama, *Rough Crossings*, 132.

9. Flexner, *George Washington in the American Revolution*, 460; Quarles, *Negro in the American Revolution*, 158.

10. Schama, *Rough Crossings*, 125; Christopher Hibbert, *George III: A Personal History* (New York, 1998), 162–65.

11. Hochschild, *Bury the Chains*, 101; Stahr, *John Jay*, 171, 294; Ferling, *John Adams*, 243–45.

12. Quarles, *Negro in the American Revolution*, 160–61; George Washington to François Joseph Paul, Comte de Grasse, February 6, 1782, in Washington Papers, LC; Thomas O. Ott, *The Haitian Revolution, 1789–1804* (Knoxville, TN, 1973), 61 n. 27; Laurent Dubois, *Avengers of the New World: The Story of the Haitian Revolution* (Cambridge, MA, 2004), 67.

13. Fraser, *Charleston*, 167; Gordon, *South Carolina and the American Revolution*, 176; Nash, *Forgotten Fifth*, 42–43; Olwell, *Masters, Slaves, and Subject*, 269; Jones, "British Withdrawal," 273.

14. Frey, *Water from the Rock*, 179–80; Landers, *Black Society in Spanish Florida*, 158–59.

15. Massey, *John Laurens*, 222; Pybus, *Epic Journeys of Freedom*, 60; Schama, *Rough Crossings*, 133.

16. Frey, *Water from the Rock*, 180; Quarles, *Negro in the American Revolution*, 176; Wright, *African Americans in the Colonial Era*, 183; Nash, *Unknown American Revolution*, 405.

17. Jones, "British Withdrawal," 280; Quarles, *Negro in the American Revolution*, 177; North Callahan, *Flight from the Republic: The Tories of the American Revolution* (Indianapolis, IN, 1967), 142; Ball, *Slaves in the Family*, 236; Frey, *Water from the Rock*, 182–83.

18. O'Shaughnessy, *An Empire Divided*, 151, 143; Frey, *Water from the Rock*, 186–87.

19. Ferling, *The First of Men*, 243; Paul H. Smith, "Sir Guy Carleton and the Evacuation of New York," *Canadian Historical Review* 50 (September 1969): 247.

20. Christopher L. Brown, *Moral Capital: Foundations of British Abolitionism* (Chapel Hill, NC, 2006), 298; Schama, *Rough Crossings*, 151.

21. Hodges, *Black Loyalist Directory*, xiv–xv; Hodges, *Root and Branch*, 156; Boston King, "Memoirs of the Life of Boston King, a Black Preacher, Written by Himself," *Methodist Magazine* 21 (1789): 4.

22. Paul R. Reynolds, *Guy Carleton: A Biography* (New York, 1980), 144; Philip Ranlet, *The New York Loyalists* (Knoxville, TN, 1986), 164; Edward G. Lengel, *General George Washington: A Military Life* (New York, 2005), 344; George Washington to Guy Carleton, April 21, 1783, in Washington Papers, LC; Guy Carlton to George Washington, April 24, 1783, ibid.

23. Paul David Nelson, *General Sir Guy Carleton, Lord Dorchester: Soldier-Statesman of Early British Canada* (Madison, NJ, 2000), 171; Hochschild, *Bury the Chains*, 102; George Washington to Guy Carleton, May 6, in Washington Papers, LC.

24. Unknown to Lord Hardwicke, 1783, in Rhodehamel, *American Revolution*, 792; George Washington to Guy Carleton, May 6, in Washington Papers, LC; Reynolds, *Guy Carleton*, 146–47.

25. Unknown to Lord Hardwicke, 1783, in Rhodehamel, *American Revolution*, 792; Foote, *Black and White Manhattan*, 222; Wiencek, *An Imperfect God*, 257.

26. George Washington to Marquis de Lafayette, May 10, 1783, in Washington Papers, LC; Hodges, *Root and Branch*, 157; Winks, *Blacks in Canada*, 32–33; Ball, *Slaves in the Family*, 239; Hodges, *Black Loyalist Directory*, 111–112, 196.

27. George Washington to Benjamin Harrison, May 6, 1783, in Washington Papers, LC; Foote, *Black and White Manhattan*, 217; Hodges, *Black Loyalist Directory*, xix–xx; Horton and Horton, *Hard Road to Freedom*, 71–72; Schama, *Rough Crossings*, 222–23.

28. Hill, *Freedom Seekers*, 10–12; Hodges, *Black Loyalist Directory*, xxi; Ranlet, *New York Loyalists*, 178; James W. St. G. Walker, *The Black Loyalists: The Search for a Promised Land in Nova Scotia and Sierra Leone, 1783–1870* (Toronto, 1992), 22–23.

29. Winks, *Blacks in Canada*, 35; McColley, *Slavery and Jeffersonian Virginia*, 87.

30. Winks, *Blacks in Canada*, 45; Hill, *Freedom Seekers*, 13.

31. Hodges, *Black Loyalist Directory*, xxii–xxiii; Horton and Horton, *In Hope of Liberty*, 64.

32. Winks, *Blacks in Canada*, 38; Bolaria, *Racial Oppression in Canada*, 190; Walker, "Blacks as American Loyalists," 65.

33. Ball, *Slaves in the Family*, 240; "Account of Mr. the Life of Mr. David George," 5.

34. Mary L. Clifford, *From Slavery to Freetown: Black Loyalists After the American Revolution* (Jefferson, NC, 1999), 53–55; Schama, *Rough Crossings*, 242–43; "Account of the Life of Mr. David George," 5.

35. Winch, *A Gentleman of Color*, 61; David S. Cecelski, *The Waterman's Song: Slavery and Freedom in Maritime North Carolina* (Chapel Hill, NC, 2001), 32–33; Bolster, *Black Jacks*, 71–73; Davis, *Inhuman Bondage*, 151.

36. Mary Beth Norton, "The Fate of Some Black Loyalists of the American Revolution," *Journal of Negro History* 58 (October 1973): 406–7; Pybus, *Epic Journeys of Freedom*, 86–87.

37. Davis, *Inhuman Bondage*, 151; Brown, *Moral Capital*, 294–95; Carretta, *Equiano the African*, 218–21; Lascelles, *Granville Sharp*, 81; A. P. Kup, "John Clarkson and the Sierra Leone Company," *International Journal of African Historical Studies* 5 (1972): 203.

38. Stephen J. Braidwood, *Black Poor and White Philanthropists: London's Blacks and the Foundation of the Sierra Leone Settlement, 1786–1791* (Liverpool, UK, 1994), 63–67; Carretta, *Equiano the African*, 220–22; Pybus, *Epic Journeys of Freedom*, 107–8.

39. Carretta, *Equiano the African*, 222; Schama, *Rough Crossings*, 186–87; Hochschild, *Bury the Chains*, 26, 145–46; Norton, "Black Loyalists," 408; Judith B. Williams, "The Development of British Trade with West Africa, 1750 to 1850," *Political Science Quarterly* 50 (June 1935): 201.

40. Norton, "Black Loyalists," 419; Equiano, *Interesting Narrative*, 226–27; Ellen G. Wilson, *The Loyal Blacks* (New York, 1976), 142–43; Walvin, *An African's Life*, 144–46; Carretta, *Equiano the African*, 225–31.

41. Pybus, *Epic Journeys of Freedom*, 117–18; Schama, *Rough Crossings*, 196–205; Winks, *Blacks in Canada*, 62.

42. Norton, "Black Loyalists," 421; Kup, "John Clarkson," 210; Clifford, *From Slavery to Freetown*, 74–76; Hochschild, *Bury the Chains*, 178–79; Schama, *Rough Crossings*, 205–7.

43. Nash, *Unknown American Revolution*, 426; Hochschild, *Bury the Chains*, 200.

44. Michael J. Turner, "The Limits of Abolition: Government, Saints and the 'African Question,' 1750–1820," *English Historical Review* 112 (April 1997): 327; Hodges, *Black Loyalist Directory*, xxxii; Walker, *Black Loyalists*, 94–95; James T. Campbell, *Middle Passages: African American Journeys to Africa, 1787–2005* (New York, 2006) 26; Winks, *Blacks in Canada*, 63.

45. Nash, *Unknown American Revolution*, 427; Wilson, *Loyal Blacks*, 198–99.

46. Walker, *Black Loyalists*, 127.

47. Turner, "Limits of Abolition," 327; Kup, "John Clarkson," 204; Clifford, *From Slavery to Freetown*, 77; Braidwood, *Black Poor*, 226; Pybus, *Epic Journeys of Freedom*, 144.

48. Campbell, *Middle Passages*, 26; Walker, *Black Loyalists*, 129–30; Nash, *Unknown American Revolution*, 427–28.

49. Wilson, *Loyal Blacks*, 231; Hochschild, *Bury the Chains*, 204–5; Nash, *Unknown American Revolution,* 428.

50. Walker, *Black Loyalists*, 151; Schama, *Rough Crossings*, 348; Pybus, *Epic Journeys of Freedom*, 170–71; Hochschild, *Bury the Chains*, 206–7; Kup, "John Clarkson," 207; Monday B. Abasiattai, "The Search for Independence: New World Blacks in Sierra Leone and Liberia, 1787–1847," *Journal of Black Studies* 23 (September 1992): 109.

51. Pybus, *Epic Journeys of Freedom*, 169–72; Wilson, *Loyal Blacks*, 283–85; Clifford, *From Slavery to Freetown*, 162.

52. Pybus, *Epic Journeys of Freedom*, 178–79; Walker, *Black Loyalists*, 175–77; Abasiattai, "Search for Independence," 109.

53. Hochschild, *Bury the Chains*, 248–49; Wilson, *Loyal Blacks*, 318–19; Schama, *Rough Crossings*, 380–81; Lascelles, *Granville Sharp*, 87.

54. Pybus, *Epic Journeys of Freedom*, 191–93; Clifford, *From Slavery to Freetown*, 189.

55. Pybus, *Epic Journeys of Freedom*, 195–96; Schama, *Rough Crossings*, 390; Abasiattai, "Search for Independence," 11; Turner, "Limits of Abolition," 329.

56. Wilson, *Loyal Blacks*, 389–91; Clifford, *From Slavery to Freetown*, 193; Walker, *Black Loyalists*, 232; Christopher Fyfe, *A History of Sierra Leone* (London, 1962), 76.

57. Wilson, *Loyal Blacks*, 393; Clifford, *From Slavery to Freetown*, 194–95; Walker, *Black Loyalists*, 233.

58. Clifford, *From Slavery to Freetown*, 195–96; Fyfe, *History of Sierra Leone*, 85; Wilson, *Loyal Blacks*, 394.

59. Schama, *Rough Crossings*, 394–95; Pybus, *Epic Journeys of Freedom*, 201; Wilson, *Loyal Blacks*, 394–95; Abasiattai, "Search for Independence," 110.

60. Pybus, *Epic Journeys of Freedom*, 202; Clifford, *From Slavery to Freetown*, 197; Turner, "Limits of Abolition," 328.

Chapter 9: A Suspicion Only

1. Cunningham, *In Pursuit of Reason*, 77; Malone, *Jefferson the Virginian*, 373–74; Thomas Jefferson, "Autobiography," in Peterson, *Jefferson: Writings*, 55.

2. Thomas Jefferson to François, marquis de Barbé-Marbois, March 24, 1782, in Jefferson Papers, LC; Cunningham, *In Pursuit of Reason*, 77; Ronald L. Hatzenbuehler, *I Tremble for My Country: Thomas Jefferson and the Virginia Gentry* (Gainesville, FL, 2006), 70; Malone, *Jefferson the Virginian*, 373.

3. Hatzenbuehler, *I Tremble for My Country*, 70–71; Jefferson, *Notes on the State of Virginia*, 289; Andrew Burstein, *Jefferson's Secrets: Death and Desire at Monticello* (New York, 2005), 125; John Adams to Thomas Jefferson, May 22, 1785, in Cappon, *Adams-Jefferson Letters*, 21.

4. Jefferson, *Notes on the State of Virginia*, 264–65.

5. Burstein, *Jefferson's Secrets*, 120–21; Jefferson, *Notes on the State of Virginia*, 264–66.

6. Miller, *Wolf by the Ears*, 76–77; Jefferson, *Notes on the State of Virginia*, 266–79.

7. Thomas Jefferson to Francis C. Gray, March 4, 1815, in Jefferson Papers, LC; Jefferson, *Notes on the State of Virginia*, 270; see, for example, Cunningham, *In Pursuit of Reason*, 79; Bernstein, *Thomas Jefferson*, 60–62.

8. Isaac, *Transformation of Virginia*, 308; Barbara J. Fields, "Slavery, Race, and Ideology in the United States of America," *New Left Review* 181 (May/June 1990): 95–118; MacLeod, *Slavery, Race, and the American Revolution*.

9. Kolchin, *American Slavery*, 90–91; Wright, *African Americans in the Colonial Era*, 194–95.

10. Malone, *Jefferson the Virginian*, 267; Burstein, *Jefferson's Secrets*, 124.

11. Wright, *African Americans in the Colonial Era*, 195; Stephen Jay Gould, *The Mismeasure of Man* (New York, 1981), 35; Waldstreicher, *Runaway America*, 138; Burstein, *Jefferson's Secrets*, 121.

12. David Grimsted, "Anglo-American Racism and Phillis Wheatley's 'Sable Veil,' 'Length'ned Chain,' and 'Knitted Heart,'" in *Women in the Age of the American Revolution*, ed. Ronald Hoffman and Peter J. Albert (Charlottesville, VA, 1989), 419; White, *Somewhat More Independent*, 58; Frey, *Water from the Rock*, 240.

13. David Brion Davis, *In the Image of God: Religion, Moral Values, and Our Heritage of Slavery* (New Haven, CT, 2001), 347; McColley, *Slavery and Jeffersonian Virginia*, 123; Essah, *A House Divided*, 65.

14. Jefferson, *Notes on the State of Virginia*, 269–70; Miller, *Wolf by the Ears*, 52; William Cohen, "Thomas Jefferson and the Problem of Slavery," 525.

15. Jordan, *White over Black*, 288–89; Jefferson, *Notes on the State of Virginia*, 189; Thomas Jefferson to François-Jean de Beauvoir, June 7, 1785, in Jefferson Papers, LC.

16. Charles A. Miller, *Jefferson and Nature: An Interpretation* (Baltimore, 1988), 72; David Freeman Hawke, *Benjamin Rush: Revolutionary Gadfly* (Indianapolis, IN, 1970), 104–5; Benjamin Rush to the Pennsylvania Abolition Society, January 4, 1795, in *Letters of Benjamin Rush*, ed. L. H. Butterfield (Princeton, NJ, 1951), 2:758; St. George Tucker, *A Dissertation on Slavery*, 87 n. b; Cunningham, *In Pursuit of Reason*, 62; Ellis, *American Sphinx*, 87.

17. Andrew Burstein, *The Inner Jefferson: Portrait of a Grieving Optimist* (Charlottesville, VA, 1995), 279; Thomas Jefferson to Francis C. Gray, March 4, 1815, in Jefferson Papers, LC; "Register of Births," in *Thomas Jefferson's Farm Book, with Commentary and Relevant Extracts from Other Writings*, ed. Edwin M. Betts (Princeton, NJ, 1953), 31.

18. Larry Tise, *The American Counterrevolution: A Retreat from Liberty, 1783–1800* (Mechanicsburg, 1998), 443–44; Larry Tise, *Proslavery: A History of the Defense of Slavery in America, 1701–1840* (Athens, GA, 1988), 34–35.

19. Tise, *American Counterrevolution*, 444; Jacobson, *Whiteness of a Different Color*, 26.

20. Richard B. Morris, *The Forging of the Union, 1781–1789* (New York, 1987), 182; Jacobson, *Whiteness of a Different Color*, 28; Davis, *Revolutions*, 29.

21. Okoye, "Chattel Slavery," 24–25; McManus, *Negro Slavery in New York*, 184–85; Wright, *African Americans in the Colonial Era*, 202; Mary Beth Norton, *Liberty's Daughters: The Revolutionary Experience of American Women, 1750–1800* (Ithaca, NY, 1996), 192–93; Sweet, *Bodies Politic*, 180–81.

22. John Dickinson's Draft, in *Journals of the Continental Congress, 1774–1779*, ed. Worthington C. Ford (Washington, DC, 1905), 5:554.

23. Collier, *Roger Sherman's Connecticut*, 159; Blackburn, *Overthrow of Colonial Slavery*, 123; Donald Fehrenbacher, *The Slaveholding Republic: An Account of the United States Government's Relations to Slavery* (New York, 2001), 22.

24. Collier, *Roger Sherman's Connecticut*, 157–58; Fehrenbacher, *Slaveholding Republic*, 24–25.

25. Collier, *Roger Sherman's Connecticut*, 272; Robinson, *Slavery in the Structure of American Politics*, 156–57.

26. Fehrenbacher, *Slaveholding Republic*, 32–33; Goldstone, *Dark Bargain*, 104.

27. Charles Warren, *The Making of the Constitution* (Boston, 1929), 561; Blumrosen and Blumrosen, *Slave Nation*, 151–52.

28. Rappleye, *Sons of Providence*, 233; Gerald H. Clarfield, *Timothy Pickering and the American Republic* (Pittsburgh, 1980), 80; Timothy Pickering to Rufus King, March 6, 1785, in *The Life and Correspondence of Rufus King*, ed. Charles R. King (New York, 1894), 1:45–56.

29. Cohen, "Thomas Jefferson and the Problem of Slavery," 511; Timothy Pickering to Rufus King, March 6, 1785, in King, *Correspondence of Rufus King*, 1:45–46.

30. Peter S. Onuf, *Statehood and Union: A History of the Northwest Ordinance* (Bloomington, IN, 1987), 46–47; Richard P. McCormick, "The 'Ordinance' of 1784?" *WMQ* 50 (January 1993): 113; Goldstone, *Dark Bargain*, 140–41; Malone, *Jefferson the Virginian*, 412–14; Miller, *Wolf by the Ears*, 28–29.

31. Morris, *Forging of the Union*, 231; Goldstone, *Dark Bargain*, 141.

32. Rappleye, *Sons of Providence*, 216; Paul Finkelman, "Slavery and the Northwest Ordinance: A Study in Ambiguity," *Journal of the Early Republic* 6 (1986): 349.

33. Finkelman, "Slavery and the Northwest Ordinance," 345; Staughton Lynd, "The Compromise of 1787," *Political Science Quarterly* 81 (1966): 231–32.

34. Miller, *Wolf by the Ears*, 29; Finkelman, "Slavery and the Northwest Ordinance," 362–63.

35. Charles A. Beard, *An Economic Interpretation of the Constitution of the United States* (New York, 1935), 151; Eric Foner, *The Story of American Freedom* (New York, 1999), 35.

36. Haw, *John and Edward Rutledge*, 203; Einhorn, *American Taxation, American Slavery*, 170; Greene, "Slavery or Independence," 206.

37. John J. Reardon, *Edmund Randolph: A Biography* (New York, 1974), 101; Blumrosen and Blumrosen, *Slave Nation*, 172–73; William M. Wiecek, *The Sources of Antislavery Constitutionalism in America, 1760–1848* (Ithaca, NY, 1977), 66.

38. Mason, *Slavery and Politics*, 32–33; Rappleye, *Sons of Providence*, 243; Adams, *Gouverneur Morris*, 159.

39. Flexner, *George Washington and the New Nation*, 129; Goldstone, *Dark Bargain*, 126; Haw, *John and Edward Rutledge*, 203–4; Wiecek, *Sources of Antislavery Constitutionalism*, 68.

40. Wiecek, *Sources of Antislavery Constitutionalism*, 68; Earl M. Maltz, "Slavery, Federalism, and the Structure of the Constitution," *American Journal of Legal History* 36 (October 1992): 469; George Mason, "In Opposition to a Motion Aimed at Counting Slaves Equal to Whites," July 11, 1787, in Rutland, *Papers of George Mason*, 3:923.

41. Waldstreicher, *Runaway America*, 233–34; Robinson, *Slavery in the Structure of American Politics*, 178; Morris, *Forging of the Union*, 282.

42. Lynd, "Compromise of 1787," 235; Maltz, "Slavery, Federalism, and the Structure of the Constitution," 470; George Mason, "Fugitive Slave Clause Will Be No Security to Such Property," June 23, 1787, in Rutland, *Papers of George Mason*, 3:1113.

43. Flower, *John Dickinson*, 242; Wiecek, *Sources of Antislavery Constitutionalism*, 70–71; Newman, *The Transformation of American Abolitionism*, 47.

44. Ketcham, *James Madison*, 224; George Mason, "State Controls on Slavery Traffic Should Be Surrendered to the National Government," August 22, 1787, in Rutland, *Papers of George Mason*, 3:965–66.

45. McLeod, *Slavery, Race, and the American Revolution*, 38; Rutland, *George Mason*, 86–87; Calvin Jillson and Thornton Anderson, "Realignment in the Convention of 1787: The Slave Trade Compromise," *Journal of Politics* 39 (1977): 715; Roger Wilkins, *Jefferson's Pillow: A Black Patriot Confronts the Myths of the Founding Fathers* (Boston, 2001), 61.

46. Luther Martin, "Genuine Information," in *The Complete Anti-Federalist*, ed. Herbert J. Storing (Chicago, 1981), 2:45; Luther Martin, Speech of August 21, 1787, in *The Records of the Federal Convention of 1787*, ed. Max Farrand (New Haven, CT, 1937), 3:280.

47. Davis, *Problem of Slavery*, 125; John Rutledge and Charles Pinckney, Speeches of August 21, 1787, in Farrand, *Records of the Federal Convention*, 3:280.

48. Broadwater, *George Mason, Forgotten Father*, 192; Adams, *Gouverneur Morris*, 159; Richard Brookhiser, *Gentleman Revolutionary: Gouverneur Morris, the Rake Who Wrote the Constitution* (New York, 2003), 82.

49. Broadwater, *George Mason, Forgotten Father*, 192; Oliver Ellsworth, Speech of August 22, 1787, in *Records of the Federal Convention*, 3:280.

50. Richard B. Morris, *Witness at the Creation: Hamilton, Madison, Jay, and the Constitution* (New York, 1983), 214; Morris, *Forging of the Union*, 285; Paul

Finkelman, "Making a Covenant with Death: Slavery and the Constitutional Convention," in *Beyond Confederation: Origins of the Constitution and American National Identity*, ed. Richard Beeman (Chapel Hill, NC, 1987), 214–15; Collier, *Roger Sherman's Connecticut*, 271.

51. Carl Van Doren, *The Great Rehearsal: The Story of the Making and Ratifying of the Constitution of the United States* (New York, 1948), 157; Collier, *Roger Sherman's Connecticut*, 259; Finkelman, "Making a Covenant with Death," 221; George Mason to Thomas Jefferson, May 26, 1788, in Jefferson Papers, LC.

52. Goldstone, *Dark Bargain*, 169; Edmund Randolph, James Wilson, Hugh Williamson, and Charles Cotesworth Pinckney, Speeches of August 22, 1787, in Farrand, *Records of the Federal Convention*, 3:280.

53. Carol Berkin, *A Brilliant Solution: Inventing the American Constitution* (New York, 2002), 113; Rappleye, *Sons of Providence*, 211–12.

54. Charles Pinckney and James Wilson, Speeches of August 22, 1787, in Farrand, *Records of the Federal Convention*, 3:280; Nash, *Race and Revolution*, 28–29; Van Doren, *Great Rehearsal*, 193.

55. Kolchin, *American Slavery*, 80; Staughton Lynd, *Class Conflict, Slavery, and the United States Constitution* (Indianapolis, IN, 1967), 159.

56. Morris, *Witness at the Creation*, 192; Wright, *African Americans in the Colonial Era*, 196; Ferling, *A Leap in the Dark*, 288; Finkelman, "Making a Covenant with Death," 193; Kevin P. Phillips, *The Cousins' Wars: Religion, Politics, and the Triumph of Anglo-America* (New York, 2000), 327.

57. "An Act to Establish an Uniform Rule of Naturalization," March 26, 1790, in *Annals of Congress*, 1st Cong., 2nd Sess., 103–4, 1148–9; Jacobson, *Whiteness of a Different Color*, 22, 25; Appleby, *Inheriting the Revolution*, 47.

58. Jacobson, *Whiteness of a Different Color*, 25; Frey, *Water from the Rock*, 235.

Chapter 10: Eli Whitney's Cotton Engine

1. Ellsworth S. Grant, "Eli Whitney," in Garraty and Carnes, *American National Biography*, 23:298; Jeannette Mirsky and Allan Nevins, *The World of Eli Whitney* (New York, 1952), 46–47; Constance McL. Green, *Eli Whitney and the Birth of American Technology* (New York, 1956), 40–41.

2. Green, *Eli Whitney*, 45; Eli Whitney to Eli Whitney Sr., September 11, 1793, in "Correspondence of Eli Whitney Relative to the Invention of the Cotton Gin," *American Historical Review* 3 (October 1897): 99.

3. Boles, *Black Southerners*, 60–61; Joyce E. Chaplin, "Creating a Cotton South in Georgia and South Carolina, 1760–1815," *Journal of Southern History* 57 (May 1991): 177–78.

4. Charles S. Aiken, "The Evolution of Cotton Ginning in the Southeastern United States," *Geographical Review* 63 (April 1973): 196–97; Daniel H. Thomas, "Pre-Whitney Cotton Gins in French Louisiana," *Journal of Southern History* 31 (May

1965): 136–37; Angela Lakwete, *Inventing the Cotton Gin: Machine and Myth in Antebellum America* (Baltimore, 2003), 42–45.

5. Boles, *Black Southerners*, 59; Introduction, "Correspondence of Eli Whitney," 91–92; Green, *Eli Whitney*, 42; John B. Boles, *The South Through Time: A History of an American Region* (New York, 1995), 151–52.

6. Mirsky and Nevins, *World of Eli Whitney*, 66; Green, *Eli Whitney*, 46–48; Eli Whitney to Eli Whitney Sr., September 11, 1793, in "Correspondence of Eli Whitney," 99; Eli Whitney to Josiah Stebbins, March 7, 1803, ibid., 123.

7. Lakwete, *Inventing the Cotton Gin*, 56; Eli Whitney to Thomas Jefferson, November 24, 1793, in "Correspondence of Eli Whitney," 100; Thomas Jefferson to Eli Whitney, November 16, 1793, in Jefferson Papers, LC.

8. Phineas Miller to Eli Whitney, May 11, 1797, in "Correspondence of Eli Whitney," 105; Eli Whitney to Josiah Stebbins, December 20, 1801, ibid., 112; Lacy K. Ford, "Self-Sufficiency, Cotton, and Economic Development in the South Carolina Upcountry, 1800–1860," *Journal of Economic History* 45 (June 1985): 262–63.

9. Fraser, *South Carolina*, 271.

10. Wright, *African Americans in the Colonial Era*, 200; Jordan, *White over Black*, 317; Allan Kulikoff, "Uprooted Peoples: Black Migrants in the Age of the American Revolution, 1790–1820," in *Slavery and Freedom*, 316–17; Dunn, "Black Society in the Chesapeake," ibid., 81.

11. Patricia S. Brady, "The Slave Trade and Sectionalism in South Carolina, 1787–1807," *Journal of Southern History* 38 (1972): 601–5; Deyle, *Carry Me Back*, 16; Kulikoff, "Uprooted Peoples," 151.

12. Deyle, *Carry Me Back*, 27–28; Thomas Jefferson to Joel Yancey, January 17, 1819, in Jefferson, *Thomas Jefferson's Farm Book*, 42–43.

13. McColley, *Slavery and Jeffersonian Virginia*, 164–65; Michael Tadman, *Speculators and Slaves: Masters, Traders, and Slaves in the Old South* (Madison, WI, 1989), 15–16.

14. Ketcham, *James Madison*, 315; Ellis, *His Excellency*, 201; Waldstreicher, *Runaway America*, 236.

15. *Annals of Congress*, 1st Cong., 2nd Sess., 1239–40; Waldstreicher, *Runaway America*, 237.

16. *Annals of Congress*, 1st Cong., 2nd Sess., 1240, 1243–4; Mason, *Slavery and Politics*, 22; Jordan, *White over Black*, 326.

17. *Annals of Congress*, 1st Cong., 2nd Sess., 1242, 1245; Ellis, *Founding Brothers*, 101.

18. *Annals of Congress*, 1st Cong., 2nd Sess., 1246; Ellis, *Founding Brothers*, 82; James Madison to Robert Walsh, November 27, 1819, in *The Writings of James Madison*, ed. Gaillard Hunt (New York, 1910), 9:1; James Madison to Benjamin Rush, March 20, 1790, in *Hutchinson, Papers of James Madison*, 13:109.

19. Ellis, *His Excellency*, 202; Fehrenbacher, *Slaveholding Republic*, 59.

20. Welch, *Theodore Sedgwick*, 101–2.

21. *Annals of Congress*, 1st Cong., 2nd Sess., 1465–66.

22. Ibid., 1465–66, 1500–1523.

23. *Annals of Congress*, 2nd Cong., 2nd Sess., 730; Newman, *Transformation of American Abolitionism*, 49; Wolf, *Race and Liberty*, 5–6; Davis, *Problem of Slavery*, 100–101.

24. *Annals of Congress*, 3rd Cong., 1st Sess., 76, 483.

25. Prince Hall, "To the Honorable Senate and House of the Commonwealth of Massachusetts," October 17, 1787, in Aptheker, *Documentary History*, 19–20.

26. No author, "To the Honorable David Ramsay," January 1791, in Aptheker, *Documentary History*, 20–21; "To the Honorable David Ramsay," December 1793, ibid., 30–31; State Free Negro Capitation Tax Books, Charleston, 1821, p. 30, SCDAH.

27. Eugene D. Genovese, *From Rebellion to Revolution: Afro-American Slave Revolts in the Making of the Modern World* (Baton Rouge, LA, 1979), xviii–xxii.

28. Frey, *Water from the Rock*, 192; Ott, *The Haitian Revolution*, 8–9; Laurent Dubois, *Avengers of the New World*, 91–96.

29. Dubois, *Avengers of the New World*, 124, 171–72; Martin Ros, *Night of Fire: The Black Napoleon and the Battle for Haiti* (New York, 1991), 29–56; Stewart King, "Toussaint Louverture Before 1791: Free Planter and Slave-Holder," *Journal of Haitian Studies* 3–4 (1997–98): 68.

30. Donald R. Hickey, "America's Response to the Slave Revolt in Haiti, 1791–1806," *Journal of the Early Republic* 2 (1982): 362–63; John H. Coatsworth, "American Trade with the European Colonies in the Caribbean and South America, 1790–1812," *WMQ* 24 (1967): 245–46; Isaac Weld, *Travels Through the States of North America* (1807; reprint, New York, 1968), 1:175–76.

31. Edward Pearson, *Designs Against Charleston: The Trial Record of the Denmark Vesey Slave Conspiracy of 1822* (Chapel Hill, NC, 1999), 89; David P. Geggus, *Slavery, War, and Revolution: The British Occupation of Saint Domingue, 1793–1798* (New York, 1982), 305; Berlin, *Slaves Without Masters*, 40; John Cowper to James Monroe, March 11, 1802, in Executive Papers, LV; Daniel Bedinger to Unknown, March 5, 1797, in Bedinger Letters, Duke University Library.

32. White, *Somewhat More Independent*, 31; Nash and Soderlund, *Freedom by Degrees*, 180; Gary B. Nash, "Reverberations of Haiti in the American North: Black Saint Dominguan in Philadelphia," *Pennsylvania History* 65 (1998): 50.

33. Kolchin, *American Slavery*, 156; Genovese, *From Rebellion to Revolution*, 11–12; *Boston Gazette and Country Journal*, June 4, 1792; Aptheker, *American Negro Slave Revolts*, 210 n. 6; Thomas Newton Jr. to Henry Lee, May 19, 1792, in *Calendar of Virginia State Papers and Other Manuscripts*, ed. H. W. Flournoy (Richmond, VA, 1875–93), 5:552; Smith Snead to Henry Lee, May 21, 1792, ibid., 5:555.

34. Littleton Savage to Smith Snead, May 5, 1792, in Flournoy, *Calendar of Virginia State Papers*, 5:535; Thomas Newton to Henry Lee, May 10, 1792, ibid., 5:540; Smith Snead to Henry Lee, May 5, 1792, ibid., 5:534; Thomas Newton to Henry Lee, May 19, 1792, ibid., 5:552; Littleton Savage to Henry Lee, May 17, 1792, ibid., 5:546–47; Charles Royster, *Light-Horse Harry Lee and the Legacy of the American Revolution* (New York, 1981), 126; Smith Snead to Henry Lee, May 21, 1792, in Flournoy, *Calendar of Virginia State Papers*, 5:555.

35. Dubois, *Avengers of the New World*, 157–59; Frey, *Water from the Rock*, 229; Miles King to Henry Lee, July 9, 1793, in Flournoy, *Calendar of Virginia State Papers*, 6:436; Thomas Newton to Henry Lee, July 6, 1793, ibid., 6:437; Willis Wilson to Henry Lee, August 21, 1793, ibid., 6:490; Elias Langham to Henry Lee, August 3, 1793, ibid., 6:470.

36. Sidbury, *Ploughshares into Swords*, 43; James Wood to William Moultrie, August, 1973, Records of the General Assembly, Governor's Messages, SCDAH; William Nelson to Thomas Newton, August 8, 1793, ibid.; Secret Keeper Richmond to Secret Keeper Norfolk, n.d. (copy), ibid.

37. Papenfuse, *Evils of Necessity*, 24; William Moultrie to General Assembly, November 30, 1793, in Records of the General Assembly, Governor's Messages, SCDAH; Peter Oram to William Moultrie, August 16, 1793, ibid.; Unsigned Notation, September 27, 1793, ibid.; Deposition of John Randolph, July 22, 1793, in Flournoy, *Calendar of Virginia State Papers*, 6:452–53.

38. Thomas Newton to James Wood, n.d., Records of the General Assembly, Governor's Messages, SCDAH; Willis Wilson to Henry Lee, August 21, 1793, in Flournoy, *Calendar of Virginia State Papers*, 6:490.

39. Miles King to James Wood, September 10, 1793, in Flournoy, *Calendar of Virginia State Papers*, 6:524; John Marshall to Henry Lee, September 26, 1793, in *The Papers of John Marshall*, ed. Charles T. Cullen (Chapel Hill, NC, 1977), 2:211; William Nelson to Henry Lee, August 24, 1793, in Flournoy, *Calendar of Virginia State Papers*, 6:494; Joseph Jones to Henry Lee, August 17, 1793, ibid.; Robert Mitchell to John Marshall, September 23, 1793, in Cullen, *Papers of John Marshall*, 2:210–11; Henry Lee to John Marshall, September 26, 1793, ibid., 2:211; James Wood to John Marshall, August 23, 1793, ibid., 2:200–1.

40. Nash, *Unknown American Revolution*, 431; Nash, "Reverberations of Haiti," 53; Furstenberg, *In the Name of the Father*, 209–10.

41. Alfred N. Hunt, *Haiti's Influence on Antebellum America: Slumbering Volcano in the Caribbean* (Baton Rouge, LA, 1988), 110–11; Papenfuse, *Evils of Necessity*, 24–25; Klein, *Unification of a Slave State*, 211.

42. White, *Somewhat More Independent*, 145; Don R. Gerlach, "Black Arson in Albany, New York, November 1793," *Journal of Black Studies* 7 (March 1977): 303.

43. White, *Somewhat More Independent*, 145; Gerlach, "Black Arson in Albany," 304–10.

44. Harris, *In the Shadow of Slavery*, 68–69; Nash, "Reverberations of Haiti," 61; Hodges, *Root and Branch*, 180.

45. Saillant, *Black Puritan, Black Republican*, 120–21; Gellman, *Emancipating New York*, 140–41; Clarfield, *Timothy Pickering and the American Republic*, 264.

46. Timothy Pickering to John Adams, June 7, 1799, in Adams Papers, MHS; Timothy Pickering to Rufus King, April 22, 1799, ibid.; Toussaint Louverture to John Adams, November 6, 1798, in "Letters of Louverture," *American Historical Review* 16 (1910): 66–67. I am grateful to John Langdon of Le Moyne College for his translation of Louverture's letters.

47. Rufus King to Henry Dundas, December 8, 1798, in *The Life and Correspondence of Rufus Rufus King*, ed. Charles R. King (New York, 1896), 2:483–84; Edward Stevens to Thomas Maitland, May 23, 1799, in "Letters of Louverture," 73; Robert Goodloe Harper to Constituents, March 20, 1799, in "Papers of James A. Bayard, 1796–1815," in *American Historical Association Annual Report for the Year 1913*, ed. Elizabeth Donnan (Washington, DC, 1915), 2:90; George Washington to Timothy Pickering, July 11, 1798, in Abbot, *Papers of George Washington: Retirement Series*, 2:397.

48. Timothy Pickering to John Adams, June 7, 1799, in Adams Papers, MHS; Timothy Pickering to Rufus King, March 12, 1799, in King, *Life and Correspondence of Rufus King*, 2:557; John Quincy Adams to William Vans Murray, July 14, 1799, in Adams Papers, MHS.

49. Garry Wills, *"Negro President": Jefferson and the Slave Power* (New York, 2003), 40; Oliver Wolcott to John Adams, February 20, 1798, in *Memoirs of the Administrations of Washington and John Adams,* ed. George Gibbs (1846; reprint, New York, 1971), 2:300–1; Philadelphia *Aurora*, January 28, 1799; *Abridgements of the Debates in Congress* (New York, 1851), 2:335–39, 347; Thomas Jefferson to James Madison, February 5, 1799, in Jefferson Papers, LC; Thomas Jefferson to James Madison, February 12, 1799, ibid.

50. Timothy Pickering to Edward Stevens, February 26, 1799, in Timothy Pickering Papers, MHS; Timothy Pickering to John Adams, February 20, 1799, in Adams Papers, MHS; Edward Stevens to Timothy Pickering, May 3, 1799, in "Letters of Louverture," 67; Timothy Pickering to Toussaint Louverture, March 4, 1799, in Timothy Pickering Papers, MHS; Edward Stevens to Timothy Pickering, June 23, 1799, in "Letters of Louverture," 75–76.

51. Tise, *American Counterrevolution*, 485; Ott, *Haitian Revolution*, 114; Stanley Elkins and Eric McKitrick, *The Age of Federalism: The Early American Republic, 1788–1800* (New York, 1993), 659; Edward Stevens to Timothy Pickering, May 24, 1800, in "Letters of Louverture," 98–99; Edward Stevens to Timothy Pickering, February 13, 1800, ibid., 93.

52. Alexander Hamilton to Timothy Pickering, February 21, 1799, in Syrett, *Papers of Alexander Hamilton*, 22:492–93; Tobias Lear to James Madison, July 17, 1801, in James Madison, *The Papers of James Madison: Secretary of State Series*, ed. Robert J. Brugger (Charlottesville, VA, 1986), 1:427–29.

53. Wills, *"Negro President,"* 131–32; Susan Dunn, *Jefferson's Second Revolution: The Election Crisis of 1800 and the Triumph of Republicanism* (New York, 2004), 192, 242.

54. Robert W. Tucker and David C. Hendrickson, *Empire of Liberty: The Statecraft of Thomas Jefferson* (New York, 1990), 126; Michael Zuckerman, *Almost Chosen People: Oblique Biographies in the American Grain* (Berkeley, CA, 1993), 204–5; Tobias Lear to James Madison, July 17, 1801, in Brugger, *Papers of James Madison: Secretary of State Series*, 1:427–29.

55. Ros, *Night of Fire*, 203–13; Alexander Hamilton, "Purchase of Louisiana," *New-York Evening Post*, July 5, 1803, in *Hamilton Papers*, 26:130; Dubois, *Avengers of the New World*, 298–99.

56. Robert L. Paquette, "Revolutionary Saint Domingue in the Making of Territorial Louisiana," in *A Turbulent Time: The French Revolution and the Greater Caribbean*, ed. David Barry Gaspar and David P. Geggus (Bloomington, IN, 1997), 206–11; Glover Moore, *The Missouri Controversy, 1819–1821* (Lexington, KY, 1953), 47–48; McColley, *Slavery and Jeffersonian Virginia*, 125.

57. Ros, *Night of Fire*, 185; Testimony of Price's John at Trial of Young's Gilbert, September 22, 1800, in Executive Papers, Negro Insurrection, LV.

Epilogue: General Gabriel's Flag

1. John Adams to Thomas Jefferson, August 24, 1815, in Cappon, *Adams-Jefferson Letters*, 455.

2. David P. Szatmary, *Shays' Rebellion: The Making of an Agrarian Insurrection* (Amherst, MA, 1980); Slaughter, *The Whiskey Rebellion*; Testimony of Price's John at Trial of Young's Gilbert, September 22, 1800, in Executive Papers, Negro Insurrection, LV.

3. Thomas Prosser, Henrico County Personal Property Tax, 1783, LV; Richmond *Virginia Argus*, September 23, 1800.

4. Patrick Henry Account Book, 1762–1770, folio 39, LV (I am grateful to Philip J. Schwarz for this citation); Cynthia M. Leonard, *The General Assembly of Virginia, July 30, 1619 to January 11, 1978* (Richmond, VA, 1978), 91 n. 6; Charles Copland Petition, December 5, 1798, Af 119, Richmond City Legislative Petitions, LV.

5. Norton, *Liberty's Daughters*, 30; Norton, Gutman, and Berlin, "Afro-American Family," 181–82; Boles, *Black Southerners*, 145; Richmond *Virginia Argus*, September 23, 1800; *Norfolk Herald*, September 16, 1800; James T. Callender to Thomas Jefferson, September 13, 1800, in Jefferson Papers, LC.

6. Thomas Prosser, Henrico County Personal Property Tax, 1783, LV. On "abroad marriages," see Deborah Gray White, *Ar'n't I a Woman?: Female Slaves in the Plantation South* (New York, 1999), 154.

7. Richmond *Virginia Gazette*, October 9, 1798, February 7, 1800; Thomas Henry Prosser, Henrico County Personal Property Tax, 1800, LV; James T. Callender to Thomas Jefferson, September 13, 1800, in Jefferson Papers, LC.

8. *Richmond Recorder*, April 9, 13, 1803; William Bowler Jr. to James Monroe, September 27, 1800, in Executive Papers, Negro Insurrection, LV.

9. Berlin, *Slaves Without Masters*, 28; Sean Wilentz, *Chants Democratic: New York City and the Rise of the American Working Class, 1788–1850* (New York, 1984), 28; Gary Nash, *The Urban Crucible: Social Change, Political Consciousness, and the Origins of the American Revolution* (Cambridge, MA, 1979), 4, 18.

10. Bogger, *Free Blacks in Norfolk*, 76–78; Testimony of Prosser's Ben at Trial of Gabriel, October 6, 1800, in Executive Papers, Negro Insurrection, LV; Confession of Prosser's Solomon, September 15, 1800, ibid.

11. Thomas Jefferson to William Smith, November 13, 1787, in Jefferson Papers, LC; Testimony of Ben Woolfolk at trial of Nicholas' King, October 3, 1800, in Executive Papers, Negro Insurrection, LV.

12. Alex Lichtenstein, " 'That Disposition to Theft, with Which They Have Been Branded': Moral Economy, Slave Management, and the Law," *Journal of Social History* 21 (Spring 1988): 413–40; Schwarz, *Twice Condemned*, 260; Trial of Gabriel, October 7, 1799, in Henrico County Court Order Book, LV.

13. Kathryn Preyer, "Crime, the Criminal Law, and Reform in Post-Revolutionary Virginia," *Law and History Review* 1 (1983): 54 n. 6; Trial of Gabriel, October 7, 1799, in Henrico County Court Order Book, LV.

14. Trial of Gabriel, October 7, 1799, in Henrico Country Court Order Book, LV.

15. John Randolph to Joseph Nicholson, September 26, 1800, in Nicholson Papers, LC; Furstenberg, *In the Name of the Father*, 212; Mason, *Slavery and Politics*, 17.

16. Confession of Prosser's Solomon, September 15, 1800, in Executive Papers, Negro Insurrection, LV: Testimony of Prosser's Ben at trial of Gabriel, ibid. The two standard accounts of this conspiracy are Sidbury, *Ploughshares into Swords*, ch. 2–4, and my own *Gabriel's Rebellion: The Virginia Slave Conspiracies of 1800 and 1802* (Chapel Hill, NC, 1993), ch. 2–4.

17. Testimony of Ben Woolfolk at Trial of Sam Byrd Jr., September 27, 1800, in Executive Papers, Negro Insurrection, LV; William Prentis to James Monroe, n.d., ibid.; *Norfolk Herald*, October 18, 1800; Testimony of Prosser's Ben at Trial of Burton's Isham, September 15, 1800, in Executive Papers, Negro Insurrection, LV.

18. Testimony of Ben Woolfolk at Trial of George Smith, September 19, 1800, in Executive Papers, Negro Insurrection, LV; Testimony of Ben Woolfolk at Trial of Sam Byrd Jr., September 27, 1800, ibid.; William Prentis to James Monroe, September 24, 1800, ibid.; Confession of Young's Gilbert, September 23, 1800, ibid.; James Monroe to William Prentis, October 11, 1800, ibid.

19. Confession of Young's Gilbert September 23, 1800, in Executive Papers, Negro Insurrection, LV; Richmond *Virginia Argus*, October 10, 1800; *Norfolk Herald*, October 2, 1800; Trial of John, October 22, 1800, in Carolina County Court Order Book, LV; James Monroe to William Prentis, October 11, 1800, in Executive Papers, Negro Insurrection, LV.

20. Richmond *Virginia Argus*, October 3, 1800; Testimony of Price's John at Trial of Sam Graham, September 29, 1800, in Executive Papers, Negro Insurrection, LV; Testimony of Prosser's Ben at Trial of Wilkinson's Jupiter, ibid.;

Confession of Ben Woolfolk, September 17, 1800, ibid.; *Norfolk Herald*, October 18, 1800; Testimony of Ben Woolfolk at Trial of Gabriel, October 6, 1800, ibid.

21. Testimony of Prosser's Sam at trial of Jack Ditcher, October 29, 1800, in Executive Papers, Negro Insurrection, LV; Testimony of Ben Woolfolk at Trial of Sam Byrd Jr., September 27, 1800, ibid.; *Norfolk Herald*, September 27, 1800; William Bowler to James Monroe, September 17, 1800, in Executive Papers, Negro Insurrection, LV; Testimony of Price's John at trial of Jack Ditcher, October 29, 1800, ibid.

22. *Norfolk Herald*, October 2, 1800; Testimony of Prosser's Ben at Trial of Gabriel, October 6, 1800, in Executive Papers, Negro Insurrection, LV; Fredericksburg *Virginia Herald*, September 23, 1800.

23. Wood, *Revolutionary Characters*, 27.

24. Richmond *Virginia Argus*, October 10, 1800; James Monroe to General Assembly, December 5, 1800, in Letterbook, Executive Communications, LV; James T. Callender to Thomas Jefferson, September 13, 1800, in Jefferson Papers, LC; Testimony of Prosser's Ben at trial of Prosser's Gabriel, October 6, 1800, in Executive Papers, Negro Insurrection, LV.

25. Thomas Newton to James Monroe, September 24, 1800, in Executive Papers, Negro Insurrection, LV; New York *Spectator*, October 11, 1800; Council Journal, October 16, 1800, LV.

26. Testimony of Ben Woolfolk at Trial of Gabriel, October 6, 1800, in Executive Papers, Negro Insurrection, LV; Sentence of Gabriel, October 6, 1800, ibid.; *Norfolk Herald*, October 11, 1800.

27. Robert Sutcliff, *Travels Through Some Parts of North America, in the Years 1804, 1805, and 1806* (Philadelphia, 1812), 50.

28. Fredericksburg *Virginia Herald*, October 14, 1800; Certification of Death for Gabriel, October 20, 1800, Condemned Slaves 1800, Auditor's Item 153, Box 2, LV; List of Slaves Reprieved for Transportation and Sold by the Commonwealth, March 8, 1806, Executive Papers, LV; Philip J. Schwarz, "The Transportation of Slaves from Virginia, 1801–1865," *Slavery and Abolition* 7 (December 1986): 223.

29. On August 30, 2007, the anniversary of the planned uprising, Virginia governor Timothy M. Kaine issued a posthumous pardon for Gabriel, stating that Gabriel was motivated by "his devotion to the ideals of the American Revolution." See "Kaine Issues Pardon in Slave Revolt," August 31, 2007, *Richmond Times Dispatch*. The "Negro Burial Ground" was discovered by historian Elizabeth Cann Kambourian in 2004.

INDEX

Ball, Joseph, 32
Ball, Lebbeus, 76
Baltimore, 29, 126–28, 157, 175, 178, 189, 191
Banneker, Benjamin, 224
Baptists, 32, 138, 180–88, 217–18
Barbados, 15, 29–30, 35, 39, 53–54, 103, 108, 121, 154
Barbé-Marbois, François, 222–23
Barber, Francis, 39
Barjonah, Isaiah, 76
Barrington, William, 69
Barrow, David, 183, 274
Beddenhurst, Alexander, 278
Belinda (slave), 109
Belknap, Jeremy, 109, 141
Benezet, Anthony, 26, 45, 48, 51–52, 78, 98–99, 101–2, 122–30
Berlin, Ira, 18
Bermuda, 54, 148–49, 196, 206, 221
Bernard, Francis, 20
Bestes, Peter, 58
Bett (slave), 120
Bett, Mum. See Freeman, Elizabeth
Billey (slave), 131
Billy, Gloucester, 140
Birch, Samuel, 205
Bishop, Abraham, 264
Bishop, Jacob, 176
Blair, Jean, 87
Body of Liberties (1641), 21, 24, 107
Boisrond-Tonnerre, Louis Félix, 270
Bonaparte, Napoleon, 269
Boston, 11, 45–47, 51–54, 56, 58–59, 69, 76, 93–94, 108–9, 141, 155, 160, 174, 178, 180, 196, 206, 228, 247, 257
Boston Massacre, 54–56
Boston Tea Party, 59
Boudinot, Elias, 230
Boukman (slave), 258–59, 276
Brom (slave), 105
Brown Fellowship Society, 179, 192
Brown, John, 22
Brown, Morris, 192–93
Brown, Moses, 109–10
Brown, Nicholas, Jr., 22
Brown, Nicholas, Sr., 22
Brueff, Oliver, 208
Bryan, Andrew, 184–85, 193
Bryan, George, 99–101
Bryan, Jonathan, 184
Bryan, William, 184
Bull, Stephen, 151

Bull, William, Jr., 50
Bulloch, Archibald, 68
Bunel, Joseph, 267
Bunker Hill, battle of, 56, 76
Burghardt, Jack, 170, 172, 174
Burgoyne, John, 80
Burr, Aaron, 112–13, 117–18
Butler, Pierce, 239, 244
Byrd, Jesse, 277
Byrd, Reuben, 277
Byrd, Sam, Jr., 273, 277, 280
Byrd, Sam, Sr., 277

Caldwell, Isabell, 93–94, 106
Caldwell, James, 93, 108
Caldwell, John, 94, 104, 106
Caldwell, Seth, 94, 104, 106
Caleb, 260
Campbell, William, 61
Canada, 17–19, 21, 53, 124, 196–97, 206–9, 211, 214–16, 218
Carleton, Guy, 195–96, 202–5, 207, 214
Carter, Landon, 63
Carter, Robert, 71, 139–40, 143, 146
Champlin, Dick, 77
Champlin, Jack, 77
Charleston, 23, 33, 35, 38, 49–50, 73, 80, 82, 85–89, 91, 111, 149, 152, 154, 156–58, 160–68, 174, 179, 181, 186, 192–93, 219, 241, 247, 249, 252, 257, 259–60, 262, 264–65, 273
Chase, Samuel, 232–34
Cheron, Marie, 19
Chew, Benjamin, 178, 189
Children (black), 15, 18–19, 23–24, 26, 31, 34, 38, 43, 59, 71–72, 84, 86, 89, 93, 100, 102, 110, 116–19, 123, 140, 142, 144, 165, 172, 174–77, 179–80, 190–91, 193, 196, 201, 206, 208, 210, 218, 233, 247, 256–57, 260, 272–73
Christian, John, 52–53
Christophe, Henri, 258, 276
Christopher (slave), 10
Clarkson, John, 214–18
Clarkson, Thomas, 17, 211, 214–19
Clinton, Eliza, 114
Clinton, George, 112–15, 204, 265
Clinton, Henry, 84–87, 89–91, 198, 203–5, 214
Coartación, 59
Cocke, Bowler, 50
Cocker, Daniel, 182
Code Noir, 18, 20

Coercive (Intolerable) Acts, 56, 59

Coffin, Obed, 79

Colbert, Jean Baptiste, 18

Collins, Josiah, 155

Colonization (of blacks), 119, 137, 141–42, 223

Congamochu (slave), 28

Congress, U.S., 97, 246, 253–56

Connecticut, 21–22, 47, 56, 60, 76–77, 79–80, 87, 95, 105, 138, 141, 187, 196–97, 232–33, 240, 243, 245, 248, 250, 257, 264; manumission of slaves in, 110

Constitution, U.S., 13, 237, 281; and slavery, 13, 236, 238–46, 269

Continental Army, 68, 74–75, 78, 84, 235, 276

Continental Congress, 6, 41, 57, 62, 73–75, 78, 81–82, 97, 232, 234

Cooper, David, 101, 119

Cooper, James, 79

Corlies, John, 65–67

Cornwallis, Charles, Earl of, 85–86, 89–91, 197–98, 202–3, 211, 271

Coste, John Paul, 264

Cotton (production), 19, 34, 156–57, 248–51, 257–58, 260, 270

Cotton gin, 249–52, 270

Court cases, 51–53, 93–95, 103–9, 275, 280

Cox, Nancy, 138

Craik, James, 11

Crevecoeur, Michel-Guillaume-Jean de, 35

Cruden, John, 88, 91

Cuffee, Paul, 103, 109

Cugoano, Quobna Ottobah, 212

Cushing, William, 107–9

Custis, George Washington Parke, 5, 7, 11

Custis, John Parke, 31

Cuthbert, John, 219

Cutler, Manasseh, 236

Daccarette, Milly, 19

Dandridge, Ann, 29

Dandridge, John, 29

Dane, Nathan, 236–37

Davie, William, 239

Dawes, William, 76

Dawes, William (lieutenant), 217, 220

Deane, Silas, 79–80

Decatur, Stephen, 78

Declaration of Independence, 13, 41, 43, 62–63, 95, 97, 125, 132, 159, 225, 230, 264

Delaware, 28–29, 95, 102, 116, 122–26, 128, 174, 178, 183, 188–89, 227, 240, 260; slave population in, 125

DeSaussure, Henry William, 160, 264

Dessalines, Jean-Jacques, 268

Dialogue Concerning the Slavery of the African (1776), 47

Diana (slave), 93

Dickinson, John, 26, 126, 232

Diderot, Denis, 223

Ditcher, Jack, 14, 273–74, 278–80

Drake, Francis, 138

Drayton, Henry, 192

Drayton, William Henry, 82, 148

Drinker, Elizabeth, 265

Du Bois, William Edward Burghardt, 170

Duke's Law (1664), 24

Dunmore, John Murray, Earl of, 6, 66, 68–73, 80, 84, 86, 91, 129–30, 195, 198, 200, 202, 214, 223

Education (of blacks), 50, 98, 110, 112, 122–23, 177–80, 190, 222, 257

Edwards, Jonathan, 112

Eliot, John, 109, 160

Ellesworth, Oliver, 233, 243–45

Elliot, Matthew, 208

Elson, William, 144

Emanuel (slave), 60

Episcopalians, 99, 187, 190

Equiano, Olaudah, 15–18, 25–26, 28–34, 36–41, 43, 49–50, 52, 97, 125, 175, 180, 182, 212

Essaka, 16

Estabrook, Prince, 56

Eve, Joseph, 249

Ewald, Johann, 86–87, 90

Faber, Catherine, 163

Faber, Polydore, 163, 273

Fairfax, Fernando, 141, 146

Families (black), 7, 24, 31–32, 144, 153, 164, 169, 172, 174–76, 178, 193, 206, 208, 210, 250–51

Farmer, Thomas, 36

Fehrenbacher, Donald, 233

Festivals, 25, 28

Fithian, Philip Vickers, 31

Florida, 36, 82, 142, 151–52, 197, 200–201, 241

Flynn, John, 125

Foote, Thelma, 84

Ford, West, 11

Fort Sumter, 63, 157

Forten, James, 78

Foster, Ariel, 255

Sharp, Granville, 17, 51–52, 80, 98, 211, 213–15

Sharp, Henry, 184

Shays, Daniel, 145, 170, 272

Shepard, Elisha, 67

Sheppard, Mosby, 279–80

Sherman, Roger, 62, 110, 233, 240, 243–45

Sierre Leone, 36, 195, 199, 211–12, 214–15, 217–20

Simmons, John, 113

Simpson, Archibald, 151–52

Simpson, John, 151

Slater, Samuel, 249

Slave clothing, 6, 10, 39, 42, 65

Slave housing, 5, 24, 31–32, 39, 123, 161, 174

Slave labor, 11, 21, 31, 34, 38, 96, 129, 135, 164; domestics, 6, 19, 21; gang system, 34, 38–39, 80, 161; and gender, 34, 38, 161, 166; hiring system, 161–65; task system, 34, 153, 160, 167; urban, 19, 161–63

Slave laws and codes, 18, 20–21, 24, 26, 30–32, 35, 37, 95, 102–3, 107, 110, 116, 118, 132, 134, 168. *See also* specific colonial and state law codes.

Slave populations and percentages, 14, 18–20, 23, 25, 28–29, 33, 36–37, 39, 42, 89, 97, 103, 111, 116, 126, 128–29, 168

Slave trade, 21, 28, 40, 49, 56–57, 61–62, 88, 104, 113, 130, 154–57, 201–2, 244, 255–56; in Africa, 15, 156, 217; domestic, 28, 120, 143, 242, 252–53, 257–58; transatlantic, 19, 21–24, 33–34, 56, 97, 102, 110, 134, 145, 150, 160, 210, 230, 241–42, 246, 254

Slaveholding, patterns of, 22–25, 111, 161, 164; and gender, 24

Slew, Jenny, 46, 104

Smeathman, Henry, 211–12, 214

Smith, Adam, 45, 47–48

Smith, George, 277–78, 280

Smith, Melancton, 115

Smith, Dr. William, 10

Smith, Rev. William, 20

Smith, William Loughton, 230, 254–57

Smyth, J.F.D., 32

Snead, Smith, 261

Snow, William, 210

Solomon, 272–73, 275–76, 279

Somerset, James, 51–54, 98, 275; impact of decision, 52–53, 55, 59, 61, 66, 71, 107, 203

South Carolina, 16, 23–24, 31, 33, 35–38, 40, 49–50, 52, 61, 70, 73, 80–84, 86–87,

89, 91, 116, 120, 125, 135, 148–59, 161–62, 167–68, 180–84, 186, 192, 196, 199, 201, 203, 206–7, 219, 228, 230, 232–33, 238–49, 251, 254–55, 257–58, 260, 262, 264

Spence, Peter, 182

Spirit of the Laws (1748), 45

Squire, Matthew, 69–70

St. Augustine, 69, 84, 151–52, 200–201

St. Croix, 39

St. Kitts, 38, 53–54

St. Vincent, 80

Stamp Act, 46, 49–50, 54

Stearns, William, 106–7

Steuart, Charles, 51–52

Steuben, Friedrich Wilhelm von, 78

Stevens, Edward, 267

Stone, Zedekiah, 93, 106

Strong, Caleb, 106

Sturgis, Stokely, 188

Suffrage, 11, 13, 104, 112–13, 121, 142, 176, 179, 209, 215, 224, 231, 247

Sugar (production), 15, 18–19, 29, 35–36, 38–39, 45, 53–54, 87–88, 149, 152, 210, 251, 259, 268

Sugar Act, 53

Sullivan, James, 142

Surry (freed slave), 56

Tacky's Revolt, 53–54

Talleyrand, Charles Maurice de, 269

Tarleton, Banastre, 87–88, 90

Tayloe, John, 133

Theory of Moral Sentiments (1759), 45

Thistlewood, Thomas, 37

Thomas, Margaret, 7–8

Thompson, Benjamin, 91

Thompson, Thomas, 212, 214

Thornton, John, 135–36

Thornton, Henry, 216

Titus. *See* Tye, Colonel.

Tobacco (production), 12, 28–29, 31–32, 71, 126–29, 138, 140, 150, 155–56, 158, 207, 212, 242, 250, 272, 273, 279

Tobago, 38, 54

Tom (slave), 279

Toney (slave), 60

Toogood, Tom, 176

Torture, 18, 31, 35, 37–39, 61, 158, 184, 259

Toussaint (slave), 19

Townshend Revenue Act, 49

Townshend, Thomas, 204

Troup, Robert, 114